193
P681w   Pitcher, George
         Wittgenstein.

12422

MODERN STUDIES IN PHILOSOPHY

WITTGENSTEIN

The *Philosophical Investigations*

Modern Studies in Philosophy is a series of anthologies presenting contemporary interpretations and evaluations of the works of major philosophers. The editors have selected articles designed to show the systematic structure of the thought of these philosophers, and to reveal the relevance of their views to the problems of current interest. These volumes are intended to be contributions to contemporary debates as well as to the history of philosophy; they not only trace the origins of many problems important to modern philosophy, but also introduce major philosophers as interlocutors in current discussions.

Modern Studies in Philosophy is prepared under the general editorship of Amelie Rorty, Douglass College, Rutgers University.

GEORGE PITCHER, Associate Professor of Philosophy at Princeton University, was born in Newark, New Jersey and educated at the U. S. Naval Academy and Harvard University, where he received his Ph.D. He has been associated with Princeton since 1956. Dr. Pitcher is author of *The Philosophy of Wittgenstein* and editor of *Truth*.

MODERN STUDIES IN PHILOSOPHY

WITTGENSTEIN

The *Philosophical Investigations*

A COLLECTION OF CRITICAL ESSAYS

EDITED BY GEORGE PITCHER

ANCHOR BOOKS
DOUBLEDAY & COMPANY, INC.
GARDEN CITY, NEW YORK

This anthology has been especially prepared for Anchor Books
and has never before appeared in book form

Anchor Books edition: 1966

Library of Congress Catalog Card Number 66–24340

Copyright © 1966 by George Pitcher

All Rights Reserved

Printed in the United States of America

PREFACE

This is a collection of articles about Ludwig Wittgenstein (1889–1951). They deal not with his life and character, but with his philosophy. Anyone interested in the man should consult Norman Malcolm's superb little book *Ludwig Wittgenstein: A Memoir* (London: Oxford University Press, 1958), in which there is included the fine biographical sketch by G. H. von Wright; he may also wish to see some of the pieces in *Ludwig Wittgenstein: The Man and His Philosophy*, an anthology forthcoming from the Dell Publishing Company and edited by K. T. Fann.

What is more, the present book is not concerned with all of Wittgenstein's philosophy, and this fact requires an explanation. If I were forced to distinguish the aspects or phases of Wittgenstein's work for the purpose, say, of writing a chapter in a history-of-philosophy text, I might make the following broad divisions:

1. *Tractatus* period, from just before 1913 to about 1929, when "Some Remarks on Logical Form" was published.*

2. Transitional period, from 1929 through 1935. Here, the ideas of the *Tractatus* were being criticized and largely rejected, and the leading themes of his later work were being developed.

3. *Investigations* period, from about 1936 until his death.

* See Part I of the bibliography at the end of this book for a list of Wittgenstein's own writings.

4. Later philosophy of mathematics, roughly from 1936 until 1944.

The emphasis of this collection falls solidly on 3, for the following reasons. Philosophy of mathematics (4) is a specialist's subject and most of its problems are intelligible only to specialists. Since this book is addressed primarily to those with a more general interest in philosophy, I have included only four articles that deal with Wittgenstein's philosophy of mathematics. They are not highly technical and were selected because they throw considerable light on certain problems discussed in the *Philosophical Investigations*. (Parts VII and VIII of the bibliography are devoted to this aspect of Wittgenstein's philosophy.)

The transitional period (2) is mainly, although by no means exclusively, of interest in so far as it shows the ideas of the *Investigations* coming to life; so I felt justified in slighting it in favor of the later period, when those thoughts came, as it were, to maturity. My reason, finally, for ignoring the *Tractatus* period (1), both in the main body of this book and in the bibliography, is simply stated: I. Copi and R. W. Beard have edited a book called *Readings on Wittgenstein's Tractatus*, to be published by The Macmillan Company, in which are collected most of the articles that anyone save a *Tractatus* expert would care to read in an effort to understand that deeply esoteric work. And their bibliography is complete. I thought it best not to attempt half measures when they have done the whole job so well. But in order to give the reader who may be unfamiliar with the *Tractatus* a general idea of what goes on there, so that he may know the sort of position Wittgenstein was reacting against in his later writings—and also to present a synoptic view of the *Investigations* itself—I have included a long selection from Anthony Quinton's clear and perceptive chapter in *A Critical History of Western Philosophy*.

The main purpose of the following collection, then, is to offer in one inexpensive and easily available volume a group of essays from widely scattered sources that serve to increase the scope and depth of our understanding of the *Investigations*. Since that book belongs on any reasonable list of the most important philosophical works of the century, and since it is also, in its way, one of the more difficult, the existence of the present book, limited as it is with respect to Wittgenstein's full corpus, seems to me to be amply justified.

One further possible qualm ought perhaps to be eased. Six of the following nineteen articles deal primarily with the battery of arguments Wittgenstein directed against the notion of what he called a "private language," and some of the others have important bearings on those arguments. This emphasis is warranted not only by the fact that the subject is central in Wittgenstein's later thought, but also because his treatment of it is anything but perspicuous, and yet raises new and fascinating questions—to which one can become fairly addicted—about some very old and very basic philosophical concerns. If anyone should nevertheless still think that the weighting is excessive, I would point out to him that fully thirty per cent of the articles that have so far appeared in the literature about the later Wittgenstein have directed themselves squarely to this subject.

I wish to thank the authors of the essays here presented for their kindness in allowing me to print them. My gratitude is due also, and for the same reason, to the publishers of the books and to the editors of the journals in which pieces have previously appeared. I gratefully acknowledge the kind permission of Basil Blackwell, publishers of Wittgenstein's *Philosophical Investigations*, *The Blue and Brown Books*, and *Remarks on the Foundations of Mathematics*, to reprint the numerous quotations from those works scattered throughout the articles collected here; and that of the Athlone Press (University of London), publishers of David Pole's *The Later Philosophy of Wittgenstein*, to reprint the passages from that book quoted in

Stanley Cavell's article. I am most particularly indebted to Anthony Kenny, who wrote his article especially for this volume.

G. P.

Princeton, New Jersey

CONTENTS

EXCERPT FROM "CONTEMPORARY BRITISH PHILOSOPHY"

A. M. QUINTON

LOGICAL ANALYSIS

During the inter-war years in Britain, while realism was the official form of academic philosophy, logical analysis, first in its atomist and then in its positivist stage, developed as an increasingly powerful opposition. By the early 1920's, idealism was in full retreat, at any rate outside Scotland, its most fertile field of recruitment. It was sustained as an effective philosophical force only by the isolated, if splendid, rearguard actions of McTaggart and Collingwood. With the publication of the great works of Russell's middle period, between *Our Knowledge of the External World* (1914) and *The Analysis of Mind* (1921), and of Wittgenstein's *Tractatus Logico-Philosophicus* (1922), logical atomism emerged with striking rapidity to occupy the vacant place and to cast a Jacobin shadow over the realist's triumph. The comprehensive scope of its challenge to realism was due to the special intensity of Wittgenstein's philosophical genius. He did not put forward a few piecemeal criticisms of the realist creed but set out a complete and integrated system of dissenting answers to all the major questions that it claimed to have settled. His blunt remark in his preface

From D. J. O'Connor, ed., *A Critical History of Western Philosophy* (London: Collier-Macmillan Ltd., 1964), pp. 535–538 and 540–545. Reprinted by permission of The Free Press of Glencoe. Copyright © 1964 by The Free Press of Glencoe, a division of The Macmillan Company.

to the *Tractatus*—"the book deals with the problems of philosophy"—made a justified claim about the fullness of its reach.

In all its forms the philosophy of logical analysis consisted essentially in the application of the new formal logic of Frege and Russell to the radical empiricism of Hume. Hume's ideas had been continued or revived by Mill, Mach, and William James, and their inheritance by way of these intermediaries does something to explain the characteristic differences between the British, European, and American versions of the doctrine. This analytic and empiricist movement was logical in two principal respects. In the first place it took *Principia Mathematica* as its model for the proper form of a theory of knowledge and aimed to represent the whole of human knowledge in a logically articulated system in which everything was derived by explicit definitions and rules of inference from a minimum initial stock of undefined basic concepts and undeniable basic propositions. Secondly, it made use of three technical features of Russell's logic in order to carry out its analyses. (i) It adopted the principle of extensionality suggested by Russell's account of compound propositions as truth-functions of elementary ones, asserting that all compounds were no more than assemblages of these elements, and so went on to accept the Russellian classification of the possible forms of propositions. (ii) It made a generalized use of the technique devised by Russell for the analysis of definite descriptions, in which problematic expressions were eliminated in principle from discourse by the adoption of rules for translating sentences in which they occurred into sentences from which they were absent. By means of these definitions in use, references to material objects, minds, classes, and numbers were shown to be "incomplete symbols" and the entities to which they seemed to refer were reductively analyzed into the unquestionably empirical data of sensation. (iii) It took over, again in a generalized way, Russell's theory of types which added logical to grammatical limitations on the possible

ways of combining expressions to form meaningful assertions. The logical paradoxes had led Russell to see that
grammatically well-formed sentences could nevertheless be
meaningless, and the logical analysts concluded that an
essential preliminary to a theory of knowledge laying
down conditions for the distinction between the true and
the false was a theory of meaning to distinguish between
the significant and the senseless.

The bible of the logical analyst movement was Wittgenstein's *Tractatus*. Like other sacred texts, it combined
prophetic fervor with sibylline obscurity in a way that
invited and received many conflicting interpretations. Expressed in pregnant aphorisms, it used familiar terms in
new but unexplained senses. It seemed that Wittgenstein,
assuming the posture of the founder of a religion rather
than that of the exponent of a philosophy, was more unwilling than unable to make the task of understanding him
an easy one. The book, whose English translations have a
certain faded eloquence, was not diminished in its influence by the large variety of mutually inconsistent interpretations to which it gave rise.

Broadly speaking, the *Tractatus* sets out a general theory
of language in relation to the world. It gives an answer to
the Kantian-looking question: how is language, and so
thinking, possible? Wittgenstein was not, as Russell supposed in his introduction to the book, projecting an ideal
language in conformity with the most stringent standards
of logical perfection. He was attempting, rather, to reveal
the essential structure that must be possessed by any language capable of being significantly used and which must,
therefore, be hidden behind the familiar surface of our
actual language.

Its general outlines are best described in the order in
which Wittgenstein himself set them out, although this is
not the order of their logical dependence on one another.

1. To start with, there is an ontology, a theory of the
ultimate contents of the world. For Wittgenstein, the
world is composed not simply of objects but of objects

arranged or configurated in facts. These facts are distinct
from and independent of one another. Objects are incomplete in the sense that they only exist in the relation to
other objects that constitutes facts. There is a limit to an
object's possibilities of combination. A possible combination of objects is a state of affairs and a fact is the actual
obtaining of a state of affairs. He did not specify the concrete nature of facts; indeed he even implied that they
may be unknown to us, but he did suggest that they are
all of the same kind or level. Russell took them to be the
occurrences of a particular kind of event, private and momentary sense-experiences. But although Wittgenstein
seems to have come round to this view later, it is not
contained in the *Tractatus*. Another gap in the theory that
was filled by Russell concerns the classification of the objects of which facts are made. Wittgenstein did not distinguish them into kinds, but Russell divided them into
particular objects, the simple, if non-persistent, entities
referred to by unanalyzable names, and general objects like
attributes and relations. In Russell's view, the names of
simple objects were intelligible on their own but general
terms could only be understood as "propositional functions," fragments of propositions of the form "x has the
attribute F" or "y stands in the relation R to z."

2. The next, and crucial stage, was the theory of elementary propositions. These are the propositions which
owe their meaning and truth not to their relation to other
propositions but to their relation to the world. That there
must be such simple, unanalyzable propositions if any
propositions are to have a definite sense and not merely
stand in internal logical relations to one another, is the
cardinal axiom of Wittgenstein's philosophy. It may be
seen as a highly generalized analogue of the traditional
empiricist principle that if any concepts or propositions
are to make sense some must be derived from experience of
the world. What makes it possible for a sentence to express
an elementary proposition is its being a picture of a possible state of affairs, a possible arrangement of objects which,

if it obtains, constitutes a fact. The proposition, as an arrangement of names, pictures the state of affairs, as an arrangement of objects. If the objects it names are so arranged, then the proposition is true. Propositions and the states of affairs that they depict must have a common form, but this cannot itself be described in propositions, it can only be shown. Names, like objects, are incomplete and can only be combined in a limited number of ways. Our ability to arrange names in ways in which objects are not arranged explains false belief, and our ability to rearrange them explains our understanding of sentences whose meaning has not been explained to us. If we are to think or speak at all, then, there must be fundamental propositions owing their meaning and truth to their pictorial correspondence to states of affairs and facts respectively. From this first principle Wittgenstein derived both his ontology of facts and objects, in one direction, and his theory of the non-elementary parts of language in the other.

3. Sentences that do not express elementary, pictorial propositions are either collections, overt or concealed, of elementary propositions or they express no propositions at all and are devoid of meaning. Those that do express compound propositions are all truth-functions of elementary propositions, generated from the latter by the operations of denial and conjunction and owing their meaning and truth-value wholly to that of their elementary components. To assert a compound proposition is to do no more than conjointly to assert or deny a collection of elementary propositions. There is nothing more to a compound assertion than what is contained by its elements. It follows that the logical concepts "not," "and," "if," and "all" are not descriptive of anything in the world, they are simply structural devices for the convenient assertion of elementary propositions, the ultimate bearers of meaning and truth. Wittgenstein's account of compound propositions is the pure, formal theory of reductive analysis and established the program of the whole movement. Philosophy conceived as the analysis of propositions becomes a search for the

translations of various kinds of sentence into explicit truth-functions of elementary propositions.

4. Within the domain of compound propositions, there are two noteworthy limiting cases in which the truth-value of the compound remains the same whatever the truth-value of the elementary components. These are tautologies, such as "*p* or not-*p*," which are always true, and contradictions, such as "*p* and not-*p*," which are always false. The truth or falsity of these limiting cases is determined simply by their truth-functional structure; we do not need to know how things are in the world to tell whether they are true or false and, in consequence, they tell us nothing about the world. Their truth or falsity is thus of a degenerate kind which leads Wittgenstein to call them senseless, though this is not to say that they are nonsensical. In a fully explicit notation, where the elementary constitution of compound propositions would be made clear by the sentences expressing them, tautologies, true in every state of affairs, and contradictions, true in no state of affairs, would be superfluous. A particularly important class of tautologies is the laws of logic. These tautologous conditionals, like other tautologies, say nothing about the world. Their truth is determined by the meaning and arrangement of the non-descriptive logical terms that occur in them. In these conditionals, the consequent is simply a repetition of some or all of the antecedent and, as laws of logic, they license the deduction of the consequent from the antecedent. Deductive inference, therefore, is no more than a reiteration, partial or total, in the conclusion, of what was asserted in the premises. Deduction gives no new information and in a fully explicit notation it would be dispensable, since we could tell what the logical consequences of a proposition were by simple inspection. Wittgenstein held mathematics to consist of equations which were dispensable in principle in the same way. The identity of meaning between expressions asserted by mathematical propositions would be conveyed by the identity of the expressions themselves. In general, logically necessary

connections exist because we have different, alternative ways of saying the same thing. Obscurity of logical connection is the price we have to pay for the conveniences of abbreviation. Wittgenstein interpreted probability as a particular kind of logical relation between hypothesis and evidence. Take all the distinctly conceivable states of affairs relevant to the truth or falsity of hypothesis and evidence. The proportion of those states of affairs in which both are true to those in which the evidence, taken by itself, is true is the probability of the hypothesis on that evidence. Wittgenstein did not raise the question of the justification of induction, but he defined induction as the propensity to look for the simplest theories consistent with what we know already.

5. The abyss into which he cast all sentences that are not either elementary themselves or equivalent in meaning to some set of elementary sentences is not an entirely amorphous one. There are within it the makings of a threefold distinction between varyingly deplorable kinds of nonsense. (i) Least excusable is the nonsense of which traditional metaphysics is made up. "Most of the propositions and questions to be found in philosophical works are not false but nonsensical . . . [they] arise from our failure to understand the logic of our language." (ii) A more tolerable kind of nonsense is exhibited by the semantic sentences about the pictorial relations between language and the world which make up the *Tractatus* itself. With the fervor of Epimenides, he declares: "my propositions serve as elucidations in the following way: anyone who understands me eventually recognises them as nonsensical, when he has used them—as steps—to climb up beyond them." In other words, Wittgenstein's philosophy is indispensable nonsense and not just idle nonsense like traditional metaphysics. In an attempt to elude the self-destructiveness of this doctrine Wittgenstein maintains that philosophy is not a theory, does not issue in a body of assertible truths, but an activity, that of making the meaning of propositions clear. The ground for these puzzling conclusions is the un-

argued and, in its literal sense, false contention that the relation between a picture and what it depicts cannot be depicted. (iii) Finally, there is what might be called deep nonsense, the transcendental or mystical profundities of morality and religion. "Ethics cannot be put into words." "God does not reveal himself *in* the world." "It is not *how* things are in the world that is mystical, but *that* it exists." In his detestation of traditional academic philosophy, Wittgenstein exaggerated its distinctness both from his own theory and from what he dignifies as the mystical. By far the greater part of it can be classified either as neutral and technical analysis of the kind he practiced himself or as spiritual edification. . . .

THE LATER PHILOSOPHY OF WITTGENSTEIN

After the publication of the *Tractatus* Wittgenstein seems to have more or less given up philosophy until his return to Cambridge in 1929. From then until his retirement in 1947 he gradually worked out the profound, obscure, and inconclusive set of ideas published after his death in the *Philosophical Investigations* (1953). These new opinions were communicated orally to small groups of followers, and manuscripts of his lectures circulated surreptitiously. Wittgenstein's dedication to esotericism both in the communication and in the expression of his thoughts ensured that they would be hard to understand and frequently misunderstood.

At first glance, obscurity seems to be all that the *Tractatus* and the *Investigations* have in common. Certainly they are obscure in different ways. While the earlier book is presented in a style of marmoreal deductive rigor, with its constituent aphorisms expressed in the unvarying tone of a prophetic revelation, the later book is loose, colloquial, and varied in mood, with arguments cropping up here and there within a mass of questions, persuasive insinuations, and occasional vatic pronouncements in the earlier style.

Furthermore, the content of the two books seems directly opposed. Where the *Tractatus* saw language as a logically rigid essence concealed behind the contingent surface of everyday discourse, a skeleton to be excavated by penetrating analysis, in the *Investigations* language is accepted as it actually and observably is, as a living, unsystematic, and polymorphous array of working conventions for a large and not simply classifiable range of human purposes.

Yet both are, in their very different ways, examinations of the same topic: the relation of language to the world. Although Wittgenstein came to reject most of the particular doctrines of the *Tractatus*, the fact that he spent so much of his time in the *Investigations* in refuting them, shows that even if the answers of the earlier book were wrong the questions that they were given to were not. And Wittgenstein did not abandon everything in the *Tractatus*. In particular, he reaffirmed, if in a new way, the earlier book's thesis of the impossibility of philosophy. What had been perhaps the least digestible feature of the *Tractatus*, its self-refuting contention that the sentences of which it was composed were meaningless attempts to say what could only be shown and at best a ladder to be climbed up on and then kicked away, took the form in the *Investigations* of the philosophical theory that it was no part of philosophy to propound theories but only to describe facts about language that were perfectly familiar already, arranging these familiar descriptions in a fashion designed to break the hold on our minds of philosophical confusions and paradoxes.

British philosophy in the last forty years would have been a very different, and poorer, thing if Wittgenstein had taken his own prohibitions literally. In fact, perfectly good sense can be made of most of the sentences in the *Tractatus*, and the *Investigations* is mercifully a great deal more than the tissue of detailed reminders about the actual use of words which the author believed that it ought to have been. It is full of large, original, and highly discussable philosophical theories and of arguments in support of them. In practice, even the most loyal of his disciples (and he exacted very high standards of loyalty) treat his passionate revulsion from the idea of himself as a philosophical theorist as the aberration which those who admire the rest of his work openly proclaim it to be. Historically considered, the two generations of British philosophers who have come under his influence have in effect simply ignored these self-denying ordinances. Making the exclusions from the body of his utterances that are needed to make the remainder intelligible, they have derived from each of his books a coherent and comprehensive philosophical system: from the *Tractatus* the logical analysis of the 1930's, from the *Investigations* the linguistic philosophy of the period from 1945 to 1960.

The system of the *Investigations* has three main parts which are broadly distinguishable despite their numerous and complicated interrelations. First, there is a theory of meaning in direct opposition to the logical atomism of the *Tractatus*, a theory which looks for the meaning of a word in its use, in public acts of communication between the users of language, and not in any objects for which it may be used to stand, whether these are understood to be in the world outside us or to be within our minds. Secondly, there is a theory about the nature of philosophy which is not, as we have seen, a matter of propounding theories but has rather the negative purpose of dispelling metaphysics, philosophy in its traditional sense, the confused and perplexed affirmation of paradoxical statements that are in conflict with ordinary common-sense beliefs that we know perfectly well to be true. Finally, there is a theory of mind, the part of the *Investigations* in which Wittgenstein breaks wholly new ground, which interprets our descriptions of mental acts and states not as referring to something private within our streams of interior consciousness but as governed by criteria that mention the circumstances, behavior, and propensities to behave of the persons described. If anything in Wittgenstein's earlier work anticipates his later theory of mind it is his cryptic dis-

posal of the problem about the analysis of belief-sentences
that caused Russell in his introduction to the *Tractatus* so
much heart-searching.

The fundamental point of Wittgenstein's new theory of
meaning is that the meaning of a word is not any sort of
object for which the word stands. Certainly it is a feature
of the meaning of some words to stand for things, but
these, the proper names, constitute only a small, specialized, and unrepresentative part of language as a whole. And
even in their case, the object they stand for is not their
meaning, which is, rather, their conventionally established
capacity to stand for objects. We are over-impressed, Wittgenstein believes, by the model of ostensive definition, the
direct correlation of words with elements of the world and,
underlying this, with the idea of pointing to an object as
being a somehow self-explanatory way of giving the meaning of a word uttered at the moment of the act of pointing.
But ostensive definition is just one conventional use of the
act of pointing to things, which can also be used to give
orders rather than introduce new words. That is to say,
before pointing can give meaning to a word it must itself
be understood as having meaning.

"What is the meaning of a word?" is a typically philosophical question; it calls for an inquiry we do not know
how to conduct. To find out what meaning is, we should
consider questions that arise about meaning outside philosophical discussions: how is the meaning of a word learned
or explained, how do we tell whether someone understands
the meaning of a word? If we approach the question in
this way, by considering the common and familiar occurrences of the word "meaning," we shall see that to talk
about the meaning of a word is to talk about the way in
which it is used. To say of a man that he has learned or
understands the meaning of a word is simply to say that
he has learned or understands how to use it, that he has
become party to a certain established social convention.
The identification of meaning with the way a word is used

is vague, but this is inevitable, for words are used in many different ways and have many different sorts of meaning.

The form of the original question suggests that there is one pre-eminent way in which words mean, and this assumption leads to such views as that the basic task of words is to describe, or, as in the *Tractatus*, to picture. But if we can only divert our attention from the misleading form of the original question and look at our use of words as it actually is in all its multifariousness, we shall see that language has many other uses than that of describing things. We use them to give orders, to express our feelings, to warn, to excite, to ask questions. It should not be assumed that there is some common element to all these different uses of language, some residual essence of meaning that is present in them all. The uses of language, in Wittgenstein's famous simile, are like games. Because we use one word to apply to all the vast variety of games, we are inclined to imagine that they all have some common property if only we could put our fingers on it. But this is not so. Games have only a family resemblance; there is a large collection of similarities only a few of which will obtain between any two of the practices we call games. To bring out this multiplicity of uses, Wittgenstein ran the two terms of his simile together in the notion of a language-game, this being a simplified model of some particular aspect of our language, studied in isolation by being conceived as the total language of some group of people. These are artificial abstractions from language as it is, since the uses of language overlap even more than most games do. The pieces, i.e., the words, we use in any one language-game may each be used in many different language-games as well.

Wittgenstein's insistence on the multiplicity of different uses of words has an egalitarian flavor. It is opposed to the idea that certain forms of language are specially privileged, meaningful in some unique, fundamental sense. He rejects, therefore, his earlier doctrine of elementary sentences made up of unanalyzable logically proper names and the atomic facts and simple objects supposed to correspond to them. No type of discourse is intrinsically simple or basic. Simplicity is always a relative notion, relative in particular to what we have a clear apprehension of already. There is not, therefore, any unique analysis of propositions into their intrinsically unanalyzable elements. What sort of analysis will be useful and provide a real clarification depends on the circumstances, on just what is problematic about the propositions under examination. Indeed, he would not accept "analysis" as a proper description of his later inquiries into meaning. The assumption that translation is the ideal technique for the clarification of meaning rests on another oversimplified image of the workings of language, one which treats language as a logical calculus, which is as confusing and irrelevant as that which sees the essence of significance to lie in picturing. The language we use is not, except in certain special technical areas, logically regimented in the manner of a calculus. It would be wholly unable to fulfil the purposes it now does if it were. The elasticity of language from a formal point of view is what makes it possible for us to convert it to new uses, to superimpose new tasks on to those it already has. He sums up his theory of meaning by saying that the language-games, within which alone words have meaning, are forms of life, modes of activity governed by systems of rules. A form of life involves attitudes, interests, and behavior; it is something far more comprehensive than the manipulation of a clearly specified calculus.

Wittgenstein's theory of meaning makes it clear that philosophy, understood as the clarification of meaning, will be something very different from the construction of a rigidly formal hierarchy of forms of discourse carried out in the *Tractatus*. It would have to be more complicated and more various in its technique than the philosophy of logical analysis with its ambition of arriving at exact rules of translation. But nothing said so far entails the extreme asceticism of the view of philosophy which he actually arrived at. Philosophy is not just any inquiry into meaning. It con-

sists of inquiries into meaning directed toward a particular
purpose, the resolution of a special kind of perplexity or
puzzlement. It is this condition of relevance to metaphysical confusions that distinguishes Wittgenstein's idea of the
proper method of philosophy from Austin's. For Austin
seemed to be interested in the rules of language for their
own sake and displayed a corresponding Baconian empiricism about language in his actual philosophical practice.
Many of the delicate discriminations in his writings are no
more than associated with the philosophical problems he
is concerned with and play no part in advancing the main
line of argument. Wittgenstein's view is that men are naturally led into metaphysics, into the making of assertions
which worry us by the collision between their apparent
deductive inevitability on the one hand and their incompatibility with familiar and deep-seated common-sense beliefs on the other. He agrees with Moore that, in this
collision, it is the metaphysical paradoxes that must give
way. They are, he holds, the outcome of our misunderstandings of the logic of our language and arise from the
misleading influence of insidious verbal analogies. We are
led by the surface grammar of words, as he calls it, the
overt likenesses between forms of discourse with very different uses, to assimilate and so misrepresent their depth
grammar. The task of philosophy is to undermine these
intoxicating analogies by the revelation of depth grammar,
by recalling our attention to the actual working of the perplexing words in all its variety. He goes on to repudiate the
metaphor involved in the phrase "depth grammar" by insisting that the facts about language from which misleading
analogies divert our attention are not hidden in the ordinary sense of being concealed. The situation is rather that
we ignore the pattern present in a whole range of uses by
fixing our gaze on one particular, favored corner of it, as
one might ignore the pattern in a carpet by looking at it
in the wrong way. We do not need to look at the carpet
with special instruments or to turn it over and examine its
underside, which was roughly the proposal of the *Tractatus*,

but to change our attitude toward it and to free ourselves from the constriction of a routine, mechanical response to it. Metaphysics is often produced by our considering words in strange connections which only occur in the writings of philosophers. In such cases, language is idling, there are no established rules for the use of words in these connections, and so we are compelled to resort to more or less untrustworthy analogies to provide a use for them. To overcome this kind of confusion we need to examine language at work, about its familiar everyday business.

Wittgenstein concludes that it is no part of the business of philosophy to reform language. It must leave everything as it is. He is not saying that language cannot be changed but rather that such changes must arise from the concrete needs of language users and not from abstract reflection about the nature of language. A further conclusion is that the philosopher must not simply replace old, bad, misleading analogies by new ones, for he seems to assume that these will be no improvement in the end on the theories they replace. What he must do is simply describe language about its everyday work, assemble reminders so that the actual pattern of uses is made clear to us. Everything in the pattern is perfectly familiar to us already; what the philosopher has to do is to make us aware of it as a pattern. Both of these conclusions have been criticized. In so far as philosophers in the past have been led into false or meaningless assertions by misunderstandings of the actual use of words, then to that extent proper, corrective philosophy will be concerned to clear up these misunderstandings by bringing that actual use into the open. But the original thesis about the causes of metaphysics is not very convincingly established. Furthermore, no very effective test of what is metaphysical in the bad sense is provided. Certainly there are philosophers who have revelled in the surprising and counter-intuitive appearance of their conclusions, Bradley and McTaggart, for example. But others, Aristotle and Kant are perhaps the most notable instances, have always aimed to reconcile their conclusions with the body of commonly accepted knowledge. Wittgenstein offers some tests for metaphysics, but they are of an imprecise and subjective character: the feeling of a particular sort of puzzlement, of not knowing one's way about. His rejection of the whole notion of philosophy as a criticism of ordinary ways of thinking is brought out in his attitude toward the problem of justifying kinds of belief. To discover what justifies a certain kind of belief, he says, all we have to do is to see what is generally accepted as justifying it. The role of philosophy, then, is purely negative. It is the removal of obstacles to understanding, not a business of making discoveries. In another of his influential similes, he likened philosophy to psychoanalytic therapy, which does not simply find out what is wrong with neurotics and tell them but gradually induces them to recognize the real significance of their words and actions. But, to turn to Wittgenstein's other conclusion, that philosophy must simply describe and remind, not theorize, the psychoanalyst has a theory himself about the nature of his patient's disorder which the patient can come to understand. Wittgenstein does not make out the case for a parallel in the situation of his metaphysical patients to repression or resistance to analysis. His view that philosophical analysis must use more various and complex techniques than the strict translation of the 1930's is better founded than his doctrines that it can only describe the established use of words, not explain, criticize, or attempt to improve on it, and that this description can only be safely carried out by the accumulation of exemplary reminders and not in any sort of general or theoretical terms. Certainly his account of previous philosophy as pathological does not seem to have been confirmed by much therapeutic success. The problems he aimed to dissolve have obstinately refused to stay dead. History refutes his view that it is no part of philosophy to interfere with our existing use of words or with our existing standards of justifying argument. The language of modern science and the criteria of evidence that it opposed to reliance on authority, scripture, and the syllogism were the creation of the philosophers of the seventeenth century. Finally, his own practice makes clear that, despite the most strenuous efforts, no sort of philosophy can confine itself to the presentation of exemplary reminders. The purpose of assembling reminders is to correct a mistaken analogy, and to do this is inevitably to put forward a correct one. If the *Philosophical Investigations* had been merely the album of accepted uses of words it ought to have been according to its author's theory, it would not have had the large and generally illuminating influence it has had.

The particular philosophical problem that takes up most of Wittgenstein's attention in the *Investigations* is that of the nature of mind or, in his terminology, of the language in which we report and describe the mental states of ourselves and others. The metaphysical doctrine against which he is arguing here is that persistent dualism of mind and body, made explicit by Plato and Descartes, but, it would seem, rather deeply lodged in our ordinary way of thinking, which holds that mental states exist in private worlds of their own of which only one person is directly aware. The paradoxes arising from this theory are, first and foremost, the idea that we can never know what is going on in the mind of another person and also perhaps the older difficulty about understanding how things can act upon each other when they are as different from one another as mental and bodily states are according to this theory. The mistaken analogy that lies behind the skeptical absurdities of dualism is that between "I see a tree" or "I touch this stone" on the one hand and "I feel a pain" and "I understand this calculation" on the other. Just as the first two sentences report perception of and action on physical things so, it is supposed, the other two report mental perception and action. The world is then conceived as containing, alongside material objects and acts of manipulating them, mental objects like pains and mental acts or processes like understanding, meaning and thinking.

Wittgenstein maintains that our mental vocabulary does not refer to inner acts and states. It is not so much that he denies the existence of private experiences as that he denies that they could serve as criteria for the employment of mental words. In his view, to say that someone is in a given mental state is to say that he is in any of a large collection of publicly observable situations, that he is doing or disposed to do any of a large collection of publicly observable things. There is no one recurrent kind of thing of which a mental word is the name, nor is it the name of any kind of private thing. He supports this theory with two kinds of argument. In the first place, he examines in detail the working of a representative selection of mental concepts, and, secondly, he has a general argument to prove that a private language, referring to the experiences of which only one person is aware, is an impossibility.

The most important and suggestive particular concept he investigates is that of understanding. The dualist supposes that when someone under instruction says "now I understand," he is reporting a private experience of understanding. But whatever experience he may have, Wittgenstein replies, cannot be the sense, and thus the criterion of truth, of the man's remark. What decides whether or not he really does understand, let us say, long division, is whether or not he can go on to repeat the operation for himself, preferably on new material so as to rule out his having learnt by heart the arrangement of numbers making up the long division sum. To understand something is to be able to apply it. It might be thought that this objection could be countered by a further specification of the purported experience of understanding. Could the experience not take the form of the private awareness of some image or formula which gives the gist of the operation claimed to be understood? Against this suggestion Wittgenstein argues that an image or formula does not dictate its own application. It must itself be understood, and that it has been understood is something that only its correct application can establish. An image or formula as it stands can be interpreted or understood in different ways. Only its publicly observable application can show if the interpretation made of it is the correct one. Essentially the same argument is applied to the concept of meaning something by a word. What a man means by a word is not a private experience, in particular it is not an image which is itself a symbol that can be meant, i.e., used, in very different ways. The meaning a man attaches to a word is only to be discovered by considering the things to which he applies, and from which he withholds, the word and the verbal contexts, the statements and arguments, in which he employs it. It follows from this that thinking is not an interior process that accompanies speech and is the criterion of its being intelligent speech and not babbling. For to think what one is saying is no more than to mean what one is saying. The same general treatment is extended to cover concepts of emotion such as hope and fear. All these concepts derive their significance from the surroundings of the people to whom they are ascribed and not to some private events going on within them. The concepts considered so far all relate to higher forms of mentality and, primarily at any rate, can only be ascribed to creatures that are at least human beings to the extent of being users of language. An important feature of the "surroundings" in these cases is what the people to whom they are ascribed will say. What sense is there, Wittgenstein asks, to the supposition that a dog is afraid of something that may happen next week?

Having argued that the publicly observable surroundings are in fact the criteria for our applications of mental words in these examples, Wittgenstein goes on to prove that this must be so, since there could not be a language whose use was wholly determined by private experiences. It might seem that I could resolve to utter a certain word whenever a sensation like this particular one I am having now took place. This decision would provide a criterion which I should apply whenever the same sensation recurred. But what could be meant, he asks, by the question whether a given sensation was the same as the one chosen as the criterion? We could only compare the present sensation with our memory of its predecessor, and how could we eliminate the possibility that our memory was playing us false? He concludes that language is an essentially social phenomenon. The making of noises does not become linguistic utterance unless it is governed by rules, unless there is an applicable distinction between the correct and mistaken use of words. With a private language, this condition cannot be satisfied, and the uttering of words introduced as names of private sensations would be just an "empty ceremony." It is for this reason that our mental words must be, as they are, connected with features of our situation which anyone can in principle observe. Every inner process must have its outward criteria.

The concept to which this treatment seems least applicable is that of pain, and Wittgenstein considers it at length. Here, as elsewhere, it is important to consider the way in which the use of the words under examination is learnt. Now, we learn how to use the words "it hurts" from other people who tell that we are in pain from our circumstances and behavior. But we do not tell that we are in pain ourselves in this way. In fact, Wittgenstein maintains, we do not discover or find out that we are in pain at all. It is not a thing we can be in doubt about and so not a thing of which it is appropriate to claim knowledge. We use no criteria for our utterances of "it hurts" and it is an incorrigible statement in the sense that we cannot be honestly mistaken about it. If I do hesitate about saying that I am in pain that shows that it is not exactly pain that I am suffering from but something like it, discomfort perhaps. Statements about pain in the first person, Wittgenstein says, are in fact extensions of natural pain-behavior, conventionalized alternatives to crying out which we are trained to adopt. They are not so much descriptions of pain but manifestations of it.

The will, in Wittgenstein's opinion, is no more private and internal than thought and feeling. The difference between my raising my arm and my arm's simply going up in the air does not consist in the presence in the former case of an interior act of will. What commonly characterizes voluntary movement is the absence of surprise. Intentions, again, are not private states. I ordinarily know for certain what my intentions are, but this does not rest on any sort of interior observation. There is a parallel here, he asserts, with our knowledge of the movements and positions of our bodies. We do not have to look to see where our arms are but we do not tell by some recognizable feeling either.

The bearing of this theory of mental language on the metaphysical problem about our knowledge of other minds which inspired it is that there is no such general problem. For there could be no mental language with which I could talk about my own mind unless there were a public mental language and I had mastered it. He does not say that any statement about the mind of another person strictly and deductively follows from any set of statements about his behavior. Nevertheless, what others do and say provides all the ground that is required for the justification of our beliefs about them. To believe that other people have feelings in the way we do ourselves does not consist in the acceptance of a definite set of propositions. It is shown, rather, in the way in which we treat other people, in our attitudes of pity and concern for them, for example. . . .

Wittgenstein's direct successors have remained loyal to his idea of philosophy as an activity without statable results. The Oxford philosophers of ordinary language, on the other hand, have taken from him his positive doctrines about the nature of meaning and of mental concepts but have developed them in a more systematic way than he did. They have largely accepted his view about the nature of metaphysics and its causation by misunderstandings of the actual use of words. It has led them to an even closer attention than his to its actual working. If they have not followed him in ruling out the possibility of philosophical theorizing, many, under the influence of Austin, have been profoundly suspicious of anything very general in the way of theory. But they have been more impressed by its difficulty than convinced of its impossibility. . . .

REVIEW OF WITTGENSTEIN'S
PHILOSOPHICAL INVESTIGATIONS

P. F. STRAWSON

This book is a treatment, by a philosopher of genius, of
a number of intricate problems, intricately connected. It
also presents in itself an intricate problem: that of seeing
clearly what the author's views are on the topics he discusses, and how these views are connected. The difficulty
of doing this arises partly from the structure and style of
the book. Wittgenstein himself describes the former accurately in the preface: "The best I could write could
never be more than philosophical remarks," "Thus this
book is really only an album." It would, however, be a very
strong prejudice against this disregard of the ordinary
conventions of exposition, which could survive a careful
reading of the whole book. Wittgenstein did not gloss his
thoughts; but he arranged them. And the gains in power
and concentration are great. It might even be thought that
there were good reasons why no attempt at all should be
made to present his views in a more conventional form.
But this could be true only on a very specialised view of
the nature of philosophical understanding. In what follows,
I try to trace and connect the main lines of his thought;
conscious that, at best, the result must involve a great im-
poverishment of his rich and complex thinking. I refer to
passages in Part I of the book simply by paragraph number
(*e.g.* 500); to passages in Part II by section and/or page
number (*e.g.* II. xi, p. 200). Quotations from the text are

From *Mind*, Vol. LXIII (1954), pp. 70–99. Reprinted with
the permission of the author and editor.

in double quotation marks. Comment and criticism will
be interspersed with exposition.

Meaning and Use. In the first thirty-seven or thirty-eight
paragraphs of Part I, which are concerned with meaning,
Wittgenstein is anxious to make us see "the multiplicity
of kinds of words and sentences" (23). We are prone to
assimilate different kinds. In particular, we are prone to
work with a certain idea of language as consisting of words
each correlated with something for which it stands, an
object, the meaning of the word (1). This picture, though
philosophically misleading for all words, is better suited
to some than to others. When we have it in mind, we are
primarily thinking of common nouns like 'chair' and
'bread' and of people's names; even primitive reflection
shows that it does not fit, say, logical connectives. So not
only is there a general tendency to assimilate different
kinds of words to each other; there is also a particular
direction which this assimilation tends to take. Perhaps
the general tendency is in part explained by the fact that
words look or sound much alike: from their uniform appearance on the printed page one would never guess at
their diversity of function (11). But there are more complex reasons both for the general tendency and for its
particular direction. The central point is this: *the picture
with which we are inclined to work derives essentially from
the instruction-setting of someone who has already mastered in part the technique of using the language; i.e. from
the situation in which someone is being taught the place
of one word, of which he is ignorant, in a way of using
language with which he is familiar (cf. 10, 27, 30, 32).*
In this situation, the instructor may well proceed by saying
something like 'the word x means (is the name of, stands
for, signifies, etc.) y' where the place of 'y' is taken by,
e.g. 'this' 'this number' 'a number' 'this colour' 'the colour
which . . . ,' or simply by a synonym or translation of the
word in question. In some, though not all, cases, he may
accompany these words by pointing. Or he may just answer the question 'What is y (this, this colour, this thing)

called?' by pronouncing the word. These procedures may
give us the impression of a relation of a unique kind being
established between two items, a word and something else;
and the further impression that the essence of meaning
is to be grasped by the contemplation of this unique relation. To counter this impression, to remind ourselves that
the efficacy of these procedures depends on the existence of
a prepared framework of linguistic training, we should bear
in mind such points as these two: that an ostensive definition (*many* kinds of words can be taught by indicating
situations in which they are in some sense applicable) can
always be variously interpreted (28); and that the process
of asking the names of things and being told them is itself
one language-game[1] among others, and a comparatively
sophisticated one.

Two minor comments. (1) Perhaps Wittgenstein does
not here sufficiently emphasise the point that the *natural*
place for the word 'meaning' and its derivatives in ordinary
use is in just such instruction-situations as those referred
to. One might get the impression that he was saying: 'In
philosophy you want the meaning of the word. Don't look
for the mythical, uniquely related term, but look at the
use; for *that* is the meaning' (*cf.* 43). But in view of the
natural place of 'meaning,' it might be better to say: 'In
doing philosophy, it can't be that you are ignorant of the
meaning: what you want to know is the use.' (2) Wittgenstein does not seek to give a complete explanation of why,
among all the kinds of names there are, it is substance-
names that tend to be taken as the model for meaning. A
suggestion which can perhaps be extracted from the text is
that (*a*) pointing figures largely both in ostensive explanation of words, and in that more primitive training in the
naming-game which a child goes through before it actually

[1] Wittgenstein uses this phrase to refer to any particular way,
actual or invented, of using language (*e.g.* to a particular way of
using a certain sentence, or a certain word); and also to "the
whole consisting of language and the actions into which it is
woven" (7).

uses words for any more practical purpose; and (b) pointing is more naturally used to discriminate the individual man or horse than any other kind of item. But there remains a question here.

Instead, then, of gazing at this over-simple picture of language, with its attendant assimilations, we are to look at the elements of language as instruments. We are to study their use. Only so can we solve our conceptual problems. Variants on 'use' in Wittgenstein are 'purpose' 'function' 'role' 'part' 'application.' It is not a complaint to say that this central notion is not immediately and wholly clear. The general aim is clear enough: to get us away from our fascination with the dubious relation of naming, of meaning, and to make us look at the speaking and writing of language as one human activity among others, interacting with others; and so to make us notice the different parts that words and sentences play in this activity. But here I inevitably re-introduce one of the variants: 'the parts they play.' Perhaps seeing what sorts of things count as *differences* of use will help one to get clear about the central notion. And here it will seem that there are differences between differences which Wittgenstein might have made more explicit.

Consider first what he says of different kinds of sentences. He makes the point that a formal (grammatical) likeness may cover a functional difference (21–22). Then (23): "But how many kinds of sentence are there? Say assertion, question, and command?— There are *countless* kinds: countless different kinds of use of what we call 'symbols,' 'words,' 'sentences.'" There follows a list of activities which involve the use of language. When we look at the items in the list, it becomes clear that the shift from 'kinds of sentence' in the question to 'kinds of use' in the answer was an important one. The list includes, for example, as separate uses, the activities of reading a story, play-acting, and translating from one language to another. The sentence 'It was raining' might occur in the course of any one of these activities; as it might in a factual narra-

tion. It would be absurd to speak of different *sentences*
here, let alone of different kinds of sentences. We *might*
speak of different uses of the sentence, though it would
be better to speak of different linguistic activities in each
of which the sentence occurred. Similarly, I suppose, reading aloud a story containing the sentence would involve a
different use from copying the story out; reading aloud a
translation of a story from reading aloud (*a*) an original,
(*b*) a translated factual narrative in all of which the sentence occurred; and there is also the special use involved
in sending an old man to sleep by reading aloud from a
translation of a play. Surely distinctions are needed here
to save the whole notion from sliding into absurdity. Such
points as the following call for attention: sometimes there
is a formal (grammatical) distinction to correspond to
(not to coincide with) a 'difference in use'; sometimes
there is not (in what cases would it be more or less natural
to have one, and why?); sometimes the existence of a
formal distinction would be self-defeating. There is a class
of interrogative sentences (sentences of which the standard
use is to ask questions); there is no class of translators'
sentences; there *could be* no class of copyists' sentences.

Consider next the point that we cannot in general talk
about the functions or uses of *words* in the same sort of
way as we can talk about the functions or uses of sentences.[2] (Of course, a word may *sometimes* function as a
sentence.) To suppose that we could would be like supposing that we could talk of the function of a numeral in
the same way as we could talk of the purpose of a calculation; or discuss a gambit and a piece in the same terms.
We might imagine a very simple language A, in which a
limited number of sentences could be formed from a

[2] *Cf.* Ryle, 'Ordinary Language,' *The Philosophical Review*,
April, 1953, pp. 178–180. Perhaps Professor Ryle puts too much
weight on the fact (if it is a fact) that we do not speak of the
'use' of sentences. Certainly we use them. But it is at any rate
true that there are some things we might mean by 'the use of a
word' which we could not mean by 'the use of a sentence'; and
the other way about.

limited number of words; and a second language B, containing no distinction of sentences and words, but consisting of unitary expressions such that every sentence of A could be translated into a unitary expression of B. Then it might be the case that every remark we could make about a use of a sentence in A would also be true of a use of an expression in B. We could also discuss the uses of the *words* of A; but there would be nothing to be said on this subject in the case of B. What perhaps causes confusion here is that very often when we (and Wittgenstein) discuss the use of *words* of certain classes, what we are concerned with is the *criteria* for their correct application; and this discussion is the same as the discussion of the conditions in which it is correct to use a *sentence* of a certain kind, namely, the sentence which says that we have here a case of what the word in question describes.

The fact that Wittgenstein is content to leave this central notion of use so vague is a manifestation of his reluctance to make distinctions and classifications which are not of direct assistance to the fly in the flybottle (309). Underlying this reluctance is a general, and debatable, doctrine of the nature of philosophy: to which I shall refer later.

Towards the end of these introductory paragraphs there enters one of the main themes of the book (33–36). Wittgenstein imagines an objection to the view that understanding an ostensive definition requires a mastery of the language. Someone might say that all that is necessary to this understanding is for the learner to know what the teacher is *pointing to* or *meaning* or *attending to*, when he makes his gesture—*e.g.* to the shape or to the colour of the object. Wittgenstein does not deny this; but points out that though there may be characteristic experiences (*e.g.* feelings) of 'meaning' or 'pointing to' the shape, which the learner might share with the teacher, their occurrence is not sufficient to make the situation one of 'meaning the shape.' Not just because they do not always occur. Even if they did it would still depend on the circumstances, the setting, on what happens before and afterwards, whether the case is one of intending or interpreting the definition in such and such a way. Seeing this is helped by seeing that there are in fact many things which may occur at the time, and none which must. It is in such cases, however, that we are apt to feign a *special* experience or mental act or process to answer to such a description.

This single topic, of *meaning* or *understanding something* by, say, a gesture, a word or a sentence, is the most persistently recurrent in the book. It is easy to see why. It is a place where two major preoccupations overlap, where two principal enemies may join hands. These enemies are psychologism in the philosophy of meaning, and the doctrine of special experiences in the philosophy of mind. Against them stand Wittgenstein's ideas. To grasp a meaning is to be able to practise a technique; while 'meaning, understanding something by a word' is itself a prime instance of those psychological expressions which seem to refer to something which happens at a point, or over a short period, of time, and may indeed do so; but, when they do, it is to something which gains its significance and its claim to its special title from what stretches before and after the point or the period.

But the main discussion of psychological concepts is deferred until the end of a further discussion of language and logic.

Language, Analysis and Philosophy (38–137). The general over-simple picture of meaning which Wittgenstein examines at the beginning of his book takes an intenser, tauter, form in a certain special doctrine of the *real* names of a language. This doctrine Wittgenstein now discusses; and the discussion broadens into a general repudiation of the set of philosophical ideas and ideals, roughly indicated by the title of 'logical atomism.' He begins with a consideration of two related notions: the idea of the genuine names of a language, and the idea of the simple indestructible elements of reality which can only be named, not described or defined, and which are the meanings of the genuine names. These are the primary elements referred to by Socrates in the *Theaetetus*, and are identified by Wittgenstein with Russell's 'individuals' and his own 'objects' of the *Tractatus* (46). Both ideas are subjected to destructive criticism and diagnosis in 39–59. First Wittgenstein attacks the notion of the word of which the meaning is the object it applies to: he instances the ordinary proper name and distinguishes between its bearer and its meaning (40); in this case, too, the meaning is the use (41–43). (Wittgenstein here gives the wrong reason for objecting to the identification of the, or a, meaning of a proper name with its bearer, or one of its bearers. If we speak at all of the meaning of proper names, it is only in quite *specialised* ways, as when we say that 'Peter' means a stone, or 'Giovanni' means 'John.' This is not an accident of usage, but reflects a radical difference between proper names and other names. But here, as elsewhere, Wittgenstein neglects the use of 'meaning.')

The antithesis 'simple-composite' is next examined and shown to have application only in a particular context, and to have different applications in different contexts: the *philosophical* question whether something is composite or simple is only too likely to lack a suitable context and hence a sense (47). Next (48–49) a simple model-language is constructed which might be held to answer to the specifications given in the *Theaetetus*; an arrangement of coloured squares is 'described' by an arrangement of letters, one letter for each square, the letters varying with the colour of the squares. We might perhaps say, in the context of this language-game, that the 'simple elements' were the individual squares. But then the assertion that the simple elements can only be named, not described, is at best, perhaps, a misleading way of saying that in the case of an arrangement consisting of one single square, the description consists of a single letter, the name of the coloured square; or of saying that *giving* a name to an element is different from *using* the name to describe a complex. Wittgenstein next considers the doctrine of the indestructibility, the necessary existence, of elements named by genuine names: the doctrine that the very meaningfulness of the name guarantees the existence of the item named. He is rightly not content to rely on a general repudiation of the notion of meaning-as-object, but produces answers to arguments in the doctrine's favour, and further explanations of its sources. The interest of the answers is weakened by the indescribable badness of the arguments (*cf.* 55, 56, 57). The explanations remain. If I understand them rightly, they run as follows. (1) We are inclined to get muddled over sentences like 'Turquoise exists.' This might be used to mean 'There are things which are turquoise'—an ordinary empirical proposition, which could be false—or 'There is such a colour as turquoise' (*i.e.* ' "Turquoise" does have meaning as a colour-word'). Taken the second way, it is again an empirical proposition, this time about a word. The muddle begins when we both take it this way and at the same time inconsistently take it as a proposition *using* the word 'turquoise' with the meaning it has, and thus as saying something about the colour, turquoise. Then we seem to be saying something necessary (for a word couldn't be used with, *i.e.* have, a meaning, and not have one), and also seem to be saying something about the colour, *viz.* that it necessarily exists (58). Wittgenstein does not remark that this account might apply to the abstract-noun form of *any* descriptive word (*e.g.* healthiness), and not merely to those which philosophers are prone to take as the names of ultimate elements. Perhaps this account should be regarded simply as a supplement to the other (2) which is summed up in the epigram, "What looks as if it *had* to exist is a part of the language" (50). If it were a necessary part of the activity of using a word 'W' that we, say, consulted a sample of W, then we might say that a sample of W must exist in order for the word to have meaning. From this *recherché* possibility, I take it we are to move to the truism that we could not teach a word by naming a sample unless there were a sample to name (*cf.* 50), and to join this to the reflection that there are at any rate some words which it is tempting to suppose could not be learnt except by means of an ostensive definition. Then we have the makings of a tautology which might be misconstrued as an assertion of metaphysically necessary existence.

The doctrine of elements is obviously connected with the belief in *analysis* as the inevitable method of philosophical clarification: the belief that the philosophical elucidation of an ordinary sentence is achieved when it is replaced by another, which makes explicit the complexity of the proposition expressed and reflects exactly the form of the fact described (91). This belief is an illusion, engendered by confusions about language and logic, and to be dispelled only by a clear view of the actual functioning of language. How exactly does the illusion arise? (Here Wittgenstein's answer has a kind of passionate obscurity which it is difficult to penetrate.) In logic, which is at once completely pure, exact, and general, we seem to have the clue to the essential nature of thought and language, and with this, the clue to the general *a priori* order of the world, of things empirical (97). For do not thought and language mirror the world? (The *thought* that it is raining is the thought *that it is raining*: the propositions fit the facts [95–96].) Somehow the exactness and order of which logic gives us the ideal must (we think) be hidden in every, even the vaguest-looking, sentence of ordinary language: the *sense* of each must be definite. Logic shows us in advance what the structure of language and the world is—so this structure must be found hidden, to be revealed by analysis, in what we actually say (98 *et seq.*). Wittgenstein does not suggest that what philosophers have called 'analysis' is, in fact, useless. Sometimes "misunderstanding concerning the use of words, caused, among other things, by certain analogies between the forms of expression in different regions of language . . . can be removed by substituting one form of expression for another" (90). But this fact itself contributes to the illusion that there is "something like a final analysis of our forms of language, and so a *single* completely resolved form of every expression" (91).

To dispel this illusion, we are to give up looking for the essence of language and instead are to look at what is all the time before our eyes: the actual functioning of language. Then we see that linguistic activities are as diverse as all the things which we call 'games,' and which are so called not because of any single common element, but because of "family resemblances"—a "complicated network of similarities, overlapping and criss-crossing" (66). (The sub-class of linguistic formations that we call 'propositions' is also just such a family. We are apt to think we have a clue to the general nature of the *proposition* in the idea of *whatever is true or false*. But one of these ideas cannot be used to elucidate the other: they move too closely together, they share each other's ambiguities [134–137].) Wittgenstein here makes an ingenious double use of his examination of the word 'game.' He not only uses the concept 'game' to cast light on the concept 'language' by means of direct *comparison*: games form a family, and so do the various activities which come under the general description of 'using language.' He also uses it as an *illustration*, to cast light on language in another way: by showing the parts which the notions of rules, and of exactness of meaning, play there. Thus the application of the word 'game' is not limited by any precise boundary; though a boundary could be fixed for a special purpose. We could say it was an *inexact* concept, that there was an indeterminacy in the rules for its use. But the important thing to notice is that this does not detract from its usefulness for ordinary purposes (and for extraordinary purposes, special rules can be devised). So that it would not even be *correct* in general, to speak of inexactness here; for 'inexact' is a word of dispraise, signifying that what is so-called falls short of a standard required for some particular purpose (88); and here no such special purpose has been specified. Moreover: (1) in whatever detail we give the rules for the use of a word (or for the playing of a game), cannot we always imagine a case in which there might be a doubt as to whether the rule applied to this case or not? and (2) is there not always the possibility of someone's not knowing how to interpret the rules or the explanations we give him of them, or the explanations of those explanations? The point Wittgenstein is making here is that the demand for absolute precision in the rules (a fixed meaning) or for absolute finality in their interpretation, their explanation, is senseless. What determines whether there is enough precision in the rules, or a sufficient explanation of them, is whether the concept is used successfully, with general agreement (84–87).

(One of the illustrations which Wittgenstein uses here is unfortunate. He wishes to say that I could use a proper name "without a fixed meaning," without its losing its usefulness; "asked what I understand by 'N,'" he says, I might adduce various descriptions some of which I might later be prepared to abandon as false of N [79]. Of course, I never should be asked *what* I understand by, but *whom* I mean by, 'N'; and in answering, I should not be defining 'N,' but identifying N.)

With what conception of philosophy is this revised view of the nature of language associated? The key to the solution of our problems still lies in their source, *viz.* language itself. But we are not to try to improve on, to tamper with, language; only to describe its workings. For the confusions we are troubled by arise not when language is doing its work, but when it is idling, on holiday; it is when we consider words and sentences in abstraction from their linguistic and non-linguistic contexts that they seem to conceal a mystery and invite a myth. So we are to "assemble reminders" of obvious facts about their uses; not at random, nor yet systematically; but on each occasion with some particular purpose in view, the purpose of dispelling some particular confusion. And to make clear the ways in which words actually function, it will sometimes be helpful to consider ways in which they do not, but might, function;

invented language-games will be useful objects of comparison with actual language-games (109–133).

Many philosophers would agree with much of this: it is difficult not to share the conception of philosophy held by the first philosopher of the age. Yet there are at least two very different directions in which it may seem unduly restrictive. First, there is the idea that the *sole* purpose of the distinctions we draw attention to, the descriptions we give of the different ways in which words function, is to dispel particular metaphysical confusions; and, associated with this, an extreme aversion from a systematic exhibition of the logic of particular regions of language. Now, even if we *begin* with a therapeutic purpose, our interest might not exhaust itself when that purpose is achieved; and there can be an investigation of the logic of sets of concepts, which starts with no purpose other than that of unravelling and ordering complexities for the sake of doing so. The desire to present the facts systematically here becomes important in proportion as therapeutic aims become secondary. The other direction might be suggested by what Wittgenstein himself says of certain metaphysical doctrines such as solipsism. The inventor of such a doctrine has discovered "a new way of looking at things"—something like "a new way of painting . . . or a new kind of song" (401). It is surely over-puritanical to hold that, just because the claims made for such new ways were too large, we should be concerned solely with preventing ourselves from seeing the world afresh. We might make room for a purged kind of metaphysics, with more modest and less disputable claims than the old. But one does not need to have an equal sympathy with both these possibilities in order to ask: could not the activities we call 'doing philosophy' also form a family?

Meaning and Understanding. (See first: 132–242, 319–326, 357–358, 431–436, 454. Further references are given later in this section.) Wittgenstein next reverts to the themes of *meaning* and *understanding* something by an expression—a theme announced, but not developed, at the

end of the introductory paragraphs (33–36). The main
sections which he devotes to this topic are of great bril-
liance and clarity. He begins with the point that the fundamental criteria for whether someone has understood an
expression lie in the application which he makes of it. Of
course, he may correctly be said to 'grasp the meaning in a
flash.' A picture or a paraphrase may come before his
mind; he may produce them to us. But neither picture nor
paraphrase dictates the use that is to be made of it: they
can be *variously* applied, and if we are inclined to forget
this, it is because we are inclined to think of only one
application. So the production of the picture or paraphrase,
though normally (and rightly) enough to satisfy us, is not
the final test: *that* resides in the application. Now this
may seem acceptable enough so long as we are considering
the criteria we employ for someone else's understanding.
But do we not often and correctly say of *ourselves*, when,
e.g. someone is trying to teach us how to develop a series,
things like: 'Now I understand!', 'Now I can go on!'? It is
obvious that we are not here applying to ourselves the
criterion of application: we seem to be reporting something which "makes its appearance in a moment." No
doubt there usually is some momentary experience: *e.g.*
a formula for the series may occur to us, or we may just
experience a feeling of release of tension. But, though in
certain cases, a remark such as 'The formula has occurred
to me' might have the same force, serve the same purpose
as 'Now I understand' etc., it will not do to say that in
general these expressions have the same meaning (183). In
any case it is clear that *the understanding* is not to be
identified with any such characteristic experience. (This
will seem only too clear; and is the point at which we are
tempted to look for a special experience.) If we ask what,
in the eyes of others, "justifies" me in using the words
'Now I understand' etc., what shows my use of them to be
"correct," it is not the occurrence of the experience, whatever it may be, but the circumstances under which I have
it (*e.g.* that I have worked with these formulae before,

that I now continue the series, etc.) (153–155). This
obviously does not mean that the words 'Now I can go
on!' are short for a description of all these circumstances,
or that they mean 'I have had an experience which I know
empirically to lead to the continuation of the series' (179);
my certainty that I shall be able to go on is not a matter of
induction (*cf.* 324–328). What we need (here I interpret
a little) is to look at such first-person utterances in a radically different way from the way in which we look at the
corresponding third-person utterances: to see them not as
reports about myself for giving which I have to apply
criteria, but rather as "exclamations" (323) or "signals"
(180, p. 218), naturally and appropriately made or given
in certain circumstances. Such an exclamation could even
be compared with "an instinctive sound" or "a glad start"
(323). Failure to perform successfully after the signal had
been given would not necessarily mean that it had been
incorrectly given. In some cases (*e.g.* if there had been an
unforeseen interruption or disturbance) we should accept
the plea: 'When I said I knew how to go on, I did know'
(323).

Two minor comments. (1) Wittgenstein does not en-
large on the suggestion given by the word 'signal.' One
might take as a typical case that in which a teacher turns
from the blackboard, proffers the chalk to the class with
the question 'Who can go on?'. Here the answer 'I can'
would have the same function as a silent acceptance of the
chalk. (2) Wittgenstein's continual use of phrases like
'gave him the right to say,' 'made it a correct use of,' 'justified him in saying' in connexion with these first-person
utterances might tend to obscure a little his own doctrine.
The essential point is that a person does *not* have (or
need) grounds or reasons (does not apply criteria) for saying correctly that he himself understands, in the sense in
which others must have them to say it of him. Of course,
he may himself have, or lack, reasons or justifications in
another (a social) sense.

Grasping the meaning (understanding it) should be

compared with intending the meaning (meaning it). The
two are connected in this way. We may be inclined to
think that the purpose of the explanations we give (of,
e.g. the rule for the development of the series) is really to
get the learner to catch hold of something essential, the
meaning we *intend* (210); and that the correct application
he then makes of the rule is somehow a consequence of his
catching hold of this essential thing. And here we have the
idea of the mental act of *intending, meaning* this expression of the rule in a certain way, as somehow anticipating
and predetermining all the steps of its application before
they are taken. Or the connexion may be approached in
another way. The criterion for the learner's having understood the rule aright is his application of it. But not *any*
application (anything that could possibly be represented
as an application of the expression of the rule) will do. It
must be the *correct* application. But what are the criteria
for correctness? Here again one is inclined to answer that
the correct application is the one that was meant: and
this answer may once more give us the picture of all the
steps being somehow covered in advance by the act of
meaning. This idea is *very* compelling. For does not the
sense of the rule (of the expression) determine what is to
count as the correct application of it? What does the determining here is not just the words or the symbols themselves. They are dead, inert (432, 454); they could be applied, and applied systematically, in indefinitely numerous
different ways. And the same goes for any paraphrase or
picture (433), the substitution of one expression or symbol for another: "interpretations (in this sense) by themselves do not determine meaning" (198). It is natural to
suppose that only the intention, "the psychical thing," can
do that. Natural, but of course wrong; (or at least misleading). The criterion for the correct application of the
rule is *customary practice* (199–201); the customary practice of those who have received a certain training; the way
we are taught to use the rule and do always use it. It is,
too, in the existence of this customary practice, and no-

where else, that we may find the way in which the steps are "determined in advance," and the way in which a certain application is "meant," or "intended" by the ordinary instructor who has mastered that practice. (Of course; for 'the rule determines this application' means 'the rule is not correctly understood unless used in this way.') What gives us the illusion of some other mysterious determinant is the fact that, having received a certain training, we find it so *utterly natural* to make a certain application of the expression. We draw the consequences of the rule "*as a matter of course*"; and cannot understand how anyone can make a wholly different application of the expression. ("'But surely you can see . . . ?' That is just the characteristic expression of someone who is under the compulsion of a rule" [231].) Of course, in the instructor-pupil situation, explanations are in place; but the purpose of the explanations is to get the pupil to do as we do, and find it equally natural. "Explanations come to an end somewhere"; then we just act. But equally, of course, "the pupil's capacity to learn may come to an end."

Among resistances to his views Wittgenstein notes the tendency to fall back on the words 'the same': the tendency, *e.g.* to say 'But when we explain a rule to someone by giving him examples of its application, all we want him to see is that he is *to do the same* in other cases.' In answer to this, Wittgenstein points out that the idea of a single, generally sufficient criterion of 'what is the same' is nonsense. The criteria for 'doing the same' in *the case of a particular rule* are just the criteria, whatever they may be, for the correct observance of that rule. The concepts of 'rule' and 'identity' are as closely related to each other as the word 'proposition' to the phrase 'true or false.' (See 185, 208, 215–216, 223–227.)

Now although Wittgenstein, in the sections here discussed, is directly concerned mainly with the topics of meaning or understanding something by an expression of a rule, what he says is taken by him to have much wider implications about language in general. These implications give the meaning-use equation a new significance, of the utmost importance in relation to the topics of experience and sensation which he next discusses. Roughly speaking: what he says about obeying what we would ordinarily call 'rules' is applied to obeying what philosophers are apt to call 'the rules for the use' of all expressions, whether or not they are the expressions of rules. Obeying a rule is conforming to an agreed common practice; "it is impossible to obey a rule 'privately'" (202). The emphasis is on the *agreed common practice* in the use of expressions, and this carries with it, in cases where it is appropriate to speak of criteria, the existence of *agreed common criteria* for their application. Wittgenstein notes that this in its turn demands the existence of general agreement in *judgments* (242). The great importance of these points emerges rapidly in what follows.

Before turning to Wittgenstein's discussion of his next topic, it is in place to notice some of the further things he says about 'meaning something by an expression.' To this he reverts at intervals, in a rich succession of examples, arguments and suggestions throughout the rest of the book (see especially 503–510, 525–534, 540–546, 592–598, 607, 661–693, II. ii, II. vi, II. xi, pp. 214–219). As before, the main doctrine attacked is the doctrine that what gives an expression, in use, its meaning and its life, is the user's special experience, or act, of meaning something by it. I select some principal points.

(*a*) One of the sources of the doctrine is the difference we feel between using words in an ordinary, and in an abnormal, context (*e.g.* repeating a sentence mockingly, or as a quotation, or in elocution practice, etc.). Aware of a difference of feeling in these latter cases, we are apt to suppose it consists in the absence of the normal experience of meaning what we say. Just so might we suppose, until we remember the facts, that everything that does not feel strange, feels familiar (592–598, 607; *cf.* also, on 'being influenced,' 169–170).

(*b*) In II. vi (*cf.* also 592), Wittgenstein analyses bril-

liantly the idea of a special atmosphere or feeling carried
by each particular word. (So some philosophers have
spoken, for example of an 'if-feeling.') Whatever feeling-
accompaniment the reading or uttering of a certain word
may have, it is only *as so accompanying the word* that we
are tempted to invest it with this special significance. Any
such feeling or sensation might occur in a different context
and not be recognised at all. But a feeling or atmosphere
which loses its identity (its identity as, say, the 'if-feeling')
when separated from a certain object, is *not* a special feeling or atmosphere associated with that object at all. Contrast it with a genuine case of separately identifiable but
closely associated things. Here a different association would
shock and surprise us.

(c) Wittgenstein does not deny that a sense can be
given to the notion of *experiencing* the meaning of a word.
(See II. ii and II. xi, pp. 214–216. *Cf.* also 526–534.)
This phrase might reasonably be used in connexion with
many experiences which we do have, and which profoundly
affect our *attitude* to language. Among these are: finding
the *mot juste* after rejecting a number of candidates; reading with *expression*; saying a word again and again until it
seems to 'lose its meaning.' In particular Wittgenstein
notes the game of pronouncing a word like 'March,' now
with one, now with another of its meanings. We can com-
ply with the instruction to do this, and can perhaps report
a different experience of the word. But this very game
shows how unimportant the experience is in relation to
meaning the word now in this way and now in that in the
ordinary course of events; for then we may not be able to
report any such experience. In general, the word 'meaning'
may be said to acquire a secondary use in connexion with
all these experiences which are of such significance in relation to the way we *feel* about our language. But this use
is secondary. Words could still have their meanings, language be used as a means of communication, in the absence of these phenomena.

(d) The most important of these later discussions

(661–693, and pp. 216–217) is concerned with meaning in the sense it has in such a question as 'Whom (which one) did you mean?', *i.e.* with an intended reference as opposed to an intended sense. But there are close analogies between the two. When, with reference to an earlier remark, I say 'I meant him' I refer to a definite time (the time at which I made the remark); but not to an experience which I had at that time. There may sometimes be characteristic accompaniments, looks, movements of attention; but these are not what 'meaning him' consists in. Compare 'I meant him' with the phrase 'I was speaking of him.' What makes it true that I was speaking of him is the set of circumstances in which the original remark was made, and in particular, the general set or direction of my actions, of which the explanation ('I meant him') is itself one. What is apt to confuse us here is that of course I do not discover whom I meant by studying those circumstances. But nor do I report an indubitable special experience. It is rather (here I interpret a little) that in giving the explanation of whom I meant I continue a certain chain of actions; as I might, in pointing things out on a complex diagram, discard a blunt pointer in favour of a finer one, more serviceable for my purpose. Or I might *dis-continue* that chain of action, think better of it; and substitute another name; and then I shall be said to have lied. The question *not* to ask is: How do I know whom I meant? For I have no *way* of knowing, I apply no criteria. (Wittgenstein suggests that the words 'know' and 'doubt' are both out of place here. But of course, one can in fact be said to forget whom one was speaking of, and thus to be in doubt, to be 'not sure'; and then to remember. But this is an unimportant qualification; for Wittgenstein discusses elsewhere the question of *remembering* one's intentions.)

Pain and Persons. (See 142, 243–315, 350–351, 384, 390, 398–421, II. iv, II. v.) Studying the sections in which Wittgenstein deals with sensations, one may well feel one's capacity to learn coming to an end. Wittgenstein's case

against saying that the phrases 'meaning/understanding
something by an expression' stand for or name special experiences seems to me thoroughly made out. But even the
significance of this denial comes into question if it then
appears that no word whatever stands for or names a special experience. (Experiences which characteristically accompany 'I understand!' are not to be identified with understanding. Try substituting "'I am in pain'" and 'pain'
in the appropriate places here.) Wittgenstein seems to me
to oscillate in his discussion of this subject between a
stronger and a weaker thesis, of which the first is false and
the second true. These may be described, rather than formulated, as follows. (I attach no importance to their descriptions: their significance must emerge later.) The
stronger thesis says that no words name sensations (or 'private experiences'); and in particular the word 'pain' does
not (cf. 293). The weaker thesis says that certain conditions must be satisfied for the existence of a common language in which sensations are ascribed to those who have
them; and that certain confusions about sensations arise
from the failure to appreciate this, and consequently to
appreciate the way in which the language of sensations
functions. The oscillation between the two theses is to be
explained by the fact that the weaker can be made to yield
to the stronger by the addition of a certain premise about
language, viz. that all there is to be said about the descriptive meaning of a word is said when it is indicated
what criteria people can use for employing it or for deciding whether or not it is correctly employed.

The stronger thesis is first developed by an attack on the
idea of a private language (243 et seq.). By a 'private language' we are here to understand a language of which the
individual names (descriptive words) refer solely to the
sensations of the user of the language. He may be imagined
as keeping a record of the occurrence of certain sensations.
The main point of the attack is that the hypothetical user
of the language would have no check on, no criterion of,
the correctness of his use of it. We might be inclined to

say that his memory provides a check. But what check has he on his memory? Suppose in the case of one particular word he keeps on misremembering its use. What difference will it make? There will be no way in which he can distinguish between a correct and an incorrect use. So the idea of a correct use is empty here: and with it the idea of such a language. Now the interesting thing about the attack is that Wittgenstein presents it as if it applied only or peculiarly to the idea of a private language in which all the descriptive words were supposed to stand for sensations. But of course, if it has any validity at all, it has an equal validity for the case of a private language (here this means 'a language used by only one individual') in which the words stand not for sensations at all, but for things like colours or material objects or animals. Here again the individual will have no external check on the correctness of his use of the names. (It is no good saying that he can, in this case, though not in the case of the sensation-language, make himself a physical dictionary, *e.g.* a table with names opposite pictures. Wittgenstein's own arguments in other places are here decisive. The interpretation of the table depends on the use that is made of it.) But if this is so, then Wittgenstein's arguments would at most tend to show that the idea of a language *of any kind* used only by one person was an absurdity: and this conclusion would have no special immediate relevance to the case of sensation.

But it is clear that Wittgenstein intends his arguments to have special relevance to this case. So let us look at the differences between the two supposed private languages. We may suppose (following Wittgenstein) that in the case of the first private language, the one for sensations only, there are no particular characteristic overt expressions of the sensations, manifested by the hypothetical user of the language. Now we introduce observers, studying the behaviour and surroundings of the language users. The observer (B) of the user of the second language observes a correlation between the use of its words and sentences and the speaker's actions and environment. The observer of the user of the first language does not. Observer B is thus able to form hypotheses about the meanings (the regular use) of the words of his subject's language. He might in time come to be able to speak it: then the practice of each serves as a check on the correctness of the practice of the other. But shall we say that, before this fortunate result was achieved (before the use of the language becomes a *shared* "form of life"), the words of the language had no meaning, no use? And if we do not say this of the case where this result can be achieved, why should we say it of the hypothetical case where it cannot? In each case, while the language is used by one person alone (let us say as in one of Wittgenstein's examples, to record occurrences), the meaning of the words is a matter of the customary practice of the user: in each case the only check on this customary practice is memory. But (it might be said), the hypothesis that someone was using a language of the first kind could never be tested. But what is to count as a test here? Suppose he also mastered the ordinary common language, and then *told us* that he had been (or was still) using a private language. It is also *just* worth asking, in connexion with some of Wittgenstein's arguments here: Do we ever in fact find ourselves misremembering the use of very *simple* words of our common language, and having to correct ourselves by attention to others' use?— Wittgenstein gives himself considerable trouble over the question of how a man would *introduce* a name for a sensation into this private language. But we need imagine no special ceremony. He might simply be struck by the recurrence of a certain sensation and get into the habit of making a certain mark in a different place every time it occurred. The making of the marks would help to impress the occurrence on his memory. One can easily imagine this procedure being elaborated into a system of dating. (The purpose of these remarks is to indicate the place the sensation-name might play in the private language-game.)

Another of Wittgenstein's main arguments is basically a

variant on the first. He notes two associated points, which one is not inclined to dispute: (1) "the expression of doubt has no place in the language-game" (288), *i.e.* in the language-game with 'I am in pain';[3] and (2) "what I do (when I say 'I am in pain') is not to identify my sensation by criteria" (290). Wittgenstein seems to think that these facts can only be accommodated if we regard 'I am in pain' as an *expression* or manifestation of pain, alongside such natural expressions as crying or groaning, but of course, one which, unlike these, is the result of training (244, 288, etc.). So regarded, 'pain' ceases to appear as the name or the description of a sensation. If we do *not* so regard it, then we shall require criteria of identity for the sensation; and with these there would enter the possibility of error (288). (Here one is, of course, reminded of the discussion of understanding. There are criteria of understanding, as of pain, which we apply in the case of others. But a man does not apply them to himself when he says 'I understand'—and his saying this is to be compared with an exclamation, a glad start, not a report of a mental occurrence.) Wittgenstein here seems to me to be in a muddle: the weaker thesis is being muddled with the stronger. What he has committed himself to is the view that one cannot sensibly be said to recognise or identify anything, unless one uses *criteria*; and, as a consequence of this, that one cannot recognise or identify sensations. But of course this is untrue. Consider cases where the rival pull of 'expression' or 'manifestation' is weaker or non-existent. Consider, for example, tastes; and such phrases as 'the taste of onions,' 'a metallic taste.' Here we have one thing (a taste) associated with another (a material substance), but quite certainly recognisable and identifiable in itself. Only, of course, one does not use *criteria* of iden-

---

[3] Even this is not quite true as it stands. There is no place for one kind of doubt, the kind that might be expressed in 'Am I interpreting the facts of this situation aright?' But there is sometimes place for another kind, which might be expressed in 'Does this quite deserve the *name* of "pain"?'

tity for *the taste*. If the question 'What is the criterion of
identity here?' is pushed, one can only answer: 'Well, the
taste itself' (*cf.* 'the sensation itself'). Of course, the
phrases by which we *refer* to such tastes involve allusions to
what can be seen and touched; for we speak a common language. But we do not identify the taste by means of the
associated substance by allusion to which we name it. Consider also that we discriminate and recognise different particular pains (I do not mean pains in different places)—
aches and throbs, searing and jabbing pains, etc. In many
cases, there are not, or not obviously, different characteristic natural expressions of pain to correspond to these differences in quality. The phrases by which we name these
particular pain-experiences are commonly analogical; and
this too for the reason that we want a common language.[4]
All the time here Wittgenstein is driving at the conditions
that are necessary for a common language in which pain
can be ascribed to persons, the consequent need for *criteria for the ascription* of pain, and the effects of this upon
the use of the word 'pain' of our common language. Hence
his obsession with the *expression* of pain. But he errs
through excess of zeal when this leads him to deny that
sensations can be recognised and bear names. Rather the
case is that these names must always contain in a more or
less complex way, within their logic, some allusion to what
is not sensation, to what can be seen and touched and
heard.

Why is this? The answer illuminates the nature of
Wittgenstein's mistake, and also the great extent to which
he is right.

(1) To deny that 'pain' is the name of a (type of) sen-

---

[4] The fact that there are characteristic natural expressions of
pain but not (or not obviously) characteristic differences between
natural expressions of different kinds of pain (I do not mean
different degrees or locations) is the explanation of the fact that
the descriptions of the different kinds tend to be analogical,
whereas the word 'pain' is not analogical. See below.

sation is comparable with denying that 'red' is the name of a colour.

(2) It is just the difference between the ways colours and pains enter into our lives that accounts for the fact (i) that we call the latter and not the former sensations (or, alternatively, that accounts for the very special status we assign to sensations); it is just this difference that accounts for the fact (ii) that we *ascribe* pains to those who suffer them and not colours to those who see them; and which accounts for the fact (iii) that *without* criteria for ascribing pains to persons, we could have no common language of pain. Finally, it is because our common language-game must be that of ascribing pains to persons that symptoms, expressions, of pain assume such overwhelming importance.

(3) Fact (iii), misunderstood, is reflected (upside down) in all the usual philosophers' confusions about sensations; and, over emphasised, is reflected (rightside up, but obscuring the rest of the picture) in Wittgenstein's.

To understand at least part of what is meant by 'the difference between the ways colours and pains enter our lives,' it will be helpful to consider some unrealised possibilities. Let us suppose first that we feel pain only and always under the condition that our skin is in contact with the surfaces of certain bodies. (*Cf.* Wittgenstein's 'pain-patches,' [312]. But he does not exploit this fully.) The pain begins and ends with the contact. Then our pain-language might have a logic wholly different from that which it does have. Instead of ascribing pains to sufferers, we might ascribe painfulness to surfaces, much as we at present call them rough, smooth, hard, soft, etc. Another possibility is this. We say things like 'It's hot in here,' 'It's cold out there,' and so on, ascribing temperatures (I do not mean in degrees Fahrenheit or Centigrade) to regions. Let us suppose that any person felt pain if and only if every other normal person in the same region (which could be the size of a room or a continent) at the same time also felt pain. Then we might ascribe painfulness to regions instead of pain to persons; saying, *e.g.* 'It's painful today,' or 'It's painful in here.' The point of both examples is that in each case we should have as *impersonal* a way of describing pain-phenomena as we have of describing colour-phenomena. But of course the incidence of physical pain is not like this. The causes of pain are often internal and organic. Even when pain is caused by contact, it generally requires a special kind of contact rather than contact with any special kind of thing; and it generally does not cease when contact ceases. If you have a pain and I come to the place where you are, or touch or look at what you are touching or looking at, this will not in general result in my having a pain. As Wittgenstein not infrequently points out, it is such very obvious general facts of nature which determine the logic of our concepts. I may put the point very roughly as follows. A set of people together in certain surroundings will be in general agreement on 'what it looks like here, what it feels like (to the touch) here, what it sounds like here.' In this possibility of a general agreement in judgments lies the possibility of a common impersonal language for describing what we see and hear and touch (*cf.* 242). But there is no such general agreement as to whether or not 'it's painful here,' as to what it feels like (as we misleadingly say) *within*. In the absence of general agreement in judgment, a common language is impossible; and this is why a common impersonal pain-language is impossible. But if (to speak absurdly) we are prepared to make our pain-language a language for ascribing pain to persons, then we have something (*i.e.* people's pain-behaviour) which we see and hear, and on which, in consequence, general agreement in judgment is possible. Because of certain general facts of nature, therefore, the only possible common pain-language is the language in which pain is ascribed to those who talk the language, the criteria for its ascription being (mainly) pain-behaviour. And because of *this* fact it is necessarily empty and pointless (I will *not* say meaningless) either (*a*) to speculate about the ascription of pain to anything which does not exhibit behaviour comparable in the relevant respects with human behaviour (*i.e.* the behaviour of those who use the concept), or (*b*) to raise generalised doubts about other people's experience of pain, or about one's own knowledge of this. It is the above points which I take Wittgenstein essentially to be making. (He sees [142] that, as things are, the possibility of the language-game rests on there being characteristic expressions of pain.) But the way in which he makes them is, in part at least, misleading. For from none of these facts does it follow that 'pain' is not the name of a sensation. On the contrary. It is only in the light of the fact that 'pain' is the name of a sensation that *these* facts are intelligible; or, better, to say that 'pain' is the name of a sensation is (or ought to be) just to begin to draw attention to these facts. One could say: that pain is a sensation (or, that sensations have the special status they have) is a *fact of nature* which dictates the logic of 'pain.'

This outline is of course extremely crude. What a proper treatment of the topic above all requires is extensive and detailed *comparisons* between the different types of sensible experience we have.

Thoughts and Words. (316–394, 427, 501, 540, 633–637, II. xi, pp. 211, 216–223.) Wittgenstein's treatment of this topic has close connexions with his account of 'meaning/understanding something by an expression'; and presents certain analogies with the account of pain. It should first be noted that Wittgenstein is not primarily concerned with certain rather specialised applications of the word 'thinking' which are apt to come first to mind. We sometimes contrast the thinker and the active man; or may speak of having spent a fortnight's holiday without having a single thought. But Wittgenstein is not especially concerned with the thoughts which come only to the reflective. Again, we sometimes use 'thinking' in the sense of 'thinking out how to do something,' or 'solving, or trying to solve, a problem,' when the problem may indeed be as practical a one as you please. But Wittgenstein is not especially concerned with the thinking that overcomes dif-

ficulties. His concern is not restricted in either of these
ways. He is quite as much interested in the most ordinary
case of 'having a thought' or 'thinking something,' in the
sense in which, for example, someone who, talking neither
at random nor insincerely, says that p, may be said to
have had the thought that p, or to think that p, or to have
said what he thought. The close connexion between Wittgenstein's discussions of 'meaning something' and 'thinking' should now be clear. For if a man satisfies the criteria
for meaning a sentence in a certain way (and is not insincere in uttering it), then he also satisfies the criteria for
having thought something and said what he thought. So
much of the argument on the former topic bears directly
on the latter.

There is a certain once common view of the nature of
thinking against which Wittgenstein's arguments are
mainly directed. It is this. Thinking or having a thought is
a special event or process which may accompany and be
expressed in speech or writing or relevant action, and may
also occur in the absence of these. No one can ever know
what another's thoughts are in just the way he knows what
his own are; for each man is directly cognisant only of his
own internal processes. Wittgenstein's general counter-
thesis runs as follows. It is true that having a thought is
not to be identified with any particular outward process
of speech or writing or action; nor with inner speech or
other imagery. The having of a thought is not the occurrence of any of these; but nor is it any other occurrence.
It is the occurrence of one of these in a certain context, in
certain circumstances. To see what sort of context, what
sort of circumstances are relevant here, one must consider
what criteria are used in ascribing thoughts to people. A
man's actions may show his thought (cf. 330), or his remarks may tell it; but if a monkey imitated the actions, or
a parrot repeated the words, we should not ascribe the
same thought to the monkey or the parrot. The difference
does not lie in what went on inside them, but in the difference between the rest of their behaviour. Of course, a

man does not, in telling his own thoughts, apply to himself the criteria for ascription of thoughts which he applies to others. But neither, when he says what he is or has been thinking, does he report on any concurrent or antecedent inner process. It is rather that he takes, or continues, a certain line of linguistic action, much as he might take or continue, in other circumstances, a certain line of non-linguistic action; and of course, he might 'think better of it,' *change* his line.

It is quite clear and very important that Wittgenstein does not deny the existence of those occurrences, whether observable, like an exclamation, or unobservable, like what we call a flash of insight, or inward speech, by reference to which we may *date* the occurrence of a thought. What he is most concerned to stress is the fact that these occurrences do not owe their significance or their claim to the titles they bear, to their own peculiar nature or that of some psychical accompaniment; but to their place in a general pattern of actions and events. The concept of thinking demands such a general pattern as a setting for the occurrence of thoughts. In this, which I shall call his hostility to the doctrine of immediacy, Wittgenstein is surely right. Another factor in his treatment of thinking which is, I think, quite distinct from this, and also more questionable, might be called his hostility to the doctrine of privacy. It is because of this factor that I speak of analogies with his treatment of pain. I shall try to illustrate this from some of the things he says about inward speech, *i.e.* about saying something to oneself in imagination. (I would emphasise that the hostility to the doctrine of privacy is not of peculiar importance in connexion with *thinking*. It has more general application. It is merely that it can be very clearly illustrated by some things that Wittgenstein says in the course of his discussion of thinking.)

II. xi, pp. 220–223 are largely concerned with telling or confessing what one 'has been saying to oneself in one's thoughts.' Wittgenstein says: (1) that what I say to myself in my thoughts is hidden from others only in the sense in which my thoughts are hidden from one who does not understand the language in which I speak out loud (pp. 220, 222); and (2) that when I tell another what I was saying to myself, or acknowledge that he has guessed aright, I do not describe what went on inside me: I do not tell what I was thinking from inspection of the inner process (p. 222). Now it seems to me that Wittgenstein is here equivocating with 'what I say to myself'; and that his motive for doing so is his hostility to the idea of what is not observed (seen, heard, smelt, touched, tasted), and in particular to the idea that what is not observed can in any sense be recognised or described or reported. The equivocation is made possible by the fact that 'what I was saying to myself in my thoughts' can mean either 'what I was thinking' or 'what words were going through my mind.' Now it is true that in saying what I was thinking, I do not report on 'what went on within me' (p. 222). In just the same way I do not tell what I am imagining by inspecting my image (II. iii). But also in just the same way I do not, in the case where I am talking or thinking aloud, discover what I am or have been thinking by listening to my words or their echo. As far as this goes, audible and inner speech are on the same level. (This fact indicates both the respect in which remark [1] above is justified and also the respect in which it is false.) They are on the same level in another way too. I may tell what I was saying to myself, not in the sense of telling what I was thinking, but in the sense of reporting what words were going through my mind. And here 'what went on within me' is just as much to the point, as 'what went on audibly' is when I am asked not to say what I meant when I spoke aloud, but to *repeat my words*. Of course, the difference between *these* two cases is that there is, and can be, no check (except the general reliability of my short-term memory) on my report of what words were going through my mind, whereas there can very well be a check on the correctness of my repetition of my audibly spoken words. But only a prejudice against 'the inner' would lead anyone, on the strength of this difference, to deny the possibility of the first kind of report. Only the same prejudice would lead anyone to deny that I can sometimes say something by way of description of my experiences of having imagery, as well as describing to people what I am imagining. (Having a confused and jumpy or intermittent image is not the same as imagining something as confused and jumpy or intermittent.) It is very likely true that some have not distinguished describing or reporting such experiences from telling what one is thinking, or describing what one is imagining. That a fact can be misconstrued is not, however, a reason for denying it. It is also true that when we describe 'private' or 'inner' or 'hidden' experiences, our descriptions of them (like our descriptions of their status) are often *analogical;* and the analogies are provided by what we *do* observe (*i.e.* hear, see, touch, etc.). This is in itself an important fact. It throws light once more on the conditions necessary for a common language. One could almost say that it is this fact which Wittgenstein is often stressing, often in a perverse way. But a description is none the worse for being analogical, especially if it couldn't be anything else.[5] Moreover, some of the analogies are *very good ones.* In particular the analogy between saying certain words to oneself and saying them out loud is very good. (One can even be unsure whether one has said them out loud or to oneself.) The analogy between mental pictures and pictures is, in familiar ways, less good.

Perhaps what is really operating here is the old verificationist horror of a claim that cannot be checked. Elsewhere in his treatment of thinking, Wittgenstein manifests the more intelligible aversion from a hypothesis or supposition that cannot be checked (344, 348–349).

States of Mind and Introspection. (572–587, II. i, ix, x; also 437, 465.) Wittgenstein writes on expectation, hope, belief, wishes, grief and fear. As in other cases, the main

[5] If one were *very* anxious to appease here, one *could* say they were only 'descriptions' in an analogical sense. But I think this would be being over-anxious.

hostility is to the doctrine of immediacy. Expectation, hope, grief are forms of human life, each with many variations. What the subject of these states is at any given moment doing or experiencing, gets its significance, its importance, from its surroundings (583–584), its context of situation and behaviour. The isolated occurrences could not claim these names. The falsity of the doctrine of immediacy is indeed, in some of these cases, a great deal more evident than it is in the cases of thinking or understanding. For a man may be said to expect or to believe or to be grieving over something when no thought of that thing is in his mind. There is therefore an *a fortiori* character about the non-immediacy of the states that these words name.

Among the criteria that we use for the ascription of certain of these states to another person, the *verbal* behaviour of the subject of them assumes an overwhelming importance. Wittgenstein in fact suggests that a necessary condition of the ascription of, *e.g.* hopes, wishes and some beliefs to a subject is the subject's mastery of a language for the *expression* of these (see II. i, ix and 650). His reason for this is clear. A creature's non-linguistic behaviour may certainly provide adequate criteria for the ascription of *some* states; but where descriptions of states take on a slightly higher degree of complexity, it may be difficult or impossible to imagine what sort of complication of non-linguistic criteria would be adequate in the case of beings incapable of speech. ("We say a dog is afraid his master will beat him; but not, he is afraid his master will beat him to-morrow.") In the sections on thinking Wittgenstein placed an analogous and obviously connected restriction on the ascription of thoughts. It seems that one ought here to distinguish between the thesis that there are certain *kinds* of state (say, wishing or hoping) which cannot even in their simplest forms be ascribed to beings without the power of linguistically expressing them; and the weaker thesis that there are more complex forms of certain kinds of states (wishing, believing, hoping) which cannot be ascribed to beings without this power. The weaker thesis seems to me obviously true. Still more obviously, the stronger thesis must, on *one* interpretation, be false. Words like 'wish' and 'hope' could never acquire a use at all unless there were *some* circumstances or range of circumstances, other than that of their being uttered, in and because of which it was correct to use them; and since wishes and hopes are ascribed to others, these circumstances must include *criteria*, must include the observable. Wittgenstein's general principles here refute his particular thesis. I may, however, very likely be mistaken in ascribing the stronger thesis in this form to Wittgenstein. His position may rather be the intermediate one that *some* linguistic capacities are required in the subject to whom wishes and hopes are ascribed, not the specific linguistic capacity for the conventional expressions of wishes and hopes. So amended, the doctrine cannot, of course, be refuted in this way.

What in general of the roles of first-person utterances about states of mind? Wittgenstein here draws an admirable distinction between those first-person utterances which are correctly called reports of the results of introspection, or descriptions of states of mind, on the one hand, and those which are only misleadingly so called (and only so called by philosophers), on the other. We can *come to conclusions* about our own hopes, fears, expectations, even beliefs; and in doing so we use much the same criteria as we use in coming to conclusions about others, though we may (or may not) have certain advantages in our own case. But first-person utterances about states of mind are more commonly not of this kind, but of another: not conclusions about, but conventional expressions of, states of mind, taking their (special) place among the other criteria which are used in ascribing them. I think Wittgenstein does not perhaps give quite enough weight to the *very* special nature of this place, that he tends to exaggerate a little the degree to which, or the frequency with which, these utterances are, so to speak, forced from us. We use them very often pretty deliberately, and to inform; to show others where we stand, what we may be expected to do and for what reasons. And this may safely be admitted—without either returning to the doctrine of reported special experiences, or advancing to the absurdity that *all* such utterances are *conclusions* about ourselves—just so long as we acknowledge, what Wittgenstein elsewhere examines, the nature of our certainties about our own deliberate behaviour. The utterance of 'I am embarrassed/amazed/shocked /confident/very glad,' etc. may be a social *act* (by this I mean something comparable with a polite greeting, a move to help someone, an offer of resistance, etc.); it may be a piece of deliberate self-revelation (compare exaggerating a *natural* facial expression) or an explanation of one's behaviour; it may be simply an embarrassed (amazed, etc.) *response*; it may be a conclusion about oneself, based on introspection (and only in this case does the question how one knows, arise); or it may be some, though not *any*, combination of these. I am not suggesting that Wittgenstein would dispute this diversity of function. On the contrary, much that he says (*cf.* especially II. ix on 'I am afraid') tends to emphasise it. It is rather that in his anxiety to stress the difference between most uses of these sentences on the one hand, and descriptions based on observation on the other, he tends perhaps to minimise their aspect as *deliberate exhibitions* of states of mind.

Immediately after the discussion of 'I am afraid,' Wittgenstein reverts briefly to 'I am in pain' (p. 198). These words "may be a cry of complaint and may be something else." It looks as if he were almost prepared to acknowledge here that they may be just a report of my sensations. Pain is not, like grief, a pattern of life. And a report can *also* be a complaint; or a request.

Voluntary Action and Intention. (611–660, II. viii, II. xi, pp. 223–224.) What Wittgenstein says on these difficult topics is immensely suggestive and interesting—but elusive and incomplete. He begins with a brilliant short account (611–620) of our temptation, under the pressure of such a question as 'How do you raise your arm?' and of obvious analogies, to think of willing as a special act of which the phenomenal features of ordinary actions are consequences; a very special act, for the obvious difficulties of this model then force us to think of it not as an act which we perform, but as one which just occurs, of the will as "only a mover, not a moved." Then, abruptly, the problem is stated: "what is left over if I subtract the fact that my arm goes up from the fact that I raise my arm?" This is sunk in the other question: "How do you know (when your eyes are shut) that you have raised your arm?" The answer is "I feel it," and this answer is correct, but misleading. For it suggests that you recognise the special feelings (the kinaesthetic sensations) *and can tell from recognising them* that their constant accompaniment, the raising of the arm, has occurred. And this is wrong. In fact, the certainty that you have raised your arm is itself a criterion of recognising the feeling here (625). It is important to note two things that Wittgenstein is *not* saying. He is not saying that one would have this certainty in the absence of any feeling, or in the presence of an unaccustomed feeling. It is no doubt *because* of the kinaesthetic sensations that I know; but it is not *from* them that I tell (II. viii). Nor is he saying that I could never (say, if suitably stimulated) be mistaken about this (624). Here is a case where I know, but don't have a *way* of knowing, of telling. Now he reverts to the former question, and suggests: "voluntary movement is marked by absence of surprise" (628). As a *sufficient* condition (he neither says nor denies that he means it as one), this will not do. Experience of involuntary movements in certain circumstances might lead me to be quite unsurprised by their occurrence. The answer suggested by his own remarks about knowing, may be more useful. Voluntary movements are characterised by a certainty of their having been made, which neither has *nor needs* a ground; though it may both have and, in another sense, need a cause. It is still far from clear that we have a sufficient condition; for this seems true of many compelled or involuntary movements of parts of the body. But for the purposes of Wittgenstein's enquiry, I do not think a sufficient condition is required. For his purpose, I think, is to throw light from 'knowing what one has done' on 'knowing what one is going to do (intends)' and on 'knowing what one *was* going to do (intended).' For there is no more reason to suppose that we need a *way* of knowing, of telling, in these cases than in that one. Of course, an announcement of a present intention, or a recalling of a past unexecuted intention is helped by, arises naturally from, the situation "in which it is (or was) embedded." But we do not read off or infer our intentions from these situations, any more than we tell what limb-movements we have just made from recognition of the accompanying sensations. (Nor in announcing or recalling our intentions do we report a current or remembered special experience. Look for this and it vanishes [645–646].) The point is that knowing what we intend to do is no more mysterious than knowing what we are going to do. (We as often make announcements of intention in the form 'I shall . . .' as in the form 'I intend to . . .'.) And a man may very well know what he is going to do (*be able to say*, if he is asked or if it should otherwise become desirable), and do it, without having raised the question to himself at all, without indeed having thought about it. The purpose—or one purpose—of announcing intentions is obvious: others have an interest in knowing what we will do. Remembering and telling a past unfulfilled intention is a less obvious case. An intention might be unfulfilled because I abandoned it or was interrupted or forestalled, etc.; or because my action failed of its effect. In no such case am I reporting something else that happened at the time. (This is particularly clear where my telling could be described as 'telling what I nearly did.') It is rather that I exhibit *now* a response to the past situation; and my purpose in doing this may be to reveal to my auditor "something of *myself*, which goes beyond what happened at the time" (659).

Evidently this topic—of doing and intending—could be

pursued into refinements and elaborations which Wittgenstein, with his fixed polemical purpose, neglects. But rarely has a subject been treated so powerfully and suggestively in so few pages.

Seeing and Seeing as. (II. xi, pp. 193–214.) By means of a series of examples and comments, Wittgenstein seeks to bring out some of the complexities of the concept of seeing. The cases he mostly considers are very special ones; and it is consequently difficult to see just how far his conclusions reach. One thing at least which gives under the strain of his examples is the doctrine of the purely sensory given on the one hand, and our interpretation of it on the other, as two ever-present but distinguishable elements in visual perception.

The examples of which Wittgenstein writes are examples of "the 'dawning of' (noticing of) an aspect." Sometimes when we look at a thing, we suddenly *see* it *as* something different from what we saw it as before, while also seeing that it has not in any way changed. Easily the best cases of this are provided by certain schematic pictures or diagrams; but we may also, *e.g.* suddenly recognise a face, or suddenly see its likeness to another. In none of these cases is it to be supposed that we 'get a better (or different) view.' These cases, then, are to be sharply distinguished from those in which we suddenly see something because, say, a light has been switched on, or a screen removed. They are also to be distinguished from cases in which a man is able in certain ways to *treat*, say, a figure as a such-and-such or as a picture of a so-and-so, but does not have the experience of its suddenly assuming for him the aspect of a such-and-such or of a picture of a so-and-so. The difference from the first of these contrasted cases is that when a man *sees* something *as* x and then *as* y, there is a perfectly good sense in which it looks the same to him as it did before: *viz.* that drawings showing it as it looked to him before and after the change of aspect would be indistinguishable. The difference from the second contrasted case is that a man on whom an aspect dawns is not merely prepared to make different applications of what he sees, but also sees it differently, has the 'visual experience' of a change of aspect.

Wittgenstein notes an ambiguity in 'seeing as,' which it is important to mention since it emphasises the special character of the experience he is concerned with. Suppose we have a visually ambiguous object such as Wittgenstein's duck-rabbit—a picture which can be seen as a picture of a duck or again as a picture of a rabbit. Then a man who never has the experience of the change of aspects, the dawning of an aspect, may nevertheless be said by those who know of its visual ambiguity to see it as, say, (a picture of) a rabbit. So a person may in an unimportant sense see something as something without having the experience in which Wittgenstein is interested. In neither sense is something which is not visually ambiguous—say, a conventional picture of a lion—normally said to be 'seen as' anything.

Why is the experience of the dawning of an aspect of such particular interest to Wittgenstein? He suggests that its importance resides in an analogy with 'experiencing the meaning of a word' (p. 214). Perhaps we might say that when an aspect of a figure dawns on us, we are 'experiencing an interpretation of the figure.' What we have here is something instantaneous, a visual experience; but it is also true that a *logical* condition of our having the experience is our being capable of making such-and-such applications of the figure, of reacting to it in certain ways, of *treating* it as what we *see* it as (p. 208). If we are to describe the experience correctly, we cannot isolate a 'pure visual element' in it and say that that and that alone is the momentary experience (*cf.* p. 193); we can describe the experience correctly only by referring to what does not relate to the moment. (Wittgenstein is helped in making this point by the fact that the figure in one sense presents exactly the same visual appearance—does not look different —before and after the dawning of the aspect.) We have here, Wittgenstein says, a modified concept of experience, of seeing.

What Wittgenstein is essentially opposed to is the conjunction of the three propositions: (1) that we have here (*a*) a pure sensory element, and (*b*) an interpretation (a tendency to treat what we see in certain ways); (2) that (*a*) and (*b*) are simply associated or conjoined; and (3) that (*a*) alone is the visual experience proper. What may at first seem odd is not this opposition, nor the remark that we have here a modified concept of experience (contrast for example with pains), but the remark that we have here a modified concept of seeing (209). For surely ordinary instantaneous visual experiences, such as we have when the light is switched on and we suddenly see the room and its contents, can also be correctly described only by a description which entails our possession of concepts of certain kinds, and which thus refers beyond the moment. So in what way is the concept of seeing *modified* in the special case of seeing as? I think the *difference* between the cases, which leads Wittgenstein to speak of a modification of the concept, is the presence in the case where the light is switched on of just such an instantaneous change in the way things look, in the visual appearance of things, as is absent from the case where the aspect changes. But if this is right, it is not very happy to speak of a modification of the concept of seeing in a way which suggests that a certain feature which is common to both seeing and 'seeing as' is peculiar to the latter.

Conclusion. Wittgenstein has penetrating and illuminating things to say on other subjects: for example, identity and difference of meaning, meaninglessness, negation, induction, dreams and memory. But the topics which I have selected are those which receive most extensive treatment. On these I have tried to summarise and criticise his main arguments and conclusions, aware that much of the power, vividness and subtlety with which, by means of example, comment and epigram, these conclusions are presented, must in this way be lost. For this there is no remedy but study of the book itself.

Three cardinal elements in his thought, as presented in this book, may perhaps be epitomised in these quotations:

(1) "To imagine a language is to imagine a form of life" (19) and "What has to be accepted, the given, is—so one could say—forms of life" (p. 226).
(2) "What is happening now has significance—in these surroundings. The surroundings give it its importance" (583).
(3) "An 'inner process' stands in need of outward criteria" (580).

The first may serve to remind us of a general prescription for doing philosophy: to understand a concept, a word, put the word in its linguistic context and the whole utterance in its social context and then describe, without preconceptions, what you find; remembering that each word, each utterance, may figure in *many* contexts.

The second epitomises what I earlier called the hostility to the doctrine of immediacy. It has analogies with the first. Just as a word gets its significance from the context of its use, so those elements of our experience which we are tempted to isolate (or, failing this, to fabricate) and make the self-sufficient bearers of certain names get their significance too from their setting, from the form of life to which their titles allude.

The third, though it contains much that is true, contains also the germ of mistakes. It epitomises the hostility to the doctrine of privacy. For the worn and dangerous 'outward' and 'inner' we may substitute 'shared' and 'unshared.' Then what is right and wrong in Wittgenstein here begins from the insight that a common language for describing and reporting requires general agreement in judgments. So for a (descriptive) word or phrase to belong to a common language, it is essential that *the occasions on which it is right to apply it should provide shared experi-*

ences of a certain kind, the existence of which is connected with the rightness of applying the word. The experiences need not be connected with the rightness of applying the word or phrase as *criteria* for its application. No one has *criteria* for something's looking red, though this is something on which we commonly agree. (Wittgenstein is perhaps misled here by temporarily confusing criteria which justify one in applying a word or phrase with criteria which justify one in saying that it is correctly applied. That there is a distinction is clear from much else that Wittgenstein says. For *every* expression of a common language [I speak here of non-analogical uses] there must exist, in the common practice of the use of the expression, criteria for determining whether a given use of it is correct or not. This will be so even where the expression in question has no descriptive use at all. So the existence of criteria for the correctness of the use of an expression does not entail that using it correctly is applying it on the strength of certain criteria. Wittgenstein would agree that the entailment does not *generally* hold; and there is no reason for thinking that it holds in the *special* case of descriptive or reporting uses of expressions. Moreover it could be independently argued that it *could* not hold here.) Now, when a word is not applied on the strength of shareable experiences, Wittgenstein is inclined to say that it is not applied in the way of report or description at all, but is used in some other way, is something else: *e.g.* a response, the habit of which is acquired by training, an action, a signal and so on. Sometimes, often, this is right: it is right in just those cases where the relevant shareable experiences count as criteria in the full, *logical* sense of that word. But there are other cases for which, taken as a general rule, it is wrong. For sometimes a person applies a word or phrase not on the strength of shareable experiences but on the strength of non-shareable experiences, and *is* publicly reporting or describing those experiences; and this he is enabled to do either by the existence of shared experiences which count as signs (criteria in the weaker sense) of the occurrence of the unshared experiences (the case of 'I am in pain'), or by the adoption or invention of analogical modes of description, where the analogy is with shareable experiences (*e.g.* reporting the words that pass through my mind).[6] What misleads Wittgenstein here is, I think, partly the belief that criteria are always essential to a report or description, a belief in its turn based, perhaps, on the confusion, mentioned above, between criteria for application and criteria for correctness; and partly the fear of legitimising certain metaphysical doubtings and wonderings. As for these, they are, if you like, senseless: but in their own way, and not in any other. They are pointless and unreal and you can do nothing with them (unless you strip them of their form and use them to point a contrast); and that is condemnation enough.

Right or wrong, Wittgenstein's particular doctrines are of the greatest interest and importance. But the value of the book as a model of philosophical method is greater still. (Here I do *not* refer to idiosyncracies of style and form.) It will consolidate the philosophical revolution for which, more than anyone else, its author was responsible.

[6] Of course (*a*) the antithesis 'shared' and 'unshared' which I have used here, is a shorthand no more immune from misunderstanding than any other; and (*b*) I do not suggest that it represents a sharp division: tastes, for example, might count as an intermediate case, since one has to do something rather special to get them shared on a given occasion.

WITTGENSTEIN'S
PHILOSOPHICAL INVESTIGATIONS[1]

NORMAN MALCOLM

*Ein Buch ist ein Spiegel; wenn ein Affe hineinguckt,
so kann freilich kein Apostel heraussehen.*

LICHTENBERG

An attempt to summarize the *Investigations* would be
neither successful nor useful. Wittgenstein compressed his
thoughts to the point where further compression is impossible. What is needed is that they be unfolded and the
connections between them traced out. A likely first reaction to the book will be to regard it as a puzzling collection of reflections that are sometimes individually brilliant,
but possess no unity, present no system of ideas. In truth
the unity is there, but it cannot be perceived without
strenuous exertion. Within the scope of a review the con-
nectedness can best be brought out, I think, by concentrating on some single topic—in spite of the fact that there
are no separate topics, for each of the investigations in
the book crisscrosses again and again with every other one.
In the following I center my attention on Wittgenstein's
treatment of the problem of how language is related to

From Norman Malcolm, *Knowledge and Certainty: Essays and
Lectures* (Englewood Cliffs, N.J., 1963)© 1963, pp. 96–129.
Reprinted by permission of Prentice-Hall, Inc., Englewood Cliffs,
N.J. This essay originally appeared, in slightly different form, in
The Philosophical Review, Vol. LXIII (1954), pp. 530–559.

[1] Ludwig Wittgenstein, *Philosophical Investigations*, German
and English on facing pages. Tr. by G. E. M. Anscombe (New
York, 1953).

inner experiences—to sensations, feelings, and moods. This is one of the main inquiries of the book and perhaps the most difficult to understand. I am sufficiently aware of the fact that my presentation of this subject will certainly fail to portray the subtlety, elegance, and force of Wittgenstein's thinking and will probably, in addition, contain positive mistakes.

References to Part I will be by paragraph numbers, e.g. (207), and to Part II by page numbers, e.g. (p. 207). Quotations will be placed within double quotation marks.

Private Language. Let us see something of how Wittgenstein attacks what he calls "the idea of a private language." By a "private" language is meant one that not merely is not but *cannot* be understood by anyone other than the speaker. The reason for this is that the words of this language are supposed to "refer to what can only be known to the person speaking; to his immediate private sensations" (243). What is supposed is that I *"associate* words with sensations and use these names in descriptions" (256). I fix my attention on a sensation and establish a connection between a word and the sensation (258).

It is worth mentioning that the conception that it is possible and even necessary for one to have a private language is not eccentric. Rather it is the view that comes most naturally to anyone who philosophizes on the subject of the relation of words to experiences. The idea of a private language is presupposed by every program of inferring or constructing the 'external world' and 'other minds.' It is contained in the philosophy of Descartes and in the theory of ideas of classical British empiricism, as well as in recent and contemporary phenomenalism and sense-datum theory. At bottom it is the idea that there is only a contingent and not an *essential* connection between a sensation and its outward expression—an idea that appeals to us all. Such thoughts as these are typical expressions of the idea of a private language: that I know only from my *own* case what the word 'pain' means (293, 295); that I can only *believe* that someone else is in pain, but I *know* it if I am (303); that another person cannot have *my* pains (253); that I can undertake to call *this* (pointing inward) 'pain' in the future (263); that when I say 'I am in pain' I am at any rate justified *before myself* (289).

In order to appreciate the depth and power of Wittgenstein's assault upon this idea you must partly be its captive. You must feel the strong grip of it. The passionate intensity of Wittgenstein's treatment of it is due to the fact that he lets this idea take possession of him, drawing out of himself the thoughts and imagery by which it is expressed and defended—and then subjecting those thoughts and pictures to fiercest scrutiny. What is written down represents both a logical investigation and a great philosopher's struggle with his own thoughts. The logical investigation will be understood only by those who duplicate the struggle in themselves.

One consequence to be drawn from the view that I know only from my *own* case what, say, 'tickling' means is that "I know only what *I* call that, not what anyone else does" (347). I have not *learned* what 'tickling' means, I have only called something by that name. Perhaps others use the name differently. This is a regrettable difficulty; but, one may think, the word will still work for me as a name, provided that I apply it consistently to a certain sensation. But how about 'sensation'? Don't I know only from my *own* case what *that* word means? Perhaps what I call a "sensation" others call by another name? It will not help, says Wittgenstein, to say that although it may be that what I have is not what others call a "sensation," at least I have *something*. For don't I know only from my own case what "having something" is? Perhaps my use of *those* words is contrary to common use. In trying to explain how I gave 'tickling' its meaning, I discover that I do not have the right to use any of the relevant words of our common language. "So in the end when one is doing philosophy one gets to the point where one would like just to emit an inarticulate sound" (261).

Let us suppose that I did fix my attention on a pain as I

pronounced the word 'pain' to myself. I think that thereby I established a connection between the word and the sensation. But I did not establish a connection if subsequently I applied that word to sensations other than pain or to things other than sensations, e.g., emotions. My private definition was a success only if it led me to use the word correctly in the future. In the present case, 'correctly' would mean '*consistently* with my own definition'; for the question of whether my use agrees with that of others has been given up as a bad job. Now how is it to be decided whether I have used the word consistently? What will be the difference between my having used it consistently and its *seeming* to me that I have? Or has this distinction vanished? "Whatever is going to seem right to me is right. And that only means that here we can't talk about 'right'" (258). If the distinction between 'correct' and 'seems correct' has disappeared, then so has the concept *correct*. It follows that the 'rules' of my private language are only *impressions* of rules (259). My impression that I follow a rule does not confirm that I follow the rule, unless there can be something that will prove my impression correct. And the something cannot be another impression—for this would be "as if someone were to buy several copies of the morning paper to assure himself that what it said was true" (265). The proof that I am following a rule must appeal to something *independent* of my impression that I am. If in the nature of the case there cannot be such an appeal, then my private language does not have *rules*, for the concept of a rule requires that there be a difference between 'He is following a rule' and 'He is under the impression that he is following a rule'—just as the concept of understanding a word requires that there be a difference between 'He understands this word' and 'He thinks that he understands this word' (cf. 269).

'Even if I cannot prove and cannot know that I am correctly following the rules of my private language,' it might be said, 'still it *may* be that I am. It has *meaning* to say that I am. The supposition makes sense: you and I *understand* it.' Wittgenstein has a reply to this (348–353). We are inclined to think that we know what it means to say 'It is five o'clock on the sun' or 'This congenital deaf-mute talks to himself inwardly in a vocal language' or 'The stove is in pain.' These sentences produce pictures in our minds, and it *seems* to us that the pictures tell us how to *apply* them—that is, tell us what we have to look for, what we have to do, in order to determine whether what is pictured is the case. But we make a mistake in thinking that the picture contains in itself the instructions as to how we are to apply it. Think of the picture of blindness as a darkness in the soul or in the head of the blind man (424). There is nothing wrong with it *as a picture.* "But *what* is its application?" What shall count for or against its being said that this or that man is blind, that the picture applies to him? The *picture* doesn't say. If you think that you understand the sentence 'I follow the rule that *this* is to be called "pain"' (a rule of your private language), what you have perhaps is a picture of yourself checking off various feelings of yours as either being *this* or not. The picture appears to solve the problem of how you determine whether you have done the 'checking' right. Actually it doesn't give you even a hint in that direction; no more than the picture of blindness provides so much as a hint of *how* it is to be determined that this or that man is blind (348–353, 422–426, p. 184).

One will be inclined to say here that one can simply *remember* this sensation and by remembering it will know that one is making a consistent application of its name. But will it also be possible to have a *false* memory impression? On the private-language hypothesis, what would *show* that your memory impression is false—or true? Another memory impression? Would this imply that memory is a court from which there is no appeal? But, as a matter of fact, that is *not* our concept of memory.

Imagine that you were supposed to paint a particular colour "C," which was the colour that appeared when the chemical substances X and Y combined.—Sup-

pose that the colour struck you as brighter on one day
than on another; would you not sometimes say: "I
must be wrong, the colour is certainly the same as
yesterday"? This shows that we do not always resort
to what memory tells us as the verdict of the highest
court of appeal [56].

There is, indeed, such a thing as checking one memory
against another, e.g., I check my recollection of the time
of departure of a train by calling up a memory image of
how a page of the time-table looked—but "this process has
got to produce a memory which is actually *correct*. If the
mental image of the time-table could not itself be *tested*
for correctness, how could it confirm the correctness of the
first memory?" (265).

If I have a language that is really private (i.e., it is a
logical impossibility that anyone else should understand
it or should have any basis for knowing whether I am using
a particular name consistently), my assertion that my
memory tells me so and so will be utterly empty. 'My
memory' will not even mean—my memory *impression*. For
by a memory impression we understand something that is
either accurate or inaccurate; whereas there would not be,
in the private language, any *conception* of what would
establish a memory impression as correct, any conception
of what 'correct' would mean here.

The Same. One wants to say, 'Surely there can't be a
difficulty in knowing whether a feeling of mine is or isn't
the *same* as the feeling I now have. I will call this feeling
"pain" and will thereafter call the *same* thing "pain" whenever it occurs. What could be easier than to follow that
rule?' To understand Wittgenstein's reply to this attractive
proposal we must come closer to his treatment of rules
and of what it is to follow a rule. (Here he forges a re-
markably illuminating connection between the philosophy
of psychology and the philosophy of mathematics.) Consider his example of the pupil who has been taught to
write down a cardinal number series of the form 'o, n, 2n,
3n . . .' at an order of the form '+n,' so that at the order

'+1' he writes down the series of natural numbers (185). He has successfully done exercises and tests up to the number 1,000. We then ask him to continue the series '+2' beyond 1,000; and he writes 1,000, 1,004, 1,008, 1,012. We tell him that this is wrong. His instructive reply is, "But I went on in the same way" (185). There was nothing in the previous explanations, examples and exercises that made it *impossible* for him to regard that as the continuation of the series. Repeating *those* examples and explanations won't help him. One must say to him, in effect, 'That isn't what we *call* going on in the *same* way.' It is a fact, and a fact of the kind whose importance Wittgenstein constantly stresses, that it is *natural* for human beings to continue the series in the manner 1,002, 1,004, 1,006, given the previous training. But that is merely what it is—a fact of human nature.

One is inclined to retort, 'Of course he can misunderstand the instruction and misunderstand the order "+2"; but if he *understands* it he must go on in the right way.' And here one has the idea that "The understanding itself is a state which is the *source* of the correct use" (146)— that the correct continuation of the series, the right application of the rule or formula, springs from one's understanding of the rule. But the question of whether one understands the rule cannot be divorced from the question of whether one will go on in that one particular way that we call 'right.' The correct use is a criterion of understanding. If you say that knowing the formula is a state of the mind and that making this and that application of the formula is merely a *manifestation* of the knowledge, then you are in a difficulty: for you are postulating a mental apparatus that explains the manifestations, and so you ought to have (but do not have) a knowledge of the construction of the apparatus, quite apart from what it does (149). You would like to think that your understanding of the formula determines in advance the steps to be taken, that when you understood or meant the formula in a certain way "your mind as it were flew ahead and took all the steps before you physically arrived at this or that one" (188). But how you meant it is not independent of how in fact you use it. "We say, for instance, to someone who uses a sign unknown to us: 'If by "x!2" you mean x^2, then you get *this* value for y, if you mean 2x, *that* one!'— Now ask yourself: how does one *mean* the one thing or the other by 'x!2'?" (190). The answer is that his putting down *this* value for y shows whether he meant the one thing and not the other: "*That* will be how meaning it can determine the steps in advance" (190). How he meant the formula determines his subsequent use of it, only in the sense that the latter is a criterion of how he meant it.

It is easy to suppose that when you have given a person the order 'Now do the *same* thing,' you have pointed out to him the way to go on. But consider the example of the man who obtains the series 1, 3, 5, 7 . . . by working out the formula 2x + 1 and then asks himself, "Am I always doing the same thing, or something different every time?" (226). One answer is as good as the other; it doesn't matter which he says, so long as he continues in the right way. If we could not observe his work, his mere remark 'I am going on in the same way' would not tell us what he was doing. If a child writing down a row of 2's obtained '2, 2, 2' from the segment '2, 2' by adding '2' once, he might deny that he had gone on in the *same* way. He might declare that it would be doing the same thing only if he went from '2, 2' to '2, 2, 2, 2' in *one* jump, i.e., only if he *doubled* the original segment (just as it doubled the original single '2'). That could strike one as a *reasonable* use of 'same.' This connects up with Wittgenstein's remark: "If you have to have an intuition in order to develop the series 1 2 3 4 . . . you must also have one in order to develop the series 2 2 2 2 . . ." (214). One is inclined to say of the latter series, 'Why, all that is necessary is that you keep on doing the *same* thing.' But isn't this just as true of the other series? In both cases one has already *decided* what the correct continuation is, and one calls that continuation, and no other, 'doing the same thing.'

As Wittgenstein says: "One might say to the person one was training: 'Look, I always do the same thing: I . . .'" (223). And then one proceeds to show him what 'the same' *is*. If the pupil does not acknowledge that what you have shown him is the *same*, and if he is not persuaded by your examples and explanations to carry on as you wish him to—then you have reached bedrock and will be inclined to say "This is simply what I do" (217). You cannot give him more reasons than you yourself have for proceeding in that way. Your reasons will soon give out. And then you will proceed, without reasons (211).

Private Rules. All of this argument strikes at the idea that there can be such a thing as my following a rule in my private language—such a thing as naming something of which only I can be aware, 'pain,' and then going on to call the same thing, 'pain,' whenever it occurs. There is a charm about the expression 'same' which makes one think that there cannot be any difficulty or any chance of going wrong in deciding whether A is the *same* as B—as if one did not have to be *shown* what the 'same' is. This may be, as Wittgenstein suggests, because we are inclined to suppose that we can take the identity of a thing *with itself* as "an infallible paradigm" of the *same* (215). But he destroys this notion with one blow: "Then are two things the same when they are what *one* thing is? And how am I to apply what the *one* thing shows me to the case of two things?" (215).

The point to be made here is that when one has given oneself the private rule 'I will call this same thing "pain" whenever it occurs,' one is then free to do anything or nothing. That 'rule' does not point in any direction. On the private-language hypothesis, no one can teach me what the correct use of 'same' is. I shall be the sole arbiter of whether this is the *same* as that. What I choose to call the 'same' will *be* the same. No restriction whatever will be imposed upon my application of the word. But a sound that I can use *as I please* is not a *word*.

How would you teach someone the meaning of 'same'?

By example and practice: you might show him, for instance, collections of the same colors and same shapes and make him find and produce them and perhaps get him to carry on a certain ornamental pattern uniformly (208). Training him to form collections and produce patterns is teaching him what Wittgenstein calls "techniques." Whether he has mastered various techniques determines whether he understands 'same.' The exercise of a technique is what Wittgenstein calls a "practice." Whether your pupil has understood any of the rules that you taught him (e.g., the rule; this is the 'same' color as that) will be shown in his practice. But now there cannot be a 'private' practice, i.e., a practice that cannot be exhibited. For there would then be no distinction between believing that you have that practice and having it. 'Obeying a rule' is itself a practice. "And to *think* one is obeying a rule is not to obey a rule. Hence it is not possible to obey a rule 'privately'; otherwise thinking one was obeying a rule would be the same thing as obeying it" (202. cf. 380).

If I recognize that my mental image is the 'same' as one that I had previously, how am I to know that this public word 'same' describes what I recognize? "Only if I can express my recognition in some other way, and if it is possible for someone else to teach me that 'same' is the correct word here" (378). The notion of the private language doesn't admit of there being 'some other way.' It doesn't allow that my behavior and circumstances can be so related to my utterance of the word that another person, by noting my behavior and circumstances, can discover that my use of the word is correct or incorrect. Can I discover this for myself, and how do I do it? That discovery would presuppose that I have a conception of correct use which comes from outside my private language and against which I measure the latter. If this were admitted, the private language would lose its privacy and its point. So it isn't admitted. But now the notion of 'correct' use that will exist within the private language will be such that if I *believe* that my use is correct then it is correct;

the rules will be only impressions of rules; my 'language' will not be a language, but merely the impression of a language. The most that can be said for it is that I *think* I understand it (cf. 269).

Sensations of Others. The argument that I have been outlining has the form of *reductio ad absurdum*: postulate a 'private' language; then deduce that it is not *language*. Wittgenstein employs another argument that is an external, not an internal, attack upon private language. What is attacked is the assumption that once I know from my *own* case what pain, tickling, or consciousness is, then I can transfer the ideas of these things to objects outside myself (283). Wittgenstein says:

> If one has to imagine someone else's pain on the model of one's own, this is none too easy a thing to do: for I have to imagine pain which I *do not feel* on the model of the pain which I *do feel*. That is, what I have to do is not simply to make a transition in imagination from one place of pain to another. As, from pain in the hand to pain in the arm. For I am not to imagine that I feel pain in some region of his body. (Which would also be possible.) [302]

The argument that is here adumbrated is, I think, the following: If I were to learn what pain is from perceiving my own pain then I should, necessarily, have learned that pain is something that exists only when *I* feel pain. For the pain that serves as my paradigm of pain (i.e., my own) has the property of existing only when *I* feel it.[2] That

---

[2] [This is an error. Apparently I fell into the trap of assuming that if two people, A and B, are in pain, the pain that A feels must be *numerically* different from the pain that B feels. Far from making this assumption, Wittgenstein attacks it when he says: "In so far as it makes *sense* to say that my pain is the same as his, it is also possible for us both to have the same pain" (*op. cit.*, 253). There is not some sense of "same pain" (*numerically* the same) in which A and B *cannot* have the same pain. "Today I have that same backache that you had last week" is something we say. "Same" means here, answering to the same description. We attach no meaning to the "question" of whether the backache

property is essential, not accidental; it is nonsense to suppose that the pain I feel could exist when I did not feel it. So if I obtain my *conception* of pain from pain that I experience, then it will be part of my conception of pain that *I* am the only being that can experience it. For me it will be a *contradiction* to speak of *another's* pain. This strict solipsism is the necessary outcome of the notion of private language. I take the phrase "this is none too easy" to be a sarcasm.

One is tempted at this point to appeal to the 'same' again: "But if I suppose that someone has a pain, then I am simply supposing that he has just the same as I have so often had" (350). I will quote Wittgenstein's brilliant counterstroke in full:

> That gets us no further. It is as if I were to say: "You surely know what 'It is 5 o'clock here' means; so you also know what 'It's 5 o'clock on the sun' means. It means simply that it is just the same time there as it is here when it is 5 o'clock."—The explanation by means of *identity* does not work here. For I know well enough that one can call 5 o'clock here and 5 o'clock there "the same time," but what I do not know is in what cases one is to speak of its being the same time here and there.
>
> In exactly the same way it is no explanation to

---

you had and the one I have are or are not "numerically" the same.

A more correct account of Wittgenstein's point in sec. 302 is the following: A proponent of the privacy of sensations rejects circumstances and behavior as a criterion of the sensations of others, this being essential to his viewpoint. He does not need (and could not have) a criterion for the existence of pain that he feels. But surely he will need a criterion for the existence of pain that *he* does *not* feel. Yet he cannot have one and still hold to the privacy of sensation. If he sticks to the latter, he ought to admit that he has not the faintest idea of what would count for or against the occurrence of sensations that he does not feel. His conclusion should be, not that it is a contradiction, but that it is unintelligible to speak of the sensations of others. (There is a short exposition of Wittgenstein's attack on the idea that we learn what sensation is *from our own case*, in "Knowledge of Other Minds." See pp. 378–380.)]

say: the supposition that he has a pain is simply the supposition that he has the same as I. For *that* part of the grammar is quite clear to me: that is, that one will say that the stove has the same experience as I, *if* one says: it is in pain and I am in pain [350].

Expressions of Sensation. Wittgenstein says that he destroys "houses of cards" ("Luftgebaüde": 118) and that his aim is to show one how to pass from disguised to obvious nonsense (464). But this is not all he does or thinks he does. For he says that he changes one's *way of looking at things* (144). What is it that he wishes to substitute for that way of looking at things that is represented by the idea of private language? One would *like* to find a continuous exposition of his own thesis, instead of mere hints here and there. But this desire reflects a misunderstanding of Wittgenstein's philosophy. He rejects the assumption that he should put forward a *thesis* (128). "We may not advance any kind of theory" (109). A philosophical problem is a certain sort of confusion. It is like being lost; one can't see one's way (123). Familiar surroundings suddenly seem strange. We need to command a view of the country, to get our bearings. The country is well known to us, so we need only to be *reminded* of our whereabouts. "The work of the philosopher consists in assembling reminders for a particular purpose" (127). "The problems are solved, not by giving new information, but by arranging what we have always known" (109). When we describe (remind ourselves of) certain functions of our language, what we do must have a definite bearing on some particular confusion, some "deep disquietude" (111), that ensnares us. Otherwise our work is irrelevant —to *philosophy*. It is philosophically pointless to formulate a general theory of language or to pile up descriptions for their own sake. "This description gets its light, that is to say its purpose—from the philosophical problems" (109). Thus we may not complain at the absence from the *Investigations* of elaborate theories and classifications.

Wittgenstein asks the question "How do words *refer* to

sensations?" transforms it into the question "How does a human being learn the meaning of the names of sensations?" and gives this answer: "Words are connected with the primitive, the natural expressions of the sensation and used in their place. A child has hurt himself and he cries; and then the adults talk to him and teach him exclamations and, later, sentences. They teach the child new pain-behaviour" (244). Wittgenstein must be talking about how it is that a human being learns to refer with words to his *own* sensations—about how he learns to use 'I am in pain'; not about how he learns to use 'He is in pain.' What Wittgenstein is saying is indeed radically different from the notion that I learn what 'I am in pain' means by fixing my attention on a 'certain' sensation and calling it 'pain.' But is he saying that what I do instead is to fix my attention on my *expressions* of pain and call them 'pain'? Is he saying that the word 'pain' means crying? "On the contrary: the verbal expression of pain replaces crying and does not describe it" (244). My words for sensations are used *in place of* the behavior that is the natural expression of the sensations; they do not *refer* to it.

Wittgenstein does not expand this terse reminder. He repeats at least once that my words for sensations are "tied up with my natural expressions of sensation" (256) and frequently alludes to the importance of the connection between the language for sensations and the behavior which is the expression of sensation (e.g., 288, 271). The following questions and objections will arise:

(1) What shows that a child has made this 'tie up'? I take Wittgenstein to mean that the child's utterances of the word for a sensation must, in the beginning, be frequently concurrent with some nonverbal, natural expression of that sensation. This concomitance serves as the criterion of his understanding the word. Later on, the word can be uttered in the absence of primitive expressions. ('It hurts' can be said without cries or winces.)

(2) In what sense does the verbal expression 'replace' the nonverbal expression? In the sense, I think, that other per-

sons will react to the child's mere words in the same way that they previously reacted to his nonverbal sensation-behavior; they will let the mere words serve as a *new* criterion of his feelings.

(3) I feel inclined to object: 'But has the child *learned* what the words *mean*? Hasn't he merely picked up the *use* of the word from his parents?' My objection probably arises from assimilating the learning of the meaning of words to the labeling of bottles—a tendency that is easily decried but not easily resisted. 'Learning *ought* to consist in attaching the right name to the right object,' I should like to say (cf. 26). The example of 'the beetle in the box' is pertinent here (see 293). The aim of this fantasy is to prove that attending to a private object can have nothing to do with learning words for sensations. Suppose you wanted to teach a child what a tickling feeling is. You tickle him in the ribs, and he laughs and jerks away. You say to him, 'That's what the feeling of tickling is.' Now imagine he felt something that you can't know anything about. Will this be of any interest to you when you decide from his subsequent use of the word 'tickling' whether he understands it? Others understand the word too. If each one has something that only he can know about, then all the somethings may be different. The something could even be nothing! Whatever it is, it can have no part in determining whether the person who has it understands the word. "If we construe the grammar of the expression of sensation on the model of 'object and name' the object drops out of consideration as irrelevant" (293, cf. 304).

My previous objection could be put like this: the teaching and learning of names of sensations cannot stop at the mere expressions of sensation; the names must be brought *right up* to the sensations themselves, must be applied *directly* to the sensations! Here we can imagine Wittgenstein replying, "Like *what*, e.g.?" as he replies to an analogous objection in a different problem (191). In *what* sense is Wittgenstein denying that names are applied directly to sensations? Do I have a model of what it would

be to apply the name 'directly'? No. I have this picture—
that learning the meaning of 'pain' is applying the sign
'pain' to pain itself. I have that picture, to be sure, but
what does it teach me, what is its "application"? When
shall I say that what it pictures has taken place, i.e., that
someone has learned the meaning of 'pain'? It doesn't tell
me; it is *only* a picture. It cannot conflict with, cannot
refute, Wittgenstein's reminder of what it is that determines whether a child has learned the word for a sensation.
(4) Wittgenstein says that the verbal expressions of sensation can take the place of the nonverbal expressions and
that in learning the former one learns "new pain-behavior."
This seems to mean that the words (and sentences) for
sensations are related to sensations in the same way as are
the primitive expressions of sensations. I am inclined to
object again. I want to say that the words are used to *report*
the occurrence of a sensation and to inform others of it.
The natural expressions, on the contrary, are not used to
inform others; they are not 'used' at all; they have no
purpose, no function; they *escape* from one. But I have
oversimplified the difference, because (a) a sentence can
be forced from one, can escape one's lips ('My God, it
hurts!'), and (b) a natural expression of sensation can be
used to inform another, e.g., you moan to let the nurse
know that your pain is increasing (you would have suppressed the moan if she hadn't entered the room), yet the
moan is genuine. Perhaps my objection comes to this: I
don't *learn* to moan; I do learn the words. But this is the
very distinction that is made by saying that moaning is a
"natural," a "primitive," expression of sensation.

It is a mistake to suppose that Wittgenstein is saying
that the utterance 'My leg hurts' is *normally called* an
'expression of sensation.' (Of course it isn't. For that matter, only a facial expression, not a groan, is called an '*expression* of pain.' But this is of no importance.) He is not
reporting ordinary usage, but drawing our attention to an
analogy between the groan of pain and the utterance of
those words. The important similarity that he is trying to

bring to light (here I may misinterpret him) is that the verbal utterance and the natural pain-behavior are each (as I shall express it) 'incorrigible.'[3] A man cannot be in *error* as to whether he is in pain; he cannot say 'My leg hurts' by mistake, any more than he can groan by mistake. It is senseless to suppose that he has wrongly identified a tickle as pain or that he falsely believes that it is in his leg when in fact it is in his shoulder. True, he may be undecided as to whether it is best described as an 'ache' or a 'pain' (one is often hard put to give satisfactory descriptions of one's feelings); but his very indecision *shows* us what his sensation is, i.e., something between an ache and a pain. His hesitant observation, 'I'm not sure whether it is a pain or an ache,' is itself an *expression* of sensation. What it expresses is an indefinite, an ambiguous sensation. The point about the incorrigibility of the utterance 'I'm in pain' lies behind Wittgenstein's reiterated remark that 'I *know* I'm in pain' and 'I don't know whether I'm in pain' are both senseless (e.g., 246, 408).[4] Wherever it is *meaningless* to speak of 'false belief,' it is also meaningless to speak of 'knowledge'; and wherever you cannot say 'I don't know . . .' you also cannot say 'I know. . . .' Of course, a philosopher can say of me that I *know* I am in pain. But "What is it supposed to mean—except perhaps that I *am* in pain?" (246).[5]

There are many 'psychological' sentences, other than sentences about sensations, that are incorrigible, e.g., the

[3] [I try to explain the notion of "incorrigibility," as I understand it, in "Direct Perception" (see pp. 77–86 of *Knowledge and Certainty*). I concentrate there on the seeing of after-images, but with appropriate changes the notion carries over to bodily sensations.]

[4] It is interesting to note that as long ago as 1930 Wittgenstein had remarked that it has no sense to speak of *verifying* "I have a toothache." (See G. E. Moore, "Wittgenstein's Lectures in 1930–33," *Mind*, LXIII, January 1954, 14.)

[5] [In "A Definition of Factual Memory," I mention a sense in which an adult person (but not an infant or a dog) can be said to know that he has a pain (see p. 239 of *Knowledge and Certainty*).]

truthful report of a dream is a criterion for the occurrence of the dream and, unless some other criterion is introduced, "the question cannot arise" as to whether the dreamer's memory deceives him (pp. 222–223). If one who has a mental image were asked whom the image is of, "his answer would be decisive," just as it would be if he were asked whom the drawing represents that he has just made (p. 177). When you say 'It will stop soon' and are asked whether you *meant* your pain or the sound of the piano-tuning, your truthful answer *is* the answer (666–684).

When Wittgenstein says that learning the words for sensations is learning "new pain-behavior" and that the words "replace" the natural expressions, he is bringing to light the arresting fact that my sentences about my present sensations have the same logical status as my outcries and facial expressions. And thus we are helped to "make a radical break with the idea that language always functions in one way, always serves the same purpose: to convey thoughts—which may be about houses, pains, good and evil, or anything else you please" (304).

This is not to deny that first-person sentences about sensations may, in other respects, be more or less like natural expressions of sensation. Wittgenstein's examples of the use of 'I am afraid' (pp. 187–188) show how the utterance of that sentence can be a cry of fear, a comparison, an attempt to tell someone how I feel, a confession, a reflection on my state of mind, or something in between. "A cry is not a description. But there are transitions. And the words 'I am afraid' may approximate more, or less, to being a cry. They may come quite close to this and also be *far* removed from it" (p. 189). The words 'I am in pain' "may be a cry of complaint, and may be something else" (p. 189); and 'it makes me shiver' may be a "shuddering reaction" or may be said "as a piece of information" (p. 174). If we pursue these hints, it is not hard to construct a list of examples of the use of the words 'My head hurts,' in which the variety is as great as in

Wittgenstein's list for 'I am afraid.' E.g., compare 'Oh hell, how my head hurts!' with 'If you want to know whether to accept the invitation for tonight then I must tell you that my head hurts again.' In one case the sentence 'My head hurts' belongs to an exclamation of pain, not in the other. In saying that in *both* cases it is an 'expression' of pain, Wittgenstein stretches ordinary language and in so doing illuminates the hidden continuity between the utterance of that sentence and—expressions of pain.

Criterion. That the natural pain-behavior and the utterance 'It hurts' are each incorrigible is what makes it possible for each of them to be a criterion of pain. With some reluctance I will undertake to say a little bit about this notion of 'criterion,' a most difficult region in Wittgenstein's philosophy. Perhaps the best way to elucidate it is to bring out its connection with *teaching* and *learning* the use of words. "When I say the ABC to myself, what is the criterion of my doing the same as someone else who silently repeats it to himself? It might be found that the same thing took place in my larynx and in his. (And similarly when we both think of the same thing, wish the same, and so on.) But then did we learn the use of the words, 'to say such-and-such to oneself,' by someone's pointing to a process in the larynx or the brain?" (376). Of course we did not, and this means that a physiological process is not our 'criterion' that A said such-and-such to himself. Try to imagine, realistically and in detail, how you would teach someone the meaning of 'saying the ABC silently to oneself.' This, you may think, is merely psychology. But if you have succeeded in bringing to mind what it is that would show that he *grasped* your teaching, that he *understood* the use of the words, then you have elicited the 'criterion' for their use—and that is not psychology. Wittgenstein exhorts us, over and over, to bethink ourselves of how we learned to use this or that form of words or of how we should teach it to a child. The purpose of this is not to bring philosophy down to earth (which it does), but to bring into view those features of someone's circumstances and behavior that *settle* the question of whether the words (e.g., 'He is calculating in his head') rightly apply to him. Those features constitute the 'criterion' of calculating in one's head. It is logically possible that someone should have been born with a knowledge of the use of an expression or that it should have been produced in him by a drug; that his knowledge came about by way of the normal process of teaching is not necessary. What is necessary is that there should be something on the basis of which we *judge* whether he *has* that knowledge. To undertake to describe this may be called a 'logical' investigation, even though one should arrive at the description by reflecting on that logically inessential process of teaching and learning.

If someone says, e.g., 'I feel confident . . . ,' a question can arise as to whether he understands those words. Once you admit the untenability of 'private ostensive definition' you will see that there must be a *behavioral* manifestation of the feeling of confidence (579). There must be behavior against which his words 'I feel confident . . . ,' can be checked, if it is to be possible to judge that he does not understand them. Even if you picture a feeling of confidence as an "inner process," still it requires "outward criteria" (580).

Wittgenstein contrasts 'criterion' with 'symptom,' employing both words somewhat technically. The falling barometer is a 'symptom' that it is raining; its looking like *that* outdoors (think how you would teach the word 'rain' to a child) is the 'criterion' of rain (354). A process in a man's brain or larynx might be a symptom that he has an image of red; the criterion is "what he says and does" (377, 376). What makes something into a symptom of *y* is that experience teaches that it is always or usually associated with *y*; that so-and-so is the criterion of *y* is a matter, not of experience, but of "definition" (354). The satisfaction of the criterion of *y* establishes the existence of *y* beyond question. The occurrence of a symptom of *y* may also establish the existence of *y* 'beyond question'—but in a different sense. The observation of a brain process may make it certain that a man is in pain—but not in the same way that his pain-behavior makes it certain. Even if physiology has established that a specific event in the brain accompanies bodily pain, still it *could* happen (it makes sense to suppose) that a man was not in pain although that brain event was occurring. But it will not make sense for one to suppose that another person is not in pain if one's criterion of his being in pain is satisfied. (Sometimes, and especially in science, we *change* our criteria: "what to-day counts as an observed concomitant of a phenomenon will to-morrow be used to define it" [79].)

The preceding remarks point up the following question: Do the propositions that describe the criterion of his being in pain *logically imply* the proposition 'He is in pain'? Wittgenstein's answer is clearly in the negative. A criterion is satisfied *only in certain circumstances*. If we come upon a man exhibiting violent pain-behavior, couldn't something show that he is not in pain? Of course. For example, he is rehearsing for a play; or he has been hypnotized and told, 'You will act as if you are in pain, although you won't be in pain,' and when he is released from the hypnotic state he has no recollection of having been in pain; or his pain-behavior suddenly ceases and he reports in apparent bewilderment that it was as if his body had been possessed—for his movements had been entirely involuntary, and during the 'seizure' he had felt no pain; or he has been narrowly missed by a car and as soon as a sum for damages has been pressed into his hand, his pain-behavior ceases and he laughs at the hoax; or . . . , etc. The expressions of pain are a criterion of pain in *certain* "surroundings," not in others (cf. 584).

Now one would like to think that one can still formulate a logical implication by taking a description of his pain-behavior and conjoining it with the negation of every proposition describing one of those circumstances that would count against saying he is in pain. Surely, the conjunction will logically imply 'He is in pain'! But this assumes there is a *totality* of those circumstances such that if none of them were fulfilled, and he was also pain-behaving, then he *could not but* be in pain (cf. 183). There is no totality that can be exhaustively enumerated, as can the letters of the alphabet. It is quite impossible to list six or nine such circumstances and then to say 'That is all of them; no other circumstances can be imagined that would count against his being in pain.' The list of circumstances has no 'all,' in that sense; the list is, not infinite, but *indefinite*. Therefore, entailment-conditions cannot be formulated; there are none.

The above thought is hard to accept. It is not in line with our *ideal* of what language should be. It makes the 'rules' for the use of 'He is in pain' too vague, too loose, not really *rules*. Wittgenstein has deep things to say about the nature of this 'ideal': "We want to say that there can't be any vagueness in logic. The idea now absorbs us, that the ideal *'must'* be found in reality. Meanwhile we do not as yet see *how* it occurs there, nor do we understand the nature of this 'must.' We think it must be in reality; for we think we already see it there" (101). "The strict and clear rules of the logical structure of propositions appear to us as something in the background—hidden in the medium of the understanding" (102). "The more narrowly we examine actual language, the sharper becomes the conflict between it and our requirement. (For the crystalline purity of logic was, of course, not a *result of investigation*: it was a requirement.)" (107). What we need to do is to remove from our noses the logical glasses through which we look at reality (103). We must study our language as it is, without preconceived ideas. One thing this study will teach us is that the criteria for the use of third-person psychological statements are not related to the latter by an entailment-relation.

Wittgenstein suggests that propositions describing the fulfillment of behavioral criteria are related to third-person psychological statements in the way that propositions describing sense-impressions are related to physical-object statements (compare 486 and p. 180). It does not *follow* from the propositions describing my sense-impressions that there is a chair over there (486). The relation cannot be reduced to a *simple* formula (p. 180). *Why* doesn't it follow? Wittgenstein does not say, but the reason would appear to be of the same sort as in the example of 'He is in pain.' The propositions describing my sense-impressions would have to be conjoined with the proposition that I am not looking in a mirror, or at a painted scenery, or at a movie film, or . . . , etc. Here too there cannot be an exhaustive enumeration of the negative conditions that would have to be added to the description of sense-impressions *if* 'There's a chair over there' *were* to be logically implied.

The puzzling problem now presents itself: if it does not *follow* from his behavior and circumstances that he is in pain, then how can it ever be *certain* that he is in pain? "I can be as *certain* of someone else's sensations as of any fact," says Wittgenstein (p. 224). How can this be so, since there is not a definite set of six or eight conditions (each of which would nullify his pain-behavior) to be checked off as not fulfilled? It *looks* as if the conclusion ought to be that we cannot 'completely verify' that he is in pain. This conclusion is wrong, but it is not easy to see why. I comprehend Wittgenstein's thought here only dimly. He says:

A doctor asks: "How is he feeling?" The nurse says: "He is groaning." A report on his behaviour. But need there be any question for them whether the groaning is really genuine, is really the expression of anything? Might they not, for example, draw the conclusion "If he groans, we must give him more analgesic"—without suppressing a middle term? Isn't the point the service to which they put the description of behaviour [p. 179]?

One hint that I take from this is that there can be situations of real life in which a question as to whether someone who groans is pretending, or rehearsing, or hypnotized, or

. . . , simply does not exist. "Just try—in a real case—to doubt someone else's fear or pain" (303). A doubt, a question, would be rejected as absurd by anyone who knew the actual surroundings. 'But might there not be still further surroundings, unknown to you, that would change the whole aspect of the matter?' Well, we go only *so* far—and then we are certain. "Doubting has an end" (p. 180). Perhaps we can *imagine* a doubt; but we do not take it seriously (cf. 84). Just as it becomes certain to us that there is a chair over there, although we can imagine a *possible* ground of doubt. There is a concept of certainty in these language-games only because we stop short of what is conceivable.

" 'But, if you are *certain*, isn't it that you are shutting your eyes in face of doubt?'—They are shut" (p. 224). This striking remark suggests that what we sometimes do is draw a boundary around *this* behavior in *these* circumstances and say 'Any additional circumstances that might come to light will be irrelevant to whether this man is in pain.' Just as we draw a line and say 'No further information will have any bearing on whether there is a chair in the corner —that is settled.' If your friend is struck down by a car and writhes with a broken leg, you do not think: Perhaps it was prearranged in order to alarm me; possibly his leg was anesthetized just before the 'accident' and he isn't suffering at all. Someone *could* have such doubts whenever another person was ostensibly in pain. Similarly: "I can easily imagine someone always doubting before he opened his front door whether an abyss did not yawn behind it; and making sure about it before he went through the door (and he might on some occasion prove to be right)—but that does not make me doubt in the same case" (84).

The man who doubts the other's pain may be neurotic, may 'lack a sense of reality,' but his reasoning is perfectly sound. *If* his doubts are true then the injured man is *not* in pain. His reaction is abnormal but not illogical. The certainty that the injured man is in pain (the normal reaction) ignores the endless doubts that *could* be proposed and investigated.

And it is important to see that the abnormal reaction *must* be the exception and not the rule. For if someone *always* had endless doubts about the genuineness of expressions of pain, it would mean that he was not using *any criterion* of another's being in pain. It would mean that he did not accept anything as an *expression* of pain. So what could it mean to say that he even had the *concept* of another's being in pain? It is senseless to suppose that he has this concept and yet always doubts.

Third-Person Sensation-Sentences. Wittgenstein assimilates first-person, not third-person, sensation-sentences to *expressions* of sensation. I will say one or two things more about his conception of the use of third-person sensation-sentences.

(1) "Only of a living human being and what resembles (behaves like) a living human being can one say: it has sensations; it sees; is blind; hears; is deaf; is conscious or unconscious" (281). The *human* body and *human* behavior are the *paradigm* to which third-person attributions of consciousness, sensations, feelings are related. (The use of first-person sensation-sentences is governed by *no* paradigm.) Thus there cannot occur in ordinary life a question as to whether other human beings ever possess consciousness, and I can have this question when I philosophize only if I forget that I use that paradigm in ordinary life. It is by analogy with the human form and behavior that I attribute consciousness (or unconsciousness) to animals and fish: the more remote the analogy the less sense in the attribution. (Just as it is by analogy with our ordinary language that anything is called 'language') (494). In order to imagine that a pot or a chair has thoughts or sensations one must give it, in imagination, something like a human body, face, and speech (282, 361). A child says that its doll has stomach-ache, but this is a "secondary" use of the concept of pain. "Imagine a case in which people ascribed pain *only* to inanimate things; pitied *only* dolls!"

(282; cf. 385, p. 216). Wittgenstein means, I think, that this is an impossible supposition because we should not want to say that those people *understood* ascriptions of pain. If they did not ever show pity for human beings or animals or expect it for themselves, then their treatment of dolls would not be *pity*.

(2) My criterion of another's being in pain is, first, his behavior and circumstances and, second, his words (after they have been found to be connected in the right way with his behavior and circumstances). Does it follow that my interest is in his behavior and words, not in his pain? Does 'He is in pain' *mean* behavior? In lectures Wittgenstein imagined a tribe of people who had the idea that their slaves had no feelings, no souls—that they were automatons—despite the fact that the slaves had human bodies, behaved like their masters, and even spoke the same language. Wittgenstein undertook to try to give sense to that idea. When a slave injured himself or fell ill or complained of pains, his master would try to heal him. The master would let him rest when he was fatigued, feed him when he was hungry and thirsty, and so on. Furthermore, the masters would apply to the slaves our usual distinctions between genuine complaints and malingering. So what could it mean to say that they had the idea that the slaves were automatons? Well, they would *look* at the slaves in a peculiar way. They would observe and comment on their movements *as if* they were machines. ('Notice how smoothly his limbs move.') They would discard them when they were worn and useless, like machines. If a slave received a mortal injury and twisted and screamed in agony, no master would avert his gaze in horror or prevent his children from observing the scene, any more than he would if the ceiling fell on a printing press. Here is a difference in 'attitude' that is not a matter of believing or expecting different facts.

So in the *Investigations*, Wittgenstein says, "My attitude towards him is an attitude towards a soul. I am not of the *opinion* that he has a soul" (p. 178). I do not *believe* that the man is suffering who writhes before me—for to what facts would a 'belief' be related, such that a change in the facts would lead me to alter it? I *react* to his suffering. I look at him with compassion and try to comfort him. If I complain of headache to someone and he says 'It's not so bad,' does this prove that he believes in something *behind* my outward expression of pain? "His attitude is a proof of his attitude. Imagine not merely the words 'I am in pain' but also the answer 'It's not so bad' replaced by instinctive noises and gestures" (310). The thought that behind someone's pain-behavior is the pain itself does not enter into our use of 'He's in pain,' but what does enter into it is our sympathetic, or unsympathetic, reaction to him. The fact that the latter does enter into our use of that sentence (but might not have) gives sense to saying that the sentence 'He is in pain' does not just *mean* that his behavior, words, and circumstances are such and such—although these are the criteria for its use.

When he groans we do not *assume*, even tacitly, that the groaning expresses pain. We fetch a sedative and try to put him at ease. A totally different way of reacting to his groans would be to make exact records of their volume and frequency—and do nothing to relieve the sufferer! But our reaction of seeking to comfort him does not involve a presupposition, for, "Doesn't a presupposition imply a doubt? And doubt may be entirely lacking" (p. 180).

Form of Life. The gestures, facial expressions, words, and activities that constitute pitying and comforting a person or a dog are, I think, a good example of what Wittgenstein means by a "form of life." One could hardly place too much stress on the importance of this latter notion in Wittgenstein's thought. It is intimately related to the notion "language-game." His choice of the latter term is meant to "bring into prominence the fact that the *speaking* of language is part of an activity, or of a form of life" (23; cf. 19). If we want to understand any concept we must obtain a view of the human behavior, the activities, the natural expressions, that surround the words for that

concept. What, for example, is the concept of *certainty* as
applied to *predictions?* The nature of my certainty that
fire will burn me comes out in the fact that "Nothing
could induce me to put my hand into a flame" (472). That
reaction of mine to fire shows the *meaning* of certainty in
this language-game (474). (Of course, it is *different* from
the concept of certainty in, e.g., mathematics. "The kind
of certainty is the kind of language-game" [p. 224].) But is
my certainty justified? Don't I need reasons? Well, I don't
normally think of reasons, I can't produce much in the
way of reasons, and I don't feel a need of reasons (cf. 477).
Whatever was offered in the way of reasons would not
strengthen my fear of fire, and if the reasons turned out to
be weak I still wouldn't be induced to put my hand on the
hot stove.

As far as 'justification' is concerned, "What people accept as a justification—is shown by how they think and
live" (325). If we want to elucidate the concept of justification we must take note of what people *accept* as justified; and it is clearly shown in our lives that we accept as
justified both the certainty that fire will burn and the certainty that this man is in pain—even without reasons.
Forms of life, embodied in language-games, teach us what
justification is. As philosophers we must not attempt to
justify the forms of life, to give reasons for *them*—to argue,
for example, that we pity the injured man because we
believe, assume, presuppose, or know that in addition to
the groans and writhing, there is pain. The fact is, we
pity him! "What has to be accepted, the given, is—so one
could say—*forms of life*" (p. 226). What we should say is:
"*This language-game is played*" (654).

From this major theme of Wittgenstein's thought one
passes easily to another major theme—that "Philosophy
simply puts everything before us, and neither explains nor
deduces anything" (126). "It leaves everything as it is"
(124).

Strawson's Criticism. Mr. Peter Strawson's critical no-

tice[6] of the *Investigations* contains misunderstandings that
might obtain currency. To Strawson it appears that, for
Wittgenstein, "no word whatever stands for or names a
special experience,"[7] "no words name sensations (or
'private experiences'); and in particular the word 'pain'
does not."[8] Wittgenstein "has committed himself to the
view that one cannot sensibly be said to recognize or
identify anything, unless one uses *criteria*; and, as a consequence of this, that one cannot recognize or identify sensations."[9] His "obsession with the *expression* of pain" leads
him "to deny that sensations can be recognized and bear
names."[10] Wittgenstein is hostile to "the idea of what is
not observed (seen, heard, smelt, touched, tasted), and in
particular to the idea that what is not observed can in any
sense be recognized or described or reported"[11]—although
at one place in the book (p. 189) "it looks as if he were
almost prepared to acknowledge" that 'I am in pain' "may
be just a report of my sensations."[12] His "prejudice
against 'the inner'" leads him to deny that it is possible
for a person to report the words that went through his
mind when he was saying something to himself in his
thoughts.[13] Strawson attributes Wittgenstein's errors not
only to prejudice and, possibly, to "the old verificationist
horror of a claim that cannot be checked,"[14] but also to
various confusions and muddles.[15]

It is important to see how very erroneous is this account
of Wittgenstein. The latter says, "Don't we talk about
sensations every day, and give them names?" and then

---

[6] "Critical Notice: *Philosophical Investigations*," *Mind*,
LXIII, January 1954, 70–99. (References to Strawson will be
placed in footnotes, references to Wittgenstein will remain in the
text.) [*Editor's note*: Strawson's article is reprinted in the present
volume, pp. 22–64. Page references to the article as here printed
will be placed in square brackets after the references to the original pages in *Mind*.]

[7] P. 83 [p. 42].   [8] P. 84 [p. 42].   [9] P. 86 [p. 45].
[10] P. 87 [p. 46].   [11] P. 90 [p. 52].   [12] P. 94 [p. 56].
[13] P. 91 [p. 52 f.].   [14] P. 92 [p. 53].
[15] See p. 86 [p. 45 f.] and p. 98 [p. 63].

asks, "How does a human being learn the names of sensations?—of the word 'pain' for example?" (244). So Wittgenstein does not deny that we *name* sensations. It is a howler to accuse Wittgenstein of "hostility to the idea of what is not observed" ("observed" apparently means 'perceived by one of the five senses') and of "hostility to the idea that what is not observed can in any sense be recognized or described or reported."[16] Dreams and mental pictures are not observed, in Strawson's sense; yet Wittgenstein discusses *reports* of dreams (p. 222; also p. 184) and *descriptions* of mental pictures (e.g., 367). Consider this general remark: "Think how many different kinds of things are called 'description': description of a body's position by means of its co-ordinates; description of a facial expression; *description of a sensation of touch*; of a mood" (24, my italics). And at many places in the *Investigations*, Wittgenstein *gives* descriptions of various sensations, although sensations are not observed, in Strawson's sense. Strawson's belief that Wittgenstein thinks that "one cannot sensibly be said to recognize or identify anything, unless one uses criteria,"[17] is proved false by the remarks about mental images: I have *no* criterion for saying that two images of mine are the same (377); yet there is such a thing as *recognition* here, and a correct use of 'same' (378). How can it be maintained that Wittgenstein has a prejudice against 'the inner' when he allows that in our ordinary language a man *can* write down or give vocal expression to his "inner experiences—his feelings, moods, and the rest—for his private use"? (243). Wittgenstein does not deny that there are *inner* experiences any more than he denies that there are *mental* occurrences. Indeed, he gives examples of things that he calls "*seelische Vorgänge*," e.g., "a pain's growing more or less," and in contrast with which a thing like *understanding a word* is not, he argues, a "*seelischer Vorgang*" (154). Either to deny that such occurrences exist or to claim that they cannot be named, reported, or described is entirely foreign to Wittgenstein's

16 P. 90 [p. 52].   17 P. 86 [p. 45].

outlook. For what would the denial amount to other than an attempt to "reform language," which is not his concern? It may *look* as if he were trying to reform language, because he is engaged in "giving prominence to distinctions which our ordinary forms of language easily make us overlook" (132). For example, Wittgenstein suggests that when we think about the philosophical problem of sensation the word 'describe' *tricks* us (290). Of course he does not mean that it is a mistake to speak of 'describing' a sensation. He means that the similarity in "surface grammar" (664) between 'I describe my sensations' and 'I describe my room' may mislead, may cause us to fail "to call to mind the differences between the language-games" (290).

Strawson rightly avers, "To deny that 'pain' is the name of a (type of) sensation is comparable with denying that 'red' is the name of a colour."[18] I suppose that, conversely, to affirm that 'pain' is the name of a sensation is like affirming that 'red' is the name of a color, and also that 'o' is the name of a number. This classification tells us nothing of philosophical interest. What we need to notice is the *difference* between the way that 'o' and '2,' say, function, although both are 'names of numbers' (think how easily one may be tempted to deny that o is a number), and the difference between the way 'red' and 'pain' function, although both are 'names.' "We call very different things 'names'; the word 'name' is used to characterize many different kinds of use of a word, related to one another in many different ways" (38). To suppose that the uses of 'pain' and 'red,' as *names*, are alike is just the sort of error that Wittgenstein wants to expose. If one thinks this, one will want to by-pass the *expression* of pain and will wonder at Wittgenstein's 'obsession' with it. Not that Strawson does by-pass it, but he seems to attach the wrong significance to it. He appears to think that the fact that there is a characteristic pain-behavior is what makes possible a *common* "language of pain," and he seems to

18 P. 87 [p. 46 f.].

imply that if we did not care to have a *common* language of pain each of us would still be able to name and describe his pains in "a private language-game," even if there were no characteristic pain-behavior.[19] It looks as if he thinks that with his private language he could step between pain and its expression, and apply names to the bare sensations themselves (cf. 245).

For Strawson the conception of a private language possesses no difficulty. A man "might simply be struck by the recurrence of a certain sensation and get into the habit of making a certain mark in a different place every time it occurred. The making of the marks would help to impress the occurrence on his memory."[20] Just as, I suppose, he might utter a certain sound each time a cow appeared. But we need to ask, what makes the latter sound a *word*, and what makes it the word for *cow*? Is there no difficulty here? Is it sufficient that the sound is uttered when and only when a cow is present? Of course not. The sound might refer to anything or nothing. What is necessary is that it should play a part in various activities, in calling, fetching, counting cows, distinguishing cows from other things and pictures of cows from pictures of other things. If the sound has no fixed place in activities ("language-games") of this sort, then it isn't a word for *cow*. To be sure, I can sit in my chair and talk about cows and not be engaged in any of those activities—but what makes my words *refer* to cows is the fact that I have already mastered those activities; they lie in the background. The kind of way that 'cow' refers is the kind of language-game to which it belongs. If a mark or sound is to be a word for a *sensation* it, too, must enter into language-games, although of a very different sort. What sort? Well, such things as showing the location of the sensation, exhibiting different reactions to different intensities of stimulus, seeking or avoiding causes of the sensation, choosing one sensation in preference to another, indicating the duration of the

---

[19] See pp. 84–88 [pp. 42–49].
[20] P. 85 [p. 44].

sensation, and so on. Actions and reactions of that sort constitute the sensation-behavior. They are the "outward criteria" (580) with which the sign must be connected if it is to be a sign for a sensation *at all*, not merely if it is to be a sign in a *common* language. In the mere supposition that there is a man who is "struck by the recurrence of a certain sensation" and who gets into the habit of "making a certain mark in a different place every time it occurred," no ground *whatever* has been given for saying that the mark is a sign for a sensation. The necessary surroundings have not been supplied. Strawson sees no problem here. He is surprised that "Wittgenstein gives himself considerable trouble over the question of how a man would *introduce* a name for a sensation into this private language."[21] It is as if Strawson thought: There is no difficulty about it; the man just *makes* the mark refer to a sensation. How the man does it puzzles Strawson so little that he is not even inclined to feel that the connection between the name and the sensation is queer, occult (cf. 38)—which it would be, to say the least, if the name had no fixed place in those activities and reactions that constitute sensation-behavior, for that, and not a magical act of the mind, is what *makes* it refer to a sensation.

The conception of private language that Wittgenstein attacks is not the conception of a language that only the speaker does understand, but of a language that no other person *can* understand (243). Strawson thinks that Wittgenstein has not refuted the conception of a private language but has only shown that certain conditions must be satisfied if a common language is to exist. Strawson appears to believe (I may misunderstand him) that each of us not only can have but does have a private language of sensations, that if we are to understand one another when we speak of our sensations there must be criteria for the use of our sensation-words, and that therefore the words with which we *refer* to our sensations must, in addition,

21 P. 85 [p. 44].

contain "allusions" either to behavior or to material substances that are "associated" with the sensations.[22] The
allusions must be to things that can be perceived by us all.
By virtue of this the use of sensation-words can be taught
and misuses corrected, and so those words will belong to a
common language. There is another feature of their use
(namely, their reference) that cannot be taught. Thus
sensation-words will have both a public and a private
meaning. Strawson's view appears to be accurately characterized by Wittgenstein's mock conjecture: "Or is it like
this: the word 'red' means something known to everyone;
and in addition, for each person, it means something
known only to him? (Or perhaps rather: it *refers* to something known only to him.)" (273).

But if my words, *without* these allusions, can refer to
my sensations, then what is alluded to is only *contingently*
related to the sensations. Adding the "allusions to what
can be seen and touched"[23] will not help one little bit
in making us understand one another. For the behavior
that is, for me, contingently associated with 'the sensation
of pain' may be, for you, contingently associated with 'the
sensation of tickling'; the piece of matter that produces in
you what you call 'a metallic taste' may produce in me
what, if you could experience it, you would call 'the taste
of onions'; my 'sensation of red' may be your 'sensation of
blue'; we do not know and cannot know whether we are
talking about the same things; we cannot *learn* the essential
thing about one another's use of sensation-words—namely,
their reference. The language in which the private referring
is done cannot be turned into a common language by having something grafted on to it. Private language cannot
be the understructure of the language we all understand. It
is as if, in Strawson's conception, the sensation-words were
supposed to perform two functions—to refer and to communicate. But if the reference is incommunicable, then

22 P. 86 [p. 46].
23 *Ibid.* [p. 46].

the trappings of allusion will not communicate it, and what they do communicate will be irrelevant.

Strawson's idea that expressions like 'jabbing pain,' 'metallic taste,' mean something known to everyone and, in addition, for each person, refer to something known only to him, is responsible, I believe, for his failure to understand Wittgenstein on the topic of recognizing and identifying sensations. There is *a* sense of 'recognize' and 'identify' with respect to which Wittgenstein does deny that we can recognize or identify our own sensations, feelings, images. Consider, for example, that although a man understands the word 'alcohol' he may fail to identify the alcohol in a bottle as alcohol, because the bottle is marked 'gasoline' or because the cork smells of gasoline; or, although he understands 'rabbit' and is familiar with rabbits, he may fail to recognize a rabbit as a rabbit, taking it for a stump instead; or, he may be in doubt and say, 'I don't know whether this is alcohol,' 'I'm not sure whether that is a rabbit or a stump.' But can a man who understands the word 'pain' be in doubt as to whether he has pain? Wittgenstein remarks:

> If anyone said "I do not know if what I have got is a pain or something else," we should think something like, he does not know what the English word "pain" means; and we should explain it to him.—How? Perhaps by means of gestures, or by pricking him with a pin and saying: "See, that's what pain is!" This explanation, like any other, he might understand right, wrong, or not at all. And he will show which he does by his use of the word, in this as in other cases.
>
> If he now said, for example: "Oh, I know what 'pain' means; what I don't know is whether *this*, that I have now, is pain"—we should merely shake our heads and be forced to regard his words as a queer reaction which we have no idea what to do with [288].

That a man wonders whether what he has is pain can only mean that he does not understand the word 'pain'; he cannot both understand it and have that doubt. Thus

there is a sense of 'identify' that has no application to
sensations. One who understands the word 'alcohol' may
fail to identify *this* as alcohol or may be in doubt as to its
identity or may correctly identify it. These possibilities
have no meaning in the case of pain. There is not over and
above (or underneath) the understanding of the word
'pain' a further process of correctly identifying or failing to
identify *this* as pain. There would be if Strawson's conception was right. But there is not, and this is why "That expression of doubt ['Oh, I know what "pain" means; what
I don't know is whether *this*, that I have now, is pain'] has
no place in the language-game" (288). (Strawson does not
have, but in consistency should have, an inclination to dispute this last remark of Wittgenstein's.)[24] The fact that
there is no *further* process of identifying a particular sensation is a reason why "the object drops out of consideration as irrelevant" when "we construe the grammar
of the expression of sensation on the model of 'object and
name'" (293)—a remark that Strawson misunderstands as
the thesis that "no words name sensations."[25] If my use
of a sensation-word satisfies the normal outward criteria
and if I truthfully declare that I have that sensation, then
I *have* it—there is not a further problem of my applying
the word right or wrong within myself. If a man used
the word 'pain' in accordance with "the usual symptoms
and presuppositions of pain" then it would have no sense
to suppose that perhaps his memory did not retain *what*
the word 'pain' refers to, "so that he constantly called
different things by that name" (271). If my use of the
word fits those usual criteria there is not an added problem
of whether I accurately pick out the objects to which the
word applies. In this sense of 'identify,' the hypothesis
that I identify my sensations is "a mere ornament, not
connected with the mechanism at all" (270).

It does not follow nor, I think, does Wittgenstein mean
to assert that there is *no* proper use of 'identify' or 'rec-

24 See p. 85 [p. 45].
25 P. 84 [p. 42].

ognize' with sensations. He acknowledges a use of 'recognize' with mental images, as previously noted. It would be a natural use of language, I believe, if someone who upon arising complained of an unusual sensation were to say, 'Now I can identify it! It is the same sensation that I have when I go down in an elevator.' Wittgenstein, who has no interest in reforming language, would not dream of calling this an incorrect use of 'identify.' He attacks a philosophical use of the word only, the use that belongs to the notion of the private object. In this example of a non-philosophical use, if the speaker employed the rest of the sensation-language as we all do, and if his behavior in this case was approximately what it was when he was affected by the downward motion of an elevator, then his declaration that he was feeling the elevator-sensation would be decisive; and also his declaration that it was *not* the elevator-sensation would be decisive. It is *out of the question* that he should have made a mistake in identifying the sensation. His identification of his sensation is an *expression* of sensation (in Wittgenstein's extended sense of this phrase). The identification is 'incorrigible.' We have here a radically different use of 'identify' from that illustrated in the examples of alcohol and rabbit.

The philosophical use of 'identify' seems to make possible the committing of *errors* of identification of sensations and inner experiences. The idea is that my sensation or my image is an object that I cannot show to anyone and that I identify it and from it derive its description (374). But if this is so, why cannot my identification and description go wrong, and not just sometimes but always? Here we are in a position to grasp the significance of Wittgenstein's maneuver: "Always get rid of the idea of the private object in this way: assume that it constantly changes, but that you do not notice the change because your memory constantly deceives you" (p. 207). We are meant to see the *senselessness* of this supposition: for what in the world would *show* that I was deceived constantly or even once? Do I look again—and why can't I be deceived that time,

too? The supposition is a knob that doesn't turn anything
(cf. 270). Understanding this will perhaps remove the
temptation to think that I have something that I cannot
show to you and from which I derive a knowledge of its
identity. This is what Wittgenstein means in saying that
when I related to another what I just said to myself in my
thoughts " 'what went on within me' is not the point at all"
(p. 222). He is not declaring, as Strawson thinks, that I
cannot report what words went through my mind.[26] He is
saying that it is a report "whose truth is guaranteed by the
special criteria of truthfulness" (p. 222). It is *that* kind of
report. So it is not a matter of trying faithfully to observe
something within myself and of trying to produce a correct
account of it, of trying to do something at which I might
unwittingly fail.

The influence of the idea of the private object on Strawson's thinking is subtly reflected, I believe, in his declaration that a metallic taste is "quite certainly recognizable
and identifiable in itself" and in his remark that "if the
question 'What is the criterion of identity here?' is pushed,
one can only answer: 'Well, the taste itself' (cf. 'the
sensation itself')."[27] Strawson realizes that we don't
identify a sensation by means of criteria (e.g., a metallic
taste by means of the metallic material that produces it).
He is inclined to add that we identify it by 'the sensation
itself.' This seems to me to misconstrue the 'grammar' of
'identify' here. It may be to the point to consider again
the comparison of colors and sensations. Wittgenstein says,
"How do I know that this colour is red?—It would be an
answer to say 'I have learned English' " (381). One thing
this answer does is to deny that I have *reasons* for saying
that this color before me is red. We might put this by
saying that I identify it as red by 'the color itself,' not by
anything else. The cases of red and pain (or metallic taste)
so far run parallel. Equally, I don't have reasons for saying
that this color is red or that this sensation is pain. But it

[26] See pp. 90, 91 [pp. 51, 52].
[27] P. 86 [p. 46].

can happen that I should fail to identify this color correctly, even though I have learned English (e.g., the moonlight alters its appearance). Here the parallel ends. Nothing can alter the 'appearance' of the sensation. Nothing counts as mistaking its identity. If we assimilate identifying sensations to identifying colors, because in neither instance reasons are relevant, we conceal the philosophically more important difference. To insist that the parallel is perfect, that one identifies sensations in the same sense that one identifies colors, is like saying that "there must also be something boiling in the pictured pot" (297). Identifying one's own sensation is nothing that is either in error or *not* in error. It is not, in *that* sense, *identifying.* When I identify my sensation, I do not *find out* its identity, not even from 'the sensation itself.' My identification, one could say, *defines* its identity.

We use a man's identification of his sensation as a criterion of what his sensation is. But this is a *dependent* criterion. His verbal reports and identifications would not *be* a criterion unless they were grounded in the primitive sensation-behavior that is the primary and independent criterion of his sensations. If we cut out human behavior from the language-game of sensations (which Strawson does in defending the 'private language-game') one result will be that a man's identifying a sensation as the 'same' that he had a moment before will no longer be a criterion of its being the same. Not only the speaker but *no one* will have a criterion of identity. Consequently, for no one will it have any meaning to speak of a man's being "struck by the *recurrence* of a certain sensation."[28]

[28] P. 85 [p. 44], my italics.

WITTGENSTEIN'S
PHILOSOPHICAL INVESTIGATIONS
PAUL FEYERABEND

In discussing this book I shall proceed in the following
way: I shall first state a philosophical theory T, which is
attacked throughout the book. In doing so I shall not use
the usual statement of the theory (if there is any) but
Wittgenstein's, which may, of course, be an idealization.
Secondly, I shall show how the theory is criticized by Wittgenstein—first, using an example (which plays a considerable role in the *Investigations*, but which I have used to
present arguments not presented in the book in connection
with this example), then discussing in general terms the
difficulties revealed by the example. Thirdly, I shall state
what seems to be Wittgenstein's own position on the issue.
This position will be formulated as a philosophical theory,
T', without implying that Wittgenstein intended to develop a philosophical theory (he did not). Finally I shall
discuss the relation between the theory stated and Wittgenstein's views on philosophy and I shall end up with a
few critical remarks.[1]

For brevity's sake I shall introduce three different types
of quotation marks: The usual quotation marks (". . .")

From *The Philosophical Review*, Vol. LXIV (1955), pp.
449–483. Reprinted with the permission of the author and
editors.
[1] Although many different problems are discussed in the *Investigations*, it seems to me that the criticism of T (or the assertion of T') is to be regarded as the core of the book. I shall
therefore concentrate on elaborating T and T', and I shall omit
all other problems (if there are any).

enclosing Wittgenstein's own words, daggers (†. . .†) enclosing further developments of his ideas and general remarks, asterisks (*. . .*), enclosing critical remarks. Text without any of these quotation marks is an abbreviated statement of what Wittgenstein is saying.

II

†The theory criticized is closely related to medieval realism (about universals) and to what has recently been termed "essentialism."[2] The theory, as presented by Wittgenstein, includes the following five main items:

†(1) "Every word has a meaning. This meaning is correlated with the word. It is the object, for which the word stands" (1; 90, 120).[3] Meanings exist independently of whether or not any language is used and which language is used. They are definite, single objects and their order "must be *utterly simple*" (97).

†(2) As compared with this definiteness and purity of meanings (their order "must . . . be of the purest crystal" [97]), "the actual use . . . seems something muddied" (426). That indicates an imperfection of our language.

†(3) This imperfection gives rise to two different philosophical problems: (a) The philosopher has to find out what a word 'W' stands for, or, as it is sometimes expressed, he has to discover the *essence* of the object which is designated by 'W,' when its use in everyday language is taken into account. From the knowledge of the essence of W the knowledge of the whole use of 'W' will follow (264, 362, 449). (b) He has to build an ideal language whose elements are related to the essences in a simple way. The method of finding a solution to problem (a) is analysis. This analysis proceeds from the assumption

[2] Cf. K. R. Popper, *The Open Society and Its Enemies* (Princeton, 1950), I, 31 ff.

[3] Parenthetical references are to the numbered sections of Part I of the *Philosophical Investigations*, unless otherwise indicated.

that *"the essence is hidden from us"* (92) but that it nevertheless " '*must*' be found in reality" (101). However different the methods of analysis may be—analysis of the linguistic usage of 'W'; phenomenological analysis of W ('deepening' of the phenomenon W); intellectual intuition of the essence of W—the answer to problem (a) "is to be given once for all; and independently of any future experience" (92). The form of this answer is the definition. The definition explains why 'W' is used in the way it is and why W behaves as it does (75; 97, 428, 654). The solution of (b) is presupposed in the solution of (a); for it provides us with the terms in which the definitions that constitute the solution of (a) are to be framed. A definite solution of (b) implies a certain form of problem (a). If it is assumed, e.g., that sentences are word-pictures of facts (291; cf. *Tractatus Logico-Philosophicus* 2.1; 4.04) then 'What is a question?' is to be translated into 'What kind of fact is described by a question? The fact that somebody wants to know whether . . . , or the fact that somebody is doubtful as to . . . , etc.?'

†(4) Asking how the correctness of a certain analysis may be checked, we get the answer that the essence can be *experienced*. This experience consists in the presence of a mental picture, a sensation, a phenomenon, a feeling, or an inner process of a more ethereal kind (305). 'To grasp the meaning' means the same as 'to have a picture before one's inner eye' and "to have understood the explanation means to have in one's mind an idea of the thing explained, and that is a sample or a picture" (73). The essence of the object denoted, the meaning of the denoting expression (these are one and the same thing; cf. 371, 373) follows from an analysis of this picture, of this sensation; it follows from the exhibition of the process in question (thus the essence of sensation follows from an analysis of my present headache [314]). It is the presence of the picture which gives meaning to our words (511, 592), which forces upon us the right use of the word (73, 140, 305, 322, 426, 449), and which enables us to

perform correctly an activity (reading, calculating) the essence of which it constitutes (179, 175, 186, 232). Understanding, calculating, thinking, reading, hoping, desiring are, therefore, mental processes.

†(5) From all this it follows that teaching a language means showing the connection between words and meanings (362) and that "learning a language consists in giving names to objects" (253). So far the description of *T*, as it is implicitly contained in the *Philosophical Investigations*.

III

†In criticizing *T*, Wittgenstein analyzes *T*4 and in this way shows the impossibility of the program *T*3 as well as the insolubility of the problems connected with this program. That implies that, within *T*, we shall never be able to know what a certain word 'W' means or whether it has any meaning at all, although we are constantly using that word and although the question how it is to be used does not arise when we are not engaged in philosophical investigations. But did not this paradox arise because we assumed that meanings are objects of a certain kind and that a word is meaningful if and only if it stands for one of those objects; i.e., because we assumed *T*1, 2 to be true? If, on the other hand, we want to abandon *T*1, 2, we meet another difficulty: words have, then, no fixed meaning (79). "But what becomes of logic now? Its rigour seems to be giving way here.—But in that case doesn't logic altogether disappear?—For how can it lose its rigour? Of course not by our bargaining any of its rigour out of it.—The *preconceived idea* of crystalline purity can only be removed by turning our whole examination round" (108); i.e., by changing from *T* to *T'*. It will turn out that this change cannot be described simply as the change from one *theory* to another, although we shall first introduce *T'* as a new theory of meaning.

†Before doing so we have to present Wittgenstein's

criticism of *T*. This criticism is spread throughout the
book. It consists of careful analyses of many special cases,
the connection between which is not easily apprehended.
I have tried to use *one* example instead of many and to
present as many arguments as possible by looking at this
example from as many sides as possible. All the arguments
are Wittgenstein's; some of the applications to the example in question are mine.

IV

†The philosopher is a man who wants to discover the
meanings of the expressions of a language or the essences
of the things designated by those expressions. Let us see
how he proceeds. Let us take, e.g., the word 'reading.'
"Reading is here the activity of rendering out loud what is
written or printed; and also of writing from dictation,
writing out something printed, playing from a score and
so on" (156).

†(A) According to *T1* we have to assume that the word
'reading' stands for a single object. Now, there is a variety
of manifestations of reading: reading the morning paper;
reading in order to discover misprints (here one reads
slowly, as a beginner would read); reading a paper written
in a foreign language that one cannot understand but has
learned to pronounce; reading a paper in order to judge the
style of the author; reading shorthand, reading *Principia
Mathematica*, reading Hebrew sentences (from right to
left); reading a score in order to study a part one has to
sing; reading a score in order to find out something about
the inventiveness of the composer, or to find out how far
the composer may have been influenced by other contemporary musicians; reading a score in order to find out
whether the understanding of the score is connected with
acoustic images or with optical images (which might be a
very interesting psychological problem). But this variety,
without "any one feature that occurs in all cases of reading"

(168), is only a superficial aspect. All these manifestations have something *in common* and it is this common property which makes them manifestations of *reading*. It is also this property that is the essence of reading. The other properties, varying from one manifestation to the other, are accidental. In order to discover the essence we have to strip off the particular coverings which make the various manifestations *different* cases of reading. But in doing so (the reader ought to try for himself!) we find, not that what is essential to reading is hidden beneath the surface of the single case, but that this alleged surface is one case out of a family of cases of reading (164).†

> Consider for example the proceedings which we call "games." I mean board-games, card-games, ball-games, Olympic games and so on. What is common to them all?—Don't say: "There *must* be something common or they would not be called 'games'"; but *look and see* whether there is anything common to *all*—for if you look at them you will not see something that is in common to all, but similarities, relationships and a whole series of them at that. . . . And the result of this examination is: we see a complicated network of similarities overlapping and criss-crossing. . . . I can think of no better expression to characterize these similarities than "family-resemblances"; for the various resemblances between members of a family: build, features, colours of eyes, gait, temperament, etc., etc., overlap and criss-cross in the same way.—And I shall say: "games" form a family [66 f].
>
> And in the same way we also use the word 'reading' for a family of cases. And in different circumstances we apply different criteria for a person's reading [164].

† (B) Looking at the outer manifestations of reading we could not discover the structure suggested by T1. Instead of an accidental variety centering in a well-defined core we found "a complicated network of similarities" (66). Does that fact refute T1? Surely not; for a philos-

opher who wants to defend T1, there are many possible
ways of doing so. He may admit that the *overt behavior*
of the person reading does not disclose any well-defined
center, but he may add that reading is a *physiological
process* of a certain kind. Let us call this process the reading process (RP). Person P is reading if and only if the
RP is going on within (the brain or the nervous system of)
P. (Cf. 158.) But the difficulties of this assumption are
clear. Consider the case of a person who does not look at
any printed paper, who is walking up and down, looking
out of the window and behaving as if he were expecting
somebody to come; but the RP is going on within his
brain. Should we take the presence of the reading process
as a sufficient criterion for the person's reading, adding
perhaps that we had discovered a hitherto unknown case of
reading? (Cf. 160.) It is clear that in a case like that we
should, rather, alter some physiological hypotheses. If,
again, reading is a physiological process, then it certainly
makes sense to say that P read 'ali' within 'totalitarianism,'
but did not read before he uttered those sounds and did
not read afterward either, although anybody who observed
the outer behavior of P would be inclined to say that P
had been reading the whole time. For it is quite possible
that the RP should be present only when P is uttering
'ali' (cf. 157). It seems, however, that it is quite meaningless to hypothesize that in the circumstances described a
person was reading only for one second or two, so that his
uttering of sounds in the presence of printed paper before
or after that period must not be called 'reading.'

†(C) To the failure of attempts (A) and (B) to discover the essence of reading certain philosophers will answer in the following way: Certainly—that was to be expected.† For reading is a *mental process*, and "the one real
criterion for anybody's *reading* is the conscious act of
reading, the act of reading the sounds off from the letters.
'A man surely knows whether he is reading or only pretending to read'" (159). †The idea to which they are
alluding is this: Just as the sensation *red* is present when

we are looking at a red object, so a specific mental process, the reading process (MRP), is present in the mind when we are reading. The MRP is the object of our analysis of reading, its presence makes our overt behavior a manifestation of reading (etc., as already indicated in T_4). In short, it is thought that this mental process will enable us to solve problems which we could not solve when considering material processes only: "When our language suggests a body and there is none; there, we should like to say, is a *spirit*" (36). But it will turn out that mental processes are subject to the same kind of criticism as material processes: that neither a material nor a spiritual mechanism enables us to explain how it is that words are meaningful and that their meanings can be known; that in pointing to mental processes we cling to the same scheme of explanation as in the physiological or the behavioristic theory of meaning (considered in the two last sections) without realizing that we are doing so.[4] That can be shown by very simple means: Consider the case of a person who does not look at any printed paper, who is walking up and down, looking out of the window, and behaving as if he were expecting somebody to come; but the MRP is going on in his mind (in his consciousness). Should we take the presence of this mental process as a sufficient criterion for the person's reading, adding, perhaps, that we had discovered a hitherto unknown case of reading? It is clear that we should alter, rather, some psychological hypotheses (the hypothesis that reading is always correlated with the MRP). But the last argument is a simple transformation of the first argument of section (B) with 'MRP' (the mental process which is supposed to be the essence of reading) substituted for 'RP' (the physiological process, which was supposed to be the essence of reading in section B). By this substitution the second argument can be used for the present purpose as well.

[4] This point is elaborated in some detail in G. Ryle's *Concept of Mind* (London, 1949), which should not, however, be taken to agree completely with Wittgenstein's ideas.

†(a) Let us now turn to a more detailed investigation
of the matter. Let us first ask whether really *every act of
reading is accompanied by the MRP*. A few minutes ago
I was reading the newspaper. Do I remember any particular mental process which was present all the time I was
reading? I remember that I was expecting a friend (actually I looked at my watch several times) and that I was
angry because he did not come, although he had promised
to do so. I also remember having thought of an excellent
performance of *Don Giovanni* which I had seen a few days
ago and which had impressed me very much. Then I found
a funny misprint and was amused. I also considered
whether the milk which I had put on the fire was already
boiling, etc. Nevertheless, I was *reading* all the time, and
it is quite certain that I was (cf. 171).† "But now notice
this: While I am [reading] everything is quite simple. I
notice nothing *special*; but afterward, when I ask myself
what it was that happened, it seems to have been something indescribable. *Afterward* no description satisfies me.
It is as if I couldn't believe that I merely looked, made
such and such a face and uttered words. But don't I *remember* anything else? No" (cf. 175; "being guided" instead of 'reading'). †The same applies to activities such as
calculating, drawing a picture, copying a blueprint, etc. I
know of course that I was reading, but that shows only
that my knowledge is not based on the memory of a certain sensation, impression, or the like—because there was
no such impression.† Compare now another example:
Look at the mark ∞ and let a sound occur to you as you
do so; utter it—let us assume it is the sound 'u.' †Now read
the sentence 'Diana is a beautiful girl.' Was it in a different way that the perception of the 'eau' (in 'beautiful')
led to the utterance of the sound 'u' in the second case?
Of course there was a difference! For I *read* the second
sentence whereas I did not read when I uttered the 'u' in
the presence of the ∞. But is this difference a difference
of mental content, i.e., am I able to discover a specific

sensation, impression, or the like which was present in the second case, and missing in the first case, whose presence made the second case a case of *reading*?† Of course, there were many differences: In the first case "I had told myself beforehand that I was to let a sound occur to me; there was a certain tension present before the sound came. And I did not say 'u' automatically as I do when I look at the letter U. Further that mark [the ∽] was not *familiar* to me in the way the letters of the alphabet are. I looked at it rather intently and with a certain interest in its shape" (166). But imagine now a person who has the feeling described above in the presence of a normal English text, composed of ordinary letters. Being invited to read, he thinks that he is supposed to utter sounds just as they occur to him—one sound for each letter—and he nevertheless utters all the sounds a normal person would utter when reading the text. "Should we say in such a case that he was not really reading the passage? Should we here allow his sensations to count as the criterion for his reading or not reading?" (160). From the negative answer to this question we have to conclude that, even if we were able to discover a difference between the way in which the perception of the ∽ leads to the utterance of the sound 'u' and the way in which, e.g., the perception of the 'eau' within 'beautiful' leads to the utterance of the 'u,' this difference—if it is a difference of mental content, of behavior, etc.—cannot be interpreted as justifying the assumption of an essential difference between cases of reading and not reading.[5]

---

[5] There are cases of mental disease where the patient talks correctly although with the feeling that somebody is making up the words for him. This is rightly regarded as a case of mental disease and not, as the adherents of the mental-picture theory of meaning would be inclined to say, as a case of inspiration: For one judges from the fact that the person in question *talks correctly*, although with queer sensations. Following Locke, a distinction is usually made between impressions of sensation and impressions of reflection. When Wittgenstein talks of sensations, of feelings, of a "picture in the mind" he seems to mean both. So his investiga-

(b) It may be objected to this analysis that the MRP is sometimes present quite distinctly. "Read a page of print and you can see that something special is going on, something highly characteristic" (165). This is true especially where "we make a point of reading slowly—perhaps in order to see what does happen if we read" (170). Thus one could be inclined to say that the MRP is a subconscious process which accompanies *every* case of reading but which can be brought to light only by a special effort.[6]

Answer: (1) Reading with the intention of finding out what happens when we are reading is a special case of reading and as such different from ordinary reading (cf. 170). Nevertheless reading without this intention is also a case of reading, which shows that the reason for calling it a case of *reading* cannot be the presence of a sensation which—admittedly—is present only in special cases and not in the case discussed. Finally, the description of the MRP cannot be a description of reading in general, for the ordinary case is omitted. We should not be misled by the picture which suggests "that this phenomenon comes in sight 'on close inspection.' If I am supposed to describe how an object looks from far off, I don't make the de-

_____

tions are directed against a primitive psychologism (concepts are combinations of impressions of sensation) as well as against a more advanced psychologism (concepts are combinations of impressions of reflection). They are also directed against a presentational realism (concepts are objects of a certain kind, but *having* a concept, or *using* a concept is the same as having an idea in one's mind—i.e., although concepts are not psychological events, their representations in people are), against a theory which Wittgenstein elsewhere described as implying that "logic is the physics of the intellectual realm."

[6] A psychologist or an adherent of the phenomenological method in psychology would be inclined to judge the situation in this way. His intention would be to create a kind of "pure situation" in which a special process comes out quite distinctly. It is then supposed that this process is hidden in every ordinary situation (which is not pure, but) which resembles the pure situation to a certain extent. In the case of reading the pure situation would be: reading plus introspecting in order to find out what is going on. The ordinary situation is: simply reading.

scription more accurate by saying what can be noticed about the object on closer inspection" (171).

†(2) Not every kind of introspection is judged in the same way. It is possible that a person who is supposed to find the MRP by introspection, being tired, should experience and describe quite unusual things while thinking all the time that the task which was set him by the psychologist is being performed by giving these descriptions.[7] No psychologist will welcome such a result. Instead of thinking that new and illuminating facts about reading have been discovered, he will doubt the reliability of the guinea pig. From this we have to conclude once more that the sensations experienced in connection with reading, and even those experienced as the essence of reading by the readers themselves, have nothing whatever to do with the question what reading really is.

†(3) Let us now assume that a reliable observer whom we ask to read attentively and to tell us what happens while he is reading provides us with the following report: 'The utterance is *connected* with seeing the signs, it is as if I were *guided* by the perception of the letters, etc.' (cf. 169, 170, 171). Does he, when answering our question in this way, describe a mental content, as a person who is seeing red and who tells us that he is seeing red describes a mental content? Does he say 'I am being guided by the letters' because the mental content *being guided* is present? Then one would have to conclude that every case of being guided is accompanied by *being guided*, as we assumed at the beginning of section (C) that every case of reading is accompanied by the MRP. But this last assumption has already been refuted, and the other, being completely analogous to it, can be refuted by the same arguments. We have to conclude, therefore, that the possibility of describing the process of reading as a case of being

---

[7] An illustrative example for experiences of this kind may be found in B. Russell, *History of Western Philosophy* (New York, 1945), p. 145.

guided does not imply that reading is a mental process, because being guided is not one (cf. 172).[8]

†(c) As already indicated, people usually try to escape from argument (Ca) by assuming that the MRP is a subconscious sensation which has to be brought to light by introspection. A different form of the same escape is the following one: The arguments that have been brought forward so far assume that reading and the MRP can be separated from one another. This, however, is not the case: Reading is inseparably connected with the MRP. What occurs separably from reading is not the MRP, but only an erroneous interpretation of something as reading. But how are we to decide whether the MRP itself is present or only something else erroneously interpreted as reading; or, what comes to the same thing, how are we to decide whether we are reading or only believing that we are reading? The given content of consciousness cannot be used for deciding that question, for it is *its* reliability which is to be ascertained. The only possible alternative is to call a sensation a case of the MRP if and only if it is accompanied by reading. But now we assume, contrary to

---

[8] The idea that reading is a single object (in spite of the variety of manifestations demonstrated in Sec. A) is apparently supported by the fact that one can give a definition like the one we gave at the beginning of Sec. IV, or that one can say that reading is a form of being guided. But let us not be misled by words. For the definition of reading in terms of being guided or the like supports the idea that reading is a single object only if being guided can itself be shown to be a single object. But an analysis similar to the one sketched in Sec. A will show that this is not the case.

One of the main reasons for the wide acceptance of the assumption that it is possible to discover the essence of reading by introspection is the fact that the great number of manifestations of reading is usually not taken into account. Beset by theory T we *think* (173, 66) that acute observation must disclose the essence and that what we find in acute observation is hidden in the ordinary case of reading (T4). But our knowledge of the ordinary case is much too sketchy to justify that assumption: "A main cause of philosophical disease—a one-sided diet: one nourishes one's thinking with only one kind of example" (593).

our previous assumption, that we do possess a criterion for
reading other than a sensation.

†Another argument against the assumption of a hidden
mental content, which may be brought to daylight by introspection or some other mental act, consists in developing the paradoxical consequences of such a view: "How
can the process of [reading] have been hidden when I
said 'now I am [reading]' *because* I was [reading]?! And
if I say it is hidden—then how do I know what I have to
look for?" (153; "understanding" replaced by "reading.")⁹

†(d) So far we have shown (by a kind of empirical investigation into the use of the word "reading") that there
is not a mental content which is *always* present when a
person is reading, and that therefore giving the criterion
for a person's reading cannot consist in pointing out a
particular mental content. Now we shall show that even if
there were a mental content which is present if and only
if a person is reading, we could not take this content to be
the essence of reading. Let us assume that a mental content is the essence of reading and that a person is reading
if and only if this content, namely the MRP, is present.
We shall now show that the process characterized by the
presence of the MRP cannot be reading.† First of all: If
reading is a particular experience "then it becomes quite
unimportant whether or not you read according to some
generally recognized alphabetical rule" (165). One is reading if and only if he is experiencing the MRP; nothing
else is of any importance. That implies, however, that no

⁹ The same criticism applies to the method of the phenomenol-
ogists. How do they know which phenomenon is the 'right' one?
They proceed from the assumption that the essence is not open
to general inspection but must be discovered by some kind of
analysis which proceeds from an everyday appearance. In the
course of this analysis several phenomena appear. How are we
to know which one of them is the phenomenon that we were
looking for? And if we know the answer to this question, why
then is it necessary to analyze at all?

distinction can be drawn between reading and believing that one is reading (cf. 202), or, to put it in another way, that anybody who believes that he is reading is entitled to infer that he *is* reading. The important task of a teacher would, therefore, consist in schooling the receptivity of his pupils (232), reading would be something like listening to inner voices in the presence of printed paper and acting in accordance with their advice (233). That different people who are reading the same text agree in the sounds they utter would be miraculous (233). †Our assumption that reading is a mental act leads, therefore, to the substitution of miracles for an everyday affair. It leads also to the substitution for a simple process (uttering sounds in the presence of printed paper) of a more complicated one (listening to inner voices in the presence of printed paper) i.e., it misses the aim of explaining the process of *reading.*†[10]

(e) But does introducing inner voices really solve our problem—namely, to explain why people read correctly and to justify our own reading of a text in a certain way? Usually we simply read off the sound from the letters. Now we want to be justified, and we think that a mental content might justify our procedure. But if we do not trust the signs on the paper—then why should we trust the more ethereal advice of intuition, or of the mental content which is supposed to be the essence of reading? (232, 233).

[10] In presenting the idea to be criticized we assumed, as in T4, that the MRP is also the reason for our uttering the sounds we utter. The criticism developed in the text applies also to the idea that in calculating we are guided by intuitions (Descartes' theory): It is said that the perception of '2 + 2' is followed by a nonperceptual mental event which advises us how to behave in the sequel; it whispers, as it were, into our mind's ear, 'Say 4!' But the idea cannot explain why we calculate as we do. For instead of explaining the process of obeying a rule (the rule of the multiplication table) it describes the process of obeying a kind of inspiration. In the case of an inspiration I *await* direction. But I do not await inspiration when saying that 2 + 2 are four (232).

V

†What conclusions are to be drawn from this analysis? First of all: It appears impossible to discover the essence of a thing in the way that is usually supposed, i.e., T_4 seems to be inapplicable. But if that is the case, the correctness of the analysis can no longer be checked in the usual way. There is no criterion for deciding whether a statement like '"A" stands for a' or 'the sentence "p" designates the proposition that p' is true or not; and there is no way to decide whether a certain sign is meaningful, either. But usually we are not at all troubled by such questions. We talk and solve (mathematical, physical, economic) problems without being troubled by the fact that there is apparently no possibility of deciding whether or not we are acting reasonably, whether or not we are talking sense. But isn't that rather paradoxical? Isn't it rather paradoxical to assume that a sign which we constantly use to convey, as we think, important information is really without meaning, and that we have no possibility of discovering that fact? And since its being meaningless apparently does not at all affect its usefulness in discourse (e.g., for conveying information), doesn't that show that the presuppositions of the paradox, in particular $T_1, 2$, need reconsideration?[11]

[11] There is another presupposition as well, namely that in Sec. IV *all* possibilities of experiencing the essence have been considered. Clearly, this assumption cannot be proved. But one thing is certain: We considered all possibilities of experiencing the essence which have so far been treated by philosophers who follow theory T. Cf. H. Gomperz, *Weltanschauungslehre*, II, 140 ff., where medieval realism about concepts is criticized by arguments like Wittgenstein's. Cf. also n. 23 below.

VI

†A great deal of the *Philosophical Investigations* is devoted to this task.† The phenomena of language are first studied in primitive kinds of application "in which one can command a clear view of the aim and functioning of words" (5; 130). The primitive, rudimentary languages which are investigated in the course of these studies are called "*language-games.*" Let us consider one such language-game: It is meant

> to serve for communication between a builder A and an assistant B. A is building with building-stones: there are blocks, pillars, slabs and beams. B has to pass the stones, and that in the order in which A needs them. For this purpose they use a language consisting of the words "block," "pillar," "slab," "beam." A calls them out;—B brings the stone which he has learned to bring at such-and-such a call. —Conceive this as a complete primitive language [2].

Consider first of all how A prepares B for the purpose he is supposed to fulfill. "An important part of the training will consist in the teacher's pointing to the objects, directing the [assistant's] attention to them and at the same time uttering a word, for instance the word 'slab' as he points to that shape" (6; "child" replaced by "assistant"). This procedure cannot be called an ostensive definition, because the assistant who at the beginning is supposed to be without any knowledge of any language cannot as yet *ask* what the name is (6); which shows that teaching a language can be looked at as "adjusting a mechanism to respond to a certain kind of influence" (497; cf. 5). Finally the assistant is able to play the game, he is able to carry out the orders given to him by the builder A. Let us now imagine that A teaches B more complicated orders— orders which contain color-names, number-words ('4 red slabs!') and even orders which contain what one would be inclined to call descriptions ('Give me the slab lying just in front of you!'), etc.

Now, what do the words of this language *signify?*— What is supposed to show what they signify, if not the kind of use they have? And we have already described that. So we are asking for the expression "This word signifies *this*" to be made a part of the description. In other words the description ought to take the form "the word . . . signifies . . . ." . . . But assimilating the descriptions of the uses of words in this way cannot make the uses themselves any more like one another. For, as we see, they are absolutely unlike [10].

†Compare, e.g., the way in which the word "four" is used with the way in which the word "slab" is used within the language-game in question. The difference in the uses of the two words comes out most clearly when we compare the procedures by means of which their respective uses are taught. A child who is to count correctly has first to learn the series of numerals by heart; he has then to learn how to apply this knowledge to the case of counting, e.g., the number of apples in a basket. In doing so, he has to say the series of cardinal numbers, and for each number he has to take one apple out of the basket (cf. 1). He has to be careful not to count one apple twice or to miss an apple. The numeral which according to this procedure is co-ordinated with the last apple is called 'the number of apples in the basket.' This is how the use of numerals is taught and how numerals are used in counting. Compare with this the use of a word like 'slab.' It is taught by simple ostension: The word 'slab' is repeatedly uttered in the presence of a slab. Finally the child is able to identify slabs correctly within the language-game it has been taught. Nothing is involved which has any similarity to the counting procedure which was described above. The application of the word itself to a concrete object is much simpler than the application of a number-word to a collection whose cardinal number cannot be seen at a glance.

This application does not involve any complicated technique; a person who understands the meaning of 'slab' is able to apply this word quite immediately.†

Let us now imagine that somebody, following $T1$, should argue in this way: It is quite clear: 'slab' signifies slabs and '3' signifies 3 . . . every word in a language signifies something (cf. 3). According to Wittgenstein, he has

> so far said *nothing whatever;* unless [he has] explained exactly *what* distinction [he] wish[es] to make. (It might be of course that [he] wanted to distinguish the words of [our] language[-game] from words "without meaning" [13].
>
> Imagine someone's saying: "*All* tools serve to modify something. Thus the hammer modifies the position of the nail, the saw the shape of the board and so on."— And what is modified by the rule, the glue-pot, the nails?—"Our knowledge of the thing's length, the temperature of the glue, and the solidity of the box." —Would anything be gained by this assimilation of expressions? [14].

VII

†Our example and its interpretation suggest an instrumentalist theory of language.[12] The orders which A gives to B are instruments in getting B to act in a certain way.

[12] Or an intuitionist (pragmatist, constructivist) theory of language—the expressions "intuitionist" or "pragmatist" being used in the way in which they serve to describe one of the present tendencies as regards foundations of mathematics. I am inclined to say—and there is strong evidence in favor of this view—that Wittgenstein's theory of language can be understood as a constructivist theory of meaning, i.e., as constructivism applied not only to the meanings of mathematical expressions but to meanings in general. Cf. Poincaré, *Derniers pensées* (German edition), pp. 143 ff., and especially Paul Lorenzen, "Konstruktive Begründung der Mathematik," *Math. Zs.*, Bd. LIII (1950), 162 ff. Cf. also *Philosophical Investigations*, p. 220: "Let the *proof* teach you *what* was being proved."

Their meaning depends on how B is supposed to act in the situations in which they are uttered. It seems reasonable to extend this theory—which is a corollary to T', soon to be described—to language games which contain descriptive sentences as well. The meaning of a descriptive sentence would then consist in its role in certain situations; more generally, within a certain culture (cf. 199, 206, 241, 325, p. 226). Wittgenstein has drawn this consequence—which is another corollary of T':

> What we call *"descriptions"* are instruments for particular uses. Think of a machine-drawing [which directs the production of the machine drawn in a certain way], a cross-section, an elevation with measurements, which an engineer has before him. Thinking of a description as a word-picture of the facts has something misleading about it: one tends to think only of such pictures as hang on the walls: which seem simply to portray how a thing looks, what it is like (these pictures are as it were idle) [291].

And quite generally: "Language is an instrument. Its concepts are instruments" (569). This idea has an important consequence. Instruments are described by referring to how they work. There are different kinds of instruments for different purposes. And there is nothing corresponding to the ethereal meanings which, according to $T1$, are supposed to make meaningful the use of *all* instruments alike. "Let the use of words teach you their meaning" (p. 220) is to be substituted for $T4$—and this now seems to be the new theory, T'. But in order to appreciate the full importance of T' we have first of all to consider the following objections, which seem to be inevitable. In talking, ordering, describing, we certainly use words and get other people to act in a certain way (to revise their plans which we show to be unreasonable, to obey our wishes, to follow a certain route which we point out to them on a map). But the description of the meanings of the elements of a language-game is not exhausted by pointing to the way in which we use those elements and the connection of this

use with our actions and other people's. For in uttering
the words and the sentences we *mean* something by them,
we want to express our thoughts, our wishes, etc. (cf. 501).
It is "our *meaning* it that gives sense to the sentence. . . .
And 'meaning it' is something in the sphere of the mind"
(358; cf. *T*4). What we mean seems to be independent of
the way we use our words and the way other people react
to our utterances (cf. 205, and again *T*4). Moreover, the
meanings of our utterances, being hidden beneath the surface of the various ways in which we use their elements,
can only be discovered by looking at the mental pictures,
the presence of which indicates what we mean by them.
A person who wants to understand has, therefore, to grasp
this mental picture. "One would like to say: 'Telling brings
it about that [somebody else] *knows* that I am in pain
[for example]; it produces this mental phenomenon:
everything else [in particular whether "he does something
further with it as well"—e.g., looks for a physician in order
to help me] is inessential to the telling'" (363). "Only in
the act of understanding is it meant that we are to do
THIS. The *order*—why, that is nothing but sounds, ink-
marks" (431). Meaning and understanding are, therefore,
mental processes.

†Apparently this idea makes it necessary to give an account of meaning which is independent of the description
of the way in which signs are used within a certain
language-game. Another great part of the *Philosophical
Investigations* is devoted to showing that this is not the
case. A careful analysis of the way we use phrases such as
'A intends to . . . ,' 'A means that . . . ,' 'A suddenly understands that . . . ,' shows that in trying to account for
this use we are again thrown back on a description of the
way we use certain elements of the language-game in which
those expressions occur and the connection of this use with
our actions and other people's.

VIII

†(A) The meaning we connect with a certain sign is a mental picture. We do not look into the mind of a person in order to find out what he is really saying. We take his utterances *at their face value*, e.g., we assume that, when saying 'I hate you' he is in a state of hating. "If I give anyone an order I feel it to be *quite enough* to give him signs. And I should never say: this is only words. . . . Equally, when I have asked someone something and he gives me an answer (i.e., a sign) I am content—that was what I expected—and I don't raise the objection: but that's a mere answer" (503). On our present view, this attitude is easily shown to be superficial. For it might be that on looking into the speaker's soul (or mind) we discover something quite different, e.g., love in the person who said 'I hate you.'

†Now two questions arise about this procedure. First: Why trust the language of the mind (one wonders what kind of language this may be) when we do not trust the overt language, i.e., the sentence 'I hate you'? (cf., e.g., 74 and all the passages on the interpretation of rules: 197 ff.). For whatever appears to be found in the mind can be interpreted in various ways, once we have decided *not* to proceed as we usually do, i.e., not to take parts of a certain language-game which we are playing at their face-value. Secondly: Let us assume that somebody who really loves a certain person tells her that he hates her.[13] Does this fact make 'I hate you' mean the same as 'I love you'? Or imagine a person, who abounds in slips of the tongue (or is at the moment rather occupied with a difficult problem and so not listening attentively), giving what we con-

[13] Psychoanalysis has made rather a misleading use of such cases. It has introduced a picture-language (so-called symbols) and interpreted it in such a way that it is not conceivable how the theory could possibly be refuted.

sider to be a wrong or an irrelevant answer. Doesn't that reaction of considering his answer as irrelevant show that what he says is thought to be meaningful independently of what he is thinking? For we don't say: 'He certainly gave the right answer; what he said was accompanied by the right thought-processes,' but rather 'He gave a quite irrelevant answer; maybe he didn't understand our question or expressed himself wrongly.' Or "suppose I said 'abcd' and meant: the weather is fine. For as I uttered these signs I had the experience normally had only by someone who had year-in year-out used 'a' in the sense of 'the,' 'b' in the sense of 'weather' and so on.— Does 'abcd' now mean: the weather is fine?" (509; cf. 665). How does somebody else find out what I meant by 'abcd'? Of course I can explain to him that 'abcd' means 'the weather is fine'; and I can also indicate how the parts of the first string of signs are related to the parts (the words) of the second string. But it would be a mistake to assume that such an explanation reveals what 'abcd' really means. For from the few words which I intend to be an explanation one cannot yet judge whether an *explanation* has been given or not.

†Of course I *say* ' "abcd" means "the weather is fine" ' or 'By "abcd" I mean "the weather is fine," ' and I have the intention of giving an explanation. But now imagine someone's saying 'Mr. A and Mrs. B loved—I mean lived—together for a long time.'[14] In this case he does not want to give a definition or an explanation according to which 'love' is supposed to mean the same as 'live'; rather, he committed a slip of the tongue and wanted to correct himself. In certain cases this is clear enough. In other cases it follows, e.g., from the fact that 'love' is never again mentioned in connection with Mr. A and Mrs. B, etc. When, therefore, I say, 'By "abcd" I mean "the weather is fine," ' it is not yet certain what the case is, whether I intended to give an explanation, or was just awaking from a kind of

[14] In Freud's *Vorlesungen über Psychoanalyse* one will find plenty of examples of this kind.

trance, or whatever else might be the case. The way 'I mean' is to be interpreted follows from the context in which the whole sentence is uttered and from what we find out about the further use of the sign 'abcd' (cf. 686). In order to find out whether 'abcd' really means 'the weather is fine' we have, therefore, to find out how 'abcd' is being used quite independently of any feelings on the part of the person who said 'abcd' and of any explanation given by him. Of course his explanation may be the starting point of a training in the use of a new language in which 'a,' 'b,' 'c,' 'd' really have the meanings indicated. But note now that "abcd" makes sense only within this language-game. I cannot mean 'the weather is fine' by 'abcd' before this language-game has been established. I myself could not possibly connect any sense with 'abcd' before the elements of this sign have become meaningful by being made elements of a certain language-game. And even the fact that "I had the experience normally had only by someone who had year-in year-out used 'a' in the sense of 'the,' 'b' in the sense of 'weather', and so on" (509) could not make them meaningful; I could not even *describe* this experience as I did just now, because such a description does not yet exist.

†We have to conclude that no mere mental effort of a person A can either make a string of signs mean something different from the meaning it has within a certain language-game of which it is part, played by the people who come into contact with A, or justify its being said that *he* means (intends) something different from everybody else who uses it. This seems rather paradoxical. But let us assume for a moment that two people

belonging to a tribe unacquainted with games should sit at a chess-board and go through the moves of a game of chess; and even with all the appropriate mental accompaniments. And if *we* were to see it we should say they were playing chess. But now imagine a game of chess translated according to certain rules into a series of actions which we do not ordinarily associate with a *game*—say into yells and stamping of feet. And now suppose those two people to yell and stamp instead of playing the form of chess that we are used to; and this in such a way that their procedure is translatable by suitable rules into a game of chess. Should we still be inclined to say they were playing a game? [200].

The decision of this question again depends on the situation. Imagine, e.g., that their yelling and stamping has an important role within a religious ceremony of the tribe. That any change of procedure is said to offend the gods and is treated accordingly (the offenders are killed). In this case neither the possibility of the translation nor the presence of the chess-feelings in the minds of the participants would turn this procedure into a game of chess (although it is also quite possible to imagine a tribe where people who lose games of chess are thought to be hated by the gods and are killed. But in this case a difference will be made between games and religious procedures by the fact, e.g., that only priests are admitted to the latter, or that different expressions are used for describing them, which is missing in our case). On the contrary, the strange mental state of those who are troubled by chess-feelings would be an indication either of insanity (cf. n. 5 above) or of lack of religious feeling.

†Now we can turn round our whole argument and look at the people who are sitting at a chess board and moving the pieces. Are they really playing chess? We see now that the inspection of their minds does not help us: they might be queer people, thinking of chess when they are performing a religious ceremony. Their assertion that they are playing chess, even, is not necessarily helpful, for it might be that they heard the words from somebody else and misinterpreted them to mean sitting in front of the board and making arbitrary moves with the pawns. The fact that they are using a chess board does not help us either, for the board is not essential to the game. What, then, is essential? The fact that they are playing according to cer-

tain *rules,* that they follow the rules of the chess game. Applying this result to the meaning of sentences in general we arrive at the idea that "if anyone utters a sentence and *means* or *understands* it he is operating a calculus according to definite rules" (81). Thus in analyzing the concepts of meaning, understanding, thinking, etc., we finally arrived at the concept of *following a rule.* But before turning to that concept we have to get more insight into the concepts just mentioned, and especially into the concept of *intention.*†

(B) It is the "queer thing about *intention,* about the mental process, that the existence of a custom, of a technique, is not necessary to it. That, for example, it is imaginable that two people should play chess in a world in which otherwise no games existed; and even that they should begin a game of chess—and then be interrupted" (205). The underlying idea is the same, as in the case of meaning: just as we can attach meaning to a sign by just connecting its use with a certain image which we voluntarily produce, we can also intend to do something by producing a certain mental picture. But how, we have to ask, is it possible to find out whether or not A, who just announced his intention of playing chess, was really intending to do so? Surely chess is defined by its rules (cf. 205). Should we therefore conclude that the rules of chess were present in the mind of A when he uttered his intention? (205).

†Investigation similar to that of IV Ca above will show that not every act of intending to play chess is accompanied by a special mental picture which is characteristic of the intention of playing chess. Of course, the intention to play chess is sometimes present quite distinctly (I have not played chess for a long time, I am a keen chess player, and *now* I want to play chess and won't stop looking until I have found a chess board and a suitable partner). But this is only a *special kind* of intending to play chess (cf. IV Cb above); therefore its characteristics cannot be the reason for calling other cases cases of intending to play

chess—cases, e.g., in which these characteristics are completely absent. But if we assume, on the other hand, that A has a perfect copy of the rules of chess before his inner eye—must he necessarily follow the features of this copy in such a way that the result will be a game of chess? Is it not possible that he either interprets them in an unusual way, that in going over from the reading of his mental picture to the outer world (the chess board, his actions in front of the chess board), he automatically makes a kind of translation, so that finally he is not doing what one would be inclined to call 'playing chess'? (cf. 73, 74, 86, 139, 237). And should we still say that he is intending to play chess just because, somewhere in the chain of events which in the end lead to his actions, a copy of the rules of chess enters in? Of course, we could *interpret* this copy as we are used to do. But is *he* interpreting it in the same way? And even if he could tell us how he is interpreting it do we know how to take his explanation? We see that "interpretations *by themselves* do not determine meaning" (198). We have simply to wait. And if he really acts in such a way that he regards playing chess—as we understand it—as a fulfillment of his intention, then we may say that he intended to play chess. But if it turned out that he did not know how to play chess or that, apparently intending to play chess, he sat down at the chess board and made irregular moves, we should under certain circumstances conclude that he had wrong ideas as to his intentions. Of course the phrase 'under certain circumstances' has to be inserted. For it is perfectly possible that A, intending to play chess, was introduced to a person he did not like and, with the intention of avoiding playing chess with him, acted as if he did not know the rules of chess or as if he had never intended to play chess. But what has to be criticized is the idea that such a difference might be found out by inspecting his mind (or soul) and by reading off his intention from his mental processes. It is his further actions (talking included), as well as his personal history, which teach us how we are to take his first utterance—

that he intended to play chess. But as it now turns out that our criteria for deciding whether a person, A, intends to play chess or not are "extended in time" (cf. 138), we have to conclude that intending to play chess cannot be a mental event which occurs at a certain time. *Intending is not an experience* (cf. p. 217): it has "no experience-content. For the content (images for instance) which accompany and illustrate [it] are not the . . . intending" (p. 217).

†(C) The same applies to understanding.† Let us examine the following kind of language-game (143 ff.): When A gives an order, B has to write down series of signs according to a certain formation-rule. The orders are of the kind "1, 2, 3, . . . !" or "2, 4, 6, 8, . . . !" or "2, 4, 9, 16, . . . !" or "2, 6, 12, 20, 30, 42, . . . !" etc. B is supposed to continue the series in a certain way, i.e., he is supposed to write down the series of numerals in the first case, the series of the even numerals in the second case, etc. First of all, A will teach B the rules of the language-game. He will then give orders to B, in order to check B's abilities. He will finally state that B has mastered the system, that he understands it. It should be clear that, when used in this way, 'understanding' cannot signify a mental phenomenon. For we also say that B understands (is master of) the language-game just explained when lying on his bed and sleeping (cf. 148). But the mental-act philosopher is ready with a new expression—he speaks of a *subconscious* mental phenomenon, i.e., he says that B, although dreaming perhaps of beautiful women, is nevertheless subconsciously thinking of the new language-game and its rules.

The objections to this idea are obvious. Whether subconscious or not, the alleged thinking-process may or may not determine the actual behavior of B (cf. VIII B, above); i.e., B may not be able to carry out the orders of A although a clever psychologist has found out that the thinking-process which is supposed to accompany his ability to obey the orders is present. We shall not say in this case that B has mastered the game, that we have discovered

a special case of mastering the game (cp. IV Cb2, above);
we shall simply say that he had not mastered it although
he or the psychologist thought he had. This objection being
accepted, it might be said that

> knowing the [game] is a state of the mind . . .
> by means of which we explain the *manifestations* of
> that knowledge. Such a state is called a disposition.
> But there are objections to speaking of a state of the
> mind here, inasmuch as there ought to be two dif-
> ferent criteria for such a state: a knowledge of the
> construction of the apparatus, quite apart from what
> it does [149].

What the apparatus does is in our case the actual behavior
of B when he receives certain orders.

But there is a second way in which the word 'understanding' is used. Understanding in this sense is not meant
to be understanding of a game as a whole (understanding
the rules of chess, i.e., knowing how to play chess) but
understanding the meaning of a particular move within the
game, e.g., understanding the order 2, 4, 6, . . . ! "Let us
imagine the following example: A writes series of numbers
down, B watches him and tries to find a law for the sequence of numbers. If he succeeds, he exclaims: 'Now I
can go on!'—So this capacity, this understanding is something that makes its appearance in a moment" (151), and
this suggests that 'understanding,' used in this way, might
mean a mental event. But wait: Do we find any mental
event which is common to all cases of understanding?
Imagine that A gave the order 1, 5, 11, 19, 29, . . . ! to B
and that, upon A's arriving at 19, B said, 'I understand.'
What happened to B?

> Various things may have happened; for example,
> while A was slowly putting one number after the
> other, B was occupied with trying various algebraic
> formulae on the numbers which had been written
> down. After A had written the number 19, B tried the
> formula $a_n = n^2 + n - 1$; and the next number
> confirmed his hypothesis. Or again—B does not think

of formulae. He watches A writing his numbers down with a certain feeling of tension and all sorts of vague thoughts go through his head. Finally he asks himself: "What is the series of differences?" He finds the series, 4, 6, 8, 10 and says: Now I can go on.—Or he watches and says "Yes, I know *that* series"—and continues it, just as he would have done if A had written down the series 1, 3, 5, 7, 9.—Or he says nothing at all and simply continues the series. Perhaps he had what may be called the feeling "that's easy!" [151].

We can also imagine the case where nothing at all occurred in B's mind except that he suddenly said "Now I know how to go on"—perhaps with a feeling of relief [179].

But are the processes which I have described here *understanding*? [152].

Is it not possible that a person who has the feelings just described is not able to write down the series as it was meant by A? Should we not be inclined to say that he did not really understand? "The application is still a criterion of understanding" (146). It would, therefore, be quite misleading "to call the words ['Now I can go on'] a 'description of a mental state.'—One might rather call them a 'signal'; and we judge whether it was rightly employed by what he [i.e., B] goes on to do" (180).

†Now let us use this example to discuss intention and meaning as well. What if B, in carrying out the order 2, 4, 6, 8, . . . ! wrote 1000, 1004, 1008, 1012, etc.? (cf. 185). Of course A will say: 'Don't you see? You ought to write 2, 4, 6, 8, . . . !' And if that does not lead to a change in the behavior of B, he will tell him: "What I meant was that [you] should write the next but one number after *every* number [you] wrote; and from this all those propositions follow in turn" (186). Now several conclusions may be drawn from this situation.† First of all one may be inclined to say that 2, 4, 6, 8, . . . ! was an incomplete order and that there was clearly a possibility of misunderstanding (cf. a similar argument in 19). For this order

reveals so to speak, only an external character of the series to be written down, namely the character that its first members are '2,' '4,' '6,' etc. And the training of B, too, taught him only an external character of all the series, namely, that they began in a certain way. B has therefore to *guess* how to continue, and of course he may hit upon the wrong guess. But the order "take the next but one!" seems to be of a different character. It contains so to speak the whole of the series in a nutshell. Understanding *this* order implies knowing the law of development for the whole series. But let us now investigate how the understanding of this order may be taught. Of course, A has to write down the series 2, 4, 6, 8, . . . and has to explain to B what 'next but one' means. He does so by comparing this series with 1, 2, 3, 4, . . . and by showing that '4' is the 'next but one to 2,' etc. The explanation will therefore be similar to the explanation of 2, 4, 6, 8, . . . ! Why, then, should teaching the pupil how to take 'the next but one' remove any possibility of error? On the contrary! We could imagine that B has been taught how to use 2, 4, 6, 8, . . . ! but that he does not know, what 'the next but one' means. In this case the teacher would have to explain the 'next but one' by referring to 2, 4, 6, 8, . . . ! and not the other way round. The same applies to algebraic formulae. Consider a 'difficult' series such as 1, 3, 7, 13, 21, 31, 43, ... It is not easily seen how this series might be continued. If we hear that its algebraic formula is $n^2 - n + 1$ we are able to write down the next members at once. But that only shows that we already knew how to apply the algebraic expression, but did not know how to apply 1, 3, 7, 13, 21, 31, 43, . . . if the continuation of this series is ordered. It does not show us an essential quality which, so to speak, contains the whole series in a nutshell. For an onlooker who is unacquainted with the formula as well as with the series will have to learn how to apply the formula in developing series. And the methods of teaching this ability will be similar to the methods of teaching 2, 4, 6, 8, . . . ! (cf. 146).

Let us return now to intention. The existence of algebraic formulae for the description of series is misleading in one way: A cannot write down the whole series in order to make himself understood to B. But he can use an algebraic formula or a simple expression, such as 'take the next but one.' He can write down the formula within a few seconds and one is therefore inclined to assume that meaning the series 1, 2, 3, 4, . . . *ad infinitum* can be a mental act which occurs within a few seconds.

> Here I should first of all like to say: Your idea was that that act of meaning the order had in its own way already traversed all those steps; that when you meant it your mind as it were flew ahead and completed all the steps before you physically arrived at this or that one.—Thus you were inclined to use such expressions as: "The steps are *really* already taken, even before I take them in writing or orally or in thought"[15] [188].

They "are determined by the algebraic formula" (189). But how? Surely thinking of the formula cannot help us (cf. 146), for one and the same formula may be used for different purposes (think of the different use which is made of the formula $a + b = b + a$ in different parts of mathematics: in class-theory it means the commutativity of class-disjunction; in algebra it is used for expressing the commutativity of algebraic addition; in number theory it is used for expressing a general property of numbers; in lattice-theory it has still another meaning and likewise in group-theory, etc.). The imagining of the formula (if it ever does occur) must be connected with a certain application of the formula in order to provide us with the knowledge of its meaning and with the knowledge of the speaker's intention in using it. And as it is always possible to apply a formula in many different ways we have to ob-

---

[15] Here is the core of Wittgenstein's criticism of the so-called Cantorian (cf. Poincaré *loc. cit.*) interpretation of mathematics. This criticism (it is developed in detail in his mathematical writings—in the *Philosophical Investigations* there are only a few passages, cf. 352) is another corollary of *T'*.

serve how it is applied in a particular case, by a particular
mathematician, in order to determine his way of using the
formula and thus *what he means* when he utters the
formula. But the use of a formula is "extended in time"
(138). And therefore, since following up this use is one
of the criteria we employ to find out what is meant by A
when he writes down a certain formula, we cannot say
that meaning something is a mental event. "It may now be
said: 'The way the formula is meant determines which
steps are to be taken.' What is the criterion for the way
the formula is meant? It is for example, the kind of way
we always use it, the way we are taught to use it" (190).[16]

(D) Another criticism of the idea that meaning is a
mental activity derives from the fact that sometimes it is
calculation that decides the question whether a sentence is
meaningful or not. Consider the sentence " 'I have n
friends and $n^2 + 2n + 2 = 0$.' Does this sentence make
sense?" (513). Assuming that a sentence is made meaningful by connecting its utterance with a certain mental
content, we should conclude that there is no difficulty; we
have only to look for the mental picture behind it, and
that will teach us how to judge. But that is not the case;
we are even inclined to say that we do not yet know
whether anybody will be able to connect any meaning with
the sentence, i.e., according to the theory we are discussing at present, whether anybody is justified in connecting
an image with the utterance of this sentence. We have
first to find out whether the sentence conforms to certain
general rules (the number of friends can neither be negative nor imaginary) and we do so by calculating. We also
cannot say at once whether we understand or not; we have
first to find out whether there is anything to be under-

---

[16] Cf. also 693: " 'When I teach someone the formation of
the series . . . I surely mean him to write . . . at the hundredth
place.'—Quite right; you mean it. And evidently without necessarily even thinking of it. This shows you how different the grammar of the verb 'to mean' is from that of 'to think.' And nothing
is more wrong-headed than calling meaning a mental activity!"

stood; i.e., whether we understand or not can again be found out by a process of calculation only. One has, therefore, to realize that "we *calculate*, operate with words and in the course of time turn them sometimes into one picture, sometimes into another" (449).

(E) Result: Meaning, understanding, intending, thinking (and, as we may add—remembering, loving, hoping[17]) are *not mental activities*. The criteria by which we decide whether or not A is thinking of . . . , intending to do . . . , meaning . . . , etc., do not relate only to the moment of the intention, the thought, the understanding. We cannot say "A intended . . . because" and point to a process which accompanies his utterances or his (apparently intentional) behavior. "For no *process* could have the consequences of [intending]" (cf. p. 218).

IX

†The last section was devoted to the discussion of a possible objection against an instrumentalist theory of language, as it seems to be suggested by Wittgenstein (cf. Sec. VII). The objection was founded on the idea that words are meaningful because we *mean* something when uttering them, and that quite independently of the way in which those words are used. But it turned out that in deciding whether somebody is really meaning something when uttering a sentence we are thrown back on observation of the way he uses certain elements of speech and that, therefore, an account of meaning can and must be

---

[17] "What is a *deep* feeling? Could someone have a feeling of ardent love or hope for the space of one second—*no matter what* preceded or followed this second?—What is happening now has significance—in these surroundings. The surroundings [the history of the event included—cf. the words "what preceded"] give it its importance" (583; cf. 572, 584, 591, 614 ff., esp. 638: "If someone says 'For a moment . . .' is he really only describing a momentary process?—But not even the whole story was my evidence for saying 'For a moment. . . .'").

given within the instrumentalist interpretation of language. Meaning is not something that needs consideration *apart* from the description of the way certain expressions are used by the speaker or by other people with whom he is trying to communicate. At the same time a tendency was discovered, namely the tendency "to hypostatize feelings where there are none" (598).[18] No objection to the instrumentalist interpretation seems to be left, but one: When playing a language-game we certainly obey certain *rules*. Thus the idea is suggested "that if anyone utters a sentence and *means* or *understands* it, he is operating a calculus according to definite rules" (81), and the rules seem to be something which *directs* the activities within a language-game, which therefore cannot be described in terms which are useful for describing the working of the language-game itself. It is this idea which we have to treat last. The discussion of this idea in the *Philosophical Investigations* is interwoven with the discussion of the other ideas treated in the book because there are arguments which apply to several ideas at once.†

Assuming that in talking, calculating, etc., we are acting in accordance with certain rules leads at once to the following question: "How am I able to obey a rule?" (217). For, on the one hand, it seems to be the case that "the rule, once stamped with a particular meaning, traces the lines along which it is to be followed through the whole of space . . . all the steps are really already taken" (219). But "if something of that sort really were the case, how would it help?" (219). For is there not always the possibility of interpreting the rule in a different way? And how are we to know which interpretation is the right one? Once the rule is separated from our activity it seems impossible that it can determine this activity any more. For it may try to make itself known to us by mental events ('grasping'

---

[18] Cf. 295: "When we look into ourselves as we do philosophy, we often get to see just such a picture. A full-blown pictorial representation of our grammar. Not facts; but as it were illustrated turns of speech."

the rule), by a book which contains all rules of the language-game to be played, etc. In any one of those cases we can proceed in many different ways depending on how we interpret, i.e., how we use, the mental picture, the book, etc., in the course of our further activities (cf. 73, 74, 86, 139, 237). Thus it seems that "no course of action [can] be determined by a rule because every course of action can be made out to accord with the rule" (201; "could" replaced by "can").

But "What this shows is that there is a way of grasping a rule which is *not* an *interpretation*, but which is exhibited in what we call 'obeying the rule' and 'going against it' in actual cases" (201). That will become clear from the following example (cf. 454): "A rule stands there like a signpost. Does the signpost leave no doubt open about the way I have to go? Does it show which direction I am to take when I have passed it?" (85). How do I know which direction I have to go? "If that means 'Have I reasons?' the answer is: My reasons will soon give out. And then I shall act, without reasons" (211). "When someone whom I am afraid of orders me [to follow the signpost], I act quickly, with perfect certainty, and the lack of reasons does not trouble me" (212, with "to continue the series" replaced by "to follow the signpost"). "When I obey a rule, I do not choose. I obey the rule *blindly*" (219). Let us now assume a land where everybody, on seeing a signpost: →, follows it in this direction: ←, where children are advised to follow the signpost in the way indicated, where foreigners who are in the habit of going → when they see a signpost like this: → are taught that they are acting wrongly, that '→' means 'go ←.' Should we say that the inhabitants of our imaginary country are misinterpreting the signpost? Obviously this would not be the right description of the situation, for without being related to human activities (language-games included) the signpost is a mere piece of matter and the question as to its *meaning* (and therefore the question as

to whether a certain interpretation is the right one) does
not arise at all.

Now it is using the signpost in a certain way, i.e., behaving in a certain way in the presence of the signpost,
that gives a meaning to it and that separates it from the
other parts of nature which are meaningless in the sense
that they are not parts of human language-games. But
behaving in this way is also called *obeying the rules*. "And
hence also 'obeying a rule' is a practice. And to *think* one
is obeying a rule is not to obey a rule. Hence it is not
possible to obey a rule 'privately': otherwise thinking one
was obeying a rule would be the same thing as obeying it"
(202).

Apply this to language-games in general. It follows, that
"to obey a rule, to make a report, to give an order, to play
a game of chess, are *customs* (uses, institutions)" (199)
and "not a hocus-pocus which can be performed only by
the soul" (454). "To understand a sentence means to understand a language. To understand a language means to
master a technique" (199). And so we are back at the
instrumental interpretation of language: "Every sign *by
itself* seems dead. *What* gives it life?—In use it is *alive*. Is
life breathed into it there?—Or is the *use* its life?" (432).
And questions of meaning, of understanding, of following
a rule are to be treated by taking into account the *use* of
signs within a certain language-game.

X

†Thus we arrive at the following result. According to T
meanings are objects for which words stand. Rules are of a
similar ethereal character. Understanding the meanings,
grasping the rules, is an activity of the mind, which is the
organ for finding our way about in the realm of meaning
as the senses are organs for finding our way about in the
physical world. We found that either there is no representation of the meanings or the rules in the mind or,

assuming that a representation does exist, that it cannot determine the way in which we proceed because there are always many possibilities of interpretation. According to *T'* the meaning of the elements of a language-game emerges from their *use* and that use belongs to a quite different category from a single mental event or a mental process, or any process whatever (cf. p. 196).

†Now a sign can be part of different language-games just as a button can be used in a game of chess (instead of a pawn, e.g., which has been lost) or a game of draughts. Do we try in this case to abstract from the differences between these two kinds of use in order to discover a common quality which will explain to us how it is possible for the button to function both as a pawn and as a piece in draughts? The question does not arise because it seems obvious that the button *changes* its function according to the game within which it is used. But in the case of a language-game, theory *T* seduces us into thinking that the sign '2,' e.g., is in any case of its use within language connected with a single element, its meaning, and that the varieties of its use ('Give me *two* apples!'—as said in a grocery; $\int_0^2 x^3 dx = 4$; 'Two hours ago I met him in the street'; 'The number of solutions of the equation $x^2 + 5x + 4 = 0$ is *two*') are only a superficial aspect. Once this idea has been dropped, once it has been realized that the meaning of a sign is constituted by its use within a certain language-game, words can be looked at as the button was above. And instead of trying to grasp the *essence* of a thing which is to explain the varieties of the use of the sign which stands for the thing we ought simply to describe the language-game of which the sign is part. "We must do away with all *explanation*, and description alone must take its place" (109). "Our mistake is to look for an explanation where we ought to look at what happens as a 'proto-phenomenon.' That is, where we ought to have said: *This language-game is played*" (654). "Look on the language-

game as the *primary* thing. And look on the feelings, etc.,
as you look on a way of regarding the language-game, as
interpretation" (656).[19]

†Wittgenstein's position has not yet been described correctly. Wittgenstein was said to hold a theory, T', which
emphasizes the instrumental aspect of language and which
points to use in a language-game as the essential thing.
And describing the language-game, so one is inclined to
say, according to the presentation which has been given
so far, is the task of philosophy. From that description
quite a few philosophical problems will become clear
which seemed hopelessly muddled when seen from the
point of view of theory T. Philosophy, then, seems to be
the theory of language-games (a kind of general syntax or
semantics in Carnap's sense) and T' seems to be its most
important part. But according to Wittgenstein this assumption would involve a misunderstanding. For the supposed theory of language-games could do no more than
enable people to run through the single moves of a game,
as a player who is acquainted with the game runs through
its moves. But for such a player there is no problem. If
he asks, e.g., " 'How do sentences manage to represent?'—
the answer might be: 'Don't you know? You certainly see
it, when you use them.' For nothing is concealed" (435).
Everything "lies open to view" (92; 126). "Philosophy"
therefore "may in no way interfere with the actual use of
language; it can in the end only describe it . . . it leaves
everything as it is" (124).

†Let us assume that somebody begins to construct a
theory of Language-games. This theory, if formulated in
the terms of T', will be thought to serve as an explanation
of how meaning is conferred upon single signs by the way
in which these signs are incorporated into a language-

19 Note that the idea of an ideal language becomes obsolete as
soon as it has been recognized that all language-games are on a
par. Vague concepts, e.g. (cf. 71), cannot be regarded as inad-
missible any longer. They have a definite function, and that is
all we can demand from them.

game. The theory (or description, as it may also be called) will involve a new kind of use of terms such as 'sentence,' 'fact,' 'meaning.' But has a useful explanation or description really been found? We must realize that the supposed theory introduces a *new* use of 'meaning,' 'fact,' 'sentence,' etc. If this use involves even a slight deviation from the use of these words within the language-games to be described (explained) the supposed description in fact involves a change in the phenomenon to be described. But if on the other hand the change is a considerable one (and that is to be expected if one is trying to develop a fully-fledged instrumentalist philosophy of meaning) a new language-game for the expression 'sentence,' 'meaning,' etc., has been established and the task of describing the given language-game is not fulfilled either. Thus "we must do away with all *explanation*" and with *T'* as well. The description, however, which Wittgenstein invites us to give instead of the explanation, consists only in "put-[ting] everything before us" (126), and as "everything lies open to view, there is nothing to explain" (126). We might therefore say, rather hyperbolically, that the "language disguises thoughts" of the *Tractatus* (4.002) is now replaced by "language is already thought, nothing is concealed."

†But the situation is not quite as simple as that. For there *are* philosophical systems, philosophical theories; and it needs to be explained how it is that they come into existence if "nothing is concealed."

†In describing how philosophical theories come into being, Wittgenstein refers to the fact that "we *do not command a clear view* of the use of our words" (122). Given the answer that nothing is concealed, "one would like to retort: 'Yes, but it all goes by so quick, and I should like to see it as it were laid open to view" (435). On the other hand, "we remain unconscious of the prodigious diversity of all the everyday language-games because the clothing of our language makes everything alike" (p. 224). "What confuses us is the uniform appearance of words when we

hear them spoken or meet them in script and print. For their *application* is not presented to us so clearly" (11). Take the following example: The sentences 'Washington is a city' and 'Two is an even number' are of a similar structure. This suggests that just as in the first case 'Washington' is the name of a real thing, 'two' is the name of a more abstract object, notwithstanding the fact that the uses of the two signs are "absolutely unlike" (10).

> In the use of words one might distinguish "surface-grammar" from "depth-grammar." What immediately impresses itself upon us about the use of a word is the way it is used in the construction of the sentence, the part of its use—one might say—that can be taken in by the ear.—And now compare the depth-grammar, say of the word "to mean," with what its surface-grammar would lead us to suspect. No wonder we find it difficult to know our way about [664].

This difficulty is the reason why we resort to philosophical theories. Why we invent theories of meaning. And why we try to conceive an ideal form behind the complexities of our language-games.

†But it is clear "that every sentence in our language 'is in order, as it is.' That is to say, we are not *striving after* an ideal, as if our ordinary vague sentences had not yet got a quite unexceptionable sense . . . there must be perfect order even in the vaguest sentence" (98). It should also be clear that the "philosophy of logic speaks of sentences and words in exactly the sense in which we speak of them in ordinary life, when we say, e.g., 'Here is a Chinese sentence' or 'No, that only looks like writing; it is actually just an ornament' and so on" (108). Thus the proper task of philosophy will be to unmask philosophical theories, to "bring words back from their metaphysical to their everyday use" (116), to destroy the "houses of cards" and to clear up "the ground of language on which they stand" (118). And philosophy becomes a "battle against the bewitchment of our intelligence by means of language" (109). This battle is carried through by "assembling reminders for a particular purpose" (127)—for the

purpose of "seeing connexions" (122); and "different therapies" (133), not "*a* philosophical method" (133), are used in order to finish it victoriously.

†But in these therapies the statement of *T'* (or rather of the several corollaries of *T'* which have been mentioned so far) plays the most important part. So far we have interpreted the statement of *T'* as the exposition of a new (instrumentalist, nominalist, or whatever you like to call it) *theory of meaning*. This interpretation is not unreasonable in itself and taken as such it is a very interesting contribution to traditional philosophy (actually I think that everything that is interesting in the book attaches to the treatment of *T'* in this way). But this interpretation would go against the way in which his book is meant to be used by Wittgenstein. That may be seen from the following considerations: In Section IV the idea was criticized that reading is a mental process. If we stick to *T'* and interpret it as a theory we cannot understand why the discussion in Section IV should be a *criticism*. For we could argue in the following way: Wittgenstein says that the meaning of a word becomes clear from the way in which it is used within a specific language-game. Let us, therefore, look at the language-game which contains both of the expressions 'reading' and 'mental process,' and in which the sentence occurs 'Reading is a mental process.' Wittgenstein's presentation—so one would be inclined to say—is a description of certain features of this language-game and includes, of course, the remark that 'mental process' as used *in this language-game* has nothing whatever to do with toothaches.

†But that is not the right account of what Wittgenstein does. Wittgenstein does criticize—but his criticism is of a particular kind. It is not the kind of criticism which is directed, e.g., against a wrong mathematical calculation. In the latter case the result of the criticism is that a certain sentence is replaced by its negation or by a different sentence. But Wittgenstein does not want his reader to discover that reading is *not* a mental process. For if 'mental process' is used in a metaphysical way in 'reading is a men-

tal process,' it is used just as metaphysically in "reading is
not a mental process" (cf. 116). For him "the results of
philosophy are the uncovering of one or another piece of
plain nonsense and of bumps that the understanding has
got by running its head against the limits of language"
(119), and his aim is "to teach you to pass from a piece of
disguised nonsense to something that is patent nonsense"
(464) and in this way to clear up "the ground of language"
(118). But that can only mean that "the philosophical
problems should *completely* disappear" (133); for if the
aim has been reached, "everything lies open to view [and]
there is nothing to explain" (126). This implies that the
formulation of T' as used within the critical procedure
cannot be interpreted as a new theory of meaning, for it is
applied with the intention of making the language-games
(e.g., that with 'reading') "lie open to view," i.e., lead to a
situation where language-games are simply played, without any question arising as to how it is that words become
meaningful as part of a certain language-game, etc. That
being so, the formulation of T' loses its function as soon as
"*complete clarity*" has been arrived at. But without a function the signs which are part of the formulation of T' are
without meaning. Thus one could say of the sentences
which are part of T': These sentences "are elucidatory in
this way: he who understands me finally recognizes them
as senseless . . . (He must so to speak throw away the
ladder, after he has climbed up on it.) He must sur-
mount these [sentences] . . . ; then he sees the world
rightly" (*Tractatus* 6.54). And seeing the world rightly
means playing the language-games without being troubled
by philosophical *questions* or by philosophical *problems.*†

XI

*Note, now, that in the preceding section the idea of
the essence has been reintroduced. In traditional philosophy the essence was hidden beneath the various ways

of describing it. Now it is the "everyday use" (116) that "has to be accepted," "is given" (p. 226); but this everyday use is likewise hidden, beneath the "houses of cards" of philosophical theories (118)[20], and it too has to be brought to light. Just so, traditional philosophers (i.e., the adherents of theory T) tried to bring to light the clear and sharp meanings which were hidden beneath the "muddied" use of the words which stand for them (426). If we assume, now, that in removing those philosophical coverings we finally arrive at *"complete* clarity" (133), we assume that there is a *sharp line* between the "houses of cards" on the one hand and the language-games on which they are built on the other. Now while Wittgenstein usually criticizes the idea that, e.g., "there *must* be something common [to games], or they would not be called 'games'" (66; cf. IV A above) and points to the fact that if we "look and see" (66) we find a "complicated network of similarities overlapping and criss-crossing" (66), he seems to assume, nonetheless, that at least philosophical difficulties have something in common, that there is a definite boundary between the card-houses of philosophy and the solid ground of everyday language, such that it becomes possible to "bring words back from their metaphysical [use] to their everyday use" (116).

*To Wittgenstein we can apply the comment (which he used to characterize the adherents of T) that "a *picture* held [him] captive" (115). For if it is the use, the practice, which constitutes meaning, if "what has to be accepted, the given, is . . . *forms of life*" (p. 226), then one may ask why Wittgenstein tries to eliminate theory T, which certainly must be regarded as a form of life if we look at the way in which it is used by its adherents. Nevertheless Wittgenstein tries to eliminate this theory as well as other philosophical theories. But this attempt can only be justified by assuming that there is a difference between using a sign

[20] "Language disguises the thought" is the position of the *Tractatus* (4.002). One could say that according to the *Investigations*, the (philosophical) thought disguises language.

(playing a language-game) and proceeding according to theory *T*. The procedures which are connected with theory *T* are supposed not to be taken as parts of a language-game they constitute a sham-game which is to be destroyed. How is this attitude to be understood?

*I think we can understand it by looking at the ideas which Wittgenstein has about philosophy (at his *"picture"* of philosophy as one might call it, using his own word). This picture is the picture of the *Tractatus*: "The word 'philosophy' must mean something which stands above or below, not beside the natural sciences" (*Tractatus* 4.111). In the *Investigations* we may replace "natural sciences" by "language-games," and we arrive at: "Philosophy must be something which stands above or below, not beside the language-games"; philosophy *cannot* be a language-game itself; e.g., it cannot be theory *T'*. I submit that this idea is still present in the *Investigations* and that it makes it clear why Wittgenstein, having found that a sign can only be meaningful if it is incorporated into a language-game, cannot admit that there are philosophical theories.[21] This observation (as well as others which have not been mentioned[22]) suggests that the *Investigations* (apart from their substitution of language-games for the one language of the *Tractatus*) are after all not as different from the *Tractatus* as they seem to be at first sight. I am even inclined to say (without being able to substantiate this contention at the moment) that the *Investigations* basically contain an application of the main ideas of the *Tractatus* to several concrete problems, the only difference being the use of language-games instead of the language of the natural sciences which formed the theoretical background of the *Tractatus*.

[21] There are some passages which seem to contradict this interpretation of Wittgenstein's views, e.g., "If one tried to advance *theses* in philosophy it would never be possible to question them, because everyone would agree to them" (128), according to which philosophical theses are not meaningless, but *trivial*.

[22] Cf. the similarity of "shows itself" in the *Tractatus* and "lies open to view" in the *Investigations*.

*Trying to evaluate the book, we might say that the criticisms of *T* and the statement of *T'* which it contains, as well as the application of this theory to the discussion of concrete problems (remembering, obeying an order, the problem of sensation, etc.), are a great achievement, which, however, has its predecessors.[23] *Here we are within traditional philosophy*. But Wittgenstein wants us to see his criticisms in a different light. In the end we should forget them as well as *T*, we should forget philosophy entirely. Although the formulation of what can be regarded as a *theory* (theory *T'*) led us to the proper understanding of our difficulties, it must not be taken as the formulation of a *theory* but only as a proper means of getting rid of our philosophical troubles. *T'* has, therefore, to disappear together with those troubles. This new idea, which is Wittgenstein's own and which can be found in the *Tractatus* as well, is due, first, to the *picture* that philosophy must be something quite extraordinary and, second, to certain difficulties, already mentioned, which could be solved by taking into account the difference between object-language and meta-language (used by Tarski to get rid of similar difficulties, but never recognized by Wittgenstein [cf. 121]). Using this device we find that the philosophical language-games do not necessarily disturb the language-games they are supposed to describe. We also find that philosophy is not necessarily on a level with the language-games it is about. On the contrary, the assumption that the philosophical language-games are on a level with the language-games they deal with leads to contradictions. This solution would not agree with Wittgenstein's, but it would retain several elements of his philosophy: (1) his criticisms of *T*; (2) his statement of *T'*; (3) his observation, that

---

[23] Cf., e.g., H. Gomperz, *Weltanschauungslehre*, vol. II, where further references are given; E. Mach, *Erkenntnis u. Irrtum*, 3d ed., pp. 126 ff.; D'Alembert, *Traité de dynamique* (1743); the tenets of the various nominalistic schools, old and new, etc. Cf. also K. Popper's criticism of essentialism, developed as early as 1935.

language-games may be disturbed by other language-games which are supposed to explain or to describe them. It would, however, interpret the statement of T′ as a special theory of meaning and formulate it by taking account of the difference between object-language and meta-language. It would be possible still to have philosophical theories and philosophical problems without being open to Wittgenstein's criticisms, except perhaps the one criticism, that the distinction introduced is purely artificial.*

THE AVAILABILITY OF
WITTGENSTEIN'S LATER PHILOSOPHY

STANLEY CAVELL

> Epochs are in accord with themselves only if the
> crowd comes into these radiant confessionals which
> are the theatres or the arenas, and as much as possi-
> ble, . . . to listen to its own confessions of cowardice
> and sacrifice, of hate and passion. . . . For there is no
> theatre which is not prophecy. Not this false divina-
> tion which gives names and dates, but true prophecy,
> that which reveals to men these surprising truths:
> that the living must live, that the living must die, that
> autumn must follow summer, spring follow winter,
> that there are four elements, that there is happiness,
> that there are innumerable miseries, that life is a real-
> ity, that it is a dream, that man lives in peace, that
> man lives on blood; in short, those things they will
> never know.
>
> JEAN GIRAUDOUX

In June of 1929 Wittgenstein was awarded a Ph.D.
from Cambridge University, having returned to England,
and to philosophy, less than a year earlier. His examiners
were Russell and Moore, and for his dissertation he had
submitted his *Tractatus*, published some seven or eight
years earlier, written earlier than that, and now famous.
The following month, he refused to read a paper ("Some
Remarks on Logical Form") which he had prepared for
the joint session of the Mind Association and Aristotelian

From *The Philosophical Review*, Vol. LXXI (1962), pp. 67–
93. Reprinted with the permission of the author and editor.

Society, and which obviously goes with the ideas he had
worked out in the *Tractatus*. Years later he said to Moore
"something to the effect that, when he wrote [the paper on
logical form] he was getting new ideas about which he was
still confused, and that he did not think it deserved any
attention."[1]

In January of 1930 he began lecturing at Cambridge
about those new ideas, and in the academic session of
1933–1934 he dictated a set of notes in conjunction with
his lectures; during 1934–1935 he dictated privately
another manuscript, longer than the former, more con-
tinuously evolving and much closer in style to the *Philosophical Investigations*. These two sets of dictations—
which came, because of the wrappers they were bound in,
to be called, respectively, the *Blue Book* and the *Brown
Book*—are now publicly available, bearing appropriately the
over-title *Preliminary Studies for the "Philosophical Investigations."*[2] But the extent to which the ideas in these
pages are available, now seven years after the publication
of the *Investigations*, is a matter of some question even
after the appearance of the first book on the later philosophy, for none of its thought is to be found in David
Pole's *The Later Philosophy of Wittgenstein*.[3]

What I find most remarkable about this book is not the
modesty of its understanding nor the pretentiousness and
condescension of its criticism, but the pervasive absence
of any worry that some remark of Wittgenstein's may not
be utterly obvious in its meaning and implications. When,
on the opening page, I read, "[Despite the fact that] he

[1] The biographical information in this (and in the final) paragraph comes from the first of Moore's three papers called "Wittgenstein's Lectures in 1930–33," *Mind*, LXIII (1954) and LXIV
(1955); from R. R(hees)'s introduction to *The Blue and Brown
Books*; and from a biographical sketch by G. H. von Wright,
published together with Norman Malcolm's moving memoir,
Ludwig Wittgenstein (Oxford, 1958).

[2] Ludwig Wittgenstein, *The Blue and Brown Books* (New
York, 1958). Cited here as *BB*.

[3] London, 1958.

. . . has been popularly portrayed as a kind of fanatic of subtlety if not, worse, an addict of mystification . . . I shall maintain that Wittgenstein's central ideas . . . are essentially simple," I was, although skeptical, impressed: that would be a large claim to enter and support in discussing any difficult thinker, but it could be very worth trying to do. About Wittgenstein the claim is doubled up. For not only is one faced with the obvious surface difficulties of the writing, one is also met by a new philosophical concept of difficulty itself: the *difficulty* of philosophizing, and especially of the fruitful *criticism* of philosophy, is one of Wittgenstein's great themes (and, therefore, doubtless, simple, once we can grasp it). My disappointment was, accordingly, the sharper when I had to recognize that Pole was conceiving the task of steering toward a deep simplicity to be itself an easy one. Disappointment mounted to despair as I found the famous and exciting and obscure tags of the *Investigations* not only quoted without explanation, but quoted as though they *were* explanations:

> At least this much is clear, first that Wittgenstein distinguishes in some sense between the structural apparatus and the content of language; and secondly that he holds that philosophers are prone to the error of seeing the one in terms of the other. We make a picture of an independently existing reality. "We predicate of the thing what lies in the mode of presentation" [p. 37].

It would, for example, have been worth while to try to point to the relation of that idea—which is usually entered as summary of philosophical disorder—to the idea (cited by Pole, p. 54) that "grammar tells us what kind of object anything is" (§ 373)[4]—which hints at what philosophy might positively accomplish and at the kind of importance it might have.

[4] All references preceded by "§" are to paragraph numbers in Part I of *Philosophical Investigations*; references to Part II are preceded by "II."

Criticism is always an affront, and its only justification lies in usefulness, in making its object available to just response. Pole's work is not useful. Where he is not misdescribing with assurance, his counters may be of the "He says . . . , but I on the other hand say . . ." variety ("For Wittgenstein . . . an expression has as much meaning as we have given it. . . . Now as against this, I shall claim that there is always more meaning in an expression than we have given it" [pp. 83–88]), as though the issues called for the actions of a prophet or a politician, as though it were *obvious* that what Wittgenstein means by "as much meaning" denies the possibility Pole envisages as "more meaning," and that the issue before us is not one of criticism but of commitment. The distortion to which Wittgenstein's thought is subjected is so continuous that no one error or misemphasis seems to call, more than others, for isolated discussion. This paper therefore takes the following form. The next two sections discuss the main concepts Pole attacks in his description and interpretation of Wittgenstein's view of language; the two sections which then follow comment on positions toward "ordinary language philosophy" which Pole shares with other critics of Wittgenstein; the final section suggests a way of understanding Wittgenstein's literary style which may help to make it more accessible.

RULES

The main effort of Pole's work is to expose and discredit Wittgenstein's views about language. There is no problem about what those views are:

Broadly the thesis is that a language . . . consists of a complex set of procedures, which may also be appealed to as rules. Normative notions—rightness, validity, and we may perhaps add truth—are significant inasmuch as there exist standards which we can appeal to and principles we can invoke. But where a new move is first made, a new development takes place, clearly no such standard can be applicable; we have moved beyond existing practice. Wittgenstein, it seems, is committed to holding that no such step can be called right or wrong; no evaluative assessment is possible [p. 55 f.].

We are to think of two factors in language; on the one hand particular moves or practices which are assessed by appeal to the rules, and on the other hand those rules themselves. Beyond these there is no further appeal; they are things we merely accept or adopt.

Where there are no rules to appeal to we can only decide; and I suppose that it is primarily on this account that this step is called a decision [p. 61].

This sounds vaguely familiar. Its Manichean conception of "rules" reminds one of Carnap's distinction between "internal" and "external" questions and of the recent writing in moral philosophy which distinguishes between the assessment of individual actions and of social practices; its use of "decision" is reminiscent of, for example, Reichenbach's "volitional decisions" and of Stevenson's "choice" between rational and persuasive methods of supporting moral judgments. Were Pole's description meant to apply to these views, it would merely be crude, failing to suggest their source or to depict their power. As a description of Wittgenstein it is ironically blind; it is not merely wrong, but misses the fact that Wittgenstein's ideas form a sustained and radical criticism of such views—so of course it is "like" them.

Pole's description seems to involve these notions:

1. The correctness or incorrectness of a use of language is determined by the rules of the language, and "determined" in two senses:

   a) The rules form a complete system, in the sense that for every "move" within the language it is obvious that a rule does or does not apply.

   b) Where a rule does apply, it is obvious whether it has been followed or infringed.

2. Where no existing rules apply, you can always adopt a new rule to cover the case, but then that obviously changes the game.

This is rough enough, and what Wittgenstein says about games, rules, decisions, correctness, justification, and so forth, is difficult enough, but not sufficiently so that one must hesitate before saying that Pole has not tried to understand what Wittgenstein has most painfully wished to say about language (and meaning and understanding). For Pole's description seems, roughly, to suggest the way correctness is determined in a *constructed* language or in the simplest games of chance. That everyday language does not, in fact or in essence, depend upon such a structure and conception of rules, and yet that the absence of such a structure in no way impairs its functioning, is what the picture of language drawn in the later philosophy is about. It represents one of the major criticisms Wittgenstein enters against the *Tractatus*; it sets for him many of the great problems of the later philosophy—for example, the relations between word, sentence, and language—and forces him into new modes of investigating meaning, understanding, reference, and so forth; his new, and central, concept of "grammar" is developed in opposition to it; it is repeated dozens of times. Whether the later Wittgenstein describes language as being roughly like a calculus with fixed rules working in that way is not a question which can seriously be discussed.

Then what are we to make of the fact that Wittgenstein constantly compares moments of speech with moves in a game? Pole makes out this much:

[the] comparison . . . serves his purpose in at least two ways. It serves him first in that a game is usually a form of social activity in which different players fill different roles; secondly in that games observe rules [p. 29].

But what purpose is served by these points of comparison? Let us take the points in reverse order:

A. Where the comparison of language with games turns on their both "observing rules," Wittgenstein invokes and invents games not as contexts in which it is just clear what "observing rules" amounts to, but contexts in which that phenomenon can be *investigated*. In particular, the analogy with games helps us to see the following:

i) In the various activities which may be said to proceed according to definite rules, the activity is not (and could not be) "everywhere circumscribed by rules" (§ 68). Does this mean that the rules are "incomplete"? It tells us something about what "being governed by rules" is like.

ii) "Following a rule" is an activity we learn against the background of, and in the course of, learning innumerable other activities—for example, obeying orders, taking and giving directions, repeating what is done or said, and so forth. The concept of a rule does not exhaust the concepts of correctness or justification ("right" and "wrong") and indeed the former concept would have no meaning unless these latter concepts already had. Like any of the activities to which it is related, a rule can always be misinterpreted in the course, or in the name, of "following" it.

iii) There is a more radical sense in which rules do not "determine" what a game is. One may explain the difference between, say, contract and auction bridge by "listing the rules"; but one cannot explain what *playing a game* is by "listing rules." Playing a game is "a part of our [that is, we humans'] natural history" (§ 25), and until one is an initiate of this human form of activity, the human gesture of "citing a rule" can mean nothing. And we can learn a new game without ever learning or formulating its rules (§ 31); not, however, without having mastered, we might say, the concept of a game.

iv) There is no one set of characteristics—and this is the most obvious comparison—which everything we call "games" shares, hence no characteristic called "being determined by rules." Language has no essence (§ 66).

B. For Wittgenstein, "following a rule" is just as much a "practice" as "playing a game" is (§ 199). Now what are its rules? In the sense in which "playing chess" has rules, "obeying a rule" has none (except, perhaps, in a special code or calculus which sets up some order of precedence in the application of various rules); and yet it can be done correctly or incorrectly—which just means it can be done or not done. And whether or not it is done is not a matter of rules (or of opinion or feeling or wishes or intentions). It is a matter of what Wittgenstein, in the *Blue Book*, refers to as "conventions" (p. 24), and in the *Investigations* describes as "forms of life" (e.g., § 23). That is always the ultimate appeal for Wittgenstein—not rules, and not decisions. It is what he is appealing to when he says such things as:

If I have exhausted the justifications I have reached bedrock, and my spade is turned. Then I am inclined to say: "This is simply what I do" [§ 217; cf. § 211].

What has to be accepted, the given is—so one could say—*forms of life* [II, p. 226].

Pole hears such phrases as meaning:

That [a given language-game] is played is no more than a matter of fact; it is always conceivable that it should not have been played. It might be said that the question raised is as to whether it ought to be played, and this formulation—one that Wittgenstein does not discuss—comes nearer, I believe, to the heart of the matter.

If your heart is on your sleeve, that is. Wittgenstein does not discuss whether language games *ought* to be played, for that would amount to discussing either (1) whether human beings ought to behave like the creatures we think of as human; or (2) whether the world ought to be different from what it is. For the "matters of fact" Wittgenstein is concerned with are what he describes in such ways as these:

> What we are supplying are really remarks on the natural history of human beings; we are not contributing curiosities however, but observations which no one has doubted, but which have escaped remark only because they are always before our eyes [§ 415].

> I am not saying: if such-and-such facts of nature were different people would have different concepts (in the sense of a hypothesis). But: if anyone believes that certain concepts are absolutely the correct ones, and that having different ones would mean not realizing something that we realize—then let him imagine certain *very general facts of nature* to be different from what we are used to, and the formation of concepts different from the usual ones will become intelligible to him [II, p. 230, my italics].

"It is always conceivable" that, for example, the game(s) we now play with the question "What did you say?" should not have been played. What are we conceiving if we conceive this? Perhaps that when we ask this of A, only A's father is allowed to answer, or that it is answered always by repeating the next to the last remark you made, or that it is answered by saying what you wished you had said, or perhaps that we can never remember what we just said, or perhaps simply that we have no way of asking that question. What sense does it make to suggest that one or the other of these games ought or ought not to be played? The question is: what would our lives look like, what very general facts would be different, if these conceivable alternatives were in fact operative? (There would, for example, be different ways, and purposes, for lying; a different social structure; different ways of attending to what is said; different weight put on our words; and so forth.)

Even with these hints of echoes of shadows of Wittgenstein's "purpose" in investigating the concept of a rule, we can say this much: (1) It allows him to formulate one source of a distorted conception of language—one to which, in philosophizing, we are particularly susceptible, and one which helps secure distortion in philosophical theorizing:

> When we talk of language as a symbolism used in an exact calculus, that which is in our mind can be found in the sciences and in mathematics. Our ordinary use of language conforms to this standard of exactness only in rare cases. Why then do we in philosophizing constantly compare our use of words with one following exact rules? The answer is that the puzzles which we try to remove always spring from just this attitude towards language [*BB*, pp. 25–26].

Or again:

> The man who is philosophically puzzled sees a law [=rule] in the way a word is used, and, trying to apply this law consistently, comes up against cases where it leads to paradoxical results [*BB*, p. 27].

(2) He wishes to indicate how inessential the "appeal to rules" is as an explanation of language. For what has to be "explained" is, put flatly and bleakly, this.

We learn and teach words in certain contexts, and then we are expected, and expect others, to be able to project them into further contexts.[5] Nothing insures that this projection will take place (in particular, not the grasping of universals nor the grasping of books of rules), just as nothing insures that we will make, and understand, the same projections. That on the whole we do is a matter of our sharing routes of interest and feeling, modes of response, senses of humor and of significance and of fulfillment, of what is outrageous, of what is similar to what else, what a rebuke, what forgiveness, of when an utterance is an assertion, when an appeal, when an explanation—all the whirl

[5] What "learning" and "teaching" are here is, or ought to be, seriously problematic. We say a word and the child repeats it. What is "repeating" here? All we know is that the child makes a sound which we accept. (How does the child recognize acceptance? Has he learned what that is?)

of organism Wittgenstein calls "forms of life." Human speech and activity, sanity and community, rest upon nothing more, but nothing less, than this. It is a vision as simple as it is difficult, and as difficult as it is (and because it is) terrifying. To attempt the work of *showing* its simplicity would be a real step in making available Wittgenstein's later philosophy.

DECISION

Having begun by miscasting the role of rules, and then taking "decision" to be a concept complementary to the concept of a rule, Pole will not be expected to have thrown light either on the real weight (and it is not much) Wittgenstein places on the concept of decision or on Wittgenstein's account of those passages of speech in which, in Pole's words, "a new move is first made."

The only passage Pole actually cites (on page 44, and again on page 61) to support his interpretation of "decision" is this one from the *Remarks on the Foundations of Mathematics*: "Why should I not say: in the proof I have won through to a decision?" (II, § 27). What I take Wittgenstein to be concerned with here is the question: "What makes a proof convincing?" Without discussing either the motives of that question or the success of his answer to it, it is clear enough that Wittgenstein takes the conviction afforded by a proof to be a function of the way it can "be taken in," "be followed," "be used as a model," "serve as a pattern or paradigm." But what can be "taken in," and so forth, in this way is *not something we have a choice about, not something that can be decided.* Saying that "the problem we are faced with in mathematics is essentially to decide what new forms to fashion" (p. 44) is as sensible as saying that the problem we are faced with in composing a coda is to decide what will sound like a cadence, or that the problem faced in describing a new object is to decide what will count as a description.

What is wrong with Pole's interpretation of Wittgenstein as suggesting that the mathematician decides "to use a certain rule" is not that it takes "too literally what Wittgenstein says of standards or rules" (p. 60), but that it is not what Wittgenstein says. ("Deciding to use a certain rule" correctly describes a logician's decision to use, say, Universal Generalization, which involves certain liabilities but ones he considers outweighed by other advantages.) What Wittgenstein says is that "the expression, the result, of our being convinced is that we *accept a rule*." We no more *decide* to accept a rule in this sense than we decide to be convinced. And we no more decide what will express our conviction here than we decide what will express our conviction about anything else—for example, that the road to New Orleans is the left one, that the development section is too long, and so forth.

Pole snaps at the word "decision" because he fears that it denies the rationality of choice; he despises this implication of its use in recent philosophizing (see p. 62). I share this concern about recent moral philosophy. But what is wrong in such discussions is not the use of the word "decision"; it is, rather, the implications which arise from an *unexamined* use of it, a use in which the concept of choice is disengaged from its (grammatical) connections with the concepts of commitment and of responsibility. How and why this has happened is something else.[6]

Wittgenstein does speak of forms of expression which

[6] If we asked, "In what kind of world would decision be unrelated to commitment and responsibility?" we might answer, "In a world in which morality had become politicalized." It is no secret that this has been happening to our world, and that we are perhaps incapable of what would make it stop happening. That is a personal misfortune of which we all partake. But the pain is made more exquisitely cruel when philosophers describe relations and conversations between persons as they would occur in a totally political world—a world, that is, in which relationships are no longer personal, nor even contractual—and call what goes on between such persons by the good (or bad) name of morality. That concedes our loss to have been not merely morality, but the very concept of morality as well.

we might think of as representing "a new move" in a shared language, to wit, those whose "grammar has yet to be explained" (*BB*, p. 10). (Adding "because there are no rules for its employment" adds nothing.) But he no more says of such expressions that in explaining them we decide to adopt the rules which confer meaning on them than he says about the concept of decision itself what Pole wishes him to say.

Some examples Wittgenstein gives of such expressions are: "I feel the visual image to be two inches behind the bridge of my nose" (*BB*, p. 9); "I feel in my hand that the water is three feet under the ground" (*ibid.*); "A rose has teeth in the mouth of a beast" (II, p. 222). What he says about them is this:

> We don't say that the man who tells us he feels the visual image two inches behind the bridge of his nose is telling a lie or talking nonsense. But we say that we don't understand the meaning of such a phrase. It combines well-known words but combines them in a way we don't yet understand. The grammar of [such phrases] has yet to be explained to us [*BB*, p. 10].

He does not say, and he does not mean, that there is "no right or wrong" about the use of such expressions. The question "Right or wrong?" has no application (yet) to such phrases, and so the statement that "such phrases are neither right nor wrong" itself says nothing. "Neither right nor wrong" may mean something like "unorthodox" or "not quite right and not quite wrong," but to use such critical expressions implies a clear sense of what would be orthodox or exactly right instances of the thing in question. Are the phrases in question unorthodox ways of saying something? What are they unorthodox ways of saying?

Pole compounds critical confusion by taking the irrelevance of the question "Right or wrong?" to mean that "no evaluative assessment is possible." (If it did mean that, then we should have made no evaluative assessment of a poem when we have found it trite or incoherent or wanting a summary stanza, nor of a decision when we have shown it thoughtless or heartless or spineless. Pole's insistence on right and wrong as the touchstones of assessment represents another attempt to meet an academic distrust of morality by an academic moralism. The positions are made for one another.) Is it no assessment of a phrase to say that its grammar has yet to be explained? But that is a very particular assessment, a new category of criticism. And there is no suggestion from Wittgenstein that *any* explanation will be acceptable. He calls one explanation of the diviner's statement a "perfectly good" one (*BB*, p. 10).

Such phrases are not the only ones in which our failure to understand is attributable to our failure to understand grammar; they are only the most dramatic or obvious ones. Once we see that the grammar of an expression sometimes *needs* explaining, and realize that we all know how to provide perfectly good explanations, we may be more accessible to the request to investigate the grammar of an expression whose meaning seems obvious and ask ourselves how it *is* to be explained.

Such an investigation will doubtless be reminiscent of procedures which have long been part of the familiar texture of analytical philosophizing; in particular, it sounds something like asking for the verification of a statement—and indeed Pole suggests (p. 96) that it is not, at bottom, importantly different in its criticism of metaphysics; and it sounds like Russell's asking for the "real [that is, logical] form of a proposition"—and, of course, the Wittgenstein of the *Tractatus* had also asked for that. A profitable way, I think, to approach the thought of the later Wittgenstein is to see how his questions about grammar differ from these (and other) more familiar questions. The sorts of differences I have in mind may perhaps be suggested this way: (1) It is true that an explanation of the grammar of an assertion can be asked for by asking "How would you verify that?" But first, where that is what the question asks for, it is not to be assumed that the question itself makes good sense; in particular it is not sensible unless there is some doubt about how that assertion is conceived to be verified, and it therefore leads to no theory of meaning at all (cf. § 353). Second, it is not the only way in which an explanation of grammar can be requested; it is equally indicative of our failure to understand the grammar of an assertion if we cannot answer such questions as: "How would you teach someone what that says?"; "How would you hint at its truth?"; "What is it like to wonder whether it is true?" (2) In the *Tractatus* Wittgenstein, if I understand, was asking: "Why is the logical form of a proposition its real form?" But in the later philosophy he answers, in effect: "It is not." And he goes on to ask: "Why do we (did I) think it was?"; and "What does tell us the real form (= grammar) of a proposition?"

It is part of the accomplishment of Pole's critical study of Wittgenstein that it omits any examination of the twin concepts of "grammar" and of "criteria." For what Wittgenstein means when he says that philosophy really is descriptive is that it is descriptive of "our grammar," of "the criteria we have" in understanding one another, knowing the world, and possessing ourselves. Grammar is what language games are meant to reveal; it is because of this that they provide new ways of investigating concepts, and of criticizing traditional philosophy. All this, it should go without saying, is difficult to be clear about (Wittgenstein's own difficulty is not willful); but it is what any effort to understand Wittgenstein must direct itself toward.

THE RELEVANCE OF THE APPEAL TO EVERYDAY LANGUAGE

Two of Pole's claims seem to be shared by many philosophers whom Wittgenstein offends, and it would be of use to do something toward making them seem less matters for common cause than for joined investigation. The claims I have in mind concern these two questions: (1) In what sense, or to what extent, does an appeal to "our everyday use" of an expression represent a mode of criticizing the use of that expression in philosophical contexts? (2) What sort of knowledge is the knowledge we have (or claim) of "how we ordinarily use" an expression? The present section is concerned with the first of these questions, the following with the second.

Pole says, or implies, that Wittgenstein regards ordinary language as "sacrosanct," that he speaks in the name of nothing higher than the "status quo" and that he "has forbidden philosophers to tamper with [our ordinary expressions]" (p. 57). Other philosophers, with very different motives from Pole's, have received the same impression, and their impatience has not been stilled by Wittgenstein's having said that

> a reform of ordinary language for particular purposes, an improvement in our terminology designed to prevent misunderstandings in practice, is perfectly possible. But these are not the cases we have to do with [§ 132]

for they persist in reading Wittgenstein's appeal to our everyday use of expressions as though his effort consisted in scorning the speech of his charwoman out of solicitude toward that of his Nanny.

It takes two to give an impression; if this is a distortion of Wittgenstein's thought, it is a distortion of *something*. Of what? Pole's reference for his claim about what Wittgenstein "forbids" is to a passage which begins this way:

> Philosophy may in no way interfere with the actual use of language; it can in the end only describe it [§ 124].

There is a frame of mind in which this may appear as something intolerably confining.[7] Then one will hear Witt-

---

[7] It is significant that Wittgenstein thought of his methods as liberating. "The real discovery is the one that makes me capable of stopping doing philosophy when I want to.— The one that gives philosophy peace, so that it is no longer tormented by questions which bring *itself* in question" (§133). The reason

genstein's statement as though it meant either that philosophy ought not to change it (in which case Wittgenstein will be accused of an intellectual, even social conservatism) or that the actual use of language may in no way be changed (in which case Wittgenstein will be accused of lacking imagination or a sufficient appreciation of scientific advance). What the statement means is that, though of course there are any number of ways of changing ordinary language, philosophizing does not change it. That charge cannot be evaded by making it sound like a Nanny bleating "ou-ou-ought."

And yet it is a very perplexing indictment which Wittgenstein has entered. Why does Wittgenstein think it is one? Why do philosophers respond to it as though it were? Have they claimed to be, or thought of themselves as, changing or interfering with language?

The force of the indictment can best be seen in considering the ancient recognition that a philosophical thesis may, or may seem to, conflict with a "belief" which we take to be the common possession of common men, together with the equally ancient claim on the part of philosophers that in this conflict philosophy's position is superior to that common possession; that, for example, such claims as "We know that there are material objects," "We directly see them," "We know that other persons are sentient," all of which are believed by the vulgar, have been discovered by philosophers to lack rational justification.

But the *nature* of this discovery and the *kind* of conflict involved are problems as constant as epistemology itself.

---

why methods which make us look at what we say, and bring the forms of language (hence our forms of life) to consciousness, can present themselves to one person as confining and to another as liberating is, I think, understandable in this way: recognizing what we say, in the way that is relevant in philosophizing, is like recognizing our present commitments and their implications; to one person a sense of freedom will demand an escape from them, to another it will require their more total acceptance. Is it obvious that one of those positions must, in a given case, be right?

Their most recent guise is perhaps brought out if we can say this much: There would be no sense of such a discovery[8] unless there were a sense of conflict with "what we all formerly believed," and there would, in turn, be no sense of conflict unless the philosopher's words meant (or were used as meaning) what they ordinarily meant. And don't they?

The ordinary language philosopher will say: "They don't; the philosopher is 'misusing words' or 'changing their meanings'; the philosopher has been careless, hasty, even wily[9] in his use of language." The defender of the tradition may reply: "Of course they don't; the philosopher uses technical terms, or terms with special senses, in order to free himself from the vagueness and imprecision of ordinary language and thereby to assess the beliefs it expresses." Neither of these replies is very satisfactory. The former is, if not too unclear altogether to be taken seriously as an explanation of disorder, plainly incredible. I do not see how it can with good conscience be denied that ordinary language philosophers (for example, Austin and Ryle) have found and made trouble for traditional philosophy. But the understanding of the trouble, and so an assessment of its seriousness or permanence, is a project of a different order. And I know of no effort of theirs at this task which carries anything like that immediate conviction which is so large a part of the power of their remarks when they are working within an investigation of ordinary language itself.

On the other hand, someone who imagines that he is

8 The importance and role of the sense of discovery in philosophical paradox (one of the constant themes in the philosophizing of John Wisdom), in particular the pervasive significance of the fact that this sense is not accounted for by the familiar criticisms made by ordinary language philosophers against the tradition, was brought in upon me in conversations with Thompson Clarke. He has also read this paper and done what he could to relieve its obscurities.

9 Austin, "Other Minds," in Flew (ed.), *Logic and Language* (London, 1953), Second Series, p. 133.

defending the tradition by maintaining its right and need to introduce technical terms (or, as Pole suggests, to invent special philosophical language games—on, for example, pages 96–97) probably has in mind the philosopher's use of such terms as "sense data," "analytic," "transcendental unity of apperception," "idea," "universal," "existential quantifier"—terms which no ordinary language philosopher would criticize on the ground that they are not ordinary. But is the word "seeing" in the statement "We never directly see material objects" *meant* to be technical? Is "private" in "My sensations are private"? Are any of the words in such a statement as "We can never know what another person is experiencing"? Are such statements used in some special language game? The assumption, shared by our ordinary language critic and our defender of the tradition, that such words are not meant in their ordinary senses, destroys the point (not to say the meaning) of such statements. For on that assumption we cannot account for the way they seem to conflict with something we all (seem to, would say that we) believe; it therefore fails to account for what makes them seem to be discoveries or, we might say, fails to suggest what the hitherto unnoticed fact is which philosophy has discovered. Why would Descartes have professed "astonishment" at his "realization" that he might be dreaming if he had not meant to be denying or questioning what anyone who said "I believe, for example, that I am seated before the fire," and the like, would mean? And what cause, otherwise, would there have been for Hume to despair of his skeptical conclusions, regarding them as a "malady which can never radically be cured" (*Treatise*, I, iv, 2), were they not skeptical about (or, as he puts it, "contrary" to) "such opinions as we . . . embrace by a kind of instinct or natural impulse"?

It may be objected to this that scientific theories, however technical their language, have no trouble conflicting with common beliefs. But it is of crucial importance that neither Hume nor the Descartes of the *Meditations*, nor

indeed anyone in that continuous line of classical episte-
mologists from Descartes and Locke to Moore and Price,
seems to be conducting scientific investigations. In particular, they do not set out a collection of more or less ab-
struse facts and puzzling phenomena which they undertake to explain theoretically. Their method is uniformly
what Hume describes as "profound and intense *reflection*"
from which, he says, "skeptical doubt arises *naturally*" (*op.
cit.*; my italics). They all begin from what seem to be
facts of such obviousness that no one could fail to recognize
them ("We all believe that there are material objects
which continue to exist when they are unperceived"), employ examples of the homeliest extraction ("We should
all say that I am now holding an envelope in my hand, and
that we all see it") and considerations whose import anyone can grasp who can speak ("But no two of us see exactly the same thing"; "But there is much that I can
doubt"). (Wittgenstein's originality does not come from
his having said that philosophy's problems concern something we all already know.) That such facts and examples
and considerations "naturally" lead to skepticism is the
phenomenon concerning us here. What the relation may
be between this way of coming into conflict with common
belief, and science's way, is a fascinating question and one,
so far as I know, as yet unexamined.

Perhaps this can now be said: If, in the nonscientific
(skeptical) conflict with common belief, words are in
some way deprived of their normal functioning, a conceptualization of this distortion will have to account for this
pair of facts: that the philosopher's words must (or must
seem to) be used in their normal way, otherwise they
would not conflict with what should ordinarily be meant
in using them; and that the philosopher's words cannot be
used in (quite) their normal way, otherwise the ordinary
facts, examples, and considerations he adduces would not
yield a general skeptical conclusion.

It is such a pair of facts, I suggest, that Wittgenstein is
responding to when he says of philosophical (he calls them

"metaphysical") expressions that (roughly) they are "used apart from their normal language game," that their "grammar is misunderstood," that they "flout the common criteria used in connection with these expressions." Such assertions do not say that the philosopher has "changed the meaning of his words" (what meaning do they now have?). Nor are they met, if any truth is caught by them, by saying that the words are being used in special senses, for none of Wittgenstein's critical assertions would be true of technical terms. They represent new categories of criticism.

Wittgenstein is, then, denying that in the (apparent) conflict between philosophy and the common "beliefs" (assumptions?) of ordinary men, philosophy's position is superior. This does not mean, however, that he is defending common beliefs against philosophy. That "there are material objects" or that "other persons are sentient" are not propositions which Wittgenstein supposed to be open either to belief or to disbelief. They seem to be ordinary "beliefs" only when the philosopher undertakes to "doubt" them. I am not saying that this is obviously not real doubt, but merely suggesting that it is not obvious that it is, and that it is completely unobvious, if it is not real doubt, what kind of experience it is and why it presents itself as doubt.

Nor is Wittgenstein saying that philosophy's position is inferior to that of common men. Perhaps one could say that he wishes to show that, in its conflict with "what we all believe," the philosopher has no position at all, his conclusions are not false (and not meaningless), but, one could say, not *believable*—that is, they do not create the stability of conviction expressed in propositions which are subject (grammatically) to belief. (That was agonizingly acknowledged, as is familiar to us, by Hume, who wanted, but confessed failure in trying to find, an explanation of it. When he left his study he forgot, as he knew and hoped he would, the skeptical conclusions of his reflections. But what kind of "belief" is it whose convincingness fades as soon as we are not explicitly attending to the considerations which led us to it?) For Wittgenstein, philosophy comes to grief not in denying what we all know to be true, but in its effort to escape those human forms of life which alone provide the coherence of our expression. He wishes an acknowledgment of human limitation which does not leave us chafed by our own skin, by a sense of powerlessness to penetrate beyond the human conditions of knowledge. The limitations of knowledge are no longer barriers to a more perfect apprehension, but conditions of knowledge *überhaupt*, of anything we should call "knowledge." The resemblance to Kant is obvious, and I will say another word about it below.

THE KNOWLEDGE OF OUR LANGUAGE

How can we come to such an acknowledgment of limitation? Wittgenstein's answer is: "What we do is to bring words back from their metaphysical to their everyday use" (§ 116). I have, in effect, asked: why does that help? And my suggestion, essentially, was: it shows us that we did not know what we were saying, what we were doing to ourselves. But now I want to ask: how do we accomplish the task of bringing words back home? How do we know when we have done it?

Well, how does the logician know that (a) "Nobody is in the auditorium" must be transcribed differently from (b) "Peabody is in the auditorium"? By intuition? Careful empirical studies? Perhaps he will say: "But obviously we do not want the same sorts of inferences to be drawn from (a) as from (b), in particular not the inference that somebody is in the auditorium." But how does he know *that*? However he knows it—and he does—that is how Wittgenstein knows that the grammar of, say, "pointing to an object" is different from the grammar of "pointing to a color" (*BB*, p. 80; § 33). Failing an awareness of that difference we take the obvious difference between them to be a function of some special experience which accompanies the act of pointing. How does Wittgenstein know that? The way Russell (and we) know that if you do not catch the difference in logical form between "Pegasus does not exist" and "Whirlaway does not whinny," you will take the obvious difference between them to indicate the presence of some special realm of being which accompanies the ordinary world.

But what kind of knowledge is this? What kind of knowledge is the knowledge of what we ordinarily mean in using an expression, or the knowledge of the particular circumstances in which an expression is actually used? Pole has this to say:

> Consider the great purpose of all this—this descriptive setting forth of language-games. It is to bring us to see that some particular move which we took for a move in the game has no proper place in it. Such a move is to be shown as failing to connect with the rest of the pattern. Wittgenstein compares it to a wheel spinning idly, disengaged from the machine it should belong to. Here we have a luminous metaphor—and yet no more than a metaphor. For there can be no way of testing whether this or that linguistic wheel has failed to engage, except to grasp the pattern in each case; to arrive at some sort of insight into that unique set of relations which it professes but fails to form a part of [p. 81].

This is thought to show that if we

> once allow that it might be right to reject a proposition or mode of speech because the pattern has no place for it, . . . it must follow that it must sometimes be right to accept others on the same ground— that the pattern requires them. There is no inherent difficulty in the notion. . . . Yet here we have a way of seeing language that the whole bent of Wittgenstein's thought was opposed to [p. 82].

If I understand what Pole is getting at (he gives no examples, here or elsewhere), he has been even less impressed by Wittgenstein's conception of language than we have seen. It is not the "bent" of Wittgenstein's thought that is opposed to the idea that the "requirement of the pattern" justifies the use we make of an expression, but the straight thrust of his whole teaching: "The more narrowly we examine actual language, the sharper becomes the conflict between it and our requirement. (For the crystalline purity of logic was, of course, not a *result of investigation:* it was a requirement" [§ 107].) "A *picture* [= pattern?] held us captive. And we could not get outside it, for it lay in our language and language seemed to repeat it to us inexorably" (§ 115). Not only is there "no inherent difficulty in the notion" of "grasping a pattern," the difficulty is to get ourselves not to take our feelings of what is called for or what must be appropriate, at face value.

Other philosophers have taken the knowledge of everyday language, since it is obviously knowledge of "matters of fact," to be straightforwardly empirical, requiring the observations and verifications which we are told that any empirical judgment requires. Such philosophers find the appeal to what we should ordinarily say and mean, when this appeal is not backed by scientific collection of "our" utterances, archaically precious, while philosophers dependent upon that appeal will find the invitation to science at this point cheaply *moderne*. This conflict is not a side issue in the general conflict between Wittgenstein (together with, at this point, "ordinary language philosophy") and traditional philosophy; it is itself an instance, an expression, of that conflict, and one therefore which we will not suppose it will be simple to resolve. Wittgenstein does not speak very explicitly about the knowledge we have of our language, but when we see what kind of claim this knowledge involves, we realize that its investigation lies at the heart of the later philosophy as a whole. I shall try to suggest what I mean by that.

Neither Wittgenstein nor the ordinary language philosopher, when he asks "What should we say (would we call) . . . ?" is asking just any question about the use of language. He is, in particular, not predicting what will be said in certain circumstances, not, for example, asking how often a word will be used nor what the most effective slogan will be for a particular purpose. (Those questions can, of course, be asked; and their answers will indeed require ordinary empirical methods for collecting sociological data.) He is asking something which can be answered by remembering what is said and meant, or by trying out his own response to an imagined situation. Answers arrived at in such ways will not tell you everything, but why assume that they are meant to tell you what only the collection of new data can tell you? The problems of philosophy are not solved by "[hunting] out new facts; it is, rather, of the essence of our investigation that we do not seek to learn anything *new* by it. We want to *understand* something that is already in plain view. For *this* is what we seem in some sense not to understand" (§ 89).

What do such answers look like? They will be facts about what we call (how we conceive, what the concept is, what counts as), for example, a piece of wax, the same piece of wax, seeing something, not really seeing something, not seeing all of something, following, finding, losing, returning, choosing, intending, wishing, pointing to something, and so on. And we could say that what such answers are meant to provide us with is not more knowledge of matters of fact, but the knowledge of what would count as various "matters of fact." Is this empirical knowledge? Is it a priori? It is a knowledge of what Wittgenstein means by grammar—the knowledge Kant calls "transcendental."

And here I make a remark which the reader must bear well in mind, as it extends its influence over all that follows. Not every kind of knowledge *a priori* should be called transcendental, but that only by which we know that—and how—certain representations (intuitions or concepts) can be employed or are possible purely *a priori*. The term "transcendental," that is to say, signifies such knowledge as concerns the *a*

priori possibility of knowledge, or its *a priori* employment [*Critique of Pure Reason*, trans. by N. Kemp
Smith, p. 96].

That is not the clearest remark ever made, but I should
think that no one who lacked sympathy with the problem
Kant was writing about would undertake to make sense of
Wittgenstein's saying:

> Our investigation . . . is directed not towards phe-
> nomena, but, as one might say, towards the "possibili-
> ties" of phenomena [§ 90].

As the "transcendental clue to the discovery of all pure
concepts of the understanding" (*Critique*, pp. 105 ff.)
Kant uses the idea that "there arise precisely the same
number of pure concepts of the understanding in general,
as . . . there have been found to be logical functions in
all possible judgments" (p. 113). Wittgenstein follows the
remark quoted above with the words: "We remind ourselves, that is to say, of the *kind of statement* that we
make about phenomena. . . . Our investigation is therefore a grammatical one" (§ 90). And where Kant speaks
of "transcendental illusion"—the illusion that we know
what transcends the conditions of possible knowledge—
Wittgenstein speaks of the illusions produced by our employing words in the absence of the (any) language game
which provides their comprehensible employment (cf.
§ 96). ("The results of philosophy are the uncovering of
one or another piece of plain nonsense and of bumps that
the understanding has got by running its head up against
the limits of language" [§ 119].)

If his similarity to Kant is seen, the differences light up
the nature of the problems Wittgenstein sets himself. For
Wittgenstein it would be an illusion not only that we do
know things-in-themselves, but equally an illusion that we
do not (crudely, because the concept of "knowing something as it really is" is being used without a clear sense,
apart from its ordinary language game). So problems
emerge which can be articulated as: "Why do we feel we

cannot know something in a situation in which there is nothing it makes sense to say we do not know?"; "What is the nature of this illusion?"; "What makes us dissatisfied with our knowledge as a whole?"; "What is the nature and power of a 'conceptualization of the world'?"; "Why do we conceptualize the world as we do?"; "What would alternative conceptualizations look like?"; "How might they be arrived at?" It was, I suggest, because he wanted answers to such questions that he said, "It did not matter whether his results were true or not: what mattered was that 'a method had been found'" (Moore, "Wittgenstein's Lectures," *Mind*, LXIV [1955], 26).

And he also said: "There is not *a* philosophical method, though there are indeed methods, like different therapies" (§ 133). The sorts of thing he means by "methods" are, I take it, "[imagining or considering] a language-game for which [a given] account is really valid" (for example, § 2, § 48); "finding and inventing intermediate cases" (§ 122); "[inventing] fictitious natural history," (II, p. 230); investigating one expression by investigating a grammatically related expression, for example, the grammar of "meaning" by that of "explanation of the meaning" (*BB*, pp. 1, 24); and so on. But in all of these methods part of what is necessary is that we respond to questions like "What would we say if . . . ?" or "But is anyone going to call . . . ?" To suppose that what is then being asked for is a prediction of what will be said, and a prediction for which we have slim evidence, would be as sensible as responding to the request "Suppose you have three apples and I give you three more. How many will you have?" by saying, "How can I answer with confidence? I might drop one and have five, or inherit an orchard and have thousands."

What is being asked for? If it is accepted that "a language" (a natural language) is what the native speakers of a language speak, and that speaking a language is a matter of practical mastery, then such questions as "What should we say if . . . ?" or "In what circumstances would

we call . . . ?" asked of someone who has mastered the
language (for example, oneself) is a request for the person
to say something about himself, describe what he does.
So the different methods are methods for acquiring self-
knowledge; as—for different (but related) purposes and in
response to different (but related) problems—are the
methods of "free" association, dream analysis, investigation
of verbal and behavioral slips, noting and analyzing "transferred" feeling, and so forth. Perhaps more shocking, and
certainly more important, than any of Freud's or Wittgenstein's particular conclusions is their discovery that knowing oneself is something for which there are methods—
something, therefore, that can be taught (though not in
obvious ways) and practiced.

Someone may wish to object: "But such claims as 'We
say . . . ,' 'We are not going to call . . . ,' and so forth,
are not merely claims about what *I* say and mean and do,
but about what *others* say and mean and do as well. And
how can I speak for others on the basis of knowledge about
myself?" The question is: why are some claims about myself expressed in the form "We . . ."? About what can I
speak for others on the basis of what I have learned about
myself? (This is worth comparing with the question: about
what can I speak for others on the basis of what I decide
to do? When you vote, you speak for yourself; when you
are voted in, you speak for others.) Then suppose it is
asked: "But how do I know others speak as I do?" About
some things I know they do not; I have some knowledge
of my idiosyncrasy. But if the question means "How do I
know at all that others speak as I do?" then the answer is,
I do not. I may find out that the most common concept is
not used by us in the same way. And one of Wittgenstein's
questions is: what would it be like to find this out?[10] At
one place he says:

[10] The nature and extent of this fact, and of the different
methods required in meeting it, is suggested by the differences of
problems presented to psychoanalysts in the cases of neurotic and
of psychotic communication (verbal and nonverbal). See, e.g.,

One human being can be a complete enigma to another. We learn this when we come into a strange
country with entirely strange traditions; and, what is
more, even given a mastery of the country's language.
We do not *understand* the people. (And not because
of not knowing what they are saying to themselves.)
We cannot find our feet with them [II, p. 223].

In German the last sentence employs an idiom which
literally says: "We cannot find ourselves in them." We,
who can speak for one another, find that we cannot speak
for them. In part, of course, we find this out in finding
out that we cannot speak *to* them. If speaking *for* someone else seems to be a mysterious process, that may be because speaking *to* someone does not seem mysterious
enough.

If the little I have said makes plausible the idea that the
question "How do we know what we say (intended to say,
wish to say)?" is one aspect of the general question "What
is the nature of self-knowledge?" then we will realize that
Wittgenstein has not first "accepted" or "adopted" a
method and then accepted its results, for the nature of
self-knowledge—and therewith the nature of the self—is one
of the great subjects of the *Investigations* as a whole.

It is also one of the hardest regions of the *Investigations*
to settle with any comfort. One reason for that, I think, is
that so astonishingly little exploring of the nature of self-
knowledge has been attempted in philosophical writing
since Bacon and Locke and Descartes prepared the habitation of the new science. Classical epistemology has con-

---

Frieda Fromm-Reichmann, *Principles of Intensive Psychotherapy*
(Chicago, 1950), esp. ch. 8 and *passim*. Perhaps it is suggestive
to say: the neurotic disguises the expression of particular com-
munications (e.g., makes something fearful to him look and
sound attractive), while the psychotic distorts his entire grammar.
The neurotic has reason, and the strength, to keep what he
means from himself; the psychotic has to keep what he knows he
means from others. Wittgenstein is concerned with both of these
kinds of incongruence.

centrated on the knowledge of objects (and, of course, of mathematics), not on the knowledge of persons. That is, surely, one of the striking facts of modern philosophy as a whole, and its history will not be understood until some accounting of that fact is rendered.[11] In a smart attack on the new philosophy, Russell suggests that its unconcern with the methods and results of modern science betrays its alienation from the original and continuing source of philosophical inspiration: "Philosophers from Thales onward have tried to understand the world" (*My Philosophical Development* [New York, 1959], p. 230). But philosophers from Socrates onward have (sometimes) also tried to understand themselves, and found in that both the method and goal of philosophizing. It is a little absurd to go on insisting that physics provides us with knowledge of the world which is of the highest excellence. Surely the problems we face now are not the same ones for which Bacon and Galileo caught their chills. Our intellectual problems (to say no more) are set by the very success of those deeds, by the plain fact that the measures which soak up knowledge of the world leave us dryly ignorant of ourselves. Our problem is not that we lack adequate methods for acquiring knowledge of nature, but that we are unable to prevent our best ideas—including our ideas about our knowledge of nature—from becoming ideologized. Our incapacity here results not from the supposed fact that ordinary language is vague; to say so is an excuse for not recognizing that (and when) we speak vaguely, imprecisely, thoughtlessly, unjustly, in the absence of feeling, and so forth.

[11] Bernard Williams, in a review of Stuart Hampshire's *Thought and Action* in *Encounter*, XV (Nov., 1960), 38–42, suggests one important fact about what I have, parochially, called "modern philosophy" (by which I meant the English and American academic traditions, beginning with Descartes and Locke and never domesticating Hegel and his successors) which, I think, is related to its unconcern with the knowledge of persons and in particular with self-knowledge; viz., its neglect of history as a form of human knowledge.

Since Wittgenstein's investigations of self-knowledge and of the knowledge of others depend upon his concept of "criteria," it is worth noting that although Pole ventures a discussion of Wittgenstein's ideas about "inner experience" he prudently withholds any opinion about the role of "criteria" in those ideas. He does suggest that Wittgenstein supposed words to have meaning "in the complete absence of conscious feeling" (p. 88), as though Wittgenstein supposed the users of language to be anaesthetized; and he finds Wittgenstein supposing that "experiential elements play no part" in determining the way language is used (p. 88; cf. p. 86), whereas what Wittgenstein says is, in these terms, that what is experiential in the use of a word is not an element, not one identifiable recurrence whose presence insures the meaning of a word and whose absence deprives it of meaning. If that were the case, how could we ever assess our feelings, recognize them to be inappropriate to what we say? Feelings (like intentions and hopes and wishes, though not in the same way) are expressed in speech and in conduct generally; and the (actual, empirical) problem of the knowledge of oneself and of others is set by the multiple and subtle distortions of their expression. Here, what we do not know comprises not our ignorance but our alienation.

Since Wittgenstein does fuller justice to the role of feeling in speech and conduct than any other philosopher within the Anglo-American academic tradition, it is disheartening to find his thought so out of reach. Pole extends the line of those who, shocked at the way academic reasoning is embarrassed by the presence of feeling—its wish to remove feeling to the "emotive" accompaniments of discourse, out of the reach of intellectual assessment—counter by taking feelings too much at face value and so suffer the traditional penalty of the sentimentalist, that one stops taking his feelings seriously. Other philosophers, I believe, are under the impression that Wittgenstein denies that we can know what we think and feel, and even that we can know ourselves. This extraordinary idea comes, no doubt, from such remarks of Wittgenstein's as: "I can know what someone else is thinking, not what I am thinking" (II, p. 222); "It cannot be said of me at all (except perhaps as a joke) that I *know* I am in pain" (§ 246). But the "can" and "cannot" in these remarks are grammatical; they mean "it makes no sense to say these things" (in the way we think it does); it would, therefore, equally make no sense to say of me that I do not know what I am thinking, or that I do not know I am in pain. The implication is not that I cannot know myself, but that knowing oneself— though radically different from the way we know others— is not a matter of cognizing (classically, "intuiting") mental acts and particular sensations.

THE STYLE OF THE *INVESTIGATIONS*

I mentioned, at the beginning of this paper, the surface difficulties one has in approaching the writings of Wittgenstein. His literary style has achieved both high praise and widespread alarm. Why does he write that way? Why doesn't he just say what he means, and draw instead of insinuate conclusions? The motives and methods of his philosophizing, as I have been sketching at them, suggest answers to these questions which I want, in conclusion, to indicate.[12]

The first thing to be said in accounting for his style is that he *writes*: he does not report, he does not write up results. Nobody would forge a style so personal who had not wanted and needed to find the right expression for his thought. The German dissertation and the British essay— our most common modern options for writing philosophy —would not work; his is not a system and he is not a spectator. My suggestion is that the problem of style is set for him by the two aspects of his work which I have

[12] Wittgenstein speaks of this as a problem in his preface to the *Investigations.*

primarily emphasized: the lack of existing terms of criticism, and the method of self-knowledge.[13]

In its defense of truth against sophistry, philosophy has employed the same literary genres as theology in its defense of the faith: against intellectual competition, Dogmatics; against Dogmatics, the Confession; in both, the Dialogue.[14] Inaccessible to the dogmatics of philosophical criticism, Wittgenstein chose confession and recast his dialogue. It contains what serious confessions must: the full acknowledgment of temptation ("I want to say . . ."; "I feel like saying . . ."; "Here the urge is strong . . .") and a willingness to correct them and give them up ("In the everyday use . . ."; "I impose a requirement which does not meet my real need"). (The voice of temptation and the voice of correctness are the antagonists in Wittgenstein's dialogues.) In confessing you do not explain or justify, but describe how it is with you. And confession, unlike dogma, is not to be believed but tested, and accepted or rejected. Nor is it the occasion for accusation, except of yourself, and by implication those who find themselves in you. There is exhortation ("Do not say: 'There *must* be something common' . . . but *look* and *see* . . ." [§ 66]) not to belief, but to self-scrutiny. And

[13] Perhaps another word will make clearer what I mean by "terms of criticism." Wittgenstein opens the *Investigations* (and the *Brown Book*) by quoting a passage from Augustine's *Confessions* in which he describes the way he learned to speak. Wittgenstein finds this important but unsatisfactory. Is there any short way of answering the question: What does Wittgenstein find wrong with it? (Does it commit a well-known fallacy? Is it a case of hasty generalization? Empirical falsehood? Unverifiable?)

[14] The significance of the fact that writing of all kinds (not just "literature") is dependent, in structure and tone and effect, on a quite definite (though extensive) set of literary forms or genres is nowhere to my knowledge so fully made out as in Northrop Frye's *Anatomy of Criticism* (Princeton, 1957); the small use I have made of it here hardly suggests the work it should inspire. More immediately I am indebted to Philip Rieff's introduction to the Beacon Press edition of Adolf Harnack's *Outlines of the History of Dogma* (Boston, 1959) and to the reference to Karl Barth's *Church Dogmatics* cited by Rieff.

that is why there is virtually nothing in the *Investigations*
which we should ordinarily call reasoning; Wittgenstein asserts nothing which could be proved, for what he asserts is
either obvious (§ 126)—whether true or false—or else concerned with what conviction, whether by proof or evidence
or authority, would consist in. Otherwise there are questions, jokes, parables, and propositions so striking (the way
lines are in poetry) that they stun mere belief. (Are we
asked to believe that "if a lion could talk we could not
understand him"? [II, p. 223]) Belief is not enough.
Either the suggestion penetrates past assessment and becomes part of the sensibility from which assessment proceeds, or it is philosophically useless.

Such writing has its risks: not merely the familiar ones
of inconsistency, unclarity, empirical falsehood, unwar-
ranted generalization, but also of personal confusion, with
its attendant dishonesties, and of the tyranny which subjects the world to one's personal problems. The assessment
of such failures will exact criticism at which we are un-
practiced.

In asking for more than belief it invites discipleship,
which runs its own risks of dishonesty and hostility. But I
do not see that the faults of explicit discipleship are more
dangerous than the faults which come from subjection to
modes of thought and sensibility whose origins are unseen
or unremembered and which therefore create a different
blindness inaccessible in other ways to cure. Between control by the living and control by the dead there is nothing
to choose.

Because the breaking of such control is a constant purpose of the later Wittgenstein, his writing is deeply practical and negative, the way Freud's is. And like Freud's
therapy, it wishes to prevent understanding which is un-
accompanied by inner change. Both of them are intent
upon unmasking the defeat of our real need in the face of
self-impositions which we have not assessed (§ 108), or
fantasies ("pictures") which we cannot escape (§ 115).
In both, such misfortune is betrayed in the incongruence

between what is said and what is meant or expressed; for both, the self is concealed in assertion and action and revealed in temptation and wish. Both thought of their negative soundings as revolutionary extensions of our knowledge, and both were obsessed by the idea, or fact, that they would be misunderstood—partly, doubtless, because they knew the taste of self-knowledge, that it is bitter. It will be time to blame them for taking misunderstanding by their disciples as personal betrayal when we know that the ignorance of oneself is a refusal to know.[15]

[15] Material for this paper was prepared during a period in which I received a grant from the Henry P. Kendall Foundation, to which I take this opportunity of expressing my gratitude.

UNIVERSALS AND
FAMILY RESEMBLANCES

RENFORD BAMBROUGH

I believe that Wittgenstein solved what is known as "the problem of universals," and I would say of his solution, as Hume said of Berkeley's treatment of the same topic, that it is "one of the greatest and most valuable discoveries that has been made of late years in the republic of letters."

I do not expect these claims to be accepted by many philosophers.

Since I claim that Wittgenstein solved the problem I naturally do not claim to be making an original contribution to the study of it. Since I recognise that few philosophers will accept my claim that Wittgenstein solved it, I naturally regard it as worth while to continue to discuss the problem. My purpose is to try to make clear what Wittgenstein's solution is and to try to make clear that it is a solution.

Philosophers ought to be wary of claiming that philosophical problems have been finally solved. Aristotle and Descartes and Spinoza and Berkeley and Hume and the author of the *Tractatus Logico-Philosophicus* lie at the bottom of the sea not far from this rock, with the skeletons of many lesser men to keep them company. But nobody suggests that their journeys were vain, or that nothing can be saved from the wrecks.

In seeking for Wittgenstein's solution we must look

From *Proceedings of the Aristotelian Society*, Vol. LXI (1960–61), pp. 207–222. Reprinted with the permission of the author and editor.

mainly to his remarks about "family resemblances" and to his use of the example of games. In the *Blue Book* he speaks of "our craving for generality" and tries to trace this craving to its sources:

This craving for generality is the resultant of a number of tendencies connected with particular philosophical confusions. There is—

(*a*) The tendency to look for something in common to all the entities which we commonly subsume under a general term.—We are inclined to think that there must be something in common to all games, say, and that this common property is the justification for applying the general term "game" to the various games; whereas games form a *family* the members of which have family likenesses. Some of them have the same nose, others the same eyebrows and others again the same way of walking; and these likenesses overlap. The idea of a general concept being a common property of its particular instances connects up with other primitive, too simple, ideas of the structure of language. It is comparable to the idea that *properties* are *ingredients* of the things which have the properties; *e.g.*, that beauty is an ingredient of all beautiful things as alcohol is of beer and wine, and that we therefore could have pure beauty, unadulterated by anything that is beautiful.

(*b*) There is a tendency rooted in our usual forms of expression, to think that the man who has learnt to understand a general term, say, the term "leaf," has thereby come to possess a kind of general picture of a leaf, as opposed to pictures of particular leaves. He was shown different leaves when he learnt the meaning of the word "leaf"; and showing him the particular leaves was only a means to the end of producing "in him" an idea which we imagine to be some kind of general image. We say that he sees what is in common to all these leaves; and this is true if we mean that he can on being asked tell us certain features or properties which they have in common. But we are inclined to think that the general idea of a leaf is something like a visual image, but one which only contains what is common to all leaves. (Galtonian composite photograph.) This again is connected with the idea that the meaning of a word is an image, or a thing correlated to the word. (This roughly means, we are looking at words as though they all were proper names, and we then confuse the bearer of a name with the meaning of the name.) (Pp. 17–18.)

In the *Philosophical Investigations* Wittgenstein again speaks of family resemblances, and gives a more elaborate account of the similarities and differences between various games:

66. Consider for example the proceedings that we call "games." I mean board-games, card-games, ball-games, Olympic games, and so on. What is common to them all?—Don't say: "There *must* be something common, or they would not be called 'games'"—but *look and see* whether there is anything common to all. —For if you look at them you will not see something that is common to *all*, but similarities, relationships, and a whole series of them at that. To repeat: don't think, but look!—Look for example at board-games, with their multifarious relationships. Now pass to card-games; here you find many correspondences with the first group, but many common features drop out, and others appear. When we pass next to ball-games, much that is common is retained, but much is lost.— Are they all "amusing"? Compare chess with noughts and crosses. Or is there always winning and losing, or competition between players? Think of patience. In ball-games there is winning and losing; but when a child throws his ball at the wall and catches it again, this feature has disappeared. Look at the parts played by skill and luck; and at the difference between skill in chess and skill in tennis. Think now of games like ring-a-ring-a-roses; here is the element of amusement, but how many other characteristic features have disappeared! And we can go through the many, many other groups of games in the same way; can see how similarities crop up and disappear.

And the result of this examination is: we see a complicated network of similarities overlapping and criss-crossing: sometimes overall similarities, sometimes similarities of detail.

67. I can think of no better expression to character-ise these similarities than "family resemblances"; for the various resemblances between the members of a family: build, features, colour of eyes, gait, temperament, etc. etc. overlap and criss-cross in the same way. —And I shall say: "games" form a family.

Wittgenstein expounds his analogy informally, and with great economy. Its power can be displayed in an equally simple but more formal way by considering a situation that is familiar to botanical taxonomists.[1] We may classify a set of objects by reference to the presence or absence of features ABCDE. It may well happen that five objects *edcba* are such that each of them has four of these properties and lacks the fifth, and that the missing feature is different in each of the five cases. A simple diagram will illustrate this situation:

e	*d*	*c*	*b*	*a*
ABCD	ABCE	ABDE	ACDE	BCDE

Here we can already see how natural and how proper it might be to apply the same word to a number of objects between which there is no common feature. And if we confine our attention to any arbitrarily selected four of these objects, say *edca*, then although they all *happen* to have B in common, it is clear that it is not in virtue of the presence of B that they are all rightly called by the same name. Even if the actual instances were indefinitely numerous, and they all happened to have one or more of the features in common, it would not be in virtue of the pres-

[1] I have profited from several discussions with Dr. S. M. Walters on taxonomy and the problem of universals. On the more general topics treated in this paper I have had several helpful discussions with Mr. R. A. Becher. Miss G. E. M. Anscombe kindly lent me the proofs of her essay on Aristotle, which appears in *Three Philosophers* by Miss Anscombe and Mr. P. T. Geach (Oxford, 1961).

ence of the common feature or features that they would
all be rightly called by the same name, since the name also
applies to *possible* instances that lack the feature or features.

The richness of the possibilities of the family resemblances model becomes more striking still if we set it out
more fully and formally in terms of a particular family
than Wittgenstein himself ever did. Let us suppose that
"the Churchill face" is strikingly and obviously present in
each of ten members of the Churchill family, and that
when a family group photograph is set before us it is unmistakable that these ten people all belong to the same
family. It may be that there are ten features in terms of
which we can describe "the family face" (high forehead,
bushy eyebrows, blue eyes, Roman nose, high cheekbones,
cleft chin, dark hair, dimpled cheeks, pointed ears and
ruddy complexion). It is obvious that the unmistakable
presence of the family face in every single one of the ten
members of the family is compatible with the absence
from each of the ten members of the family of one of the
ten constituent features of the family face. It is also obvious that it does not matter if it happens that the feature
which is absent from the face of each individual member
of the family is present in every one of the others. The
members of the family will then have no *feature* in common, and yet they will all unmistakably have *the Churchill face* in common.

This example is very artificial, and it may seem at first
sight that its artificiality plays into my hands. But on the
contrary, the more natural the example is made the more
it suits my purpose. If we remember that a family face
does not divide neatly into ten separate features, we
widen rather than reduce the scope for large numbers of
instances of the family face to lack a single common feature. And if we remember that what goes for faces goes
for features too; that all cleft chins have nothing in common except that they are cleft chins, that the possible
gradations from Roman nose to snub nose or from high

to low cheekbones are continuous and infinite, we see that there could in principle be an infinite number of unmistakable Churchill faces which had no feature in common. In fact it now becomes clear that there is a good sense in which *no two* members of the Churchill family need have *any* feature in common in order for *all* the members of the Churchill family to have the Churchill face.

The passages that I have quoted contain the essence of Wittgenstein's solution of the problem of universals, but they are far from exhausting his account of the topic. Not only are there other places where he speaks of games and of family resemblances: what is more important is that most of his philosophical remarks in *The Blue and Brown Books* and in the *Philosophical Investigations* are concerned with such questions as "What is the meaning of a word?" "What is language?" "What is thinking?" "What is understanding?" And these questions are various forms of the question to which theories of universals, including Wittgenstein's theory of universals, are meant to be answers. There is a clear parallel between what Wittgenstein says about games and what he says about reading, expecting, languages, numbers, propositions; in all these cases we have the idea that there is a common element or ingredient, and Wittgenstein shows us that there is no such ingredient or element. The instances that fall under each of these concepts *form a family*.

It is already clear that the point Wittgenstein made with the example of games has a much wider range of application than that example itself. But exactly how wide is its application meant to be? Wittgenstein's own method of exposition makes it difficult to answer this question. In his striving to find a cure for "our craving for generality," in his polemic against "the contemptuous attitude towards the particular case," he was understandably wary of expressing his own conclusions in general terms. Readers and expositors of Wittgenstein are consequently impelled to make use of glosses and paraphrases and interpretations if they wish to relate his work to philosophical writings and doctrines that are expressed in another idiom; that is to say, to most other philosophical writings and doctrines.

I believe that this is why Wittgenstein's solution of the problem of universals has not been widely understood, and why, in consequence, it has not been widely seen to be a solution.[2] In avoiding the generalities that are characteristic of most philosophical discussion he also avoided reference to the standard "problems of philosophy" and to the "philosophical theories" which have repeatedly been offered as answers to them. He talks about games and families and colours, about reading, expecting and understanding, but not about "the problem of universals." He practised an activity which is "one of the heirs of the subject which used to be called 'philosophy,'" but he did not relate the results of his activity to the results of the enquiries to which it was an heir. He did not, for example, plot the relation between his remarks on games and family resemblances and the doctrines of those philosophers who had been called Nominalists and Realists.

When I claim that Wittgenstein solved the problem of universals I am claiming that his remarks can be paraphrased into a doctrine which can be set out in general terms and can be related to the traditional theories, and which can then be shown to deserve to supersede the traditional theories. My purpose in this paper is to expound such a doctrine and to defend it.

But first I must return to my question about the range of application of the point that is made by the example of games, since it is at this crucial first stage that most readers of Wittgenstein go wrong. When we read what he says about games and family resemblances, we are naturally inclined to ask ourselves, "With what kinds of con-

[2] Of recent writings on this topic I believe that only Professor Wisdom's *Metaphysics and Verification* (reprinted in *Philosophy and Psycho-analysis*) and Mr. D. F. Pears' *Universals* (reprinted in Flew, *Logic and Language*, Second Series) show a complete understanding of the nature and importance of Wittgenstein's contribution.

cepts is Wittgenstein *contrasting* the concepts of game, language, proposition, understanding?" I shall consider three possible answers to this question.

The first answer is suggested by Professor Ayer's remarks about games and family resemblances on pp. 10–12 of *The Problem of Knowledge*. Ayer contrasts the word "game" with the word "red," on the ground that the former does not, while the latter does, mark "a simple and straightforward resemblance" between the things to which the word is applied. He claims that, "The point which Wittgenstein's argument brings out is that the resemblance between the things to which the same word applies may be of different degrees. It is looser and less straightforward in some cases than in others." Now this contrast between simple and complicated concepts is important, and the games example is a convenient means of drawing attention to it, but I am sure that this is not the point that Wittgenstein was making with his example. In the *Brown Book* (p. 131) he asks, "Could you tell me what is in common between a light red and a dark red?" and in the *Philosophical Investigations* (Section 73) he asks, "Which shade is the 'sample in my mind' of the colour green—the sample of what is common to all shades of green?" Wittgenstein could as easily have used the example of red things as the example of games to illustrate "the tendency to look for something in common to all the entities which we commonly subsume under a general term." Just as cricket and chess and patience and ring-a-ring-a-roses have nothing in common *except that they are games*, so poppies and blood and pillar-boxes and hunting-coats have nothing in common *except that they are red*.

A second possible answer is implied by a sentence in Mr. P. F. Strawson's *Individuals*: "It is often admitted, in the analytical treatment of some fairly specific concept, that the wish to understand is less likely to be served by the search for a single strict statement of the necessary and sufficient conditions of its application than by seeing its applications—in Wittgenstein's simile—as forming a family, the members of which may, perhaps, be grouped around a central paradigm case and linked with the latter by various direct or indirect links of logical connexion and analogy" (p. 11). The contrast is not now between simple and complex concepts, but between two kinds of complex concepts: those which are definable by the statement of necessary and sufficient conditions and those which are not. But once again the contrast, although it is important, and is one which the family resemblances simile and the example of games are well able to draw, is not the point that Wittgenstein is concerned with. In the sense in which, according to Wittgenstein, games have nothing in common except that they are games, and red things have nothing in common except that they are red, *brothers have nothing in common except that they are brothers*. It is true that brothers have in common that they are male siblings, but their having in common that they are male siblings is their having in common that they are *brothers*, and not their having in common something in addition to their being brothers. Even a concept which can be explained in terms of necessary and sufficient conditions cannot be *ultimately* explained in such terms. To satisfy the craving for an ultimate explanation of "brother" in such terms it would be necessary to define "male" and "sibling," and the words in which "male" and "sibling" were defined, and so on *ad infinitum* and *ad impossibile*.

What then *is* the contrast that Wittgenstein meant to draw? I suggest that he did not mean to draw a *contrast* at all. Professor Wisdom has remarked that the peculiar difficulty of giving a philosophical account of universals lies in this: that philosophers are usually engaged in implicitly or explicitly comparing and contrasting one type of proposition with another type of proposition (propositions about minds with propositions about bodies, propositions of logic with propositions about matters of fact, propositions about the present and the past with propositions about the future, etc.) whereas propositions involving universals cannot be compared or contrasted with propositions that do not involve universals, since *all* propositions involve universals.[3] If we look at Wittgenstein's doctrine in the light of this remark we can understand it aright and can also see why it has been misunderstood in just those ways that I have mentioned. It is because of the very power of the ways of thought against which Wittgenstein was protesting that philosophers are led to offer accounts of his doctrine which restrict the range of its application. They recognise the importance of Wittgenstein's demonstration that *at least some* general terms can justifiably be applied to their instances although those instances have nothing in common. But they are so deeply attached to the idea that there must be something in common to the instances that fall under a general term that they treat Wittgenstein's examples as special cases, as rogues and vagabonds in the realm of concepts, to be contrasted with the general run of law-abiding concepts which *do* mark the presence of common elements in their instances.

Here we come across an ambiguity which is another obstacle to our getting a clear view of the problem of universals and of Wittgenstein's solution of it. Ayer remarks, in the passage to which I have already referred, that, "It is correct, though not at all enlightening, to say that what games have in common is their being games." It is certainly correct, but I strongly deny that it is unenlightening. It is of course trivially and platitudinously true, but trivialities and platitudes deserve emphatic affirmation when, as often in philosophy, they are explicitly or implicitly denied, or forgotten, or overlooked. Now the platitude that all games have in common that they *are* games is denied by the nominalist, who says that all games have nothing in common except that they are *called* games. And it is not only the nominalist, but also his opponent, who misunderstands the central importance of the platitude that all games have

[3] Professor Wisdom has pointed out to me that further discussion would be necessary to show that claims of the form "This is Jack" are not exceptions to this rule.

in common that they are games. When he is provoked by
the nominalist's claim that all games have nothing in
common except that they are called games, and rightly
wishes to insist that games have something more in common than simply that they are called games, he feels that
he must look for something that games have in common
apart from *being* games. This feeling is entirely misplaced.
The very terms of the nominalist's challenge require only
that the realist should point out something that games
have in common apart from *being called* games, and this
onus is fully discharged by saying that they *are* games.

Although the feeling is misplaced, it is a very natural
feeling, as we can see by considering the kinds of case in
which we most typically and ordinarily ask what is in common to a set of objects. If I ask you what these three books
have in common, or what those four chairs have in common, you will look to see if the books are all on the same
subject or by the same author or published by the same
firm; to see if the chairs are all Chippendale or all three-
legged or all marked "Not to be removed from this room."
It will never occur to you to say that the books have in
common that they are books or the chairs that they are
chairs. And if you find after close inspection that the
chairs or the books do not have in common any of the
features I have mentioned, and if you cannot see any
other specific feature that they have in common, you will
say that as far as you can see they have nothing in common.
You will perhaps add that you suppose from the form of
my question that I must know of something that they have
in common. I may then tell you that all the books once
belonged to John Locke or that all the chairs came from
Ten Rillington Place. But it would be a poor sort of joke
for me to say that the chairs were all chairs or that the
books were all books.

If I ask you what *all* chairs have in common, or what *all*
books have in common, you may again try to find a feature
like those you would look for in the case of *these three*
books or *those four* chairs; and you may again think that

it is a poor sort of joke for me to say that what all books have in common is that they are books and that what all chairs have in common is that they are chairs. And yet this time it is not a joke but an important philosophical truth.

Because the normal case where we ask "What have all *these* chairs, books or games in common?" is one in which we are not concerned with their all being chairs, books or games, we are liable to overlook the extreme peculiarity of the *philosophical* question that is asked with the words "What do *all* chairs, *all* books, *all* games have in common?" For of course games *do* have something in common. They *must* have something in common, and yet when we look for what they have in common we cannot find it. When we try to say what they have in common we always fail. And this is not because what we are looking for lies deeply hidden, but because it is too obvious to be seen; not because what we are trying to say is too subtle and complicated to be said, but because it is too easy and too simple to be worth saying: and so we say something more dramatic, but something false, instead. The simple truth is that what games have in common is that they are games. The nominalist is obscurely aware of this, and by rejecting the realist's talk of transcendent, immanent or subsistent forms or universals he shows his awareness. But by his own insistence that games have nothing in common except that they are called games he shows the obscurity of his awareness. The realist too is obscurely aware of it. By his talk of transcendent, immanent or subsistent forms or universals he shows the obscurity of his awareness. But by his hostility to the nominalist's insistence that games have nothing in common except that they are called games he shows his awareness.

All this can be more fully explained by the application of what I will call "Ramsey's Maxim." F. P. Ramsey, after mapping the course of an inconclusive dispute between Russell and W. E. Johnson, writes as follows:

Evidently, however, none of these arguments are really decisive, and the position is extremely unsatisfactory to any one with real curiosity about such a fundamental question. In such cases it is a heuristic maxim that the truth lies not in one of the two disputed views but in some third possibility which has not yet been thought of, which we can only discover by rejecting something assumed as obvious by both the disputants. (*The Foundations of Mathematics*, pp. 115–116.)

It is assumed as obvious by both the nominalist and the realist that there can be no objective justification for the application of a general term to its instances unless its instances have something in common over and above their having in common that they *are* its instances. The nominalist rightly holds that there is no such additional common element, and he therefore wrongly concludes that there is no objective justification for the application of any general term. The realist rightly holds that there is an objective justification for the application of general terms, and he therefore wrongly concludes that there *must* be some additional common element.

Wittgenstein denied the assumption that is common to nominalism and realism, and that is why I say that he solved the problem of universals. For if we deny the mistaken premiss that is common to the realist's argument and the nominalist's argument then we can deny the realist's mistaken conclusion and deny the nominalist's mistaken conclusion; and that is another way of saying that we can affirm the true premiss of the nominalist's argument and can also affirm the true premiss of the realist's argument.

The nominalist says that games have nothing in common except that they are called games.

The realist says that games must have something in common, and he means by this that they must have something in common other than that they are games.

Wittgenstein says that games have nothing in common except that they are games.

Wittgenstein thus denies at one and the same time the nominalist's claim that games have nothing in common except that they are called games and the realist's claim that games have something in common other than that they are games. He asserts at one and the same time the realist's claim that there is an objective justification for the application of the word "game" to games and the nominalist's claim that there is no element that is common to all games. And he is able to do all this because he denies the joint claim of the nominalist and the realist that there cannot be an objective justification for the application of the word "game" to games unless there is an element that is common to all games (*universalia in rebus*) or a common relation that all games bear to something that is not a game (*universalia ante res*).

Wittgenstein is easily confused with the nominalist because he denies what the realist asserts: that games have something in common other than that they are games.

When we see that Wittgenstein is not a nominalist we may easily confuse him with the realist because he denies what the nominalist asserts: that games have nothing in common except that they are called games.

But we can now see that Wittgenstein is neither a realist nor a nominalist: he asserts the simple truth that they both deny and he also asserts the two simple truths of which each of them asserts one and denies the other.

I will now try to put some flesh on to these bare bones.

The value and the limitations of the nominalist's claim that things which are called by the same name have nothing in common except that they are called by the same name can be seen if we look at a case where a set of objects literally and undeniably have nothing in common except that they are called by the same name. If I choose to give the name "alpha" to each of a number of miscellaneous objects (the star Sirius, my fountain-pen, the Parthenon, the colour red, the number five, and the letter Z) then I may well succeed in choosing the objects so *arbitrarily* that I shall succeed in preventing them from having any feature in common, other than that I call them by the name "alpha." But this imaginary case, to which the nominalist likens the use of all general words, has only to be described to be sharply contrasted with the typical case in which I apply a general word, say "chair," to a number of the instances to which it applies. In the first place, the *arbitrariness* of my selection of alphas is not paralleled in the case in which I apply the word "chair" successively to the chair in which I am now sitting, the Speaker's Chair in the House of Commons, the chair used at Bisley for carrying the winner of the Queen's Prize, and one of the deck chairs on the beach at Brighton. In giving a list of chairs I cannot just mention anything that happens to come into my head, while this is exactly what I do in giving my list of alphas. The second point is that the class of alphas is a *closed* class. Once I have given my list I have referred to every single alpha in the universe, actual and possible. Although I *might* have included or excluded any actual or possible object whatsoever when I was drawing up my list, once I have in fact made my arbitrary choice, no further application can be given to the word "alpha" according to the use that I have prescribed. For if I later add an object that I excluded from my list, or remove an object that I included in it, then I am making a different use of the word "alpha." With the word "chair" the position is quite different. There are an infinite number of actual and possible chairs. I cannot aspire to complete the enumeration of all chairs, as I can arbitrarily and at any point complete the enumeration of all alphas, and the word "chair," unlike the word "alpha," can be applied to an infinite number of instances without suffering any change of use.

These two points lead to a third and decisive point. I cannot teach the use of the word "alpha" except by specifically attaching it to each of the objects in my arbitrarily chosen list. No observer can conclude anything from watching me attach the label to this, that, or the other object, or to any number of objects however large, about the nature of the object or objects, if any, to which I shall later attach it. The use of the word "alpha" cannot be learned or taught as the use of a general word can be learned or taught. In teaching the use of a general word we may and must refer to characteristics of the objects to which it applies, and of the objects to which it does not apply, and indicate which of these characteristics count for the application of the word and which count against it. A pupil does not have to consult us on every separate occasion on which he encounters a new object, and if he did consult us every time we should have to say that he was not *learning* the use of the word. The reference that we make to a finite number of objects to which the word applies, and to a finite number of objects to which the word does not apply, is capable of equipping the pupil with a capacity for correctly applying or withholding the word to or from an infinite number of objects to which we have made no reference.

All this remains true in the case where it is not I alone, but a large number of people, or all of us, who use the word "alpha" in the way that I suggest. Even if everybody always called a particular set of objects by the same name, that would be insufficient to ensure that the name was a general name, and the claim of the name to be a general name would be defeated by just that necessity for reference to the arbitrary choices of the users of the name that the nominalist mistakenly claims to find in the case of a genuinely general name. For the nominalist is right in thinking that if we always had to make such a reference then there would be no general names as they are understood by the realist.

The nominalist is also right in the stress that he puts on the rôle of human interests and human purposes in determining our choice of principles of classification. How this insistence on the rôle of human purposes may be reconciled with the realist's proper insistence on the objectivity of the similarities and dissimilarities on which any genuine classification is based can be seen by considering an imaginary tribe of South Sea Islanders.

Let us suppose that trees are of great importance in the life and work of the South Sea Islanders, and that they have a rich and highly developed language in which they speak of the trees with which their island is thickly clad. But they do not have names for the species and genera of trees as they are recognised by our botanists. As we walk round the island with some of its inhabitants we can easily pick out orange-trees, date-palms and cedars. Our hosts are puzzled that we should call by the same name trees which appear to them to have nothing in common. They in turn surprise us by giving the same name to each of the trees in what is from our point of view a very mixed plantation. They point out to us what they called a mixed plantation, and we see that it is in our terms a clump of trees of the same species. Each party comes to recognise that its own classifications are as puzzling to the other as the other's are puzzling to itself.

This looks like the sort of situation that gives aid and comfort to the nominalist in his battle against the realist. But if we look at it more closely we see that it cannot help him. We know already that our own classification is based on similarities and differences between the trees, similarities and differences which we can point out to the islanders in an attempt to teach them our language. Of course we may fail, but if we do it will not be because we *must* fail.

Now *either* (*a*) The islanders have means of teaching us their classifications, by pointing out similarities and differences which we had not noticed, or in which we had not been interested, in which case *both* classifications are genuine, and no rivalry between them, of a kind that can help the nominalist, could ever arise;

or (*b*) Their classification is arbitrary in the sense in which my use of the word "alpha" was arbitrary, in which case it is not a genuine classification.

It may be that the islanders classify trees as "boatbuilding trees," "house-building trees," etc., and that they are more concerned with the height, thickness and maturity of the trees than they are with the distinctions of species that interest us.

In a particular case of *prima facie* conflict of classifications, we may not in fact be able to discover whether what appears to be a rival classification really *is* a classification. But we can be sure that *if* it is a classification *then* it is backed by objective similarities and differences, and that if it is *not* backed by objective similarities and differences then it is merely an arbitrary system of names. In no case will it appear that we must choose between rival systems of genuine classification of a set of objects in such a sense that one of them is to be recognised as *the* classification for all purposes.

There is no limit to the number of possible classifications of objects. (The nominalist is right about this.)[4]

There is no classification of any set of objects which is not objectively based on genuine similarities and differences. (The realist is right about this.)

The nominalist is so impressed by the infinite diversity of possible classifications that he is blinded to their objectivity.

The realist is so impressed by the objectivity of all genuine classifications that he underestimates their diversity.

Of course we may if we like say that there is one complete system of classification which marks all the similarities and all the differences. (This is the realist's summing up of what we can learn by giving critical attention to the realist and the nominalist in turn.)

Or we may say that there are only similarities and differences, from which we may choose according to our pur-

[4] Here one may think of Wittgenstein's remark that "Every application of every word is arbitrary," which emphasises that we can always find *some* distinction between any pair of objects, however closely similar they may be. What might be called the principle of the diversity of discernibles guarantees that we can never be *forced* to apply the same word to two different things.

poses and interests. (This is the nominalist's summing up.)

In talking of genuine or objective similarities and differences we must not forget that we are concerned with similarities and differences between *possible* cases as well as between actual cases, and indeed that we are concerned with the actual cases only because they are themselves a selection of the possible cases.

Because the nominalist and the realist are both right and both wrong, each is driven into the other's arms when he tries to be both consistent and faithful to our language, knowledge and experience. The nominalist talks of resemblances until he is pressed into a corner where he must acknowledge that resemblance is unintelligible except as resemblance *in a respect*, and to specify the respect in which objects resemble one another is to indicate a *quality* or *property*. The realist talks of properties and qualities until, when properties and qualities have been explained in terms of other properties and other qualities, he can at last do nothing but point to the *resemblances* between the objects that are said to be characterised by such and such a property or quality.

The question "Are resemblances ultimate or are properties ultimate?" is a perverse question if it is meant as one to which there must be a simple, *single* answer. They are both ultimate, or neither is ultimate. The craving for a single answer is the logically unsatisfiable craving for something that will be the ultimate terminus of explanation and will yet itself be explained.

COMMON NAMES AND
"FAMILY RESEMBLANCES"

HAIG KHATCHADOURIAN

I

In this paper we propose to give, first, a brief analysis of Wittgenstein's notion of "family resemblances." Next we shall try to show that whether or not "family resemblances" constitute a general feature of ordinary language so far as common names are concerned, there are at least some common names such that the things named by them do have one or more features in common, though this feature or these features are not a determinate or relatively determinate *quality* or *characteristic*. Further, we shall argue that this common "feature" or these common "features," in each case, is or are what determine (at least in part) the applicability or uses of the common name concerned, as is shown by an examination of the way in which the latter is used in ordinary discourse. We shall next show how "family resemblances" themselves, where they obtain in the kinds of thing we are concerned with, can be accounted for in terms of our results. Finally, we shall apply our results to the terms 'good' and 'poor' or 'not good' in one sense of these terms, as used in ordinary language.

Briefly, Wittgenstein's notion of "family resemblances" is that the traditional view that in every case where things are called by the same name (when the name is used in

From *Philosophy and Phenomenological Research*, Vol. XVIII (1957–58), pp. 341–358. Reprinted with the permission of the author and editor.

the same "sense") there is a quality or a set of qualities
which is common to them all, by virtue of which they are
all called by that name, is mistaken. Instead of such a
common quality or a set of these, examination reveals complex patterns of resemblance different in different cases.
Thus, in speaking of "language games," Wittgenstein says:

> Instead of producing something common to all that
> we call language, I am saying that these phenomena
> have no one thing in common which makes us use the
> same word for all,—but that they are *related* to one
> another in many different ways. And it is because of
> this relationship, or these relationships, that we call
> them all "languages."[1]

This is illustrated, for instance, by what we call "games":

> If you look at them you will not see something that
> is common to *all*, but similarities, relationships, and
> a whole series of them at that. . . . Look for example
> at board-games, with their multifarious relationships.
> Now pass to card-games; here you find many corre-
> spondences with the first group, but many common
> features drop out, and others appear. When we pass
> next to ball-games, much that is common is retained,
> but much is lost. . . . (pp. 31e–32e)

Instead of finding characteristics common to all games,
"we see a complicated network of similarities overlapping
and criss-crossing: sometimes over-all similarities, sometimes similarities of detail" (p. 32e). These similarities
Wittgenstein calls "family resemblances" because "the
various resemblances between members of a family: build,
features, colour of eyes, gait, temperament, etc. etc. overlap
and criss-cross in the same way" (p. 32e). The situation
involved is like that of a thread in which different fibres
overlap but none runs through the whole length of the
thread. "And the strength of the thread does not reside in

[1] *Philosophical Investigations*, translated by G. E. M.
Anscombe, (Oxford, 1953), p. 31e.

the fact that some one fibre runs through its whole length, but in the overlapping of many fibres" (p. 32e).

It seems clear that the "features" which Wittgenstein has in mind in speaking of "family resemblances" are determinate or relatively determinate characteristics (or relations, or both), and not merely kinds of characteristic or determinables (or kinds of relation, or both). For we can imagine a "family" in which *all* the members have a determinable or a set of determinables but not any determinate or relatively determinate characteristics, in common. All the members of a human family have eyes, ears, a nose, limbs, etc. in common; but we would not (nor would Wittgenstein) say that these members have certain "family resemblances" by virtue of possessing eyes, ears, a nose, etc. For the determinables these members have in common are shared by most if not all human beings. Rather, what Wittgenstein seems to have in mind is a "family" in which some members have either (1) one or more determinate characteristics in common (say hazel eyes), or (2) relatively determinate characteristics in common (say brown eyes of different shades), and each of these members has one or more *different* determinate, or relatively determinate characteristics in common with some (at least one) or all of the other members. So that some members are directly related by qualitative resemblances to other members, while some or all are also indirectly related to other members through their direct relations to members themselves directly related to the latter.

But how determinate should a characteristic shared by *all* members of a "family" be in order that it may be said to be "something in common" to all the members? For determinateness is a matter of degrees, and is relative: what is a determinate characteristic relatively to a given characteristic may be a determinable relatively to another characteristic. If Wittgenstein is merely repudiating the view that all things called by the same name (in the same "sense") have a qualitatively *identical* "determinate" char-

acteristic (or a set of these), then traditional essentialism
will not be completely overthrown; since on the latter view
relatively determinate characteristics which are not qualitatively identical *are* counted as the "same." It is obvious
that it makes all the difference where we draw the line
between qualitative "sameness" and mere qualitative "resemblance." If anything short of qualitative identity is rejected as a common quality, even two copies of the same
book, or two dimes, may only have certain "resemblances"
but no quality "in common." On the other hand, if the
distinction is drawn higher up, so to speak, in the
determinate-determinable scale, then the members of the
family, all of whom have brown eyes of different shades,
will have a common quality and not a "resemblance" in
color of eyes. That Wittgenstein himself does not intend
to draw the distinction too finely or too stringently is seen
by considering his analysis of "games." There he seems to
consider games which are amusing as having a common
feature; similarly with games which involve competition, or
winning and losing; and so on. Yet "amusiveness," for instance, may be of different kinds. Nevertheless, the difficulty seems to remain: for on what logical basis or bases
(whether the same or different ones in different cases)
would Wittgenstein draw the line in a given case, and in
different given cases, between qualitative "resemblance"
and qualitative "identity"?

There is another point to note before we proceed further. This is that in talking about "family resemblances,"
Wittgenstein is concerned with things which are called by
the same name in one and the same sense, and not in
different (literal) senses. Obviously, if what Wittgenstein
is maintaining is simply that things which are called by
the same name, but in different senses, or with different
meanings, have only "family resemblances" of one sort or
another and not any common determinate or relatively
determinate characteristics, his view would be of relatively
little significance. For hardly anybody would hold the contrary, in the case of at least the majority of common names

which have two or more (literal) senses, or meanings. (However, the transition from one sense, or one meaning, of a term to another is subtle and not sharply defined in many cases, and it is no easy matter always to decide where the one sense, or meaning, ends and the other begins, assuming that this way of speaking is itself legitimate.)

We shall now analyze the uses or meaning of the name 'games,' in some detail, as a paradigm for the view we shall argue for; and then apply our results to one class of objects, namely manufactured—in general, man-made—objects.[2]

Wittgenstein seems to me to be quite right in holding that there are no determinate or relatively determinate *characteristics* common to all things called "games." All the games that we have, and all phenomena that we would normally call "games," are played in accordance with certain kinds of rule; so that there is a universal common to them all; but the rules involved differ as we pass from board games to ball games to card games, etc., and from one board game to another, from one ball game to another;[3] and so on. Still, there *is* a more determinate feature common to all kinds of game: namely, the capacity to serve a specific human need or needs, directly or indirectly, under what we shall call "standard" (causal) conditions or in "normal" contexts. The term 'need' is used here in a wide sense, to include emotional, intellectual, aesthetic, "practical," as well as physical and biological needs. Instead of speaking of the "capacity to serve a human need," we might speak of the "capacity to further human ends," or the "capacity to produce certain effects in other things, which, directly or indirectly, serve or can serve human

[2] Whether our results apply to natural objects and to psychological phenomena in general we shall not inquire in this paper.

[3] Cf. what Wittgenstein says about skill and luck in games. "Look at the parts played by skill and luck; and at the *difference* between skill in chess and skill in tennis." (p. 32e.) (Italics mine.)

ends." Or we might speak of the phenomena or things whose "capacities" we are talking about as having or as capable of having a specific use or uses for human beings under specified conditions. In the case of "games," this "capacity" is the capacity to evoke or produce pleasure in the player or players and/or the spectators. That this is implicit in some way to be determined later in the meaning or uses of the name 'game' can be seen in a general way by considering some remarks we ordinarily make in connection with "games"; e.g. "What sort of game is this?— it's boring!"; "He always gets angry while playing—and spoils the game"; "This is certainly a queer kind of game: I don't see what pleasure you (or the players, or the spectators) get out of it!"; "You call this a game? Well, you may call it that if you like, but it's certainly a poor game: it's positively irritating!" Also, we do not normally say: "This is a pleasant game" (though we quite frequently say: "This is a *very* pleasant game"), except perhaps to mean that *I* liked it, or that *I* find it pleasant. "This is a most unpleasant game" is possible though unusual, and makes one think of games which some would find coarse or vulgar (morally speaking) because it involves, say risqué utterances, or actions ordinarily regarded as indecent. In the last case we tend to think that the term 'game' applies only in a loose or extended or peculiar sense, or that the person making the statement is prudish, that he is judging the game in terms of extrinsic criteria, that he is approaching it in the "wrong spirit." "I found this a most unpleasant game" would, however, not be puzzling. But "This is a painful game," seems to be almost a contradiction in terms in "standard" contexts. It raises questions in the hearer's mind, and requires explanation. (It will be explained, however, if the game referred to is bear-baiting, say, and the speaker is thinking of the bear's suffering, or of the pain he feels for the bear's suffering, or of both.) If someone says: "This game made me angry," we think: "He (or his favorite team, or player) lost, that's why"; or that he did not play as well as he knew he could, so he felt frustrated. If a person does not enjoy a game, and we regard the conditions as "standard" conditions so far as the majority of spectators and/or players are concerned, we will think: He's not "in" it; he hasn't caught the "spirit" of the game; he doesn't have the "right" spirit; his mind is wandering; he is preoccupied; he is tired; he has a headache; and so on.

In order to understand these remarks in the light of what we said about "games," we have to consider our crucial qualification that what we call "games" have a common capacity to produce pleasure under *standard conditions* or in *normal contexts*. What we ordinarily call "games" certainly do not actually produce pleasure under just any and all conditions, in all contexts. It is only when certain conditions obtain that a "game" *actually* produces pleasures. This is why we said that "games" have the "capacity" to produce pleasure under "standard" conditions. The word "capacity" is meant to indicate that if certain conditions obtain, pleasure will[4] be produced. To put the matter without using the misleading word 'capacity,' what we are saying is that "games," under certain conditions, produce (either physically or psychologically, or both: in general, causally) by virtue of whatever characteristics they possess, what we call "pleasure" in the player or players, etc. The word 'capacity' is not meant to stand for a

---

[4] The statement: "If standard conditions obtain, pleasure will be produced by a game" is meant to be, and is, an analytic statement; and not either an *a priori* synthetic judgment, or an empirical generalization. For our contention is that the notion of "standard" conditions here is built into the meaning of the word 'game' in such a way as to make the above statement analytic. The essential point here is that we are not arbitrarily introducing the notion of "standard" conditions in order to guarantee the truth of the statement. Our contention is that if we analyze the uses of the term 'game,' we *discover* this notion of "standard" conditions implicit in it. That this is so is, however, an empirical assertion about the uses or meaning of 'game.' Similarly with the other common names which we shall discuss later on. (But see above for the distinction and difference between two kinds of "standard" condition which are used indiscriminately here.)

mysterious power or property, over and above the ordinary
characteristics of a game. If we were not unwilling to com-
plicate matters by using controversial notions, we would
say that games have a certain "dispositional property," or
a set of these—the property or properties of producing
pleasure.

In making the statement "This is a good game, but I
don't enjoy it," the speaker tacitly recognizes or implies
that although he is not being affected in the way which is
normal in those cases in which he would, without hesitation, call a given phenomenon a "good game," the absence
of this element in this case is not a sufficient ground for
not calling the phenomenon concerned a "good game." In
saying that it is a game or a good game, he concedes that
it can give, and perhaps is actually giving, others, some, or
even a good deal of, pleasure; and also, he implies that his
failure to have pleasure is not due to the "game" itself,
but to his mood, state of mind, etc. at the time. Thus if
somebody asked our friend: "Why do you say so?," on
hearing him make the above statement, the answer generally given will be something like: "O, I'm not in the
mood to-day"; or, "I have a toothache"; "I'm worried about
my affairs"; and the like. That is, the speaker implies that
so far as he is concerned, the conditions are not normal
or standard conditions.

But now a doubt arises: is the pleasure produced by
different games, or by different kinds of game, of the same
kind in every case? Are not the pleasures produced related
merely by certain "family resemblances," at least in the
case of the pleasure produced by games of different
"kinds"? If the answer is in the affirmative—and Wittgenstein would say that it is in the affirmative—then obviously
Wittgenstein's analysis of games would be completely true,
though here it would be the effects of games that are related by "family resemblances," rather than, or as well as,
their characteristics themselves.[5] Now it is certainly true

[5] Wittgenstein himself sometimes thinks of the characteristics,
sometimes of the effects produced, in speaking of "family re-

that different kinds of pleasure may be involved in the case of different kinds of game: some kinds, like ball games, involve or may involve both physical and psychological pleasure (a feeling of well-being, enjoyment, etc.), while others, like card games and board games, normally involve only the latter kind of pleasure. But though only some kinds of game produce or can produce physical pleasure, it seems that all games produce or can produce psychological pleasure—though the amount and intensity of pleasure produced may differ with different kinds of game, with different games of the same kind, and with different matches of the same game, depending on the context. But are all these psychological pleasures of the same kind in all cases? No, again. The nature of the specific game determines in good measure the kind of psychological pleasure derived. In chess, the pleasure is said to be "intellectual," while in the case of card games it may be "intellectual" pleasure mixed with "feeling," depending on the context. That is, psychological pleasure may be divided into subclasses, which are themselves further divisible. Nonetheless, it seems to me (though it is not possible to defend this here), that the classification into "intellectual" and "non-intellectual" (emotional) pleasure more concerns the way in which the pleasure is produced and its general intensity than marks a distinction in the kind of experience involved. Whereas, a difference in kind of experience *is* involved in the case of the distinction between psychological and physical pleasure, in addition to a difference in the kind of way they are produced in us. Thus a *relatively* determinate kind of effect seems to be produced by all kinds of games.[6] And so far as this relatively determinate

---

semblances." For instance, he asks whether all games are amusing (effects), whether they always involve winning and losing, or competition between the players, or skill, or luck (the characteristics of the games themselves). (Cf. p. 32e.)

[6] It is noteworthy that many of the phenomena Wittgenstein analyses are complex "psychological" processes, such as thinking, doubting, learning; and it may well be that there *only* "family resemblances" can be discovered. But supposing that to be true,

kind of effect is produced by all games, it seems to follow
that there is some kind of "capacity" in the games themselves, which is (at least) similar in the case of all games;
though there need not be (and we are not maintaining
that there is) any determinate or relatively determinate
characteristic or characteristics common to all games, by
virtue of which this kind of effect is produced.

What we have said applies, *mutatis mutandis*, to all
other man-devised activities, to man-devised processes, and
to man-made objects, like cooking, writing, furniture, instruments, tools, machines. That is, in the case of all activities, processes, or objects of this sort which are called
by the same name (in the same literal sense), we find a
common capacity or common capacities to serve, directly
or indirectly, some human need or some human purpose,
the capacity or capacities for being used in the same kind
of way. To put the matter abstractly and generally, suppose we take a number of such activities, processes, or objects, *a, b, c, d, e, f . . . . n*, which we ordinarily call "X."
If we analyze *a, b, c, d, e, f . . . . n*, we find that under
certain kinds of condition they possess a common capacity
or a set of common capacities (Ca) to serve some purpose
or set of purposes (P), to satisfy some need or needs (N),
directly or indirectly—in general, that they possess the capacity for being used in a common kind of way (U). What
is more, and this is the central point here, if we examine
the way 'X' is used in ordinary discourse—the situations
in which we ordinarily apply it and the situations in which
we ordinarily refrain from applying it—we find that the
conditions under which 'X' is applied are *roughly* (see p.
11 ff.) those conditions under which *a, b, c, d, e, f . . . .
n*, are capable of serving P, of satisfying N, of having U.
That is, we find that the notion of a common capacity Ca,

---

and even if in the case of games themselves, only "family resemblances" are discoverable in their effects, our position seems
to remain secure as far as the names of manufactured objects are
concerned—and also of activities which do not appreciably include psychological elements in their effects.

or alternatively, of a common use U, is implicit in the meaning or uses of 'X' in ordinary discourse. It is true that activities, processes, or objects called by *different* names may satisfy the same (kind of) need, may have the capacity of being used in the same (kind of) way; also, that activities, processes, and objects which are called by the same common name can be used in different ways. We can use a table as well as a chair for sitting, and we can use a chair as well as table for eating or writing. But sitting on tables is not ordinarily regarded as the normal or proper way of using tables, nor eating off a chair or writing on it as the normal or proper way of using chairs. (I am not using 'proper' in the sense in which it is used in books on etiquette.) The satisfaction of a certain specific need or a set of needs, the capacity of being used in a specific way, is associated with one "kind" of object, activity, or process (objects, activities, or processes called by the same name), and another or other specific needs, another or other uses, are associated with another "kind" of object, activity, or process, in the way we speak about these objects, activities, or processes. The reason is simple: it is we, the makers of tables and chairs, who design them in such a way that it becomes possible for them to satisfy the need, or to have the use in view, more efficiently or better than another or other needs or uses. This, as we said, is reflected in ordinary language: the notion of some proper function or use or another (or of the capacity to satisfy a given need) is implicit in the meaning of the common names— of the particular sort we are talking about—which we give to things. It is no accident that the names of manufactured objects (as also the names of man-devised activities, or processes) implicitly involve in their meaning the notion of a capacity to satisfy a specific need or specific needs, to have a given use or uses. "Separate seat for one," a common definition of 'chair,' illustrates this clearly.[7] In many cases, however, dictionaries give a description of the char-

---

[7] Cf. Max Black, *Language and Philosophy*, (Ithaca, New York, 1949), pp. 30–31.

acteristics which the things called by the given name were
endowed with by their inventors or original makers (hence,
when the particular name was first given to them), and/or
those characteristics which they most frequently possess,
in addition to mentioning a specific use or specific uses.
(Cf. for example the definitions of 'pen' and 'table' in *The
Concise Oxford Dictionary*.) Further, as in the case of
"games," it is seen that no single determinate or relatively
determinate *characteristic*, or set of characteristics, common to all things ordinarily called "chairs," is discoverable.
The same is true of things called "tables," "pens," and so
on. An object may be made of chromium or of plastic, may
be high or low, soft or hard, round or square or polygonal,
straight or curved: and yet will not, for that reason, be
refused the name 'chair'—so long as it can serve[8] as a
"separate seat for one"; i.e., so long as the variation in
these and other characteristics does not grossly impede or
make impossible the object's possession of the requisite
capacity. If an object is made of jelly, it cannot serve as a
chair; and we do not apply 'chair' to it in a straightforward
sense, even if it has the form of one kind of chair or another. Similarly chair-like objects only a few inches wide
and high may be called "toy chairs," but not "chairs" without qualification. They may be called "toy *chairs*" because
(1) they have the over-all form of one kind of chair or
another, and (2) they can serve to seat tiny "toy men"
and "toy women" ('toy man' and 'toy woman' being defined in the same way as 'toy chair'), or little imaginary
creatures. How much variation in form and material is
compatible with the requisite capacity, depends on the nature and range of the corresponding "standard" (causal)
conditions, and on the nature and number of the needs
the thing is intended to satisfy. In general, the more specialized and the more complex the need, the smaller the
range of variation possible; the less specialized and the less

[8] For the precise meaning of 'can' here, and for a discussion of
an important qualification of the above, see above and footnote
12.

complex the need, the greater the range of variation possible. Similarly, the range of variation is inversely proportional, roughly speaking, to the number of needs meant to be satisfied. The form of chairs designed merely with "utility" in view admits of considerably greater variation than that of chairs designed with an eye to beauty as well as to "utility"; and chairs designed only with an eye to beauty (a mere hypothetical example, however!) admit of greater variation in material than chairs designed with an eye to both beauty and "utility."

From all this we see why no determinate or relatively determinate characteristic or characteristics need run through all things called by the same name for that name to be applicable to them. Hence it is not surprising, if one fixes his attention on the *determinate* or *relatively determinate* characteristics of things, that he tends to conclude that things called by the same name have no determinate "feature" or "features" in common; or that, at most, they have certain "family resemblances." It is especially easy to fall into this line of thought since we become aware or fully aware that a common capacity is or may be involved only by considering the characteristics of a thing from a *very* general standpoint (i.e., by looking at them as general *kinds* of characteristic or as determinables), or by considering a thing in the light of the way we talk about it in actual contexts, under both "standard" and "non-standard" (causal) conditions. For as we have said, things which do satisfy a common need, or have a common use, in certain kinds of situation, may not be capable of satisfying the need or of having that use in other kinds of situation.

II

The preceding—and especially the fact that the possible range of variation in the characteristics of a thing is, roughly speaking, inversely proportional to the complexity and specialization, among other things, of the uses it is ordinarily put to, the ends it serves—gives us one explanation of why we do find "family resemblances" between things called by the same name—the feature on which Wittgenstein fixes his attention. The clearest way to show this is by considering things like chairs, tables, cups, saucers, hammers, nails, and the like. In the majority of cases we unqualifiedly[9] apply the name 'chair' to objects which have a certain kind of over-all structure and shape, and are made of kinds of material falling within some range. This general, over-all pattern imposed by the purpose for which chairs are designed—serving as a separate seat for one—gives things generally called chairs certain over-all similarities in form, and to a lesser degree, in kind of material. A "chair" is expected to have some kind of seat, to rest on some kind of support, to have some kind of support for the sitter's back; and in some cases (where we use the name 'arm-chair') to have supports for the sitter's arms. With regard to material, it has to be made of something relatively hard and firm to support the sitter's weight. But different chairs may serve different, more specialized needs, in addition to serving as a separate seat for one. The kinds of specialized need, or the kinds of specialized use, give us the basis for the ordinary *classification* of chairs into kinds. They impose further restrictions on the form and material of chairs: restrictions over and above those imposed on them by the end-in-view of serving as separate seats for one. These additional restrictions give rise to greater resemblances between chairs of the same "kind" (chairs which satisfy the same kind of specialized need, which have the same kind of specialized use), and to a lesser extent, between chairs of different "kinds" whose specialized uses overlap or are similar in certain respects. Thus a "reclining chair" bears greater resemblances to other "reclining chairs" than to ordinary, plain chairs. But "re-

---

[9] This qualification is necessary in the light of our later discussion below. But the borderline cases we shall discuss there can themselves be explained in terms of the principles underlying the above discussion.

clining chairs" may be subdivided into "deck chairs," "Morris chairs," and the like, with still greater resemblances between one "deck chair" and another, one "Morris chair" and another (one kind of still more specialized use being involved in each case). These resemblances in detail between chairs of the same "kind," and more general resemblances between chairs of different "kinds," give us at least some of the overlapping and criss-crossing of resemblances which Wittgenstein speaks about. Also, since the specialized uses of different kinds of chair may have *different* elements in common, the resemblances in form and material may be now with respect to one characteristic, or kind of characteristic, now to another.

The same applies to games, as we see when we consider the general kinds of game: board games, ball games, card games, and the like, and the particular kinds of game falling under one or another of the former: e.g. chess, tennis, bridge. But the general purpose meant to be served by a game, as a game, and the more specialized purposes meant to be served by it as a specific kind of game, determine its characteristics to a lesser degree than the corresponding purposes in the case of a chair, say, because of the former's greater complexity and greater indeterminacy. Pleasure, be it physical or psychological, can be produced in human beings in many different ways. That in the case of games it is actually produced by activities following certain kinds of rule and involving the use of certain kinds of material (such as balls, rackets, boards, cards), must be ascribed to a large extent to the genius of the inventors of games.

III

In talking about games, we gave examples of the kinds of condition which are "standard," and of others which are not "standard," relatively to games in general. It is now time to say something more general and more precise about these. The "standard" conditions, S_1, relative to a thing T, and to a given use U, are:

(1) The kinds of condition—physical, or psychological, or both—which are causally necessary for T's having U by virtue of its (T's) characteristics. "Non-standard" conditions, S_1, relative to T and U, are the kinds of condition— physical, or psychological, or both—which causally impede, or even make impossible, T's having U; assuming that T itself, as T (i.e., as called "T") is not what we would ordinarily call defective. For even under "standard" or "favorable" conditions relative to T, a thing T, lacking some part it ordinarily possesses, may be incapable of having U. Thus even under "standard" conditions, relative to chairs, a chair with a missing leg, for instance, cannot, as it stands, be used as a chair.

(2) There is no hard and fast dividing line between "standard" and "non-standard" conditions relative to T and U. Also, there does not exist a unique set of conditions which is "standard," and another unique set of conditions which is "non-standard," relatively to T and U. A good deal of flexibility is possible; though mainly in situations where psychological factors are important. A pen cannot be used as a writing instrument without some kind of writing fluid; but a game of baseball may be played and enjoyed even in relatively bad weather, if the players and spectators are in the mood for playing or watching, respectively.

(3) In the case of any given common name 'X' (of the kind we are concerned with in this paper) there are certain conditions, fixed by linguistic usage, which determine whether or not 'X' shall properly apply to a given thing T: conditions under which we would *refrain* from calling a thing an "X" if it did not have a use U the notion of which is implicit in the meaning of 'X.' These conditions may be called the "standard conditions for the use or application of 'X' to a thing T" (symbolized by 'S_2'). In general, S_1 and S_2 coincide. More clearly, conditions S_1 under which a thing T normally has a use U are, generally

speaking, the conditions under which T's having or not having use U becomes crucial for determining whether or not a name 'X' (which involves the notion of use U in its meaning) is applicable to it. If T does not have U under standard causal conditions S_1 relative to X's in general, 'X' will not, generally speaking, be applicable to it.

But S_2 and S_1 do not always coincide. For instance, there are cases where we do not refrain from calling a given thing an "X," even though it is incapable, as it stands, of having a use U under the standard causal conditions S_1 relative to X's in general, and though the notion of U is implicit in the meaning of 'X.'[10] For example, a "broken chair," or a "chair with a leg missing," is called a chair even though it cannot be sat on under causal conditions which are standard for intact chairs. The existence of such cases may seem to contradict our general position in sections I and II. But actually it does not materially affect it. As a matter of fact, such apparent exceptions merely constitute borderline cases and are themselves explainable in terms of our general position.

A. Let us take a simple and clear example, that of chairs. Chairs seem unmistakably to have been invented for a specific kind of use, for use in a certain way. That is, the intended use seems to have determined the general characteristics of the original chairs. It is possible, therefore, that originally the name 'chair' did involve, in ordinary discourse, the notion of the capacity to have that use under certain physical conditions such that a thing could *not* be properly called a chair *unless* it possessed that capacity. But since a chair's *characteristics* are causally responsible

[10] There are also cases where a thing T does have a use U under (at least some of the) standard causal conditions S_1 relative to things called "X's," and yet we refrain from calling it an "X" ('X' being a name which implicitly involves the notion of U in its meaning). A log can be sat on, and yet we do not call it a chair—not without some qualification at least. About these cases we have already said something in connection with the notion of a thing's "proper" or "normal" use. Further discussion must be left to a future paper.

for the chair's possessing the capacity to be used in a given way, under certain conditions, the term 'chair' would subsequently come to apply to objects which have these kinds of characteristic, *in their own right*, making the possession of these kinds of characteristic a "necessary" condition for the applicability of 'chair,' rather than the capacity to have the use which these characteristics are designed to make possible. Once this shift in "meaning" has been effected, a further complication seems to arise. The term 'chair' now comes to be applied also to objects which merely "resemble"[11] objects hitherto called chairs, provided the "resemblance" is considerable and not tenuous (there being no sharp line of demarcation between "considerable" and "tenuous" resemblance), even though these objects, as they stand, cannot serve as chairs. By an "object which 'resembles' a chair" I have here in mind a so-called broken, battered, or incomplete chair, such as a chair with one leg missing.

B. But the shift in "meaning" described above is not sharp and complete in actual cases. The notion of certain sets of characteristics Ca, or Cb, or Cd, and so on, does not seem to usurp completely, in actual practice, the place of the notion of a given use U which Ca, or Cb, or Cd, and so on, make possible in a given thing T. In deciding whether or not to call a given thing by a certain name, or in justifying the giving of a certain name to a given thing, appeal is made now to the one, now to the other, now to both, notions. When we say: "What sort of chair is this?—it's broken; one of its legs is missing!" our tendency to

11 I am not here referring to the kind of resemblance which obtains, say, between so-called "irrational numbers" and so-called "cardinal numbers," on the basis of which (taking this merely as a hypothetical possibility) the former may have come to be called "numbers." This kind of extension of a name's meaning does not consist in the creation of borderline cases, as in the case of a so-called "broken chair's" being called a chair despite its being "broken." Incidentally, the former is one way in which the existence of "family resemblances" between things called by the same name may be accounted for.

think of the object referred to as a *broken* chair may be due either to the fact that (a) it lacks certain kinds of characteristics which are generally found in objects called "chairs" without qualification (so-called intact chairs), and/or to the fact that (b) it cannot, as it stands, serve as a chair. But we *do* speak of it as a "*chair*" because we think of it (i) as an object which used to have the kinds of characteristic a chair generally has, or was capable of serving as a chair, or both; and/or (ii) as an object capable of serving as a chair if it were to have certain characteristics it now lacks (i.e., if it were to be "repaired"). Thus if (say) just before a party a servant discovers a chair with a cracked seat, and he remarks: "We can't use this (as a chair): the seat is cracked," he may get the following reply from the hostess: "Yes we can! Get me some glue," or "Yes we can, if you get me some glue."[12] In

---

[12] It is important to note that in the above interchange 'can' is used in two different senses by the servant and the hostess respectively. The former is using the word in a narrower and stricter sense. He is saying, in effect, that *as it stands*, and under the *prevailing circumstances*, the "chair" cannot serve as a chair. The hostess, on the other hand, is using 'can' in a less stringent sense. What she says, in effect, is that the broken chair can serve as a chair, even in that particular situation, since it can be (easily) repaired, and therefore *made to serve* as a chair. In this sense of 'can,' our statement that an object (activity, process, of the kind we are concerned with) may be called "X" even if it cannot serve as an "X," etc., will be false. In this sense of 'can,' "can serve as an X *can* be taken as a (conventionally determined) "necessary" condition for properly calling a man-made or a man-devised thing an "X." However, let us add that the ordinary uses of 'can,' in our second sense, are relative to the particular situation involved. A chair with a slightly cracked seat "can (be made to) serve" as a chair, even in the urgency of preparations for a party; but a chair with a leg missing cannot (even in the second sense of 'can'). So the hostess would not say: "Yes we can, get me some glue!" if the chair referred to had a leg missing. (But she would still refer to the object as a "chair.") Still, a chair with a leg missing "can (be made to) serve" as a chair if there is plenty of time, say, to send it to a carpenter and have it repaired. Thus the distinction between 'can' and 'cannot' in this sense is not clearcut and sharp: whether or not a given object is

using qualifying adjectives like 'broken,' 'defective,' 'incomplete,' 'battered,' we reflect in ordinary language the distinction between the kind of case in which a given object called "X" can, *as it stands*, serve as an "X," and the borderline kind of case in which it cannot, as it stands, serve as an "X."

Let us note that there is no hard and fast line dividing the borderline cases themselves, where the name 'chair,' say, is still applied (though with qualification), and cases where the name 'chair' is no longer applied. Thus we uniformly speak of a "*chair* with a leg missing," a "*chair* with two legs missing," a "*chair* with three legs missing"; but we can *either* speak of a "*chair* with all of its legs missing," (or a "*legless chair*") *or* of the "*seat* and *back* of a chair"; while we do *not* seriously speak of a "chair with the legs and back missing" but rather of the "*seat* of a chair," or even of a "wooden board" (or a "wooden board having the shape of a chair's seat"), and the like. In other words, and stated generally, there is no hard and fast line in ordinary discourse between an "X with a part missing," a "part *a* of X," and a "not-X and not-*a*."

IV

Our discussion would be grossly incomplete if we do not consider, at least briefly, one use of 'good' and of 'poor' or 'not good'; namely, their use in such statements as "This is a good knife," "That wasn't a good game of tennis," "He played a poor game of chess." Such an analysis shows that there is a very intimate relationship between the uses of common names of the kind we have concerned ourselves with in this paper, and the above uses of 'good' (also 'very good,' 'excellent') and 'poor' or 'not good' (also 'very poor,' 'extremely poor,' 'not very good,' 'not good at all,' etc.).

A. If we examine cases in which we ordinarily call a

---

thought of as capable of having a given use depends on the state of the object in a particular situation.

man-made object, or a man-devised activity or process, a "good X" and not merely "X," we find, first, that we do so both (a) when the prevalent causal conditions (viz., in general, the conditions for the application of the name 'X') are standard, and (b) when the causal conditions are non-standard, for "X's" in general. In the case of (a) we further discover that in calling the given thing a *good* "X," we indicate one or both of two things: (i) that this thing "X" is capable of having, or actually has, *in an eminent or outstanding degree* (these terms being used in a relative sense) a given use U; (ii) that "X" possesses one or more *characteristics* by virtue of which it is capable of having, or actually has, a use U, in an eminent or outstanding degree. In both (i) and (ii), the use U involved is found to be the use associated with "X" *qua* "X" or the notion of which is implicit in 'X's' meaning. For instance, if we point to a knife and say: "This is a *good* knife," we ordinarily indicate that it is capable of cutting, or is actually cutting, certain kinds of thing (meat, butter, bread, and so on) well, efficiently, without effort, and/or it is either sharp or very sharp, *or* has a firm and comfortable grip, *or* has a long and wide blade, *or* its blade has a saw-like edge, or some or all of these characteristics together—that is, one or more characteristics which make it capable of cutting certain kinds of thing well, efficiently, with ease. We may also speak of a knife as a good knife it it has one or more characteristics that make it capable of being used to cut (of serving as a knife), or to cut well, *for a relatively long time*: in general, characteristics which enable it to preserve its peculiar use. Thus a knife may be said to be a good knife because it has a rust-proof blade and/or has a sturdy handle.

Examples illustrating these points can be easily multiplied. Also, these points can be readily applied, *mutatis mutandis*, to the use of 'very good,' 'excellent,' and the like, corresponding to the use of 'good' we are talking about.

In the case of (b), i.e., when we apply the term 'good'

to a thing "X" under causal conditions which are non-standard for "X's" in general, we indicate that "X" is capable of having, or actually has, use U *even though the prevalent conditions are non-standard for it qua "X,"* and therefore even though it is not expected to have U. If "X" has U, or seems capable of having it (or if it has characteristics which seem to show that it has this capacity) in an outstanding degree, even though the prevalent causal conditions are non-standard, we tend to call it a "very good X," or an "excellent X," and not merely a "good X." We will call a knife a good (or a very good) knife if it cuts (and better still, if it cuts well) things which it is not designed—and therefore not expected—to cut. Similarly, we would ordinarily apply the term 'good' (or 'very good,' etc.) to an all-purpose knife just invented, tacitly comparing its performance with the performance of ordinary knives. But once we get used to this kind of knife and ordinary knives go out of use or become rare, we tend to bestow these terms only on a specific all-purpose knife (or a whole brand of it) which cuts better the things all-purpose knives are expected to cut, or cuts more kinds of things than other all-purpose knives, under conditions which now come to be regarded as standard for *them*, but which include conditions which are non-standard for ordinary knives. (Cf. the case of quill pens and fountain pens. This example also illustrates the converse of what we have just said: we tend at present to speak of a quill pen as a *poor* pen, judging its performance in terms of the performance of fountain pens, when originally it must have been the opposite.) It may be noted that in case (b) in general, (i) the degree in which a thing "X" has or seems to have use U associated with it *qua* "X," and (ii) the degree in which the prevalent causal conditions are non-standard (or unfavorable), wherever such variation in degree in these conditions is possible, ordinarily determines the judge's assessment of *how* eminently "X" has or is capable of having U. Consequently, they determine whether 'good,' or 'very good,' or 'excellent,' shall be applied.

These points may be illustrated by the following statements: "It was a very good game of tennis! The players rarely missed the ball, despite the strong wind"; "It was an excellent game of tennis! The players rarely (or better still: "hardly ever," or "never") missed the ball, and did some fast footwork, despite the strong wind and the soggy ground."

Our remarks in (a) and (b) above apply equally, *mutatis mutandis*, to objects, activities, and processes with relatively, or highly, specialized uses, such as carving knives, chess games, sledge hammers, writing desks, arm chairs, ice cream, and so on.

B. Coming now to uses of 'poor' or 'not good' in the sense in which we are here concerned with these terms, a man-made object or a man-devised activity, or process, is ordinarily said to be a "poor X" or "not a good X" in the following situations:

(1) If it is regarded as completely incapable of having a given use U associated with it *qua* "X," provided that (a) it is regarded as intact *qua* "X," and that (b) the prevalent causal conditions are regarded as standard, that is, when "X" is expected by the person calling it a "poor X" or "not a good X" to have use U. (In this type of case, however, we generally tend to use a stronger expression than 'poor' or 'not good' alone: we say: "This isn't a good X at all," or "This X is useless," or "This is a very poor X.") A knife with a completely blunt blade is intact as a knife—it has the general structural characteristics of one kind of knife or another, though not all the characteristics which are necessary for cutting. Hence it *is* called a knife, and not, say, "junk" (except as a hyperbole). But since it is incapable of cutting things which knives are ordinarily expected to cut, it is called a poor knife or is said to be not a good knife. (On the other hand, we will probably call it "junk," or something equivalent in meaning to 'junk,' instead of a "poor knife," if it has no blade; though we might still call it a "handle-less knife" and not "junk" if it has a blade but no handle. For the possession of a blade

is regarded as—and is—causally more *necessary* for cutting,
for an object's serving as a knife, than the possession of a
handle.)

(2) If, as it stands, it is capable of having the associated
use U—or is regarded as capable of having use U—but in
a lower degree than the person calling it a "poor X" ex-
pects a thing called "X" to have, it being again assumed
that the prevalent causal conditions are standard conditions
and that "X" is intact *qua* "X." Taking knives again as our
illustration, a knife may be said to be a poor knife if its
blade, say, is rusty or is somewhat blunt, if it has a very
short handle, or a very short blade, or has several or all of
these defects together. In other words, if it lacks certain
characteristics which would have enabled it to have the
peculiar use—cutting—associated with it *qua* knife, with the
ease and efficiency expected of a knife; or has certain characteristics which prevent it from serving as expected.

The above analysis, as well as further analysis, tends to
indicate that in such statements as "*a* is a good X," "*b* is
a poor X," where 'X' and 'Y' are common names of the
kind we are dealing with in this paper, (a) 'good' does not
refer to any specific determinate or relatively determinate
characteristic or characteristics common to all things ordinarily called "good X's," by virtue of which these things
function better than is generally expected of things called
"X's," or by virtue of which they are called good "X's";
(b) that, similarly, 'poor' or 'not good' do not refer to any
specific determinate or relatively determinate characteristic
or characteristics *present* in all things called "poor Y's,"
which prevent them from functioning well or even functioning at all; nor do these terms refer to any specific determinate or relatively determinate characteristic or characteristics *absent* from all things called "poor Y's" or "not
good Y's," as a result of which they are incapable of functioning well or even functioning at all. The determinate
or relatively determinate characteristics of a knife may vary
qualitatively and in degree, and yet we may still properly
call it a good knife—so long as it serves well (and/or for a

relatively long time) as a knife. Similarly a knife may be capable of cutting things it is not ordinarily expected to cut, by possessing one or more of a variety of determinate or relatively determinate characteristics of certain kinds. The same applies to "poor knives" or "not good knives." Of course many knives said to be good knives may and do have one or more determinate or relatively determinate characteristics in common, in the same way as many knives in general (say those of the same brand) whether good or not, may and do have such characteristics in common. But our point is that we do not restrict the ordinary application of the term 'good' to knives which have one or more specific characteristics in common. What determines in ordinary usage the application—and the range of application —of 'good' is something other than the possession of certain characteristics in common: as we have been trying to show, it is the *degree*, and the *nature of the conditions* under which, a given kind of *use* is possessed. On this basis, there is no necessity, no need for all things called "good X's" to have one or more determinate or relatively determinate characteristics in common, in order that they may properly be called "good X's." Similarly, *mutatis mutandis*, with 'poor' or 'not good.'[13]

One final word. There is no hard and fast dividing line between cases where an object or phenomenon would be

[13] It is interesting to note that in English there is no meaning or sense of 'bad' (with the exception, perhaps, of 'bad' in 'bad food') which corresponds to the above meaning or sense of 'good.' The antonym of 'good' in this meaning or sense is 'not good' or 'poor,' and not 'bad.' We cannot properly say "a bad knife," "a bad game," "a bad pen," in the same way in which we speak of a "good knife," a "good game," a "good pen," and so on. In other words, there does not seem to be a meaning or sense of 'bad' in English which is synonymous with 'not good' (or 'poor') in the above sense or meaning. But there may be some languages in which we can properly say "This is a bad knife," "This is a bad game," and the like, in the sense of "This is a poor knife," "This is not a good game." As a matter of fact, this is admissible in one Asiatic language I know, namely, in *colloquial* or *conversational* (though not in literary) Armenian.

called a "poor X" and cases where it would not be called "X" at all. Consider an object having the general structure of an armchair, but with one of its legs considerably shorter than the rest. This object we call a poor armchair or not a good armchair (as well as, say, a "lame" armchair), rather than something else—say "junk." The situation here is relatively straightforward, since the object in hand does serve as a separate seat for one, etc., though less satisfactorily than anything generally called a "chair" or "armchair" without qualification. A chair is required to afford the sitter some degree of rest or comfort; whereas this particular chair is uncomfortable. But one can still sit upon it. Now suppose we have a similar object, but with one of its "legs" missing. This object cannot, as it stands, serve as a separate seat for one. Despite that, we would still call it a chair— qualified with (say) 'broken.' In this case, however, we would *not* speak of it as a "poor chair." We call it a chair though we know that it cannot, as it stands, serve as one; but at the same time we do not expect it to serve as a chair. That is why we do not call it a "poor chair." Finally, if we rip a chair apart, leaving the "seat" intact, we do not call the latter *either* a "poor chair," *or* a "broken chair," but rather, the "seat of a chair." All this goes to show that the transition from (i) "chair" (without qualification) to (ii) "poor chair" (or "not a good chair"), and, say, "chair with cracked seat" to (iii) "broken chair" (say in the case of a chair with a leg missing), but *not* "poor chair" to (iv) "junk," is not clear-cut and fixed, but gradual and continuous and blurred. This also goes to show that there is no sharp demarcation line between "standard" conditions for the use of a name 'X' (say 'chair') and "non-standard" conditions.[14]

[14] I wish to thank Professor Bernard Peach of Duke University for his criticisms of an earlier draft of this essay.

ON WITTGENSTEIN'S USE OF
THE TERM "CRITERION"

ROGERS ALBRITTON

1. An important notion in Wittgenstein's later philosophy is that of a *criterion*. For example:

> It is part of the grammar of the word "chair" that *this* is what we call "to sit on a chair," and it is part of the grammar of the word "meaning" that *this* is what we call "explanation of a meaning"; in the same way to explain my criterion for another person's having toothache is to give a grammatical explanation about the word "toothache" and, in this sense, an explanation concerning the meaning of the word "toothache."

> When we learnt the use of the phrase "so-and-so has toothache" we were pointed out certain kinds of behaviour of those who were said to have toothache. As an instance of these kinds of behaviour let us take holding your cheek. Suppose that by observation I found that in certain cases whenever these first criteria told me a person had toothache, a red patch appeared on the person's cheek. Supposing I now said to someone "I see A has toothache, he's got a red patch on his cheek." He may ask me "How do you know A has toothache when you see a red patch?" I should then point out that certain phenomena had always coincided with the appearance of the red patch.

Presented as part of a symposium on "Criteria" at the Fifty-Sixth Annual Meeting of the American Philosophical Association, Eastern Division, at Columbia University, December 29, 1959. Reprinted from *The Journal of Philosophy*, Vol. LVI (1959), pp. 845–857, with the permission of the author and editor.

Now one may go on and ask: "How do you know that
he has got toothache when he holds his cheek?" The
answer to this might be, "I say, *he* has toothache when
he holds his cheek because I hold my cheek when I
have toothache." But what if we went on asking:—
"And why do you suppose that toothache corresponds
to his holding his cheek just because your toothache
corresponds to your holding your cheek?" You will be
at a loss to answer this question, and find that here we
strike rock bottom, that is we have come down to conventions. (If you suggest as an answer to the last question that, whenever we've seen people holding their
cheeks and asked them what's the matter, they have
answered, "I have toothache,"—remember that this experience only co-ordinates holding your cheek with
saying certain words.)

This passage is from the *Blue Book* of 1933–1934.[1] It
is followed by the one passage of Wittgenstein's published
work in which he gives anything like a definition of the
term "criterion":

Let us introduce two antithetical terms in order to
avoid certain elementary confusions: To the question "How do you know that so-and-so is the case?",
we sometimes answer by giving *'criteria'* and sometimes by giving *'symptoms.'* If medical science calls
angina an inflammation caused by a particular bacillus, and we ask in a particular case "why do you say
this man has got angina?" then the answer "I have
found the bacillus so-and-so in his blood" gives us the
criterion, or what we may call the defining criterion
of angina. If on the other hand the answer was, "His
throat is inflamed," this might give us a symptom of
angina. I call "symptom" a phenomenon of which experience has taught us that it coincided, in some way
or other, with the phenomenon which is our defining
criterion. Then to say "A man has angina if this bacillus is found in him" is a tautology or it is a loose way

[1] Ludwig Wittgenstein, *The Blue and Brown Books* [hereafter
abbreviated "BB"] (Oxford, 1958), p. 24.

of stating the definition of "angina." But to say, "A man has angina whenever he has an inflamed throat" is to make a hypothesis.[2]

Wittgenstein then makes some remarks about the role of criteria in our actual use of language:

> In practice, if you were asked which phenomenon is the defining criterion and which is a symptom, you would in most cases be unable to answer this question except by making an arbitrary decision *ad hoc*. It may be practical to define a word by taking one phenomenon as the defining criterion, but we shall easily be persuaded to define the word by means of what, according to our first use, was a symptom. Doctors will use the names of diseases without ever deciding which phenomena are to be taken as criteria and which as symptoms; and this need not be a deplorable lack of clarity. For remember that in general we don't use language according to strict rules—it hasn't been taught us by means of strict rules, either. *We*, in our discussions on the other hand, constantly compare language with a calculus proceeding according to exact rules.
>
> This is a very one-sided way of looking at language. In practice we very rarely use language as such a calculus. For not only do we not think of the rules of usage—of definitions, etc.—while using language, but when we are asked to give such rules, in most cases we aren't able to do so. We are unable clearly to circumscribe the concepts we use; not because we don't know their real definition, but because there is no real 'definition' to them. To suppose that there *must* be would be like supposing that whenever children play with a ball they play a game according to strict rules.[3]

2. Suppose that a capacity to score better than fifty points on a certain test is the criterion of genius, in the sense that Wittgenstein means to give to the term "crite-

[2] *Ibid.*, pp. 24–25.
[3] *Ibid.*, p. 25.

rion." Then it will sufficiently explain how I *know* that a particular man is a genius to say that I have given him the test and found his score on it to be better than fifty. This explanation will be sufficient *not* because it is an established fact that whoever scores better than fifty on the test is a genius, but because to say that whoever scores better than fifty on it is a genius is to utter "a tautology" or "is a loose way of stating the definition" of the word "genius." The criterion of a thing is its "defining criterion." By taking this or that as the criterion by which to govern our use of a word, we "define the word." The criterion of angina, if any, is what "medical science calls angina."[4] That is, it is what medical science calls "angina." (But this is not to deny that it is called "angine" in French.)

It is plain enough, then, though Wittgenstein might have made it plainer, that in the sense of the passages I've quoted from the *Blue Book* the criterion for this or that's being so is, among other things, a logically sufficient condition of its being so. That is: If I find in a particular case that the criterion for a thing's being so is satisfied, what entitles me to claim that I thereby know the thing to be so is that the satisfaction of the criterion *entails* that it is so, in the technical sense of the word "entails" in which if a

---

[4] It might be argued that while the criterion of angina, in Wittgenstein's example, is just the presence of a particular bacillus in one's blood, what medical science is said to *call* angina is something more, namely "an inflammation caused by a particular bacillus." (My dictionary tells me that angina is "any inflammatory infection of the throat or fauces, esp. one producing suffocative spasms.") But if having angina is supposed to be having such an inflammation, it will not be "a tautology or a loose way of stating the definition of 'angina'" to say that a man has angina if the bacillus is found in him. The phrase "an inflammation caused by a particular bacillus" has more in it, under the influence of the ordinary sense of the word "angina," than Wittgenstein finds convenient for the purposes of the example, and he therefore slips without notice into the simpler supposition that what is called "having angina" is just having the bacillus in one, inflammation or no inflammation. Thus "'His throat is inflamed' . . . might give us a *symptom* of angina."

man owns two suitcases, that entails that he owns some luggage.[5]

Such expressions as "the defining criterion" and "a loose way of stating the definition of 'angina,'" or the sentence beginning "It may be practical to define a word by taking one phenomenon as the defining criterion," would seem to warrant the addition that if anything is the criterion for a thing's being so, the thing's being so entails the satisfaction of the criterion: The criterion is a logically necessary as well as a logically sufficient condition of its being so. (Thus Wittgenstein says in the *Brown Book*: "the real criterion for a person's *reading or not reading*"; "the only real criterion *distinguishing reading from not reading*."[6]

3. It might be objected that I do violence to Wittgenstein's thought by trying to force it into such jargon as that of "logically necessary and sufficient conditions." I might be reminded of his remark in the *Brown Book* about an explanation there of the term "pattern": "This explanation, as others which we have given, is vague, and meant to be vague."[7] Why shouldn't Wittgenstein's term "criterion" be more or less like those words of which, according to the *Blue Book*, one might say: "They are used in a thousand different ways which gradually merge into one another. No wonder that we can't tabulate strict rules for their use"?[8]

But I haven't offered to tabulate strict rules for the use that Wittgenstein proposes to make of the word "criterion." For example: It is a logically necessary and sufficient

---

[5] As might be expected, a criterion is in Wittgenstein's usage always a criterion for something or other's being the case, being so, though it may be described as "the criterion of X," where "X" is a noun or a substantive phrase. I follow Wittgenstein's German in writing, as a rule, "criterion *of* angina" and "criterion *of* having angina," for example, but "criterion *for* a man's having angina" (to represent the German "Kriterium dafür," with a "dasz"-clause). The expression "satisfaction of the criterion" has no parallel in Wittgenstein's idiom.

[6] *BB*, pp. 121, 122.

[7] *Ibid.*, p. 84.

[8] *Ibid.*, p. 28.

condition of there being *eight* men in a room that there should be as many men in the room as there are even integers between nine and twenty-five. But is that what anyone *calls* there being eight men in a room? The criterion of X is what is *called* "X." I have no exact account to give of Wittgenstein's use of such expressions as "is called." And if "logically necessary and sufficient condition" and "entails" are jargon, they have the company in that misery of the word "tautology," which Wittgenstein uses in the passage I've been discussing.

I should say, however, that I have no intention of committing Wittgenstein to the view that the criterion of X is a logically necessary and sufficient condition of X *in the nature of things,* so to speak. Criteria are for him primarily criteria that men "accept," "adopt," "fix," "introduce," and "use" or "apply" in connection with their use of certain *expressions.*[9] If anything is the criterion of X and therefore a logically necessary and sufficient condition of X, it is because (in some sense of "because") men agree in certain *conventions.* ("Here we strike rock bottom, that is we have come down to conventions."[10])

4. "To say, 'A man has angina whenever he has an inflamed throat' is to make a hypothesis." Wittgenstein's use of the word "hypothesis" here may suggest that in his opinion no one ought to claim to know (or know *for certain,* anyway) that *p* without something better to go on than *symptoms* of its being the case that *p.* But the suggestion a few lines earlier is that one may sometimes answer the question "How do you know that so-and-so is the case?" quite as irreproachably by "giving 'symptoms'" as by "giving 'criteria,'" and this is what Wittgenstein thinks, as far as I can find. The satisfaction of the criterion for a thing's being the case entails that it is the case, which no symptom of its being the case can do. But it doesn't follow

[9] For the quoted words, cf. *BB,* pp. 63, 64, 55, and *Philosophical Investigations,* hereafter abbreviated *PI* (Oxford, 1953): I, secs. 141, 182, 322; II, pp. 212, 222.

[10] *BB,* p. 24.

that no criterion can seem to be satisfied when it isn't or that no symptom can be perfectly reliable.

Nevertheless, the criterion for a thing's being so (if any) is in one respect the primary phenomenon by which one may judge that it is so. It is only because experience has taught us that another phenomenon "coincided, in some way or other," with the criterion that we are entitled to regard that other phenomenon as a symptom of the thing's being so. Wittgenstein's way of introducing the term "symptom" appears to involve that if anything is a symptom for us of a given thing's being so, there must be some phenomenon which is the criterion for its being so. This appearance is deceptive, as I will argue in the next section of this paper; there may be symptoms of that for which there is no *one* criterion. But if there is *no* criterion by which I might judge that I myself have a toothache, for example, then it will follow that nothing can be a symptom for me of my having one.

5. When we turn from Wittgenstein's explanation or partial explanation of what criteria and symptoms are to his account (in the third passage that I've quoted) of how language is used, it appears at first that he has brought criteria and symptoms in only to usher them out again: "In practice, if you were asked which phenomenon is the defining criterion and which is a symptom, you would in most cases be unable to answer this question," not because you don't know the answer, but because "in general we don't use language according to exact rules," and so on. Even within this account, however, one phrase implies that there are in many or most cases symptoms of a thing's being so: "It may be practical to define a word by taking one phenomenon as the defining criterion, but we shall easily be persuaded to define the word by means of what, according to our first use, was a symptom." Wittgenstein has said, only a few lines earlier, "I call 'symptom' a phenomenon of which experience has taught us that it coincided . . . with the phenomenon which is our defining criterion." So if there were symptoms of what we meant

by "X" in our first use of the word, then something, it seems, must have been the criterion of X, in that sense of "X". But "our first use" must mean our first, unruly use of the word according to *no* one defining criterion.

This apparent contradiction is confusing, but not important. Wittgenstein doesn't mean to *define* the term "symptom" by the sentence beginning "I call 'symptom' . . . ," but to explain how he uses it in such cases as the imaginary one of angina. The rest of its use is supposed to be obvious from this explanation. (The *Blue Book* was "meant only for the people who heard the lectures."[11]) What Wittgenstein then goes on to deny is that any phenomenon is *the* criterion of X, in most cases. He doesn't deny that there will generally turn out to be *criteria* of X in those cases. For example: In the preceding passage about toothache he alleges that we have, not one, specific criterion, but criteria for another person's having a toothache:[12] such phenomena as his holding his cheek, "certain kinds of behaviour." A symptom of X, in such cases, will be a "phenomenon of which experience has taught us that it coincided, in some way or other," with one or more of the phenomena which are our criteria of X. The red patch on a person's cheek, in the example of toothache, will be a symptom in this way: "Certain phenomena"—criteria of having a toothache—"had always coincided with the appearance of the red patch."[13]

[11] Wittgenstein in a letter to Russell, quoted *BB*, p. v.

[12] At *ibid.*, p. 24, l. 10, the singular, "criterion," is used as in *PI*, I, sec. 344, for example.

[13] Why, if asked "which phenomenon is the defining criterion and which is a symptom," wouldn't we be able in most cases to say at least that this or that one is a *symptom*? Wittgenstein seems to be thinking of the question as one that might be asked with reference to a couple of phenomena (or more, but the wording suggests two) so intimately associated with X that where neither of them was the defining criterion of X both would turn out to be *criteria* of X. And in that case it would be misleading to say even that *neither* of them was a symptom, since a phenomenon that is one among other criteria of X is nevertheless a symptom of X under *some* circumstances. In *PI*, I, sec. 354,

6. But what does Wittgenstein mean by *criteria* of X? If a phenomenon is a criterion among others for a thing's being so, then first, certainly, it is one among other phenomena that can *show* the thing to be so, as *the* criterion for its being so might do if there were one. (Wittgenstein says, for example: "whenever these first criteria told me a person had toothache."[14]) But it can be "used as a criterion," or "is a criterion," only *under certain circumstances:*[15] "Many different criteria distinguish, under different circumstances, cases of believing what you say from those of not believing what you say."[16] Or suppose, as Wittgenstein does (though he may not think that this one phenomenon is ever really enough, by itself), that holding one's cheek, in a certain kind of way, is a criterion of (another person's) having a toothache. Still, there are circumstances under which a man's holding his cheek, no matter how, *won't* show that he has a toothache.

In this respect a criterion among others for a thing's being so differs from the defining criterion for a thing's being so. From this difference there follows another. None of the many criteria for a thing's being so can be a logically necessary and sufficient condition of its being so. But it doesn't follow that a criterion among others of X isn't a criterion *in the same sense* as that in which the defining criterion of X, if there were one, would be a criterion of X. It may be that in Wittgenstein's sense of the term "criterion" the defining criterion of X is a logically necessary and sufficient condition of X in consequence of being the *only* criterion of X. And since Wittgenstein is content to introduce the term by explaining what it is to be the defining criterion of X, without explaining sep-

---

Wittgenstein refers to this state of affairs as "the fluctuation in grammar between criteria and symptoms," which "makes it look as if there were nothing at all but symptoms."

[14] *BB*, p. 24; cf. p. 57, ll. 6–9; 63, ll. 30–32.
[15] The quoted expressions are warranted by *ibid.*, p. 61, ll. 26–27; 135, ll. 27–28; 144, ll. 9–12.
[16] *Ibid.*, p. 144, ll. 37–39.

arately what it is to be one of many criteria of X, there is
a strong presumption that in his usage a phenomenon is a
criterion of X in some single sense of that form of words
if it is a criterion of X at all, whether it is the only one
or one among others.

What can this sense of the term "criterion" be?

7. (a) In the first sentence of the first passage that I
quoted at the beginning of this paper, the phrase "my
criterion for another person's having toothache" parallels
the preceding phrases "what we call 'explanation of a
meaning'" and "what we call 'to sit on a chair.'" Apparently, my criterion for another person's having toothache is what I *call* his having a toothache.

(b) The criterion of angina, in Wittgenstein's example,
is what "medical science calls angina," and we may say
that it is "the defining criterion of angina." In one passage
of the *Brown Book* the many criteria of a thing are also
its "defining criteria."[17] And Wittgenstein repeatedly says
or implies, in the *Blue* and *Brown Books*, that criteria of
X are phenomena that we call "X", or refer to by the
expression "X" (if not refer to *as* "X"), or describe by the
expression "X" (if not describe *as* "X"), *under various circumstances*. To save space, I will not quote any such passages, but only list those I have found, in a note.[18] There
is no hint in them that Wittgenstein is using the expressions "call," "refer to," and "describe" in abnormal senses,
or metaphorically. He means, as far as I can make out,
that a man's preparing tea for two, say, may be part of
what is properly called his "expecting someone to tea,"
as it must be the whole of what is properly called his "preparing tea for two."[19]

(c) Suppose that under certain circumstances a man's

[17] *BB*, p. 104.
[18] *Ibid.*, pp. 20, ll. 9–24; 32, ll. 24–33, l. 9; 57, ll. 32–34; 88,
ll. 14–17; 110, ll. 1–9; 112–116, secs. 62–64 (on p. 116, notice
ll. 22–33); 135, ll. 26–33; 143–144, sec. 6; 146, ll. 27–34; 147,
ll. 27–40; 152, sec. 12; 154, ll. 3–5; 157, ll. 23–25.
[19] *Ibid.*, p. 20.

saying a certain formula is a criterion for his knowing the formula, and that this is a criterion for his being able to continue a certain series, under the same circumstances. Does it follow that "He can continue . . ." *means the same as* "He knows the formula" (and that both of these sentences mean the same as "He has said the formula")? Wittgenstein replies: "We can say 'They don't mean the same, i.e., they are not in general used as synonyms as, e.g., the phrases "I am well" and "I am in good health"'; or we may say *'Under certain circumstances* "He can continue . . ." means he knows the formula.' "[20] (That is, as a version of this passage in the *Investigations* confirms,[21] under certain circumstances "He can continue . . ." means the same as "He knows the formula.") Or again, under certain circumstances "understanding . . . means the same as reacting [in such-and-such a way, e.g. to an order]."[22]

(d) Under given circumstances of X, X may *consist* in a phenomenon that satisfies a criterion of X under such circumstances; or we may say that the phenomenon *is* X under the circumstances.[23]

8. These various ways of speaking about criteria imply that to be a criterion of X is just to *be* (what is called) X, in case there is only one criterion of X, or to be (what is called) X under certain circumstances, in case there is more than one criterion of X. But on any such account of criteria there will be less truth in certain of Wittgenstein's most interesting remarks than one might have hoped or feared.

Some sixty per cent of the passages in which he attributes criteria to this or that (in all of his published work taken together) have to do with such concepts as those of understanding, imagining, and feeling—roughly: "psy-

[20] *Ibid.*, p. 115, and cf. the whole of sec. 64.
[21] *PI*, I, sec. 183.
[22] *BB*, p. 141, ll. 36–37.
[23] *Ibid.*, pp. 131, ll. 33–38; 147, ll. 36–40. Cf. pp. 110, ll. 10–15; 154, ll. 3–5.

chological" concepts. It is by no means always a kind of
behavior that he calls a criterion in this connection. But
he appears to think that there is in every case at least one
"outward" criterion of an "inner" event, state, process, or
whatever the thing "grammatically" is, though there may
be inner criteria of it as well.[24] By silently reciting a poem
to myself, I might discover that I know it by heart. For
such a thing as having a toothache, however, there is no
inner criterion.[25] A man's holding his cheek in a certain
kind of way, with a certain kind of look, is the sort of
thing that is a criterion for his having a toothache; and his
saying that he has one is an additional, derivative criterion.

But can what a man does or says be called his having a
toothache, or referred to or described as that, or even referred to or described *by* saying that he has a toothache,
under any circumstances, in a proper and literal sense of
the words said? No. (And is there no inner criterion of
having a toothache? There is something that I have *called*
having a toothache, when I had a toothache, namely *having* one.)

Or take *expecting*, another of Wittgenstein's examples.
What is expecting? If it is an empty idea that what we
call "expecting" is a queer, incorporeal something hidden
away in that remarkable medium, the mind, what *do*
we call "expecting"? For example, what do we call "expecting someone to tea"? Unfortunately, the *Blue Book* is
ready with a wrong answer: no one phenomenon, but any
one of many different "processes of expecting someone to
tea," according to the circumstances. "What happens *may*
be this: At four o'clock I look at my diary and see the
name 'B' against to-day's date; I prepare tea for two"; and
so on. (If we seize upon seeing the name, for example,
and say "Well, *that's* hidden, at least," the *Blue Book*
threatens to remind us of various phenomena *en plein air*

[24] "Whatever the thing 'grammatically' is": cf. *PI*, I, secs.
572–573.
[25] Wittgenstein does not expressly say this, but cf., e.g., *PI*,
I, secs. 289–290, 377.

that we call "seeing.") Under certain circumstances "all this is called 'expecting B from 4 to 4.30.' "[26]

But it isn't. And so the "picture" of the hidden something or other that is uniquely called "expecting" doesn't vanish;[27] or it seems to vanish, but only because the *Blue Book* has evoked a competing picture, of the plain man calling what that other man is doing over there, with his diary and teapot, "expecting."

9. In the *Remarks on the Foundations of Mathematics* and the *Philosophical Investigations*, the ways of speaking about criteria that were dominant in the *Blue* and *Brown Books* are almost entirely suppressed. Wittgenstein may have been unconscious of this change, striking as it is, since some eight scattered remarks in the *Investigations* still suggest that a criterion of X is something that may be described as "X" under certain circumstances, something in which X may consist.[28] But in general the *Investigations* and the *Remarks on the Foundations of Mathematics* do not support that account of a criterion.

There is one exceptional passage of the *Blue Book* in which Wittgenstein calls what he unquestionably regards as criteria for the truth of certain propositions "evidences for" the propositions.[29] The dominant conception of a criterion in the *Remarks on the Foundations of Mathematics* and the *Investigations* is one to which this passage points: A criterion for a given thing's being so is something that can show the thing to be so and show by its absence

[26] BB, p. 20.

[27] PI, II, p. 223; " 'I cannot know what is going on in him' is above all a *picture*."

[28] At least the following remarks more or less strongly suggest the dominant account of criteria in BB: PI, I, secs. 145, 177, 183, 444, 541, 573, 586; II, p. 174, ll. 10–14. The following remarks, however, more or less strongly suggest that that account ought to be rejected: PI, I, secs. 321–322, 369–370, 557; II, p. 211e, ll. 23–32; and perhaps I, sec. 412, ll. 10–13, with the insertion of the parenthetical clause that has been left untranslated by mistake.

[29] BB, pp. 51–52. Compare PI, I, secs. 354–356.

that the thing is not so; it is something by which one may be *justified in saying* that the thing is so and by whose absence one may be justified in saying that the thing is not so. And a criterion for a thing's being so has this relation to the thing's being so not as a matter of fact, like what Wittgenstein calls a "symptom" of its being so, but as a matter of "logical" necessity. That is, on Wittgenstein's account of such necessity, its relation to the thing's being so is "founded on a definition" or "founded on convention" or is a matter of "grammar."[30]

Something of this sort is of course what Wittgenstein's introduction of the term "criterion" prepared us to find. A criterion for so-and-so's being the case was to be something by which one might *know* that it was the case; that this or that *was* a criterion for so-and-so's being the case was to be a sort of "tautology," a matter of "convention."[31] But instead of making this conception clear, Wittgenstein distorts it, in the *Blue* and *Brown Books*, by representing the criteria for so-and-so's being the case as various things that may *be* what is called "so-and-so's being the case," as a valise and a trunk or a trunk and a birdcage may be what is called "my baggage." In the later books, this distortion is undone, for the most part, but Wittgenstein still leaves his conception of a criterion very unclear. Can it be made clear? I think so. I will try to say how, very briefly, in the space that remains to me.

Take toothaches again. What Wittgenstein calls a "criterion" of having a toothache is a phenomenon by which, under certain circumstances, one would be justified in saying that a man had a toothache or in saying, should one have occasion to do so, that one knew he had a toothache. (It is therefore a phenomenon by which one *may know* that a man has a toothache, though sometimes, to be sure, one is justified in saying that one knows a thing

[30] For the quoted phrases, cf. *PI*, I, secs. 354, 355, and for "grammar" in this connection cf., e.g., *PI*, I, sec. 520.

[31] *BB*, pp. 24–25.

and yet doesn't know it, because, as one may or may not discover, it isn't so.)

Suppose that I am justified in saying that a certain man has a toothache by his present behavior, under certain circumstances. Then I must be in a position to say that *when* a man, or a man of whom it is true that so-and-so, or at least this man, behaves thus and thus, under such and such circumstances, he always or almost always has a toothache. This general proposition may be (one might think that it *must* be) one that it would be absurd to describe as a necessary truth. (For brevity's sake, I will use the expressions "necessary" and "contingent" in this section, in familiar senses, without explanation or defense, at a cost in clarity that may be greater than I imagine.) The association of certain behavior with having a toothache may be the purest matter of fact. It may happen to be a fact, say, that whenever Jones makes an appointment with his dentist he has a toothache, or that no one ever takes a certain drug unless he has a toothache.

But suppose that a man sits rocking miserably back and forth, holding his jaw, every now and then cautiously pushing at a loose tooth on that side with certain kinds of grimaces and sharp intakes of breath, and so on, in my presence. Under a variety of kinds of circumstances I would not be justified by this behavior in saying that the man had a toothache. (I hope that I have conveyed, without attempting to describe it in detail, what behavior I mean by "this behavior.") As it happens, such circumstances are exceptional. Normally, I *would* be justified by this behavior in saying that the man had a toothache. A man who behaves in this manner, under normal circumstances, always or almost always does have a toothache. That is, a man who behaves in this manner, under circumstances that have no tendency to show that he is *not* so behaving because he has a toothache, always or almost always *is* so behaving because he has a toothache.

Is that an established fact, or a fact of common experience? It has the look of one. But in Wittgenstein's

view, if I understand him correctly, it is a necessary truth.
That a man behaves in a certain manner, under certain
circumstances, cannot entail that he has a toothache. But
it can entail something else, which there is no short way
of stating exactly, so far as I can find. Roughly, then: it
can entail that anyone who is aware that the man is behaving in this manner, under these circumstances, is *justified in saying* that the man has a toothache, in the absence
of any special reason to say something more guarded (as,
for example, that there is an overwhelming probability
that the man has a toothache). Even more roughly: That
a man behaves in a certain manner, under certain circumstances, can entail that he *almost certainly* has a toothache. (But this way of putting it may be very misleading,
since what I would ordinarily be justified in saying, by the
fact that a man almost certainly has a toothache, in this
sense, is "He has a toothache" or even "I *know* he has a
toothache.")

If it *is* a necessary truth that a man who behaves in the
manner that I indicated, under what I will call, for short,
"normal circumstances" (see the paragraph before last),
always or almost always is so behaving because he has a
toothache, then there is an immense "family" of kinds or
patterns of behavior that are associated in this way with
having a toothache. (The family includes, though this may
seem paradoxical, the behavior of replying, when asked if
one has a toothache, that one does.) And Wittgenstein also
holds, if I understand him correctly, that it is a necessary
truth that a man whose behavior does *not* include any
belonging to this family, under normal circumstances,
never or almost never has a toothache. These kinds or
patterns of behavior, then, if there are any, are "criteria"
of having a toothache, in Wittgenstein's usage, so far as I
can make out what that usage is.

I cannot discuss here the question whether there *are*
criteria, in this sense, of having a toothache. I am inclined
to think that there are not. The propositions that would
have to be necessary and not contingent if there were in

this sense behavioral criteria of having a toothache do not seem to me to be clear cases of propositions that are necessary and not contingent. On the other hand, they do not seem to me to be clear cases of propositions that are contingent and not necessary, either. They seem to me to be *neither* necessary nor contingent. It may be sufficient for Wittgenstein's philosophical purposes that these and other such propositions should have this indefinite status, though *he* appears to have thought that they had the definite status of necessary propositions. But that is another question that I have no space to discuss in this paper.

Postscript (1966): The last section of the foregoing paper assumes that if a kind of behavior, or anything else, is a criterion in Wittgenstein's sense, then between it and that of which it is a criterion some necessary connection or other must hold under what I will call an *ordinary description* of the criterion and of the circumstances, if any, to which its criterial role is confined. (I mean, for example, a description of the type envisaged in sec. 9, ⟨6.) As far as I can see now, this assumption, which guided my attempt to specify a range of "propositions that would have to be necessary and not contingent if there were . . . behavioral criteria of having a toothache" (sec. 9, ⟨9), is completely mistaken. The propositions I had in mind would not be necessary, and that does not matter in the least.

It was another mistake to think that these propositions, though not necessary, would be not quite contingent, either. They would be just contingent, no better or worse. As I imagined them, they would be formulated at very great length: "A man who sits rocking miserably back and forth, holding his jaw [and so on for pages and pages] in circumstances that have no tendency to show that he is not so behaving because he has a toothache, always or almost always is so behaving because he has a toothache." Or "If a man sits rocking [and so on] in circumstances [and so on], then anyone who is aware that the man is

behaving in this manner, in these circumstances, is justified in saying that the man has a toothache, in the absence
of any special reason to say something more guarded." (Cf.
sec. 9, ⟨7.) But their length would not save them. For
example—an objection I owe to Alvin Plantinga—what if
one had no notion *how* people with toothaches were likely
to behave, these days? Or what if rocking-and-so-on, once
so characteristic of people with severe toothaches, were
commonly mimicked to perfection by others without
toothaches? If either of these suppositions were realized,
that circumstance would have no "tendency to show" that
a man who sat rocking-and-so-on did *not* have a toothache.
Nor would it provide a "reason to say something more
guarded" than that he did have a toothache. It would
provide, rather, some reason to be quiet about the question whether he had a toothache or not, for the time
being.

Indeed, it seems conceivable that people with toothaches should cease to behave in any special way at all. "If
things were quite different from what they actually are—
if there were for instance no characteristic expression of
pain, of fear, of joy; if rule became exception and exception rule; or if both became phenomena of roughly equal
frequency—this would make our normal language-games
lose their point." So Wittgenstein says in *Philosophical
Investigations* I, § 142. He does not say that things could
not really be as different as all that. On the contrary, he
appears to treat the fact that there are characteristic expressions of pain, for example, as one among the "general
facts of nature" of which he speaks in the remark at the
foot of the same page and in section xii of Part II. And
a general fact of nature it is, as far as I can tell. Imagining
how it might be an amazing but established fact that there
were no longer any characteristic, natural expressions of
pain has its pitfalls, certainly. But one needn't fall into
them, and one needn't jump into them, either, for fear of
discovering that pain is a "private object." If there were
no characteristic, natural expressions of pain, pain might

be less public on the whole than now, but would not be any the more a "private object," if Wittgenstein is right. "Private objects" are not so easily come by.

In short, there are no necessary or not quite contingent truths of any of the types that I suggested. There are only contingent facts of those types. But Wittgenstein never meant to deny that, and no denial of it is involved, I think now, in the observation (as he took it to be) that there are behavioral criteria of having a toothache and of other such things.

If a kind of behavior is a criterion, in Wittgenstein's sense, of having a toothache, then it is part of the "use," the "grammar," of the word "toothache," among others, that in at least some circumstances another person who so behaves may be said to have a toothache. His so behaving may be taken to decide the question whether he has a toothache or not: he does. And that this behavior may be so taken is a matter of "definition," a "convention." (For "use," "grammar," "definition," and "convention," in this connection, see the *Blue Book*, pp. 23 [l.27]–24 [l.13], pp. 24 [l.38]–25 [l.12], p. 57 [ll.6–13], and *Philosophical Investigations* I, §§ 354–355.) It does not follow, however, that there lies ready to hand in the language an ordinary description of the behavior, or of it together with some possible circumstances of its occurrence, that *entails* having a toothache. (Moreover, if such descriptions were available, no philosophical skeptic would be impressed. Dancing with rage entails being in a rage, perhaps; if so, that leaves the problem of other minds where it was.) It does not follow either, as I thought it did, that there lies ready to hand an ordinary description of the behavior, or of it together with some possible circumstances of its occurrence, that entails "almost certainly" having a toothache (sec. 9, ¶7) or being warrantably describable as having a toothache, or anything whatever of interest about having a toothache, as far as I can see now. If the "convention" of describing a man who behaves in such and such a (criterial) way as a man with a toothache were cancelled, as it would be if this criterion drifted away from the others, it does not follow that the concept of a toothache would not survive. It is harder than that to destroy a concept, to replace a "use" by *another* "use."

The concept of a toothache allows for exotic reversals. ("He behaved exactly as if he had a toothache, said he did and meant it honestly, had teeth, but turned out to have no toothache." Wittgenstein, apparently, would object to "said he did and meant it honestly," but there is no reason to draw the line there, or anywhere.) The concept also allows for unnerving contingencies of a more general kind. It allows us to imagine that behaving in such and such a way that was paradigmatic for having a toothache should come to have nothing to do with toothaches. It allows us to imagine a time when adults who say they have toothaches, and mean it, will *never* have toothaches. A concept so extremely tolerant may lack dignity, but there is no help for it. Unless it is the concept of a "private object," after all. But I see no support for that suspicion in anything I have said.

CAN THERE BE A PRIVATE LANGUAGE?

A. J. AYER

In a quite ordinary sense, it is obvious that there can be private languages. There can be, because there are. A language may be said to be private when it is devised to enable a limited number of persons to communicate with one another in a way that is not intelligible to anyone outside the group. By this criterion, thieves' slang and family jargons are private languages. Such languages are not strictly private, in the sense that only one person uses and understands them, but there may very well be languages that are. Men have been known to keep diaries in codes which no one else is meant to understand. A private code is not, indeed, a private language, but rather a private method of transcribing some given language. It is, however, possible that a very secretive diarist may not be satisfied with putting familiar words into an unfamiliar notation, but may prefer to invent new words: the two processes are in any case not sharply distinct. If he carries his invention far enough he can properly be said to be employing a private language. For all I know, this has actually been done.

From this point of view, what makes a language private is simply the fact that it satisfies the purpose of being intelligible only to a single person, or to a restricted set of people. It is necessary here to bring in a reference to pur-

From *Proceedings of the Aristotelian Society*, Supplementary Vol. XXVIII (1954), pp. 63–76. Reprinted, with one footnote added, by permission of the author and editor. The article has been collected in A. J. Ayer, *The Concept of a Person and Other Essays* (London and New York, 1963).

pose, since a language may come to be intelligible only to a few people, or even only to a single person, merely by falling into general disuse: but such 'dead' languages are not considered to be private, if the limitation of their use was not originally intended. One may characterize a private language by saying that it is not in this sense meant to be alive. There is, however, no reason, in principle, why it should not come alive. The fact that only one person, or only a few people, are able to understand it is purely contingent. Just as it is possible, in theory, that any code should be broken, so can a private language come to be more widely understood. Such private languages are in general derived from public languages, and even if there are any which are not so derived, they will still be translatable into public languages. Their ceasing to be private is then just a matter of enough people becoming able to translate them or, what is more difficult but still theoretically possible, not to translate but even so to understand them.

If I am right, then, there is a use for the expression 'private language' which clearly allows it to have application. But this is not the use which philosophers have commonly given it. What philosophers usually seem to have in mind when they speak of a private language is one that is, in their view, necessarily private, in as much as it is used by some particular person to refer only to his own private experiences. For it is often held that for a language to be public it must refer to what is publicly observable: if a person could limit himself to describing his own sensations or feelings, then, strictly speaking, only he would understand what he was saying; his utterance might indirectly convey some information to others, but it could not mean to them exactly what it meant to him. Thus, Carnap who gives the name of 'protocol language' to any set of sentences which are used to give 'a direct record' of one's own experience argues, in his booklet on *The Unity of Science*,[1] that if an utterance like 'thirst now,' belonging

[1] Pp. 76 ff.

to the protocol language of a subject S_1, is construed as expressing 'only what is immediately given' to S_1, it cannot be understood by anyone else. Another subject S_2 may claim to be able to recognize and so to refer to S_1's thirst, but 'strictly speaking' all that he ever recognizes is some physical state of S_1's body. 'If by "the thirst of S_1" we understand not the physical state of his body, but his sensations of thirst, *i.e.* something non-material, then S_1's thirst is fundamentally beyond the reach of S_2's recognition.'[2] S_2 cannot possibly verify any statement which refers to S_1's thirst, in this sense, and consequently cannot understand it. 'In general,' Carnap continues, 'every statement in any person's protocol language would have sense for that person alone. . . . Even when the same words and sentences occur in various protocol languages, their sense would be different, they could not even be compared. Every protocol language could therefore be applied only solipsistically: there would be no intersubjective protocol language. This is the consequence obtained by consistent adherence to the usual view and terminology (rejected by the author).'[3]

Since Carnap wishes to maintain that people can understand one another's protocol statements, if only on the ground that this is a necessary condition for statements made in what he calls the physical language to be intersubjectively verifiable, he draws the inference that 'protocol language is a part of physical language.' That is, he concludes that sentences which on the face of it refer to private experiences must be logically equivalent to sentences which describe some physical state of the subject. Other philosophers have followed him in giving a physicalist interpretation to the statements that one makes about the experiences of others, but have stopped short of extending it to all the statements that one may make about one's own. They prefer to hold that certain sentences do serve only to describe the speaker's private experiences,

[2] *The Unity of Science*, p. 79.
[3] *Ibid.*, p. 80.

and that, this being so, they have a different meaning for him from any that they can possibly have for anybody else.

In his *Philosophical Investigations* Wittgenstein appears to go much further than this. He seems to take the view that someone who attempted to use language in this private way would not merely be unable to communicate his meaning to others, but would have no meaning to communicate even to himself; he would not succeed in saying anything at all. 'Let us,' says Wittgenstein,[4] 'imagine the following case: I want to keep a diary about the recurrence of a certain sensation. To this end I associate it with the sign "E" and write this sign in a calendar for every day on which I have the sensation.—I will remark first of all that a definition of the sign cannot be formulated.— But still I can give myself a kind of ostensive definition.— How? Can I point to the sensation? Not in the ordinary sense. But I speak or write the sign down, and at the same time I concentrate my attention on the sensation—and so, as it were, point to it inwardly.—But what is this ceremony for? for that is all it seems to be! A definition surely serves to establish the meaning of a sign.—Well, that is done precisely by the concentration of my attention; for in this way I impress on myself the connection between the sign and the sensation. But "I impress it on myself" can only mean: this process brings it about that I remember the connection *right* in the future. But in the present case I have no criterion of correctness. One would like to say: whatever is going to seem right to me is right. And that only means that here one can't talk about "right."'

Again, 'What reason have we for calling "E" the sign for a *sensation*? For "sensation" is a word of our common language, not of one intelligible to me alone. So the use of this word stands in need of a justification which everybody understands.'[5]

This point is then developed further: 'Let us imagine a table (something like a dictionary) that exists only in our

[4] *Philosophical Investigations*, I. 258.
[5] *Op. cit.*, I. 261.

imagination. A dictionary can be used to justify the translation of a word X into a word Y. But are we also to call it a justification if such a table is to be looked up only in the imagination?—"Well, yes; then it is a subjective justification."—But justification consists in appealing to something independent.—"But surely I can appeal from one memory to another. For example, I don't know if I have remembered the time of departure of a train right, and to check it I call to mind how a page of the time-table looked. Isn't it the same here?"—No; for this process has got to produce a memory which is actually *correct*. If the mental image of the time-table could not itself be *tested* for correctness, how could it confirm the correctness of the first memory? (As if someone were to buy several copies of the morning paper to assure himself that what it said was true.)

'Looking up a table in the imagination is no more looking up a table than the image of the result of an imagined experiment is the result of an experiment.'[6]

The case is quite different, Wittgenstein thinks, when the sensation can be coupled with some outward manifestation. Thus he maintains that the language which we ordinarily use to describe our 'inner experiences' is not private because the words which one uses to refer to one's sensations are 'tied up with [one's] natural expressions of sensation,'[7] with the result that other people are in a position to understand them. Similarly he grants that the person who tries to describe his private sensation by writing down the sign 'E' in his diary might find a use for this sign if he discovered that whenever he had the sensation in question it could be shown by means of some measuring instrument that his blood pressure rose. For this would give him a way of telling that his blood pressure was rising without bothering to consult the instrument. But then, argues Wittgenstein, it will make no difference whether his recognition of the sensation is right or not. Provided

[6] *Op. cit.*, I. 265.
[7] *Op. cit.*, I. 256.

that whenever he thinks he recognizes it, there is independent evidence that his blood pressure rises, it will not matter if he is invariably mistaken, if the sensation which he takes to be the same on each occasion is really not the same at all. 'And that alone shows that the hypothesis that [he] makes a mistake is mere show.'[8]

Let us examine this argument. A point to which Wittgenstein constantly recurs is that the ascription of meaning to a sign is something that needs to be justified: the justification consists in there being some independent test for determining that the sign is being used correctly; independent, that is, of the subject's recognition, or supposed recognition, of the object which he intends the sign to signify. His claim to recognize the object, his belief that it really is the same, is not to be accepted unless it can be backed by further evidence. Apparently, too, this evidence must be public: it must, at least in theory, be accessible to everyone. Merely to check one private sensation by another would not be enough. For if one cannot be trusted to recognize one of them, neither can one be trusted to recognize the other.

But unless there is something that one is allowed to recognize, no test can ever be completed: there will be no justification for the use of any sign at all. I check my memory of the time at which the train is due to leave by visualizing a page of the time-table; and I am required to check this in its turn by looking up the page. But unless I can trust my eyesight at this point, unless I can recognize the figures that I see written down, I am still no better off. It is true that if I distrust my eyesight I have the resource of consulting other people; but then I have to understand their testimony, I have correctly to identify the signs that they make. Let the object to which I am attempting to refer be as public as you please, let the word which I use for this purpose belong to some common language, my assurance that I am using the word correctly,

8 *Op. cit.*, I. 270.

that I am using it to refer to the 'right' object, must in the end rest on the testimony of my senses. It is through hearing what other people say, or through seeing what they write, or observing their movements, that I am enabled to conclude that their use of the word agrees with mine.[9] But if without further ado I can recognize such noises or shapes or movements, why can I not also recognize a private sensation? It is all very well for Wittgenstein to say that writing down the sign 'E,' at the same time as I attend to the sensation, is an idle ceremony. How is it any more idle than writing down a sign, whether it be the conventionally correct sign or not, at the same time as I observe some 'public' object? There is, indeed, a problem about what is involved in endowing any sign with meaning, but it is no less of a problem in the case where the object for which the sign is supposed to stand is public than in the case where it is private. Whatever it is about my behaviour that transforms the making of a sound, or the inscription of a shape, into the employment of a sign can equally well occur in either case.

[9] My use of a similar argument in my book *The Problem of Knowledge* has led Miss Anscombe to accuse me of committing a logical fallacy (*vide* her book *An Introduction to Wittgenstein's Tractatus*, pp. 138–139). She supposes that I argue 'from the fact that it is not possible, and *a fortiori* not necessary, that every identification or recognition should in fact be checked, to the innocuousness of the notion of an uncheckable identification.' I agree with her that this is a fallacy, but I do not think I have committed it. My argument is that since every process of checking must terminate in some act of recognition, no process of checking can establish anything unless some acts of recognition are taken as valid in themselves. This does not imply that these acts of recognition are uncheckable in the sense that their deliverances could not in their turn be subjected to further checks; but then these further checks would again have to terminate in acts of recognition which were taken as valid in themselves and so *ad infinitum*. If the inference drawn from this is that an act of recognition is worthless unless it is corroborated by other acts of recognition, the recognition of private sensations will not necessarily be excluded. For there is no reason in principle why such acts of recognition should not corroborate one another.

But, it may be said, in the one case I can point to the object I am trying to name, I can give an ostensive definition of it; in the other I cannot. For merely attending to an object is not pointing to it. But what difference does this make? I can indeed extend my finger in the direction of a physical object, while I pronounce what I intend to be the object's name; and I cannot extend my finger in the direction of a private sensation. But how is this extending of my finger itself anything more than an idle ceremony? If it is to play its part in the giving of an ostensive definition, this gesture has to be endowed with meaning. But if I can endow such a gesture with meaning, I can endow a word with meaning, without the gesture.

I suppose that the reason why the gesture is thought to be important is that it enables me to make my meaning clear to others. Of course they have to interpret me correctly. If they are not intelligent, or I am not careful, they may think that I am pointing to one thing when I really intend to point to another. But successful communication by this method is at least possible. The object to which I mean to point is one that they can observe. On the other hand, no amount of gesturing on my part can direct their attention to a private sensation of mine, which *ex hypothesi* they cannot observe, assuming further that this sensation has no 'natural expression.' So I cannot give an ostensive definition of the word which I wish to stand for the sensation. Nor can I define it in terms of other words, for how are they to be defined? Consequently I cannot succeed in giving it any meaning.

This argument is based on two assumptions, both of which I believe to be false. One is that in a case of this sort it is impossible, logically impossible, to understand a sign unless one can either observe the object which it signifies, or at least observe something with which this object is naturally associated. And the other is that for a person to be able to attach meaning to a sign it is necessary that other people should be capable of understanding it too. It will be convenient to begin by examining the second of these assumptions which leads on to the first.

Imagine a Robinson Crusoe left alone on his island while still an infant, having not yet learned to speak. Let him, like Romulus and Remus, be nurtured by a wolf, or some other animal, until he can fend for himself; and so let him grow to manhood. He will certainly be able to recognize many things upon the island, in the sense that he adapts his behaviour to them. Is it inconceivable that he should also name them? There may be psychological grounds for doubting whether such a solitary being would in fact invent a language. The development of language, it may be argued, is a social phenomenon. But surely it is not self-contradictory to suppose that someone, uninstructed in the use of any existing language, makes up a language for himself. After all, some human being must have been the first to use a symbol. And even if he did so as a member of a group, in order to communicate with the other members, even if his choice of symbols was socially conditioned, it is at least conceivable that it should originally have been a purely private enterprise. The hypothesis of G. K. Chesterton's dancing professor about the origin of language, that it came 'from the formulated secret language of some individual creature,' is very probably false, but it is certainly not unintelligible.

But if we allow that our Robinson Crusoe could invent words to describe the flora and fauna of his island, why not allow that he could also invent words to describe his sensations? In neither case will he be able to justify his use of words by drawing on the evidence provided by a fellow creature: but while this is a useful check, it is not indispensable. It would be difficult to argue that the power of communication, the ability even to keep a private diary, could come to him only with the arrival of Man Friday. His justification for describing his environment in the way that he does will be that he perceives it to have just those features which his words are intended to describe. His knowing how to use these words will be a mat-

ter of his remembering what objects they are meant to
stand for, and so of his being able to recognize these objects. But why should he not succeed in recognizing them?
And why then should he not equally succeed in recognizing
his sensations? Undoubtedly, he may make mistakes. He
may think that a bird which he sees flying past is a bird of
the same type as one which he had previously named,
when in fact it is of a different type, sufficiently different
for him to have given it a different name if he had observed it more closely. Similarly, he may think that a sensation is the same as others which he has identified, when
in fact, in the relevant aspects, it is not the same. In
neither case may the mistake make any practical difference to him, but to say that nothing turns upon a mistake
is not to say that it is not a mistake at all. In the case of the
bird, there is a slightly greater chance of his detecting his
mistake, since the identical bird may reappear: but even so
he has to rely upon his memory for the assurance that it is
the identical bird. In the case of the sensation, he has only
his memory as a means of deciding whether his identification is correct or not. In this respect he is indeed like
Wittgenstein's man who buys several copies of the morning paper to assure himself that what it says is true. But
the reason why this seems to us so absurd is that we take
it for granted that one copy of a morning paper will duplicate another; there is no absurdity in buying a second
newspaper, of a different type, and using it to check the
first. And in a place where there was only one morning
newspaper, but it was so produced that misprints might
occur in one copy without occurring in all, it would be perfectly sensible to buy several copies and check them
against each other. Of course there remains the important
difference that the facts which the newspaper reports are
independently verifiable, in theory if not always in practice. But verification must stop somewhere. As I have already argued, unless something is recognized, without being referred to a further test, nothing can be tested. In
the case of Crusoe's sensation, we are supposing that be-

yond his memory there is no further test. It does not follow that he has no means of identifying it, or that it does not make sense to say that he identifies it right or wrong.

So long as Crusoe remains alone on the island, so long, that is, as he communicates only with himself, the principal distinction which he is likely to draw between 'external' objects and his 'inner' experiences is that his experiences are transient in a way that external objects are not. He will not be bound to draw even this distinction; his criteria for identity may be different from our own; but it is reasonable to suppose that they will be the same. Assuming, then, that his language admits the distinction, he will find on the arrival of Man Friday that it acquires a new importance. For whereas he will be able to teach Man Friday the use of the words which he has devised to stand for external objects by showing him the objects for which they stand, he will not, in this way, be able to teach him the use of the words which he has devised to stand for his sensations. And in the cases where these sensations are entirely private, in the sense that they have no 'natural expressions' which Man Friday can identify, it may well be that Crusoe fails to find any way of teaching him the use of the words which he employs to stand for them. But from the fact that he cannot teach this part of his language to Man Friday it by no means follows that he has no use for it himself. In a context of this sort, one can teach only what one already understands. The ability to teach, or rather the ability of someone else to learn, cannot therefore be a prerequisite for understanding.

Neither does it necessarily follow, in these circumstances, that Man Friday will be incapable of learning the meaning of the words which Crusoe uses to describe his private sensations. It is surely a contingent fact that we depend upon ostensive definitions, to the extent that we do, for learning what words mean. As it is, a child is not taught how to describe his feelings in the way he is taught to describe the objects in his nursery. His mother cannot point to his pain in the way that she can point to his cup and spoon. But she knows that he has a pain because he cries and because she sees that something has happened to him which is likely to cause him pain; and knowing that he is in pain she is able to teach him what to call it. If there were no external signs of his sensations she would have no means of detecting when he had them, and therefore could not teach him how to describe them. This is indeed the case, but it might easily be otherwise. We can imagine two persons being so attuned to one another that whenever either has a private sensation of a certain sort, the other has it too. In that case, when one of them described what he was feeling the other might very well follow the description, even though he had no 'external' evidence to guide him. But how could either of them ever know that he had identified the other's feeling correctly? Well, how can two people ever know that they mean the same by a word which they use to refer to some 'public' object? Only because each finds the other's reactions appropriate. Similarly one may suppose that Man Friday sympathizes when Crusoe's private sensation is painful, and congratulates him when it is pleasant, that he is able to say when it begins and when it stops, that he correctly describes it as being rather like such and such another sensation, and very different from a third, thereby affording proof that he also understands the words that stand for these sensations. Admittedly, such tests are not conclusive. But the tests which we ordinarily take as showing that we mean the same by the words which we apply to public objects are not conclusive either: they leave it at least theoretically open that we do not after all mean quite the same. But from the fact that the tests are not conclusive it does not, in either case, follow that they have no force at all. It is true also that such tests as the expressed agreement about the duration of the experience require that the two men already share a common language, which they have no doubt built up on the basis of common observations. It would indeed be difficult, though still, I think, not necessarily impossible,[10] for them to establish communication if all their experiences were private, in Wittgenstein's sense. But even if their understanding each other's use of words could come about only if some of the objects which these words described were public, it would not follow that they all must be so.

It is not even necessary to make the assumption that Man Friday comes to know what Crusoe's sensations are, and so to understand the words which signify them, through having similar sensations of his own. It is conceivable that he should satisfy all the tests which go to show that he has this knowledge, and indeed that he should actually have it, even though the experience which he rightly ascribes to Crusoe is unlike any that he has, or ever has had, himself. It would indeed be very strange if someone had this power of seeing, as it were, directly into another's soul. But it is strange only in the sense that it is something which, on causal grounds, we should not expect to happen. The idea of its happening breaks no logical rule. An analogous case would be that of someone's imagining, or seeming to remember, an experience which was unlike any that he had ever actually had. To allow that such things are possible is, indeed, to admit innate ideas, in the Lockean sense, but that is not a serious objection. The admission is not even inconsistent with the prevalent varieties of empiricism. It can still be made a rule that in order to understand a word which signifies a sensation one must know what it would be like to have the sensation in

[10] I have come to doubt this. See the following footnote to 'Privacy' [reprinted in *The Concept of a Person and Other Essays*]: Having tried to construct a language of this kind [viz., a language all of whose words refer to nothing but private things], I have come to doubt whether it is feasible. I am now inclined to think that in any language which allows reference to individuals there must be criteria of identity which make it possible for different speakers to refer to the same individual. This would not prevent the language from containing private sectors, but it would mean that my idea that these private sectors could be made to absorb the public sectors was not tenable.

question: that is, one must be able to identify the sensation when one has it, and so to verify the statement which describes it. The peculiarity of the cases which we are envisaging is just that people are credited with the ability to identify experiences which they have not previously had. There may indeed be causal objections to the hypothesis that this can ever happen. The point which concerns us now is that these objections are no more than causal. The ways in which languages are actually learned do not logically circumscribe the possibilities of their being understood.

If the sort of insight which we have been attributing to Man Friday were commonly possessed, we might well be led to revise our concepts of publicity and privacy. The mistake which is made by philosophers like Carnap is that of supposing that being public or being private, in the senses which are relevant to this discussion, are properties which are somehow attached to different sorts of objects, independently of our linguistic usage. But the reason why one object is publicly and another only privately accessible is that in the one case it makes sense to say that the object is observed by more than one person and in the other it does not.[11] Tables are public; it makes sense to say that several people are perceiving the same table. Headaches are private: it does not make sense to say that several people are feeling the same headache. But just as we can assimilate tables to headaches by introducing a notation in which two different persons' perceiving the same table becomes a matter of their each sensing their own private 'tabular' sense-data, so we could assimilate headaches to tables by introducing a notation in which it was correct to speak of a common headache, which certain people only were in a condition to perceive. As things are, this notation would not be convenient. But if people were so constituted that they were communally exposed to headaches in the way that they are communally exposed to the weather,

[11] This is an over-simplification; see 'Privacy.'

we might cease to think of headaches as being necessarily private. A London particular might come to be a local headache as well as, or instead of, a local fog. Certain persons might escape it, just as certain persons, for one reason or another, may fail to perceive the fog. But the fog exists for all that, and so, given this new way of speaking, would the public headache. The conditions which would make this way of speaking useful do not, indeed, obtain; but that they do not is, once again, a purely contingent fact.

The facts being what they are, we do not have a use for such expressions as 'S_2's feeling S_1's thirst' or 'S_2's observing the sensation of thirst which S_1 feels.' On the other hand, we do attach a meaning to saying that the same physical object, or process, or event, for instance a state of S_1's body, is observed by S_2 as well as by S_1. Does it follow, as Carnap thinks, that for this reason S_2 cannot understand a statement which refers to S_1's feeling of thirst, whereas he can understand a statement which refers to the condition of S_1's body? Suppose that we modified our rules for identity, in a way that many philosophers have proposed, and allowed ourselves to say that what was ordinarily described as S_1 and S_2's observing the same physical event was 'really' a case of each of them sensing his own sense-data which, while they might be qualitatively similar, could not be literally the same. Should we thereby be committed to denying that either could understand what the other said about this physical event? Surely not. And equally the fact that S_2 cannot feel, or inspect, S_1's feelings in no way entails that he cannot understand what S_1 says about them. The criteria for deciding whether two people understand each other are logically independent of the fact that we do, or do not, have a use for saying that literally the same objects are perceived by both.

I conclude, first, that for a person to use descriptive language meaningfully it is not necessary that any other person should understand him, and, secondly, that for anyone to understand a descriptive statement it is not necessary that he should himself be able to observe what it describes. It is not even necessary that he should be able to observe something which is naturally associated with what it describes, in the way that feelings are associated with their 'natural expressions.' If we insist on making it a necessary condition for our understanding a descriptive statement that we are able to observe what it describes, we shall find ourselves disclaiming the possibility of understanding not merely statements about other people's private sensations, but also statements about the past; either that, or reinterpreting them in such a way that they change their reference, as when philosophers substitute bodily states for feelings, and the future for the past. Both courses, I now think, are mistaken. No doubt it is a necessary condition for my understanding a descriptive statement that it should be, in some way, verifiable. But it need not be directly verifiable, and even if it is directly verifiable, it need not be directly verifiable by me.

CAN THERE BE A PRIVATE LANGUAGE?

R. RHEES

The problem about private languages is the problem of how words mean. This is much the same as the question of what a rule of language is.

When we talk about something, our language does not point to it, nor mirror it. Pointing or mirroring could refer to things only within a convention, anyway: only when there is a way in which pointing is understood and a way in which mirroring is understood. I point for the sake of someone who understands it. Apart from that it were an idle ceremony; as idle as making sounds in front of things.

Our words refer to things by the way they enter in discourse; by their connexions with what people are saying and doing, for instance, and by the way they affect what is said and done. What we say makes a difference. What expressions we use makes a difference. And the notion of a rule goes with that. If it made no difference what sound you made or when, you could not be understood and you would have said nothing. If you have said something, your utterance will be taken in one way and not in another. In many cases you will have committed yourself to saying other things, to answering in certain ways if you are asked, or to doing certain things. That belongs to the regular use of your words, and that is why it would not have been just the same if you had used others instead. That is also why it is possible to learn the language.

From *Proceedings of the Aristotelian Society*, Supplementary Vol. XXVIII (1954), pp. 77–94. Reprinted with the permission of the author and editor. This article is a reply to Ayer's of the same title, reprinted above.

When we speak of "use" we may think of general practice and we may think of rules. Sometimes these can be left together, but sometimes there are differences we ought to notice. When I learn the use of an expression, or learn what it means—that is how other people speak. Yet I do not say I have learned what other people do; I have learned what it means. I may learn what it means *by* observing what other people do, and of course if I know what it means I know that others who speak the language will use it in that way. But I have not learned what generally happens. I have learned a rule.

That is in some ways like learning the rules of a game, although in some ways it is very different. It is different from learning the rules of a calculus, too. In fact in some ways it is misleading to talk of rules at all here. But it does make some things clearer—that it is possible to use an expression wrongly, for instance.

A rule is something that is *kept*. That is why we can know what we are talking about. When you have learned how the expression is used, then you can not merely behave as other people do, you can also *say* something. That is not a matter of behaving in a particular way. "This is red" does not mean "Everyone calls this red." If that were all there were to it nothing would mean anything.

And yet, that there should be rules at all does depend on what people do, and on an agreement in what they do. If you teach someone the meaning of a colour word by showing him samples of the colour, then he will probably understand; and if he understands he will go on to use the word in new situations just as you would. If he remembered your instruction all right but differed wildly from you in what he called "the same as" the samples you had shown him, and if this went on no matter how often you repeated your explanation, then he could never learn what that colour word means. And this holds generally, not just with colours. It is a point to which Wittgenstein is referring in *Investigations* 242. Of course that situation practically never arises. And if it were at all general we could not speak.

I am not saying, "People see that their reactions tally, and this makes communication possible." That would assume considerable understanding and language already. The agreement of which I am speaking is something without which it would not be possible for people to "see" that their reactions tallied or that anything else tallied. We see that we understand one another, without noticing whether our reactions tally or not. *Because* we agree in our reactions, it is possible for me to tell you something, and it is possible for you to teach me something.

The consensus of reactions is in this sense prior to language, but the reactions themselves are not languages, nor are they language. Neither does the agreement in reactions come first or anticipate language. It appears as the language does, it is a common way of taking the expressions of the language. They are common reactions within the course of language—not to anything there might have been before language or apart from it.

Because there is this agreement we can understand one another. And since we understand one another we have rules. We might perhaps speak of being "trusted" to go on in the way that is for us the only natural one. But if you have learned the language you take it for granted. If any one did not, we could never understand him.

Because there is this agreement it is possible to say something. When I tell you that the patch on the patient's skin is red, I am not saying that it is called red, but that it *is* red. But I could mean nothing definite by that, and you could not understand me, unless people who have learned the words as we have would agree in calling this red. If people could not be brought to use the word in any regular way, if one man who had been taught as we have should go on to give the name to what we should call the complementary colour, if another used it as we do on Monday but in a different way on Tuesday, and if others did not show even these degrees of regularity—then it would not mean anything to say that someone had used the word mistakenly. There would be no distinction between mistakenly and correctly. And there would be no distinction between saying that it is red and saying anything else.

It is not a statement about what I do or about what people generally do. But unless the words had a regular use I should not know it was red, and I should not know what colour it was, because there would be nothing to know. I know what colour it is because I know red when I see it; I know what red is. A bull may charge at a red flag, and rats may be trained to react in one way to red lights and in another way to blue lights, but neither the bull nor the rat knows what red is, and neither knows that this is red. We might put this by saying that neither of them has the concept "red" and neither of them has the concept "colour." No one can get the concept of colour just by looking at colours, or of red just by looking at red things. If I have the concept, I know how the word "red" is used. There must *be* a use, though; there must be what I have been calling common reactions. The phrase "the same colour" must mean something and be generally understood, and also "a different colour." I must know when it makes sense to talk about different shades of the same colour; and so on. Unless I did know what it makes sense to say, unless I were used to talking about colours and to understanding people when they did, then I should not know what red is and I should not know red when I see it.

Of course the colour red is not the word "red." And I suppose if a man cannot see he will never know what it is. But the colour red is not *this*, either. This is red. But if I say "This is the *colour* red," that is a definition—I am giving you a definition by showing you a sample. And the point of that depends upon the definition's being taken in a particular way; and also on its connexion with other uses of language. If I had just shown you that sample without saying anything, and without your asking—what would you have learned from this? Not what the colour red is, anyway.

Someone might say, "I know what *I* mean by 'red.' It is what I experience when I look at this. Whether I have this experience under the same circumstances as lead you to use the word—that is a further question, which may be important in deciding the description of physical objects. But I know what colour *I* see in these circumstances." (It would be hard to keep from asking, "Well, what colour *do* you see?") I suppose the point would be that I know this independently of having learned the (public) language. If I know what I mean, in this way—if I know what colour *I* am referring to—then apparently I have done something like giving myself a definition. But I must also have confused giving a definition and following a definition. It is this which allows me to evade the difficulty of what I am going to *call* "following the definition." Which is a real difficulty: what could it mean to say that I had followed the definition—"my" definition—incorrectly? But if that has no sense, then what on earth is the point of the definition? And what does the definition *establish*?

Suppose someone asked "What colour is red?" and thought it was like asking "What colour is blood?" This, he might think, is something which I can learn only by my own experience, my immediate experience. And although I can tell you what colour blood is, I cannot tell you what colour red is. I can only suggest things that may enable you to find out for yourself. Well, but in this case what is the sense of "what colour red *is*"? If it is something nobody can say, then nobody can ask it either. Suppose I ask it only of myself—but whatever is it I am asking? Something I should like to know? But if that has no sense, then there is nothing I tell myself either. Perhaps I say "What a colour!", but that is all.

I cannot learn the colour unless I can see it; but I cannot learn it without language either. I know it because I know the language. And it is similar with sensations. I know a headache when I feel it, and I know I felt giddy yesterday afternoon, because I know what giddiness is. I can remember the sensation I had, just as I can remember the colour I saw. I feel the same sensation, and that is the same colour. But the identity—the sameness—comes from the language.

A rule is something that is kept. The meaning of a word is something that is kept. It is for this reason that I can say this is the same colour I saw a moment ago. I can see the same colour just because I know red when I see it. And even with shades for which we have no special names, the same thing holds: I know the same colour when I see it.

It is similar, I have said, with sensations. I can say what I felt and I can say what I feel, and I can say it is the same sensation this time—because I know what sensations I am speaking of. It might be said that I can know it is the same only if it *feels* the same; and that is something no language can tell me. Nor can I know whether you are feeling the same as you have felt before. Only you can tell me that, because you are the only one who knows what it feels like. Well, I agree that no language can tell me whether this feels the same. No language can tell me whether those two are the same colour, either. And my familiarity with methods of measurement will not tell me whether those two plots have the same area before I have measured them. But without language I could not have told whether this feels the same, either; if only because I could not have asked.

Of course recognizing a sensation is a different sort of thing from recognizing a colour. This holds whether I am speaking of my own or another's. It is different from recognizing what anything looks like or what is going on. When I say the dog is in pain I am not describing what the dog is doing, any more than I describe what I am doing when I give expression to pain. It is more like an expression of pity. At any rate, feeling pity, trying to ease him and so on—or perhaps turning away from the sight—is all part of believing that he is in pain. And to say that I was

obviously justified in that—or maybe that I was mistaken—
is a different sort of thing from saying that I was justified
or mistaken in believing that he had a fracture. "Mistake"
means something different here, although it is just as definite. If I made a mistake in thinking the boy was in pain,
well, he was shamming and my pity was misplaced. The
mistake was not that I supposed something was going on
in him when nothing was. I may have supposed that too,
perhaps that he had a cramp, but that is a different mistake. The dog's pain is not something going on. It is just
his *being* in pain. I know for certain that he is in pain, and
I know this because I know what pain is and what suffering is. There is an important difference between seeing
that he is in pain and being in pain myself, because I do
not see that I am in pain, and while it is conceivable that
I am mistaken about him, that makes no sense in my own
case. But this does not mean that I know something about
myself which I cannot know about him.

We do not speak of sensations in the same way as we
speak of processes or of colours. The name of a sensation is
a different sort of name from the name of a colour. But
if it means anything to say I am in pain again or that he is
in pain again, this is because the word "pain" has a regular
use and because we know this when we know what pain is.
If it were something I knew only in myself, then I might
say "This is something different now" or "This is the same
again" or I might say neither, and in any case it would not
make any difference. This is not a question of whether I
can trust my memory. It is a question of when it makes
sense to speak of remembering; either of a good memory
or a faulty one. If I thought I could not trust my memory,
then of course I might look for confirmation. But there
cannot be any question of confirmation here, nor any question of doubting either. There is just no rule for what is
the same and what is not the same; there is no distinction
between correct and incorrect; and it is for that reason
that it does not make any difference what I say. Which
means, of course, that I say nothing.

I cannot say anything unless I know the language. But I cannot know the language—any language—privately. I may have a secret code, but that is not the point here. It is a question of whether I can have a private understanding; whether I can understand something which *could* not be said in a language anyone else could understand. ("He may understand the language I speak, but he will not understand what I understand.") I say I cannot know a language privately, for what would there be to *know?* In language it makes a difference what you say. But how can it make any difference what you say privately? (I do not mean talking to yourself.) It seems that in a private language everything would have to be at once a statement and a definition. I suppose I may define a mark in any way I wish. And if every use of the mark is also a definition—if there is no way of discovering that I am wrong, in fact no sense in suggesting that I might be wrong—then it does not matter what mark I use or when I use it.

One might ask, "Why can I not give myself a definition and decide for myself what following the definition is going to be?" But when? Each time? If I decide once and for all, that only renews the problem: what is "according to my decision"? But what would the decision be anyway? In ordinary language I may decide to use an expression in a particular way, and I know how to keep to this. I do this in connexion with established usages and rules. That is why "in a particular way" means something. That is also why I can decide to use the expressions of a secret language or the signs of a code in a particular way. For I am dealing with expressions that can be understood, and I know how the matter could be said in ordinary language. I know whether I am saying the same as I said before, and I know what I am deciding. But not when it is something which *could* not be said in ordinary language. Here there would be no point in saying, for instance, "I am going to use S to mean that," because I do not know what "meaning that" could be.

The reason is not that others must see what my words

refer to. It is just that if my words are to refer to anything they must be understood. They cannot refer at all except in connexion with a use, a use which you learn when you learn what the word means. They cannot refer to anything unless there is a way in which the language is spoken. That is why there cannot be a private understanding. If it makes no difference what is said, nothing is understood.

There is of course no reason why I should not give an account of something which only I can see. Or of something which only I can feel: as when I tell a doctor what I feel in my abdomen. He does not feel my sensations (if that means anything), but he knows what I am talking about; he knows what sensations they are.

Ayer asks why Crusoe should not invent names for his sensations. (He actually says "names to *describe* his sensations," but I do not understand this.) *I* can invent names for my sensations. But that is because I speak a language in which there are names for sensations. I know what the name of a sensation is. Inventing a name or giving it a name is something that belongs to the language as we speak it.

It is possible, certainly, to invent new expressions, and even in one sense new languages. But it is a different question whether anyone could have invented language. If language were a device or a method which people might adopt, then perhaps he could. But it is not that. And you could as easily speak of someone's inventing commerce; more easily, in fact. For he would have to invent what we call use and meaning. And I do not say so much that this would be beyond anyone's powers as rather that it is unintelligible.

The expressions of a language get their significance and their force from their application, from their extensive uses. Many of them enter in almost everything we do. And this gives them the force and obviousness they have in new contexts. So even if someone dreamed of a language before there was any, how could he put that forward as "a practical proposition"? Or *what* would he put forward? Marks and sounds would be so much gibberish. To invent a vocabulary he would have at least to invent ways of using these sounds in various circumstances—in circumstances of a social life which has in fact grown up *with* language and could no more be invented than language could. And people would have to understand them. They would have to see not just that this sign occurs here and that there; they would have to see the difference it makes if you use the one or the other. And once again the difficulty is that there would be nothing to understand; because there would be no established use, and nothing we should call "the difference it makes."

Wittgenstein did not say that the ascription of meaning to a sign is something that needs justification. That would generally be as meaningless as it would if you said that language needs justification. What Wittgenstein did hold was that if a sign has meaning it can be used wrongly. On the other hand, if anyone had tried to invent language and teach it to others, then you might say the language and the use of expressions did stand in need of justification.

But why could not a dominant individual have brought people to behave as the people in one of Wittgenstein's primitive language games do? Why could he not force them to that as we train animals? Why could he not train them to respond in regular ways when ordered, and perhaps to answer?

Well, no animals have been trained to do even the primitive things that are done in those language games. Those people are not just going through a complicated trick; what they say depends upon what they need and what they find. They are not just carrying out orders. They use the expressions they do because they have something to say, and because that use is understood by all parties. Whereas although you may train animals to make the "correct" responses to different words or signs, the animals themselves do not *use* different words. A dog may respond in one way to "Slippers!" and in another way to "Basket!", but he does not himself have one sound for the one and a different sound for the other; neither does he do anything like always giving two barks when he wants food and one bark when he wants a drink. No training has brought an animal to speak, even in a primitive way. This is not a question of the capacities of animals. If any animals do learn to speak, they will not learn it just as they learn tricks. A dog "knows what you want him to do" when you utter the word, but he does not know what it means.

If people merely carried out orders and made certain utterances when they were ordered—if this were "making the signs they were supposed to make when they were supposed to make them"—they would not be speaking. I suppose people might be trained to do that with Greek sentences without knowing Greek. And the people in our example would not understand what they were saying. They could not do that unless they used the expressions themselves, and using them is not just doing what you are told with them. What we call following a rule in language is not following orders. That is why we talk about "taking part in" a language—the language is not any one man's doing more than another's, and the rules, if they are rules of language, are not one man's rules. This is essential for understanding.

It might be that when people had been trained as we imagined they would eventually begin to speak. But that would not be what was invented, and it would not have come about by invention. It would have grown up through the initiative and spontaneous reactions of various people, none of whom was inventing language.

We might ask for *whom* would anyone invent language? Or for what? For animals, for instance? Or for people who have a social life as we have? If it is the latter, he need not trouble, for we have it. But unless it is for those who have the kind of social life people with languages do have —then what is the point and what is he inventing? What would a "language" for a flock of parrots be, for instance? Can you get anywhere except by absurdly imagining them to live as human beings do, as in children's stories?

The point is that no one could invent just *language*. Language goes with a way of living. An invented language would be a wallpaper pattern; nothing more.

A man might invent marks to go with various objects. That is not language. And when Ayer's Crusoe invents *names* to *describe* flora and fauna, he is taking over more than he has invented. He is supposed to keep a diary, too. Ayer thinks that if he could do that when Friday was present he could surely have done it when he was still alone. But what would that be—keeping a diary? Not just making marks on paper, I suppose (or on a stone or what it might be). You might ask, "Well what is it when I do it? And why should it not be the same for him, only a bit more primitive?" But it cannot be that. My marks are either marks I use in communication with other people, or they stand for expressions I use with other people. "What difference does that make? He can *use* them just as I do." No, because I use them in their various meanings. He cannot do that.

What is it he cannot do? What is it that I can do and he cannot? There seems to be nothing logically absurd in supposing that he behaves just as I do. To a large extent I agree. But it is absurd to suppose that the marks he uses mean anything; even if we might want to say that he goes through all the motions of meaning something by them.

I should agree that if "meaning something" were something psychological, he might conceivably do that. If it were a question of what is put into my mind by my association with other people, then there is nothing logically absurd in supposing this to come into someone's mind without that association.

"What is it that I can do . . . ?" To say that meaning something must be something *I* do is rather like saying it is something that happens at the moment. The point is that I speak a language that is spoken. What I say has significance in that language, not otherwise. Or in other words, if I *say* anything I must say it in some language. If there were no more than my behaviour, the marks I make and so on, then I should not mean anything either.

If I say there is "more" than that—it is that I use the expressions in the meanings they have. If Crusoe used the same expressions he would not do that. Nor can he use different expressions but in these meanings. He does not use expressions in any meanings at all.

Using them in their meanings is what we call following a rule. For language there must be "the way the expressions are used," and this goes with the way people live. I need not live that way myself when I use them. Defoe's Crusoe could have kept a diary, but Ayer's could not. Defoe's Crusoe's diary need never be read by anyone, and the meaning of what he writes does not depend on that. What he writes down may never play a part in the lives of other people. But the language in which he has written it does. And for that reason he can understand what he writes, he knows what he is saying. He knows the use or application of the expressions he uses, and it is from that they get the significance they have for him. He knows what he is talking about. Ayer's Crusoe does not and cannot.

Ayer's Crusoe may use marks for particular purposes—to show where he has hidden something, perhaps—and with as great regularity as we care to think. This is not what we mean by the regular use of an expression in a language. If he should suddenly do something which *we* should call using these marks entirely differently, it would have no sense to say that he had done anything wrong or anything inconsistent with what he had done before. We could not speak of his using them in the same meaning or in a different meaning. If he always uses them for the same purpose—as he might always gather wood for the same purpose—this is not what we mean by using an expression in the same way. *Using an expression in the same way does not mean using it for the same purpose.* (What I said about identity is connected with this.) And if there is any sort of discrepancy between what I said at one time and what I say at another—this does not mean that what I do with a mark or sound at one time is different from what I did with it before. If I have always done this with the mark, there is nothing of a rule of language in that.

"But if he uses them just *as* they would be used by someone who spoke the language, so that they *could* be understood, what is the trouble with saying that he uses them in their meanings?" The first trouble is that he does not understand them. And this really means that he does *not* use them just as someone who spoke the language would. For he cannot be guided by his signs in just the way in which you and I may be guided by words.

This is not a question of something beyond his powers. If we ask whether a machine could follow words, or whether a machine might speak, we are not asking what a machine might be designed to do. It is not a question of capacity or performance at all.

If you say something to me I understand you. If a tape recorder plays back what you have said, I understand what I hear but I do not understand the tape recorder. Which is a grammatical statement: I do not fail to understand either. If I say that you have said something but the tape recorder has not, I am not saying that something has happened in your case which did not happen in the other. But I do have an entirely different attitude towards you and towards what I hear from you, and I behave towards you in a host of ways as I should never behave towards a machine—for instance I may answer you, and I should never answer the recorder. I should not try to answer you either, nor should I suppose you had said anything, unless I assumed you knew the language; or unless I thought you said something in a language I did not understand. And I take it for granted you are speaking the language as it is spoken.

I am hardly ever in doubt whether you said something, if I have heard you. But I should begin to doubt if I found that you did not follow my answer, and that you did not seem to know anything about the matters to which your words referred. What I should be doubtful about, in that case, would not be whether something went on in you. I should be doubtful whether you knew what you were saying. But for all I know you may have "done" all that you would have done if you had. The trouble is that your utterance was not a move you were making in the conversation or in the language at all.

If I doubt whether you know the language, or if I doubt whether you ever know what you are saying, then in many ways I must regard you more as I should regard the tape recorder. This is not because you do not do anything that other people do. It is because you do not take part in what they do. You do not speak the language they speak. And *speaking* the language they speak is not just uttering the words; any more than understanding the language is just "recognizing" the words. It is carrying on a conversation, for instance; or it may be writing reports, or listening to a play in a theatre. It is being someone to whom the rest of us can speak and get an answer; to whom we can tell something and with whom we can make a joke and whom we can deceive. All this, and of course immeasurably more, belongs to speaking the language. And it belongs to being able to follow words. You can follow words because you know how to speak. And for the same reason a machine cannot follow words. This has nothing to do with any question of what physics and engineering may achieve. It is just that it makes no sense to say that a machine might follow words.

One can say that absolutely of a machine, but not of Crusoe, because Crusoe might learn a language. But so long as he never has learned a language, in the sense of taking part in a language, it is as meaningless to say of him that he follows words as it would be to say this of an electronic computor.

I cannot ask whether a machine has made a mistake or whether it meant what it said. A machine may be out of order, and then you cannot rely on it. But it is not making a mistake. (And when I make a mistake myself there is nothing out of order.) A machine may "correct mistakes" in connexion with the operation of negative feed-back. But there is nothing there like a mistake in understanding; nor like a mistake in calculation either. This is one reason why a machine cannot follow words—why that makes no sense. I can follow words only where a mistake or a misunderstanding is at least conceivable. ("Yes, of *course* that's what it means.") Otherwise there would be nothing like what we call understanding them.

I may react to words, rightly or wrongly, when I do not understand them. They may be words in a language I do not know, but I may have been taught to obey the orders of someone who shouts them. Maybe no one else would use them in these orders as he does, and that is of no consequence to me. It would have been exactly the same if he had used sounds of his own instead of words. I may react wrongly, as an animal might. But if I call this making a mistake, it is not like mistaking the meaning of the words he uses; any more than I have shown I understand the words if I make no mistake. I know what he wants, that is all. (I know enough to get out of the way of a barking dog, too.) If I had understood the words I should probably know what they would mean in other situations; and at any rate I should know what they would mean if somebody else used them too. The latter is the important point. It is connected with the fact that if I understand the words I should be able to use them, at least in some measure, myself. That is essential if I am guided by the words or if I follow them. But if that is necessary for understanding the words, it is also necessary for misunderstanding them; by which I mean again that it makes no sense to talk about misunderstanding apart from that. Misunderstanding or mistaking the meaning belongs to taking part in the language. You cannot speak of it otherwise.

Ayer's Crusoe may make the kind of mistakes animals do. He may mistake a bird which he does not like to eat for one which he likes. This is not like a mistake in understanding the meaning of an expression, or a mistake in following what was said.

"Why not? He calls the edible bird *ba*, and when he sees the inedible one he says 'ba' and kills it."

That is not a mistake in following the meanings of words. He could have made the same mistake without using words at all. (Perhaps it is roughly the kind of mistake that is corrected through negative feed-back.) You cannot ask whether he made the other kind of mistake; any more than you could ask this of a machine.[1]

I can mistake the meanings of the words you use, because I might use those words myself. If different people can use the same words, then the meanings are independent. I may also take your words in the wrong way. That is rather different, but it is connected with this. He said, "I wonder how long it can last," and she thought he was finding their affair intolerable, whereas he meant the opposite. She knew the meanings of the words he was using, and she could not have misunderstood him in that way unless she had. He might have used the same words to mean what she thought he meant. But he could not have meant either the one or the other unless his words had meant what they do independently; unless they had been the words of a language. I call their meanings "independent," partly because they have to be learned. That is characteristic of language.

Unless the meanings of words were independent—unless they had to be learned—they could not be misunderstood. You do not misunderstand just a sound. You mistake the cry of an animal for the cry of a bird. You may mistake the call of an enemy for the call of a friend. That is not misunderstanding, not in the present sense. If one spoke of learning the meaning of a sound, that would not be like learning the meaning of a word. Perhaps it would not be nonsense to say that he "knew instinctively" that it

[1] Ayer says Crusoe may think that a bird is "of the same type as one which he had previously named, when in fact it is of a different type, *sufficiently* different *for him to have* given it a different name if he had observed it more closely." What do the words I have italicized mean here?

was the cry of an animal. But it is nonsense to say that he knew instinctively the meaning of a word.

You can misunderstand what you can learn. And you are misunderstanding a rule—not a matter of fact. Mistaking the cry of a bird for an animal cry is not misunderstanding a rule.

If one spoke of the independent existence of a tree, this might mean partly that I could think there was no tree there and be wrong. But the meanings of words are not quite comparable with that, and by their independence I do not mean quite the same. If I am wrong about the tree, I may run into it. If I am wrong about the meaning of a word, it is not like that. It is just that I use the word incorrectly, or understand it incorrectly. And that seems almost like saying that if I am wrong I am wrong. Which in a sense is just what I do mean. That is why it is better in this case to say that "the meanings are independent" means just that they have to be learned; as a rule has to be learned. And that is why it is natural to speak of *misunderstanding* here; as it is not, so much, when you are speaking of a mistake in fact.

If anyone did not understand what kind of mistake it is, he would not understand the difference between correct and incorrect; and vice versa. But then he would not understand what words are.

Now since you have learned the meanings of the expressions you use, it may happen that you do not mean what you say. At least it makes sense to ask of anyone who has spoken whether he meant it. If he does not mean what he says, this is familiar and definite enough, but you cannot describe it by describing what he is doing. You can describe it only by taking into account his relation to other people. In this case it is not simply that various people use the same words, although that is a large part of it. What is important is the special rôle or part played by the person in saying them. That is what his "not meaning them" is. And it is as characteristic and essential for language as independent meanings are. I have said it is essential that different people may use the same words. But if those people were all doing the same thing, it would not be language. There must be something more like an organisation, in which different people are, as we may put it, playing different rôles. (The simile limps, but it has something important too. It must serve here.) That belongs to the use of language. Without it there would not be words and there would not be meaning.

Language is something that is spoken.

WITTGENSTEIN ON PRIVACY

JOHN W. COOK

Recent discussions of Wittgenstein's treatment of the idea of a private language have made it clear that the point of what Wittgenstein is doing has been widely misunderstood. I should here like to take one step toward remedying that situation. A chief complaint against Wittgenstein is that he does not make it sufficiently clear what the idea of a private language includes—what is meant by "a private language."[1] It is this complaint that I mean to examine, and I will argue that there can be no such genuine complaint even though it is true that Wittgenstein does not say clearly what is meant by "a private language." He does not try to make this clear because the idea under investigation turns out to be irremediably confused and hence can be only suggested, not clearly explained. Moreover, the philosophical idea of a private language is confused not merely in that it supposes a mistaken notion of language

From *The Philosophical Review*, Vol. LXXIV (1965), pp. 281–314. Reprinted with the permission of the author and editors.

[1] See, e. g., the papers by H. N. Castañeda and J. F. Thomson in *Knowledge and Experience*, ed. C. D. Rollins (Pittsburgh, 1964). Thomson (pp. 121–123) asks, "What kind of language is here being envisaged?" and concludes that Wittgenstein's account is "obscure." The controversy over whether there can be a private language rages, he thinks, over "some unexplained sense of 'private language,'" and so "the claim that Wittgenstein answered it [must be] obscure." Castañeda (p. 129) says that "the idea of a private language is so obscure that there are many senses of 'privacy,'" and he implies that "Wittgenstein's definition of a private language" is not "an honest effort at giving the idea of a private language a full run" (p. 90).

(or meaning) but in its very notion of the privacy of sensations. It is this last point which is generally missed and which I mean here to insist on.

I

The philosophical idea of a private language is a consequence of the following argument (hereafter called A):

> No one can know that another person is in pain or is dizzy or has any other sensation, for sensations are private in the sense that no one can feel (experience, be acquainted with) another person's sensations.

The conclusion of argument A leads, in turn, to the further conclusion that no one can be taught the names of sensations; each of us must give these words their meanings independently of other people and of other people's use of sensation words. (The missing premise here is that in order to teach another person the name of a sensation, it would be necessary to check his use of the word, and this would require knowing from time to time what sensation the learner is having.) The result is the idea that anyone who says anything about his sensations is saying something which he alone can understand. Names of sensations, the word "sensation" itself, and the expression "same sensation" will have no genuine public use, only a private use.

It is this consequence of A that Wittgenstein refers to in Section 243 of the *Investigations*[2] when he asks whether we could imagine a language whose words "refer to what can only be known to the person speaking; to his immediate private sensations. So another person cannot understand the language." But having raised this question, he almost immediately (PI 246–254) launches attacks against both the premise and the conclusion of A.

[2] *Philosophical Investigations* (New York, 1953), hereafter abbreviated as *PI*. Unless otherwise indicated, numbered references will refer to sections of Part I.

That is, he undertakes to show that the very notion of privacy on which the description of this language depends is a tangle of confusions. Hence, when he returns in Section 256 to the consideration of "the language which describes my inner experiences and which only I myself can understand," he points out that (contrary to argument A) our ordinary use of sensation words is not such a language. Thus, the temptation behind the idea of a private language has already been disposed of. What Wittgenstein goes on to do, then, in the ensuing discussion of this "language which only I myself can understand" is to "assume the abrogation of the normal language-game," that is, to consider what the result would be "if we cut out human behavior, which is the expression of sensation" (PI 288). He introduces the discussion as follows: "But suppose I didn't have my natural expression of sensation, but only had the sensation? And now I simply *associate* names with sensations and use these names in descriptions" (PI 256). Here we have what might be an allusion to Descartes, who assumes that even if his philosophical doubts be justified, so that he has "no hands, no eyes, no flesh, no blood, nor any senses," still he can privately understand and inwardly speak a language. It is this picture of language as a phenomenon made possible by "some remarkable act of mind" (PI 38) that Wittgenstein means to investigate. In rejecting this idea of a private language, then, what he rejects is not our normal language game but a philosophically truncated version of it. Defenders of argument A, however, because they must regard sensations as only privately namable, must regard Wittgenstein's rejection of this either as a rejection of our normal language game or as committing him to an extremely odd account of our normal language game. Thus, on the one hand, Wittgenstein has been "refuted" on the grounds that since sensations are private, and since each of us does have names of sensations in his vocabulary, there could not be any real difficulty in the idea of a private language: "the ordinary language of pains is . . . a counter-example against Witt-

genstein's thesis."[3] On the other hand, it has been argued
that since sensations are private, and since Wittgenstein
denies the possibility of naming private objects, he must
be denying that ordinary language contains any genuine
names of sensations: on Wittgenstein's view "private sensations do not enter into pain language games."[4]

In order to expose the errors of these two views, it is
necessary to bring out the force of Wittgenstein's attack
on argument A. I have given the argument in a form commonly found, but as it stands certain of its premises are
suppressed. The premise

(P_1) No one can feel (experience, be acquainted
with) another person's sensations

does not entail the conclusion

(C) No one can know what sensations another person
is having.

Argument A, as it stands, is really no better than (and I
will show that it cannot be made to be better than) the
following argument: "No one can have another person's
shadow, and therefore no one can know anything about
another person's shadow." This argument is unsatisfactory for the obvious reason that the premise has no bearing
on how one gets to know something about another person's shadow. In the same way, the premise of A has no
bearing on how one gets to know about another person's
sensations. And yet it is just this bearing that (P_1) is
thought to have by those who advance argument A. What,
then, are their suppressed premises? One of them must be
this:

(P_2) The proper and necessary means of coming to
know what sensation another person is having is to
feel that person's sensation.

3 Castañeda, op. cit., p. 94.
4 George Pitcher, The Philosophy of Wittgenstein (Englewood
Cliffs, 1964), p. 299.

With this premise added, argument A purports to be denying that anyone can avail himself of the sole proper means of ascertaining what sensations another person is having. Hence, what the argument must also show, if it is to be at all plausible, is that the sole proper means of ascertaining whether another person is in pain, for example, is to feel his pain. This is usually thought to be shown as follows:

> (P_3) Anyone who has a sensation *knows* that he has it because he feels it, and whatever can be known to exist by being felt cannot be known (in the same sense of "known") to exist in any other way.

With these two premises added, is argument A complete? In recent defenses of the argument it has been common to add to (P_1) the qualification that the impossibility of experiencing another person's sensations is a *logical* impossibility. What bearing this qualification has on the form of the argument will depend on which of the several current interpretations is placed on "logical impossibility." I will examine these interpretations in Sections II and III and will show that they fail to make sense of the claim that no one can feel another person's sensations. Therefore, I will give no further attention here to the qualification that (P_1) expresses a logical impossibility. In the remainder of this section I will try to bring out the force of Wittgenstein's attack on the premises (P_2) and (P_3) which purport to state a necessary condition for knowing what sensation another person is having.

What these premises say is that I can *know* that I am in pain because I *feel* my pain and that if anyone else is to know that I am in pain, he too will have to feel my pain. What the argument presupposes, then, is that there is a genuine use of the verb "to know" as an expression of certainty with first-person present-tense sensation statements. This is essential to the argument, for what the conclusion (C) states is that no one can know, in this sense of "to know" appropriate to first-person sensation statements, what sensations another person is having. Hence, if this presupposition of the argument should turn out to be indefensible, we must reject not only (P_2) and (P_3) but also the conclusion. For if the alleged use of "to know" is spurious, then all three are infected by the confusion.

Does it make sense, then, to say "I know that I am in pain"? Consider the following. A man has been complaining for several days that his stomach hurts dreadfully, though he has sought no relief for it. His wife has nagged him repeatedly, "You're in pain, so go to a doctor!" Might he not at last exclaim in exasperation, "I *know* I'm in pain, but we can't *afford* a doctor"? No one would want to maintain that this expression of exasperation was unintelligible. What argument A presupposes, however, is not that "I know I am in pain" be intelligible as an expression of exasperation but that it be intelligible as an expression of certainty. What, then, would be necessary for it to be an expression of certainty? Consider the following case. Someone asks you whether it is raining; you tell him that it is, and then he asks, "Are you certain?" Here one might reply, "Yes, I know it's raining; I'm looking out the window." (This might be a telephone conversation, for example.) Now, what is the function of "I know" here? To put it roughly and briefly, the function of these words is to indicate that in answering the question one is not merely guessing or taking someone's word for it or judging from what one saw ten minutes before or something else of the sort. Their function is to indicate that one is in as good a position as one could want for answering the question "Is it raining?" What makes it possible to use "I know" here as an expression of certainty is that it would be intelligible for someone to suppose that the speaker is not, in the particular instance, in as good a position as one could want for correctly answering a certain question or making a certain statement. More generally, for "I know that . . ." to be an expression of certainty, it is at least necessary that the sense of the sentence filling the blank allow the speaker to be ignorant in some circumstances of the truth value of statements made by means of the sentence (or equivalents thereof). But now, it is just this, as Wittgenstein points out (*PI* 246 and pp. 221–222), that does *not* hold for "I am in pain."

It should be noticed that Wittgenstein is not saying that the addition of the words "I know" to "I am in pain" would be *pointless* and therefore senseless. That might be said of the following case. The two of us are seated in such a way that you cannot see out the window, although I can. As you notice that it is time for you to leave, you ask me whether it is still raining. I peer out the window, straining to see in the failing light, and then go to the window, open it, and put my hand out. As I close the window, wiping the drops from my hand, I say, "Yes, it is raining rather hard." Because you have watched me take the necessary pains to answer your question, you would have nothing to gain by asking, "Are you certain?" or "Do you *know* that it is?" For the same reason, I would not be telling you anything by adding to my answer the words "I know . . . ." If I were to add them, you might cast about for an explanation: did he think I didn't see him put his hand out? Or: is adding those words some eccentricity of his, like the character in one of Dostoevsky's novels who is always adding "No, sir, you won't lead me by the nose"? If no explanation is found (and it would not be an explanation to say that I added those words because they were *true*), my utterance of them would have to be judged senseless. But for all that, in the situation we began by describing, if someone in the street had seen me put my hand out, he might have said of me, "He knows it's raining." Or had my wife called from the next room to ask whether I knew it was raining, I could have answered that I do know.

Now the point that Wittgenstein is making about "I am in pain" can be made clear by the contrast with "It is raining." The sense of the latter sentence is such that, although in a given situation my *saying* to a particular person "I *know* it is raining" may be senseless, still in that same situation I could be said by some other person to know that it is raining. In that same situation I may be asked by someone whether I know it is raining and may sensibly answer the question. By contrast, the sense of "I am in pain" (or of any other first-person present-tense sensation statement) does not provide for *any* situation such that the addition of the words "I know" would be an expression of certainty. It would not be merely pointless to utter the sentence "I know I am in pain" (indeed, we have seen how its utterance might express exasperation); it is rather that no utterance of it could be sensibly taken to be an expression of certainty.[5]

Wittgenstein's point here is often missed because, instead of considering what function the words "I know" could have in "I know I'm in pain," one wants to say something like this: "Surely a man who is in pain could not be like the man who has a stone in his shoe but does not know it because he does not feel the stone. A man who has a pain *feels* it, and if he feels it, he must *know* he's in pain." But this is making a wrong assimilation of "I feel a pain in my knee" to "I feel a stone in my shoe," which will be discussed below. At any rate, what we are inclined to contrast is the case of a man in pain with the case of a man with a (possibly unnoticed) stone in his shoe, and we want to mark the contrast by saying that, invariably, the

[5] This point has been widely missed. Castañeda, for example, argues "it is odd, because pointless, to inform another person that one believes or thinks that one is in pain, or to insist that one knows that one is in pain. But this fact about ordinary *reporting* in no way shows that there are no facts that would be reported if one were to make pointless assertions. The pointlessness of the assertions is not only compatible with their intelligibility, but even presupposes it" (*op. cit.*, p. 94). I do not know what could be meant here by "pointless assertions," i.e., what would make them *assertions*. But it should be clear that Wittgenstein's point about "I know I'm in pain" is quite different from the point I have made about the sometimes senseless addition of "I know" to "It is raining," and this is the difference Castañeda has missed. The same mistake is made (in almost the same words) in Ayer's criticism of Wittgenstein in "Privacy," *Proceedings of the British Academy* (1959), p. 48.

man in pain *knows* that he is in pain. But this is a wrong way of marking the contrast. The right way is to say that whereas it makes sense to speak of ignorance and knowledge, doubt and certainty, in the case of the stone in the shoe, it does not make sense to speak this way in the case of the man in pain. Or as I would prefer to put it (see Section III below): the moves that are part of the one language game are not part of the other.

I have not here argued for Wittgenstein's point; I have merely tried to clarify it. To argue for it, I should have to go some way toward showing the "incorrigibility" of first-person sensation statements. It is not clear to me, however, what "showing this" would involve. The most one could do, I should think, is to provide reminders as to how the names of sensations are taught, for example, that such teaching contains no counterpart of teaching a child to put a color sample under a better light or to move in closer for a better look. Also, one might show a person that where he thinks we can (or do) doubt or make mistakes about our sensations, he has merely oddly described something else. For instance, I have heard it objected against Wittgenstein that we sometimes exclaim "Ouch!" in anticipation of a pain which never comes, but it would be misleading, at best, to call this "a mistake about *being* in pain." There is also the fact that such words as "stomachache," "headache," and "dizziness" are partly diagnostic. Thus, a doctor might correct someone by saying, "It's not stomach-ache you have; it's appendicitis!" Or a man might correct himself by saying, "Never mind the aspirin; I didn't have a headache, after all. It was just this tight hat I've been wearing." These are corrections of mistaken diagnoses. Another objection that is raised is that victims of accidents sometimes hysterically scream that they are in dreadful pain, although they are scarcely injured. But it should be clear that the screamings of hysterical people are no more to be counted genuine uses of language than are the ravings of delirious people or the mumblings of sleepwalkers. It is not my intention here to answer all such objections; I have no idea how many an ingenious person might propose or how far he would go to defend them.

The preceding discussion has shown, in so far as showing this is possible, that the alleged use of "to know" presupposed by argument A is not a use at all but a confusion. Thus, an essential presupposition of argument A has been defeated, and the argument will have to be abandoned. The possible criticisms of A, however, are by no means exhausted. In the remainder of this section I will deal with several points related to those already made. Sections II and III will present Wittgenstein's criticisms of (P_1) and the claim that it states a logical impossibility.

There is a use of the verb "to feel" (as in "I feel a stone in my shoe") that is related to the verb "to know" in the following way. If I am asked how I know that there is a stone in my shoe or that the grass is wet or that a certain man has a pulse beat, there will be cases in which it will be correct to answer, "I know because I feel it." I will call this the *perceptual sense* of "to feel." Now it is clear that argument A presupposes that it makes sense to speak of feeling (in the perceptual sense) a pain or an itch or dizziness. (P_3) says that I can *know* that I am in pain because I *feel* my pain. It no doubt contributes to the plausibility of this that we commonly say such things as "I feel a slight pain in my knee when I bend it." That this is not the perceptual sense of "to feel" should be clear from the fact that in all such sentences the words "I feel" may be replaced by either "I have" or "there is" without altering the sense of the sentence (cf. *PI* 246). Thus, aside from idiomatic differences, "I feel a slight pain in my knee" comes to the same as "There is a slight pain in my knee." There is no such equivalence when "to feel" is used in the perceptual sense. "I feel a stone in my shoe" implies, but does not mean the same as, "There is a stone in my shoe." It will make sense to say, "There was a stone in my shoe, but I didn't feel it," whereas it will not make sense to say, as an admission of ignorance, "There was a pain in my knee, but I didn't feel it." Sensation words cannot be the objects of verbs of perception in first-person sentences. And once this is seen, the plausibility of argument A altogether disappears. For when it is recognized that it does not make sense to say "I know that I am in pain because I feel it," it will no longer be tempting to say, "Another person can know that I am in pain only if he feels it."

There remain difficulties with argument A which have gone generally unnoticed. (P_2) purports to state the proper and necessary means of ascertaining what sensations another person is having, and what it says is that one must feel his sensation. But even within the presuppositions of the argument this is inadequate: it ought to require not only that one feel the other person's sensation but also that one correctly identify it as being *his*. The plausibility of A depends on its seeming to be analogous to something like this: to ascertain whether my neighbor's crocuses are in bloom, as opposed to merely taking his word for it, I must see his crocuses. But I must also know which are his and which are mine, and I know this by knowing where the line runs between our gardens. I identify our respective crocuses by identifying our gardens, and this is presupposed in the sense of "I saw his crocuses" and "He saw my crocuses." But how am I supposed to distinguish between the case in which I am in pain (whether he is or not) and the case in which he is in pain and I feel it? How do I know whose pain I feel? I will postpone the discussion of this question until the next section, but it is worth noticing how far the analogy with seeing my neighbor's crocuses has been carried. Thus, Russell says that "we cannot *enter into the minds of others* to observe the thoughts and emotions which we infer from their behavior."[6] The italicized phrase seems to provide a criterion of identity of the same kind as in the case of the crocuses, but of course it does not. It merely raises the further question of how one is to identify whose mind one has "entered into." What that question should show is that one is being led on by an analogy that has no application.

[6] *Human Knowledge* (New York, 1948), p. 193 (my italics).

Why, in the first place, is one tempted to speak of "feeling another's sensations"? A part of the answer is that one thinks that just as such a sentence as "My neighbor's crocuses are in bloom" has a place in its grammar for both "I know because I *saw* them" and "I didn't see them but took his word for it," so the sentence "He is in pain" should have a place in its grammar for both "I know because I *felt* his pain" and "I didn't feel his pain but took his word for it." And now if we somehow exclude "I felt his pain," it will seem that we are left with "I only took his word for it." If, instead of seeing for myself, I ask my neighbor whether certain of his flowers are in bloom, this may be owing to a garden wall. It may seem that some comparable circumstance must account for the fact that we ask people what they feel. "Other people can tell us what they feel," says Russell, "but we cannot directly observe their feelings."[7] Thus is argument A born. It makes out the difference between first- and third-person sensation statements to rest on a matter of circumstance (like being unable to see my neighbor's crocuses), whereas Wittgenstein has made us realize that the difference resides in the language game itself (PI 246–248). The difference does not rest on some circumstance, and therefore argument A, which purports to name such a circumstance with the words "being unable to feel another's sensations," is inherently confused.

There remains a difficulty with premise (P₃) related to the above. (P₃) states that I can know what sensations I am having because I feel them. Now if someone wants to defend argument A, he will have to show how it is supposed to account not only for what we have here called "sensation statements" but also for their negations: "I am not in pain" and "He is not in pain." This may not seem to pose a difficulty if one thinks he understands Russell's phrase about entering into the minds of others to observe their thoughts and emotions. For if one enters a room to observe what is there, one may also observe that nothing

[7] *The Analysis of Mind* (London, 1951), p. 118.

is there or that certain things are not there. But if one
does not pretend to understand Russell's phrase, how (on
the presuppositions of argument A) is one supposed to understand either "I am not in pain" or "He is not in pain"?
The same difficulty may be raised about negative statements containing "dream" or "image" instead of "pain"
(see PI 448). But if we stick to the case of bodily sensations, one might be tempted to substitute for the word
"mind" in Russell's phrase the word "body." One would
then suppose that if someone says, "I didn't feel any pain
in my knee that time," he is reporting an observation: I
felt around in my knee for a pain and found none. But
what is the feeling in this case? Is it the same feeling as
when feeling pain? But if not that, then what? There *is*
such a thing as making oneself receptive to pain—and even
to pain in a particular place. (Perhaps a doctor wants to
know whether your injured knee still hurts when it is bent
in a certain way.) One relaxes, stops moving and talking,
and then one feels pain—or one does not. But although
there is no difficulty with the idea of being receptive to
pain when there is no pain, it is not even prima facie
plausible to speak of a feeling which might have disclosed
a pain but did not. How, for instance, could one make
out the difference between not feeling for pain and feeling
for a pain but finding none? Here all talk about a kind of
observation appropriate to sensations becomes obvious
nonsense. On the presuppositions of argument A, then, no
account of negative sensation statements can be even suggested. It was tempting to say: "I can know that I am in
pain because I *feel* my pain, and that is what I cannot do
in the case of another person." But the plausibility of this
is lost if one says, "I can know that I am not in pain because I can *feel* the absence of pain in myself, and that is
what I cannot feel in the case of another person." One
would want to reply: perhaps you are feeling the absence
of it right now!

II

The one premise of argument A which we have so far neglected is in some respects the most pertinacious: "No one can feel (have) another person's sensations." I remarked in Section I that it is now commonplace to say that this premise expresses a "logical impossibility." This is intended, no doubt, as an improvement over older ways of talking. Russell once said of our sensations and images that they "cannot, even theoretically, be observed by anyone else."[8] But substituting "not even logically possible" for "not even theoretically possible" has proved to be an empty gesture, for the meaning of "logically impossible" has at best remained dubious. Two interpretations are current. (1) Some philosophers have held that to say that it is logically (or conceptually) impossible that p is to say no more and no less than that the sentence "p" is senseless. In the present case, this would amount to saying that such sentences as "I felt his pain" and "He feels my dizziness" are senseless.[9] (2) Others seem to hold that to say that it is logically (or conceptually) impossible that p is to say, not that "p" is senseless, but that the negation of "p" is a necessary truth. In the present case, this would amount to saying that a sentence such as "I did not feel his pain" (or perhaps "Any pain I feel is my own pain") expresses a necessary truth.[10] Both versions speak of sentences—one

[8] *The Analysis of Mind* (London, 1951), p. 117.

[9] "The barriers that prevent us from enjoying one another's experiences are not natural but logical. . . . It is not conceivable that there should be people who were capable of having one another's pains, or feeling one another's emotions. And the reason why this is inconceivable is *simply that we attach no meaning to such expressions* as 'I am experiencing your headache,' 'She is feeling his remorse,' 'Your state of anger is numerically the same as mine.'" A. J. Ayer, *The Foundations of Empirical Knowledge* (London, 1953), pp. 138–139 (my italics).

[10] For example, Castañeda, who regards it as a logical impossibility to experience another's sensations (*op. cit.*, p. 90), seems

saying that certain sentences are senseless, the other saying
that the negations of those sentences express necessary
truths. This presents a difficulty.

Any sentence may, so far as logic can foresee, find its
way into some nonphilosophical context. Thus, in the last
section a context was imagined in which the sentence "I
know I'm in pain" was uttered as an expression of exasperation. No one would want to say that in that context the
person who exclaimed, "I know I'm in pain!" was uttering
either nonsense or a necessary truth—any more than they
would want to say this of "Business is business." Now there
are, no doubt, a great many philosophical propositions for
which it would be extremely difficult, if not impossible, to
provide a nonphilosophical context. But it should be clear
that to specify merely a sentence is not to specify what
(according to which view you take) is said to be senseless
or to express a necessary truth. At this point it is tempting
to say that, in the context I imagined for it, the sentence
"I know I'm in pain" was not meant literally. Similarly,
someone might insist that if we were ever to say, "I feel
your pain," this could not, at any rate, be *literally* true.
Thus, Ayer says that "it is logically impossible that one
person should *literally* feel another's pain."[11] What is said
to be logically impossible, then, is what is expressed by "I
feel his pain" in its literal sense. But can we now apply
either of the aforementioned versions of logical impossibility? Those who adopt version (1) would find themselves in the odd position of saying that it is the literal
sense of a sentence which is senseless. (This is what Wittgenstein warns against in saying that "it is not the sense as

---

to take this view of "logical impossibilities." In his discussion of
the sentence "I believed falsely at time *t* that I was in pain at *t*'"
(which he says would be regarded as meaningless by Wittgensteinians), he gives his own position as follows: "But obviously 'I believed falsely at *t* that I was in pain at *t*' is meaningful; it expresses a conceptual contradiction; its negation is a necessary
truth" (*ibid.*, p. 93).

[11] *The Problem of Knowledge* (Edinburgh, 1956), p. 202 (my
italics).

it were that is senseless" [PI 500].) Those who adopt either (1) or (2) will somehow have to specify, for the particular sentence, what its alleged literal sense is. One way of attempting this is by presenting the parts of the sentence (either words or expressions) in some familiar context in which *they* have the desired meaning and then specifying that it is when the sentence in question combines the words or expressions as used in *these* contexts that it has its literal sense. But what could it mean to speak of transferring a word or expression *and its meaning* from a context in which it has a particular use to a sentence in which it has no use at all (except as a part of speech)—and certainly not the use it had in the context from which it was allegedly transferred? The most that would seem to be possible here is that one might be under the *impression* that he had combined the original meanings into the sentence. This, I think, is exactly the case with philosophers who declare either that certain sentences are senseless or that their negations are necessary truths.

To illustrate this point, I want to consider a fictitious philosophical argument designed both for its transparency and for its similarity to the case of someone's saying that no one can have another person's sensations. Here, then, is the argument of an imaginary philosopher:

> We commonly speak of a child as having his father's build, but this is really absurd when you come to think of it. How *could* someone have another person's build? I know what it is for someone to have his father's watch or for someone to have another man's coat, but no one could literally have another person's build. A build is not something which, like a coat, can be removed and passed around from person to person. That is not even conceivable. And this is why no one can have another person's build. So when, ordinarily, we say of someone that he has another person's build, or when we say that two people have the *same* build, we are using these words, not in their literal sense, but in a sense that is arbitrary and does not fit the meaning of the words at all. We are saying only that

the one person has a build that is *like* the other person's, not that he has the other person's build itself. It is the same when we say that a child has her mother's eyes. We don't mean this literally—that her mother's eyes have been transplanted into her head. Of course, this could theoretically be done. But having another's build, in the literal sense, is not even theoretically possible. No amount of surgical skill will enable doctors to transfer a build from one person to another. They may graft skin and bone, but each person will still have a build all his own, not someone else's. Builds, one might say, are among the most inviolable forms of private property.

Now what has happened in this argument? Our imaginary philosopher purports to have identified the "literal sense" of such sentences as "He has your build" and "You have your father's build" and to have discovered that these sentences, in their literal sense, mean something impossible. But what is being referred to here as the literal sense of "He has your build"? What I should like to suggest is that though this is no sense at all, what may strike one as being the literal sense—the real meaning—of "He has your build" is this sentence construed on analogy with such a sentence as "He has your coat." The temptation so to construe it lies, of course, in the surface similarity of the two sentences. Moreover, quite apart from these sentences, there is our familiar use of possessives in "my build," "your build," and so forth, and one may be tempted to construe this use of possessives on analogy with possessives of ownership. That this is a false analogy can be shown as follows. In order to use a possessive of ownership (as in "his coat") to make a true statement, we must correctly identify the owner of the article. It is this identification that makes the difference between saying, "*His* coat is too large for him," and saying merely, "*That* coat is too large for him." If I should say, "*His* coat is too large for him," without having made the correct identification, I can be corrected by being told, for example, "That's not *his* coat; it's his father's."

Now contrast this case with one in which I notice a child's build and comment, "His build is rather angular." Here the step of identifying an owner plays no part: I need only observe the child. And so my statement could not be challenged by someone saying, "The build *is* rather angular, but are you sure that it's *his?*" This question would be senseless because, intended as a particular kind of challenge to my statement, it wrongly presupposes that in the language game played with "his build" there is a move of the same kind as in the language game played with "his coat," that is, the identification of an owner. But now it is just this question that would have to make sense if the so-called "literal sense" of "He has his father's build" were to *be* a sense. Hence, the "literal sense" was no sense at all.

To put the matter in another way, what would not make sense would be to ask, as though requesting an identification, "Whose build does he have: his own or his father's?" But in its so-called "literal sense" the sentence "He has his father's build" was supposed to be a sentence of the kind used in answering that supposedly genuine identification question. So again, the "literal sense" was no sense at all. Here it is important to notice that in thus rejecting the "literal sense" of "He has his father's build" we must also reject its correlatives, "I have my own build" and "Everyone has his own build." For these sentences, too, in the context of the above argument, are supposed to be of the kind used in answering that supposedly genuine identification question. But as we have seen, there is no such genuine question, and so there are no answers either. The question and the answers we were made to believe in by the analogy with "He has his father's coat" are not moves in the language game played with the word "build." Hence, what we were to understand as involving some kind of impossibility—namely, "literally having another's build"— and also what we were to take as being necessarily true— namely, "I have my own build"—turn out to be illusions. Therefore the statement "Builds are private" must be given up.

The points I have made here apply, *mutatis mutandis,* to the philosophical assertion "Sensations are private," where this is meant as "No one can have another person's sensations." I will not rehearse the arguments again. It is enough to say that in order to be in a position to use correctly the expression "his pain" (as in "His pain is worse, so you had better give him a hypo"), it is sufficient to know *who* is in pain. There is no further step required here comparable to that of identifying an owner as in the use of "his coat." (Hence in the first-person case, where there is no question of *who* is in pain [PI 404–408], there is no identification of any kind.) Or to put the point in still another way, when we say of someone, "His pain is quite severe," the word "his" is performing the same function (apart from surface grammar) as the word "he" in "He is in severe pain." It was this that Wittgenstein meant to bring out when, in reply to "Another person can't have my pains," he asked: "Which pains are my pains?" (*PI* 253). He did not intend that one should *answer* that question, saying something like "All the pains I have are mine." He intended, rather, that that "answer" and the "question" that prompts it should be recognized as spurious, as not belonging to the language game.[12] Hence, for the reasons adduced in the previous case, when it is said that no one can, literally, have another person's pain, the supposed literal sense is no sense at all.

Before leaving the topic of possessives, it will be well to notice a source of frequent confusion. It was briefly mentioned in Section I that such words as "stomach-ache" and "headache" are partly diagnostic. Thus, a man might say, "Never mind the aspirin; I didn't have a headache after all. It was only this tight hat I've been wearing." Now it

[12] In another passage (*PI* 411) Wittgenstein asks us to consider a "practical (non-philosophical)" application for the question "Is this sensation *my* sensation?" Perhaps he was thinking that this form of words might be used in place of "Am I the *only* one having this sensation?" which would be like asking, "Am I the *only* one who is dizzy?"

is easy to imagine a use of possessives related to this in the following way. Philosophers have imagined wireless connections of some sort being set up between people such that when one of them is in pain the other is, too. In such cases, it is suggested, the question "Whose headache do I have?" would come to have the following use. It will be correct to answer that I have my own headache when, on detaching the wireless device, the pain continues unaffected, but if instead the pain immediately stops, it will be correct to say that I did not have my own headache, that I had Smith's headache, and so forth. Now granting all this, it is still important to be clear about two points. First, the sentence "I did not have my own headache" will not mean the same as "I was not in pain." The man who asks, "Whose headache do I have?" will be one of whom it will be true to say, "He is in pain" or even "He is in severe pain." Secondly, when we say of a person, "He is in severe pain," we also say indifferently, "His pain is severe." (As noted above, the words "he" and "his" in these two sentences perform the same function.) So the statement "His pain was severe" will be true even though it is also true that he did not have his own headache. Because "his pain" in the former statement is not an answer to an identification question of the kind provided for in the new idiom, it does not compete with the new idiom. Moreover, this would remain true even if we should lapse into using the word "pain" in the same kind of way we have here imagined the word "headache" to be used. That is, even if we should superimpose on our present use of "pain" the question "Whose pain do I have?" with the possible answer "I have Smith's pain," it will still be possible to say of me "His pain is severe" in case I am in severe pain. It is thus as a comment on this use of possessives that one can say: any pain I feel will be mine. The mistakes one is inclined to make here are, first, to suppose that this is a truth about the nature of pains or of human beings, and secondly, to suppose that the word "mine" here is a possessive of ownership. Those who have sought to avoid the first mistake by resorting to talk about "logical impossibility" have nevertheless persisted in the second mistake, and thus they have reinforced the fundamental confusion by serving it up in a terminology that commands great respect. We can see more clearly what this amounts to if we return to the argument of our imaginary philosopher. Having concluded that no one can have another person's build, he might go on to argue that therefore we need never worry that the build someone has will not last out his lifetime owing to its previous hard use by another person. Now if a more up-to-date philosopher were to take this "worry" seriously and offer further relief from it by maintaining that it is not even *logically* possible to have another's build, this would be merely a perpetuation of the original confusion. This is what happens when philosophers seek to strengthen argument A by adding that it is a *logical* impossibility to feel another's sensations.

If we can make any sense of the insistence that pains are private—that is, that any pain I feel is my own—this amounts to no more than a comment on the kind of possessive commonly used with the word "pain." Of course, this is not what philosophers have supposed they were saying with the premise "No one can feel another's pain," but since nothing but this can be intelligibly made of that premise, it can hardly do the job that philosophers have given it. There would not be even the semblance of plausibility in an argument running: no one can know what sensations another person has, because the possessives commonly used with names of sensations are not possessives of ownership.

III

The preceding section began with two criticisms of the view that "No one can have another's pain" expresses a logical impossibility. The criticisms were these: (*a*) when something is said to be logically impossible it is necessary to specify more than a sentence, but what must be specified cannot be the sense of a sentence, for it is absurd to speak of the sense as being senseless; and (b) attempts at specifying such a sense must come to grief in requiring the parts of the sentence (either words or expressions) to retain their meaning though shorn of their use. Have my own arguments of the preceding section avoided these criticisms?

The chief difficulty with the views against which these criticisms were directed is that they propose to deal with sentences, and then in order to specify what is said to be logically impossible, they find themselves resorting to talk about the literal sense of a sentence. This is what Wittgenstein meant to oppose when he wrote: "When a sentence is called senseless, it is not as it were its sense that is senseless. But a combination of words is being excluded from the language, withdrawn from circulation" (PI 500). But what does it mean to speak of "a combination of words being excluded from the language"? What is being excluded from what? When Wittgenstein says, for example, that "it can't be said of me at all (except perhaps as a joke) that I *know* I am in pain" (PI 246), he does not mean to exclude the joke. In fact, one can think of a variety of contexts for the sentence "Now he *knows* he's in pain." (Think of how a torturer might say it.) So again I ask: what is being excluded from what? The answer to this can be seen from the following segment of argument from Section II:

If I should say, "His coat is too large for him," without having made the correct identification, I can be corrected by being told, for example, "That's not *his* coat; it's his father's." Now contrast this case with one in which I notice a child's build and comment, "His build is rather angular." Here the step of identifying an owner plays no part: I need only observe the child. And so my statement could not be challenged by someone saying, "The build *is* rather angular, but are you sure it's *his*?" This question would be senseless

because, *intended as a particular kind of challenge to
my statement*, it wrongly presupposes that in the language game played with "his build" there is a move
of the same kind as in the language game played with
"his coat," that is, the identification of an owner.

What is appealed to here is the reader's familiarity with a
pair of language games. What is said to be senseless is not
merely a combination of words but rather an attempt, by
means of a combination of words, to make in one language
game a move that belongs only to the other language game.
In other words, by showing that the apparent analogy between the language games is in fact a false one, the argument shows that if one tried making the moves suggested
by the analogy, one would not be *saying* anything but
would be merely under the impression that he was. It is
this mistaken *impression* of saying something that the argument condemns as senseless, and therefore (to answer
our original question) the argument cannot be accused of
saying that the *sense* of some sentence is senseless. It
should be evident, however, that an argument of this kind,
unless it is carefully formulated, is peculiarly open to misunderstanding. For in order to specify what it is that one
is condemning as nonsense, one must repeat that nonsense
in *some* form, and if a reader insists on taking one's words
"straight" at this point and thus looks for or imagines a
sense where none was intended, then one's argument will
have the paradoxical air of trying to prove that the sense
of something is senseless.

Since the point I have been making here is important
to Wittgenstein's thought, it is worth noticing the following pair of passages. The first is from Moore's report of
Wittgenstein's 1930–1933 lectures:

[Wittgenstein] then implied that where we say "This
makes no sense" we always mean "This makes nonsense *in this particular game*"; and in answer to the
question "Why do we call it 'nonsense'? what does it
mean to call it so?" said that when we call a sentence
"nonsense," it is "because of some similarity to sen-

tences which have sense," and that "nonsense always arises from forming symbols analogous to certain uses, where they have no use."[13]

The second passage is from the *Blue Book*:

It is possible that, say in an accident, I should . . . see a broken arm at my side, and think it is mine when really it is my neighbor's. . . . On the other hand, there is no question of recognizing a person when I say I have a toothache. To ask "are you sure that it's *you* who have pains?" would be nonsensical. Now, when in this case no error is possible, it is because the move which we might be inclined to think of as an error, a "bad move," *is no move of the game at all.* (We distinguish in chess between good and bad moves, and we call it a mistake if we expose the queen to a bishop. But it is no mistake to promote a pawn to a king.)[14]

It is clear that Wittgenstein came to think that there is more than one kind of senselessness, but the description of the kind mentioned here is the description of "No one can feel another person's pain."[15]

Going back now, briefly, we can say one thing more about the so-called "literal sense" of "He has his father's build" or "I feel your pain." Seeming to see in such sentences a sense that is somehow impossible is a queer sort of illusion, produced by seeing one pattern of grammar on analogy with another and quite different pattern of grammar. This sort of illusion is not altogether peculiar to philosophy, however. Seeming to see in a sentence a meaning that is somehow impossible is the stuff of which grammatical jokes are made (cf. *PI* 111). Consider, for example, a

13 G. E. Moore, *Philosophical Papers* (London, 1959), pp. 273–274.
14 Wittgenstein, *The Blue and Brown Books* (Oxford, 1958), p. 67 (the last italics are mine).
15 Another kind of senselessness is that illustrated in Sec. I by the sometimes senseless addition of the words "I know" to "It is raining." Other examples are noticed in *PI* 117, 349, 514, 670, p. 221, and elsewhere.

cartoon by S. J. Perelman. It shows a distraught gentleman rushing into a doctor's office clutching a friend by the wrist and whimpering: "I've got Bright's disease, and he has mine." This is more than a play on the name "Bright's disease." The surface grammar reminds one of such a sentence as "I've got his hat, and he has mine," as used to report a mix-up in the coatroom. So the caption gives the illusion of making sense—of reporting an extraordinary mix-up, which the doctor is supposed to set straight. And yet "getting the joke" consists in feeling its senselessness. So there seems to be a sense that is somehow senseless. But what we understand here is not a *sense* but rather the two language games that have been (humorously) assimilated. When this is intentional and fairly obvious, it produces a laugh; when it is unintentional and unrecognized, it may seem to provide an original and penetrating insight into the nature of things. Thus, in the case of my imaginary philosopher, once he is captivated by the grammatical analogy suggested by "He has his father's build," he is led to treat the word "build" at every turn on analogy with the word "coat." The whole complex grammar of words for physical objects opens out before him as a new field for the word "build" to run in. A new range of sentences is thus opened up, suggesting what appear to be new "speculative possibilities"—builds being removed like coats, being passed around from person to person, becoming more worn and shabby with the years, and so forth. When we are captivated by such an analogy, we may succumb to temptation and play in these new fields. But we may also feel considerable resistance here, for the grammatical analogy behind it is a false one, and the signs of this may be too clear to be missed altogether. My imaginary philosopher expresses this felt resistance by insisting that "no one can literally have another's build." This, of course, does not reject the analogy; it merely denies that the supposed "speculative possibilities" can ever be realized. Nor would it improve matters to say that the impossibility involved is a *logical* one. This would be merely a new jargon for call-

ing a halt to the analogy in midcourse. One finds the same
thing when David Pole, in his commentary on the *Investigations*, writes: "In some sense experience is clearly private; one person cannot be said literally to feel another's
feelings," and this cannot be said, he thinks, because
grammar "forbids us" to say it.[16] This talk of grammar
"forbidding us" to say something is nothing but the most
recent jargon for calling a halt to an analogy whose oddness
has begun to dawn on one. Because Pole is still in the
clutches of the analogy, he is under the impression that
there is some "literal sense" of the phrase "feeling another's feelings" which grammar somehow forbids. Because
in general he thinks that grammar forbids us at many
points to express a sense that we fully understand, he
vehemently opposes Wittgenstein's expressed intention to
"bring words back from their metaphysical to their everyday use" (*PI* 116). Thus, he speaks of Wittgenstein's
"characteristic anxiety to pin language down within the
limits of its origins" and of Wittgenstein's insistence
that "existing usage is to be accepted as we find it and
never tampered with."[17] The result of this, Pole warns, is
that "the advance of speculation may well be halted;
though may well be 'contained' within its existing fron-
tiers."[18] What Pole fails to recognize is that the "metaphysical use" from which Wittgenstein wants to "bring
words back" is not a *use* but the illusion of a use. Wittgenstein himself says that to reform language "for particular practical purposes . . . is perfectly possible. But these
are not the cases we have to do with" (*PI* 132).

IV

There is another expression for the idea that sensations
are private. It is said that no two people can have (feel)

[16] *The Later Philosophy of Wittgenstein* (London, 1958), pp.
68–69.
[17] *Ibid.*, pp. 91 and 94.
[18] *Ibid.*, p. 95.

the *same* sensation. This has an analogue in the case of our
imaginary philosopher, who argues that when we say of
someone that he has his father's build or that they have
the same build, "we only mean that the one person has a
build that is *like* the other's, not that he has the other
person's build itself." He means to say that, however alike
they may be, there are two builds here, not one. This, of
course, is a mistake as to how builds are counted, but it
goes with his prior mistake of taking possessives as used
with "build" to be possessives of ownership. He reasoned
that if we say, "His build is rather angular, and so is mine,"
there must be two builds: his and mine. But this is wrong.
If one wanted to count builds, one would proceed differently—as one would proceed to count diseases or habits or
the gaits of horses. One counts in such cases in accordance
with more or less detailed descriptions. A five-gaited horse
is one that can ambulate in accordance with five descriptions of foot movements, and two horses are performing
the same gait if their foot movements fit the same relevant
description. What would not make sense (if one meant to
be using "gait" in its present sense) would be to say, "They
are performing different gaits which are exactly alike." To
say that this makes no sense is to say that the identity of a
gait is just given by a description of it. To count two gaits
among those being performed, one must make out some
difference in foot movement that would be relevant in describing (identifying) gaits. In the same way, a person has
the same build he had before if he still fits the same
(relevant) description; and if ten people fit that description, then all ten have the same build. Our imaginary philosopher's error lay in this: having confused the use of
"his build" with that of "his coat," he inevitably repeated
the mistake with "same build" and "same coat." Of course
it does make sense to speak of two coats being exactly
alike, for one may identify coats independently of descriptions of them. Now, no doubt we do say such things as
"His build is exactly like mine," but this is not used in
opposition to "He and I have the same build." It is rather

that "same" and "exactly like" are used interchangeably here, as in the case of color we might say indifferently either "The color here is exactly like the color over there" or "This is the same color here as over there." Whichever we say, there is but one color—red, for example—and it would be a mistake to say: there cannot be only *one* color, for there is *this* color *here* and also *that* color *there*.

The point is that there is no such thing as being just *the same*—no such thing as identity pure and simple. It would be a mistake to think that the same is the same whether we are speaking of builds or coats or gaits or sensations. "Same" must always be understood together with some general term, such as "build" or "coat," and the criterion of identity in any particular case is determined by the general term involved. Or when we use the phrase "the same one," it is determined by the general term that is understood in the context to have been replaced by "one." Similarly, there is no such thing as being an individual pure and simple. It is always a matter of being one build or one coat, and the criterion for counting will vary with the general term. Now one consequence of failing to be clear on this point is that we may unwittingly take the criterion of identity determined by one kind of general term as showing us the meaning of "same" by itself, with the result that we construe the use of "same" with all general terms on this one model. Thus, my imaginary philosopher supposed that if someone were to have the *same* build as his father, he would be getting an already well-worn article. He was clearly taking as his paradigm the use of "same" with words for physical objects and supposing that *that* is what "same build" must mean. The same mistake is made by Ayer when he writes:

The question whether an object is public or private is fundamentally a question of . . . the conventions which we follow in making judgements of identity. Thus physical objects are public because it makes sense to say of different people that they are perceiving the same physical object; mental images are pri-

vate because it does not make sense to say of different
people that they are having the same mental image;
they can be imagining the same thing, but it is impossible that their respective mental images should be
literally the same.[19]

When Ayer speaks of "judgements of identity" and "being
literally the same," he is taking the use of "same" with
words for physical objects as his paradigm for all uses of
"same." So he thinks that if two people were to see the
same mental image, they would be in a position to add to,
correct, and corroborate one another's descriptions in the
same kind of way as we do when two of us have seen the
same house.

But we do, of course, constantly speak of two people
having the same image or the same sensation. The identity
of an image is given by the description of that of which it
is an image (cf. PI 367), and thus we say, "There is one
image that keeps coming back to me: that little boy standing there . . . ," and someone else may remark, "I have
that same image." Again, someone descending in an elevator for the first time may complain of the funny feeling in
his stomach, and someone else tells him, "I get the same
sensation; it will go away when the elevator stops." Nor
would it be odd for someone to say, "We always get the
same pain whenever it rains: an intense aching in the
joints." Now we may also say, "He gets a pain exactly like
mine," but nothing turns on the choice of idiom. We say
indifferently either "Now I have the same pain in both
knees" or "Now there is a pain in my left knee exactly like
the one in my right knee." As Wittgenstein remarks: "In
so far as it makes sense to say that my pain is the same as
his, it is also possible for us both to have the same pain"
(PI 253). His point is that where it is correct to say, "His
pain is the same as mine," it is also correct to say, "We
have the same pain." It would be a mistake to think that
"same pain" here really means "two pains exactly alike."

19 *The Problem of Knowledge,* p. 200.

Ayer, for example, has said that though we speak of two people having the same pain or the same thought, "same" here does not have the meaning of "numerical identity."[20] Apparently he thinks that in all such cases we are comparing two pains or thoughts or images. But Ayer gives no defense of this, except by invoking the very doctrine he is trying to defend: that sensations and thoughts are private. But since Ayer wants to treat this doctrine as a thesis about language, it is begging the question to appeal to the doctrine to decide what *must* be the meaning of "same pain," "same image," and so on. If he were not captivated by the doctrine, he would see that if someone says, "He and I get the same pain in damp weather: an intense aching in the joints," then intense aching is counted as one pain. Another pain would be, for example, the searing sting of a pulled muscle.

The confusion about identity can show up in still another way, which Wittgenstein deals with as follows:

> I have seen a person in a discussion on this subject strike himself on the breast and say: "But surely another person can't have THIS pain!"—The answer to this is that one does not define a criterion of identity by emphatic stressing of the word "this" [PI 253].

What Wittgenstein describes here would be exactly analogous to our imaginary philosopher gesturing toward his body and saying: "But surely another person can't have *this* build!" Although the mistake is more obvious here, it is the same: the word "this" can be used to refer to a particular pain or build only in accordance with the criterion of identity provided by the use of the general term. The word "this" does not itself carry a criterion of identity. As we have already seen, to speak of a particular pain would be, for example, to speak of intense aching in the joints, and *that* is something that many people have. How, then, could someone think that by stressing the word "this"

[20] *The Foundations of Empirical Knowledge*, p. 139; and *The Problem of Knowledge*, p. 199.

he could refer to a pain that he alone can have? Wittgenstein remarks that "what the emphasis does is to suggest the case in which we are conversant with such a criterion of identity, but have to be reminded of it" (PI 253). That is, we might use the emphatic "*this*" to clear up a misunderstanding that has occurred because the general term involved is used at different times with different criteria of identity. To take the stock example, we might clear up in this way a misunderstanding resulting from the type-token ambiguity of the word "letter." ("No, I meant that you should count *this* letter, too.") This will succeed, of course, only if the alternative use of the general term is already well known to us, so that the emphatic "*this*" has only to remind us of it, for as Wittgenstein says, the emphasis "does not define" the kind of identity that is meant. Is there, then, a familiar use of sensation words with a criterion of identity that is reflected in "But surely another person can't have *this* pain!"?

There is a class of episode words that must be considered here. Such expressions as "dizzy spell," "toothache," and sometimes "pain" are used with a criterion of identity quite different from any described above. Although it makes sense to speak of having had the same sensation or image or dream on several occasions, it does not make sense to speak of having had the same dizzy spell on several occasions, unless this means that one was *still* having the dizzy spell. Similarly, there is a use of the word "toothache" such that if someone with a toothache should remark that he had one just like it two years ago, it could only be a joke or a confusion to suggest, "Perhaps it is the same one again." Toothaches are episodes of pain, just as dizzy spells are episodes of dizziness, so that answering the question, "How many toothaches have you had?" requires a reference to particular occasions. Moreover, the episodes are counted by reference to particular persons, so that if I were to count the number of toothaches my children had had, and on some date two of them had suffered from toothache, I should have to count two tooth-

aches for that date. This would be like having to keep
count of the number of tantrums they have or the number
of somersaults they turn in a day. To refer to a particular
tantrum or a particular somersault is to refer to what *one*
person did at some time. Thus, if a mother has described
one of her children's tantrums, someone else might remark
that her child had had a tantrum "exactly like that"; he,
too, threw himself on the floor and held his breath until
he turned blue. "Exactly like" is used here in contrast, not
with "same," but with "rather like," "rather different," and
so forth. That is, it would not be asked: "Do you suppose
they may have had the same one and not just two exactly
alike?" This kind of identification question has no place
in the grammar of "tantrum," and so neither do its two
answers: "Yes, they did have the same one" and "No,
they did not have the same one, only two exactly alike."
Now this same point holds for the grammar of "toothache": the identification question "Did they have the same
one?" has no place and so neither do its answers. That is,
it would not make sense to say, as if in answer to that
question, *either* "They had the same toothache" or "They
did not have the same toothache." Now the relevance of
this point can be seen if we bear in mind the inclination
to think of sensations as being objects of perception. If we
think of first-person sensation statements on analogy with
eyewitness reports, the question will arise whether our reports of sensations could be corroborated or denied by
other "eyewitnesses." So the question becomes "Can two
people feel the same toothache?" But as between answering that two people *can* feel the same toothache and answering that they *cannot*, we seem to be faced with a
Hobson's choice. For the former alternative will seem to
be excluded a priori—that is, we will want to say (without
knowing quite why, perhaps): "It can't be the *same* toothache if there are *two* people in pain." This, of course, is the
influence of the criterion of identity (described above) in
the use of the word "toothache." But with one of the pair
of "answers" thus excluded a priori, it will seem (quite

wrongly, as was shown above) that the other one *must* be true, and thus "No two people can feel the same toothache" comes to be called "a necessary truth." From this one easily concludes that we cannot know anything about another person's toothaches.

This, then, is the complicated story behind the idea that in "Sensations are private" we have a "necessary truth" or that "No one can feel another's pain" expresses a "logical impossibility." The notion of "logical impossibility" was meant to be contrasted with "physical impossibility," but borrowing a remark of Wittgenstein's from another context, we might say: it made the difference "look *too slight.* . . . An unsuitable type of expression is a sure means of remaining in a state of confusion. It as it were bars the way out" (*PI* 339). The "state of confusion" in the present case is that of argument A—that of thinking that (as Wittgenstein once imagined it being expressed) "a man's thinking [or dream or toothache] goes on within his consciousness in a seclusion in comparison with which any physical seclusion is an exhibition to public view" (*PI* p. 222). It seems to have caused Wittgenstein some concern that he might be misunderstood on this point, for he remarks in one place: "The great difficulty here is not to represent the matter as if there were something one *couldn't* do. As if there really were an object . . . but I were unable to show it to anyone" (*PI* 374). But there can be no doubt that Wittgenstein meant to "get rid of the idea of the private object" (*PI* p. 207). It is worth remarking, perhaps, that there is an altogether unproblematic sense in which our sensations may be private: we can sometimes keep them to ourselves. In this sense we often speak of a man's thoughts on some subject being private. No doubt most of our sensations are private in this sense once we pass beyond childhood.

V

In Section I it was mentioned that if argument A is taken to be sound, it will be seen to have the following consequence: no one can be taught the names of sensations; each of us must give these words their meanings independently of other people and their use of sensation words, and therefore no one can know what other people mean by them. With argument A now disposed of, we can also reject this consequence of it. We were taught the names of sensations by others—by others who knew what our sensations were. So we speak a common language. If one fails to see that Wittgenstein has already established this point before he takes up the question "Can there be a private language?" (*PI* 256 ff.), then one may suppose that what is in question is our actual use of sensation words. As was mentioned in Section I, it has been argued against Wittgenstein that since sensations are private, and since we do have names of sensations in our vocabularies, Wittgenstein could not have exposed any real difficulties in the idea of a private language. This argument has now been sufficiently disposed of in the preceding sections: the requisite notion of "privacy" is defective. There has recently been published, however, another version of this misunderstanding, which is likely to gain currency, and which I will therefore briefly discuss.

In his recent book on Wittgenstein, George Pitcher has taken the following view of the matter: (*a*) "Everyone acknowledges that sensations are private, that no one can experience another person's sensations, so that the special felt quality of each person's sensations is known to him alone,"[21] so (*b*) it must be acknowledged also that if there were to be genuine names of sensations, they would have to get their meanings by private ostensive definitions, but (*c*) since Wittgenstein rejects the possibility of any word

[21] *Op. cit.*, p. 297.

acquiring meaning in this way, he must be taken to be
denying that in ordinary language there are any genuine
names of sensations.[22] Therefore, (d) on Wittgenstein's
view, in the language game we play with the word "pain,"
for example, a person's "private sensations do not enter
in."[23] This means that if we have just seen a man struck
down by a car and find that "he is moaning, bleeding, crying out for help, and says he is in great pain," and if we
"rush to help him, see that doctors are called, do everything we can to make him comfortable," still that wretched
man's sensations "are completely unknown to us; we have
no idea what he might be feeling—what the beetle in his
box might be like. But this is no . . . stumbling block to
the playing of the language-game, for they are not in the
least needed. We proceed in exactly the same way no matter what his sensations may be like."[24]

If this reads like an attempted *reductio ad absurdum* of
Wittgenstein, it was not intended as such. But one is not
surprised to find Pitcher concluding that Wittgenstein's
"ideas are obviously highly controversial" and open to
"powerful objections."[25] In fact, Pitcher's "exposition" is
altogether inaccurate. Wittgenstein, as we have seen, rejects the first step (a) in the argument. As for step (b),
Wittgenstein not only rejects private ostensive definitions,
as Pitcher sees, but also explicitly presents an alternative
account of how names of sensations are possible (PI 244,
256). But since (b) is essential to reaching the conclusion
(d), how does Pitcher manage to attribute this conclusion
to Wittgenstein? The answer is that Pitcher has misunderstood certain passages in which Wittgenstein opposes the
idea of "the private object." As can be seen from the above
quotation, one of these is the passage in which Wittgenstein creates the analogy of the beetle in the box (PI
293). There are several other passages similarly misunder-

[22] *Op. cit.*, pp. 281–300.
[23] *Ibid.*, p. 299.
[24] *Ibid.*
[25] *Ibid.*, p. 313.

stood (for example, *PI* 297), but I will deal with only this one.

Pitcher quotes only the following lines from the beetle-in-the-box passage:

> Suppose everyone had a box with something in it: we call it a "beetle." No one can look into anyone else's box, and everyone says he knows what a beetle is only by looking at *his* beetle.—Here it would be quite possible for everyone to have something different in his box. One might even imagine such a thing constantly changing.—But suppose the word "beetle" had a use in these people's language?—If so it would not be used as the name of a thing. The thing in the box has no place in the language-game at all; not even as a *something*: for the box might even be empty.—No, one can "divide through" by the thing in the box; it cancels out, whatever it is [*PI* 293].

Without quoting the final, crucial sentence, Pitcher remarks: "The analogy with pain is perfectly clear."[26] By this he seems to mean at least that pains are, as it were, in a box and cut off from public view, so that they have (as Wittgenstein says of the thing in the box) "no place in the language-game at all." But so far from this being Wittgenstein's actual view, it is what he calls a "paradox" (*PI* 304). It is not our actual use of sensation words that yields this paradox, but rather the philosophical picture of that use. The intention of the passage is clearly shown in the final sentence, which Pitcher does not quote: "That is to say: if we construe the grammar of the expression of sensation on the model of 'object and name' the object drops out of consideration as irrelevant." The word "if" here is crucial, for it is not Wittgenstein's view but the one he opposes that construes the grammar of the expression of sensation on the model of "object and name," and therefore it is not Wittgenstein, as Pitcher thinks, who is committed to the paradoxical consequence that in the use of the word "pain," for example, the sensation drops out as

26 *Ibid.*, p. 298.

irrelevant. The point of the passage, then, is quite the
opposite of what Pitcher supposes. Rather than showing
that sensations cannot have names, it shows that since the
view that sensations are private allows sensations to have
"no place in the language-game" and thereby makes it impossible to give any account of the actual (that is, the
"public") use of sensation words, we must, if we are to
give an account of that language game, reject the view that
sensations are private. In Wittgenstein's words, we must
reject "the grammar which tries to force itself on us here"
(PI 304). We have seen that the idea that sensations are
private results from construing the grammar of sensation
words on analogy with the grammar of words for physical
objects. One consequence of this false grammatical analogy
is that we are led to think that the names of sensations
must get their meanings by private ostensive definitions.
Wittgenstein, on the other hand, gives this account of
learning the name of a sensation: "words are connected
with the primitive, the natural, expressions of the sensation and used in their place. A child has hurt himself and
he cries; and then adults talk to him and teach him exclamations and, later, sentences" (PI 244). It is in this way
that sensations get their place in the language game.

It is clear that Pitcher cannot have grasped this last
point, for although he quotes he does not understand Wittgenstein's remark (PI 246) that it is either false or nonsensical to suppose that no one can know whether another
person is in pain. He takes Wittgenstein to agree with him
that I cannot "determine that another person feels the
same sensation I do: to do that, I would have to be able to
feel his pain . . . , and that is impossible."[27] It is not
surprising, then, that Pitcher should fail to understand
Wittgenstein's reminder of how names of sensations are
taught. It is surprising, however, that he should think that
the view of sensation words rejected by Wittgenstein is
our "commonsensical attitude."[28] Whatever Pitcher may

[27] Op. cit., p. 288.
[28] Ibid., p. 283.

have meant by this phrase, it at least indicates that he has failed to see how very queer is the idea that sensations are essentially private. Could it be that the child who comes crying with a bumped head and who screams when it is touched is giving his peculiar expression to an itching scalp? Or that the giggling child who comes wriggling back for more tickling is really a grotesque creature coming back for more pain? Or that the person who staggers, gropes for support, blinks, and complains that the room is whirling is exhibiting, not dizziness, but a feeling of bodily exhilaration? No, the idea of the private object is not one that turns up in our common thought and practice; it turns up only in those odd moments when we are under the influence of a false grammatical analogy.

WITTGENSTEIN ON SENSATION

ALAN DONAGAN

THE PROBLEM OF SENSATION:
CARTESIANISM VS. BEHAVIOURISM

The problem of sensation with which Wittgenstein struggled in *Philosophical Investigations*[1] is a dilemma. Each of the two familiar solutions of it, to which I shall loosely refer as "Cartesianism" and "Behaviourism,"[2] accepts one of its horns, and professes to conjure the other away. The dilemma itself originates in the grammatical commonplace that the two sentences "I have the sensation *S*," and "He has the sensation *S*," can be used, by different persons, to make the same assertion. If on a given occasion I say, "I am in pain," and you say of me, "He is in pain," you have made the same assertion as I.

The position I shall call "Cartesian" is that each man has, in Rylean phrase, "privileged access" to his own sensations. Not only does he, and only he, have them; but he, and only he, directly knows that he has them. Others may, with varying degrees of certitude, infer that he has a given sensation; but he, and only he, knows whether he has it or not. This raises a problem about how a word can name

To appear in a forthcoming issue of *Mind*. Reprinted with the permission of the author and editor.

[1] In the sequel the titles of two of Wittgenstein's works are abbreviated as follows: BB—*The Blue and Brown Books* (Oxford and New York, 1958); and PI—*Philosophical Investigations*, tr. G. E. M. Anscombe (Oxford, 1953).

[2] I do not mean the well-known programme in psychology that is called "behaviourism," with which I am in sympathy, but a philosophical doctrine.

a sensation. Since nobody can display his sensations to anybody else, sensations cannot be given names by public ostensive definition. Hence Cartesians are tempted to infer that, in order to name a sensation of a given kind, for example toothache, each man must wait until he has a sensation of that kind, and then privately confer the name "toothache" on it.

The Cartesian doctrine that nobody can directly know whether another has a given sensation, say a pain, is now widely dismissed as incredible. That another is in pain can be observed in innumerable cases, as when one sees a child spill boiling water on himself, and hears his uncontrollable cry. To describe such observations as inferential, much less as dubiously inferential, would be perverse. It seems to follow that to say of somebody, "He is in pain," asserts nothing except what can be observed: that is, nothing that does not have to do with his behaviour and circumstances. But if that is so; and if the sentence, "He is in pain," said by somebody else of me, may express exactly the same statement as the sentence, "I am in pain," said by me; then when I say, "I am in pain," far from asserting something directly known only by me, I am in fact asserting something about my behaviour and circumstances of which others may be better placed than I to know. Such is the behaviourist position.

It too is widely dismissed as incredible. Can it be doubted that nobody could ever know some of your sensations, including some of your pains, unless you yourself vouchsafed information about them? And is it not manifestly false that a man learns about his own sensations by observing his behaviour? As Wittgenstein remarked: "I cannot be said to learn of [my sensations]. I *have* them" (*PI*, I § 246).

The problem of sensation, then, is this. According to the Cartesian position, knowledge of the sensations of others is impossible; according to its behaviourist opposite, a man can know what his own sensations are only in the way by which others do, namely by observing his behaviour and circumstances. The Cartesian is perplexed by the problem of other minds, the behaviourist by what Professor Buck has dubbed the problem of "non-other" minds.[3] The dilemma is that, while both positions are repugnant, it appears that one or the other must be true.

WITTGENSTEIN'S "MIDDLE PERIOD" SOLUTION

In a series of lectures delivered in 1932–33, of which G. E. Moore has left a detailed record,[4] Wittgenstein took the bold course of denying the grammatical commonplace from which the problem of sensation derives. The sentences "I have toothache" and "He has toothache" do not, he declared, both express values of the propositional function "x has toothache."[5] If he was right, the problem of sensation does not arise at all. A vestige of this solution may perhaps survive in the remark in the *Blue Book* that "To say, 'I have a pain' is no more a statement about a particular person than moaning is" (*BB*, 67).

In Part I of *Philosophical Investigations* Wittgenstein appears tacitly to have abandoned this solution. He did, indeed, continue to uphold what was true in his remark in the *Blue Book*; namely, that when a man utters the sentence, "I am in pain," he may well not be describing his sensations but making a complaint or begging for relief (cf. *PI*, I §§ 244, 290–291). However, in Part II, begun two years after Part I, Wittgenstein made it clear that a man may use the sentence, "I am in pain," to describe his state. Consider the following passage:

> I say "I am afraid"; someone else asks me: "What was that? A cry of fear; or do you want to tell me how

[3] Cf. "Non-Other Minds" by R. C. Buck, in R. J. Butler (ed.) *Analytical Philosophy* (Oxford, 1962).

[4] "Wittgenstein's Lectures in 1930–33," Parts I–II, *Mind* LXIII (1954), Part III, *Mind* LXIV (1955); all three Parts are reprinted in G. E. Moore, *Philosophical Papers* (London and New York, 1959).

[5] G. E. Moore, *Philosophical Papers*, 307.

you feel; or is it a reflection on your present state?"
—Could I always give him a clear answer? Could I
never give him one? (*PI*, II, ix, 187).

To both questions I take the correct, and intended, answer
to be "No." The implication is evident. Sometimes, but
not always, when I say, "I am afraid," I simply want to tell
somebody else how I feel; that is, to inform him of, to
describe, my feeling. And since throughout the section
from which this passage is taken Wittgenstein has interwoven remarks about fear and grief with remarks about
pain and visual sensation, he evidently intended what he
said about fear to be applied to sensation also.

Although it is not necessary, in inquiring what Wittgenstein's theory of sensation in *Philosophical Investigations*
is, to decide whether he was right in abandoning his "middle period" solution, it cannot be doubted that he was.
When a man who has betrayed no distress in the waiting
room says to his physician, "I have a pain here," while
pointing to some part of his body, manifestly he is neither
crying out with pain nor reflecting on his state, but is
describing to his physician how he feels.

BEHAVIOURIST INTERPRETATIONS OF
PHILOSOPHICAL INVESTIGATIONS

Wittgenstein forewarned his readers against interpreting
Philosophical Investigations as behaviourist (cf. *PI*, I §§
307–308), and he expressly rejected a number of crudely
behaviourist doctrines such as that the word "pain" really
means crying (*PI*, I § 244). Yet that has not prevented
most students from attributing to him a highly sophisticated form of behaviourism. In his sympathetic study, *The
Philosophy of Wittgenstein* (Englewood Cliffs, N.J.,
1964), Professor George Pitcher has perfected that interpretation.

According to Pitcher, Wittgenstein's work on sensation
in *Philosophical Investigations* is a sustained criticism of a

Cartesian theory, which he labels V, that can be stated in three propositions (Pitcher, *op. cit.*, 285). They are:

(1) Words like "toothache" and "pain" are the names, in a non-trivial sense, of sensations which people sometimes experience.

(2) When I say truly "I have toothache," or "I am in pain," I am describing the state of my consciousness.

(3) When I say of another person, "He has toothache" or "He is in pain," I claim that he is experiencing the same sort of sensation as I do when I have toothache or am in pain.

Although the view V, so stated, is natural and plausible, the reasons why Pitcher has taken Wittgenstein to deny it are fairly clear. First, he believes Wittgenstein to have held that, if V were true, the absurd consequences of Cartesianism would follow: in particular, that nobody can ever know whether another is in pain or not (cf. Pitcher, *op. cit.*, 285), or even conceive what it would be for anybody else to have a pain (*ibid.*, 286–287). If Wittgenstein had indeed believed these absurdities to follow from V, it is intelligible that he should have rejected it in favour of some behaviouristic substitute.

Even more important, in Pitcher's eyes, is Wittgenstein's repudiation of an alleged linguistic corollary of V, namely, "that the word 'pain' names or designates . . . something [frightful] that the person [who is in pain] feels, in a way which is even remotely like the way that words for publicly observable things name or designate them" (*ibid.*, 298).

According to Pitcher, although he acknowledged "that when a person is in pain he very often and perhaps always feels something frightful" (*ibid.*, 298), Wittgenstein nevertheless denied that the word "pain" stands for that frightful thing in the same sort of way as the word "red" stands for a certain colour, or the word "tree" for a certain sort of plant. His reasons, Pitcher holds, were as follows:

> [I]n the numerous language-games we play with the
> word "pain," private sensations play no part, and so
> "pain" cannot denote them in anything like the way
> that "tree," for example, denotes that kind of object.
> What does play a part in pain language-games is pain-
> behaviour . . . and pain-comforting behaviour . . . in
> short the external circumstances in which the word
> "pain" is used (Pitcher, *op. cit.*, 298–299).

If Pitcher is right, Wittgenstein's position comes to this:
the private inner happenings that the Cartesians wrongly
describe as "sensations" really do exist, but no language
either does or can have names for them. As for sensations,
for which we do have words, although perhaps not names,
they are a matter of the behaviour of those who have
them, and the behaviour of others towards them. This
position might well be described as "linguistic behaviourism," in contrast to the more familiar "ontological" behaviourism, which denies that Cartesian inner happenings
exist at all.

Before advancing my own interpretation of Wittgenstein's investigation of sensation, one piece of evidence
that has been thought strongly to favour Pitcher's ought to
be examined. Immediately after asking two brief questions
about the claim that cries of pain are uttered on account
of something frightful that "accompanies" them, Wittgenstein propounded this parable:

> Of course, if water boils in a pot, steam comes out of
> the pot and also pictured steam (*das Bild des
> Dampfes*) out of the pictured pot (*dem Bild des
> Topfes*). But what if one insisted on saying that there
> must be something boiling in the pictured pot? (*PI*,
> I § 297).

Pitcher comments: "It would be absurd to start talking
about the liquid in the pictured pot; to wonder, for example, whether it is water or tea . . . [T]he liquid in the
pot is no part of the picture—and language-games which

involve the picture do not contain references to the contents of the pot" (Pitcher, *op. cit.*, 299–300).

If Wittgenstein meant what Pitcher says he did, his parable was ill-chosen. It is true that the pictured pot does not contain, as a part, pictured boiling water. But it is not true that you can describe what the whole picture is a picture of, without referring to the contents of the pot. Nor is it always absurd to inquire what liquid is in the pot. A picture of a metal teapot on a hot plate, with steam pouring from its spout, might well illustrate how not to keep tea hot; considered as a picture of a pot of boiling water its significance would be altogether different. Language-games involving pictures more often than not contain references to the contents of what is pictured. Can we not draw a balloon filled with lighter-than-air gas?

Wittgenstein did not overlook these points: indeed, when he applied his parable to the picturing of pain, he introduced an elaborate quasi-technical terminology for making them. He began by distinguishing between a *Vorstellung* (imaginative representation[6]) and a *Bild* (picture). A *Bild* he considered to contain nothing it does not directly represent. Hence, when you draw a boiling pot, your drawing will contain a *Bild* of steam and a *Bild* of a pot, but not a *Bild* of anything boiling. A *Vorstellung*, by contrast, can represent indirectly. A toy balloon filled with lighter-than-air gas can be imaginatively represented by drawing it as round and as above a tight vertical string tied to it. This would not be a *Bild* of a balloon filled with lighter-than-air gas, because it would contain no *Bild* of the gas, but it would be a *Vorstellung* of one. In this example, a *Vorstellung* is produced by means of a *Bild*.

[6] Miss Anscombe translates "*Vorstellung*" as "image," because of its connexion with imagination, considered as a faculty intermediate between sensation and thought. Unfortunately, "image" suggests a mental counterpart of a physical picture. Pitcher's translation, "representation" (*op. cit.*, 307), blurs the distinction between "*Vorstellung*" and "*Darstellung*" (cf. *PI*, I §397). My compromise is clumsy, but not seriously misleading.

Presumably it was with such examples in mind that Wittgenstein remarked:

> A *Vorstellung* is not a *Bild*, but a *Bild* can correspond
> to it (*PI*, I § 301).

In his analysis of the representation of pain, Wittgenstein employed his distinction between *Bild* and *Vorstellung* as follows.

> It is a misunderstanding to say "The *Bild* of pain
> enters into the language-game with the word 'pain.'"
> The *Vorstellung* of pain is not a *Bild* and *this Vorstellung* is not replaceable in the language-game by anything that we should call a *Bild*. The *Vorstellung* of
> pain certainly enters into the language-game in a
> sense; only not as a *Bild* (*PI*, I § 300).

This passage can be summed up in two propositions. First, the word "pain" cannot mean what it does by way of a picture *qua* picture: there cannot be a picture of pain as there can be of pain-behaviour. Secondly, although pains cannot be directly represented in pictures, they can be indirectly represented—in "imaginative representations" (*Vorstellungen*). Since Wittgenstein immediately went on to say that although a *Vorstellung* is not a *Bild*, "a *Bild* can correspond to it" (*PI*, I § 301), we may take him to have held that a picture can correspond to the imaginative representation of a man in pain. What might such a picture depict? There are only two possibilities. It might depict a man exhibiting pain-behaviour; or it might depict others behaving to him in ways appropriate to somebody in pain.

Pitcher correctly interprets Wittgenstein's remark that "the *Vorstellung* of pain enters into the language-game . . . , only not as a picture" as meaning that one person may imaginatively represent another's pain without having an "image or picture of a private sensation . . . hovering before the other fellow's consciousness" (*op. cit.*, 307).

There cannot be a picture of a private sensation. But Pitcher goes on to suggest that, for Wittgenstein,

> The representation of pain enters in, . . . not by any reference to a mental object behind the pain-behaviour and causing it, but rather by a reference to the *circumstances*, including various sorts of *surroundings*, of the present pain-behaviour (*op. cit.*, 307).

This cannot be right. It is true that Wittgenstein denied that pain is imaginatively represented by a picture of a mental object behind the pain-behaviour; but that is not the same thing as denying that a mental object is referred to. Everything Wittgenstein said turns on his contention that the *Vorstellung* of pain represents something for which there cannot be a *Bild*. Now there can be a *Bild* of the external circumstances of pain. At the very least, Wittgenstein was maintaining that, in the *Vorstellung* of pain, reference is made to something other than the external circumstances depicted in the *Bild* that corresponds to it.

WITTGENSTEIN'S CONCESSIONS
TO CARTESIANISM

Wittgenstein was by no means as hostile to Cartesianism as the behaviourist interpretation makes out. In endeavouring to demonstrate this, I shall for the most part confine my attention to *Philosophical Investigations*, I §§ 243–308, where Wittgenstein explored the problem of sensation so thoroughly that not even he shrank from summarizing his results (cf. *PI*, I § 304).

(a) *The Privacy of Sensation.* Cartesians typically say such things as: "Another person cannot have my pains" (*PI*, I § 253), and "When I say 'I am in pain' I am at any rate justified *before myself*" (*PI*, I § 289). Although Wittgenstein rejected these claims as "grammatical fictions," as the sort of thing a philosopher is driven to say when bewitched by language, yet he did not think that grammatical fictions are baseless. He sought to do justice to the grammatical facts on which they rest.

That another person cannot have my pains is false if it means that there is a kind of pain that only I can have; as Wittgenstein pointed out, "in so far as it makes *sense* to say that my pain is the same as his, it is also possible for us both to have the same pain" (*PI*, I § 253). But if "Another person cannot have my pains" means only that, should somebody else have the same kind of toothache as I, then there would be two instances of toothache and not one, it is merely trivial. Moreover, although Wittgenstein did not trouble to point it out, this trivial fact would not serve to distinguish pains from purely bodily injuries. Two boxers cannot have the same instance of a bruise, even though they may each have identical bruises. These facts about sensations and bodily injuries have the same explanation: one of the criteria of identity of the same instance of a sensation or bodily injury is that it be the sensation or injury of the same individual. To exclaim "But surely another person can't have THIS pain!" can at best remind your audience, in a grammatically misleading way, of this criterion of identity (*PI*, I § 253).

The most striking difference between sensations and bodily processes is not in their criteria of identity, but in how they are reported. Whether you are wounded or not, and, if you are, what the nature of your wound is, are questions conclusively answered only by observing your own body. You are not necessarily in a better position to make such observations than anybody else: indeed, if you are wounded in the back, you are in a worse. It is true that you may report a wound without either observing yourself, or drawing any inference; but your report may be mistaken, and you may be in doubt about it. A soldier on the battlefield may believe that he is hit when he is not; and he may also wonder whether he has been hit. It is quite otherwise with sensation. Although in innumerable cases it can be observed whether another is in pain, in innumerable cases it cannot. Yet even when you cannot tell by

observing him whether or not another is in pain, he can
tell you (cf. *PI*, I § 357); and although what he tells you
may be false, it makes no sense at all to wonder whether
he is mistaken (*PI*, I § 246). A man can intelligibly say,
"I think I'm hit!" but not "I think I'm in pain."

Wittgenstein combatted the common Cartesian inference that a man's truthful reports of his own sensations
exemplify a peculiarly certain and desirable kind of knowledge: a kind of knowledge which, regrettably, we cannot
hope to obtain about the sensations of others. His reason
was that, since it is normally improper to claim knowledge
except as opposed to doubt or error, it is normally improper for a man to claim to know what sensations he is
having. Wittgenstein drew a parallel:

> "This body has extension." To this we might reply:
> "Nonsense!"—but are inclined to reply "Of course!"
> —Why is this? (*PI*, I § 252).

The answer is, that although it would be absurd to speak
as though this body might not have had extension, it may
be desirable to remind somebody that it would be absurd.
One way of reminding him of this would be to say, "*All*
bodies have extension," which formally entails the perplexing statement that *this* body has extension. It may be
equally desirable to remind a behaviourist that often only
the man who has a sensation can tell that he has it; and
that, if he says he has a certain sensation, it makes no
sense to wonder whether he is mistaken. These reminders
are true, even though Cartesians invalidly infer from them
such absurdities as that only I, and not you, poor devil,
can know whether I'm having a sensation; and that when
I say I'm having a sensation, it is a remarkable fact that
I can't be mistaken.

The proposition, "Sensations are private," is absurd if it
is advanced as equivalent to: "Sensations happen to be
private; it is not the case that they are public." But it is
not at all absurd if it is advanced as a reminder: as a
"grammatical statement" like "One plays patience by one-

self" (*PI*, I § 248). Wittgenstein would not have denied that the grammatical statement, "Sensations are private," is *a priori* true, when taken as summing up three reminders: (i) that it is nonsense to suppose that more than one sentient being can have the same instance of a sensation; (ii) that if a man has a sensation, it may be that only he can tell whether he is having it; and (iii) that when a man reports that he has a sensation, it is nonsense to suppose him mistaken.

(b) *Sensations as Occurrences.* Anticipating the objection that, if the occurrence of a sensation is a matter of behaviour, then the manifestly false conclusion follows that from an inspection of somebody's behaviour it is always possible to tell whether or not he is having a given sensation, behaviourists generally analyse sensation into dispositions to behave in specific ways, rather than into actual behaviour. A man in pain may be disposed to cry out; yet he may be even more strongly disposed to conceal his feelings. Behaviourists therefore identify the occurrence of pain, not with the occurrence of pain behaviour, but with dispositions to pain-behaviour that may, or may not, be held in check. It is logically possible to combine a dispositional conception of the nature of sensation with the doctrine that sensation is private, at least in the form in which Wittgenstein held it. If Wittgenstein himself had done so, it would be reasonable to classify him as a behaviourist, although an unorthodox one.

Two passages decisively demonstrate that Wittgenstein rejected any analysis of sensation as dispositional. First, with respect to pain.

> "Yes, but there is *something* there all the same accompanying my cry of pain. And it is on account of that that I utter it. And this something is what is important—and frightful."—Only whom are we informing of this? And on what occasion? (*PI*, I § 296).

Although the statement placed by Wittgenstein in quotation marks must not be taken *propria persona*, the questions that follow show him to have considered it a legitimate philosophical reminder. What could be an occasion for such a reminder? Well, a behaviourist, who holds that there is no more to pain than dispositions to such behaviour as writhing and crying out, would be hard put to it to give a reason why the pain of an amputation should not be treated by trussing and gagging the patient. It is true that a gag would not remove his disposition to cry out; but there seems to be no behaviourist reason for suppressing a disposition that will cease when the amputation has been performed, if it is more convenient to suppress its manifestations directly. The important difference between an analgesic and a gag is not that the analgesic suppresses a disposition and the gag only suppresses behaviour, but that the analgesic removes what accompanies the disposition. It is the accompaniment, not the disposition, that is frightful.

In another passage, Wittgenstein implied that visual sensation is not dispositional. In the course of answering the question how philosophers could be tempted to think that a word like "blue" could mean at one time a colour known to everybody, and at another a private visual impression, Wittgenstein wrote this:

> I don't turn the same kind of attention on the colour in the two cases. When I mean the colour impression that (as I should like to say) belongs to me alone I immerse myself in the colour—rather like when I "cannot get my fill of a colour" (*PI*, I § 277).

If the sensation of seeing blue were no more than a disposition to discriminate between blue and non-blue when they are presented to your gaze, then it would be nonsensical to say that you can turn upon the blue you see a kind of attention that can be described as "immersing" yourself in it. Once again, Wittgenstein has reminded us of a feature of visual sensation that behaviourists are prone to forget.

CARTESIAN DOCTRINES REJECTED
BY WITTGENSTEIN

Although, as we have seen, Wittgenstein strove to secure recognition for the grammatical facts from which Cartesianism derives its strength, he denounced the common Cartesian conception of sensation as a "yet uncomprehended process in [a] yet unexplored medium" (*PI*, I § 308). But what particular Cartesian doctrines did he single out for refutation?

As might have been expected, he chose to inquire into the implications of Cartesianism for language, and particularly into what it implies about the meanings of the words and phrases by which we refer to sensations: words like "pain" and "toothache," and phrases like "see the blue of the sky." According to Cartesianism, sensations are essentially private processes that take place, not in the body, but in the "yet unexplored medium" of the mind. However, since Cartesians hold each person to be infallibly acquainted with his own sensations, they apprehend no difficulty about how one may give one's sensations names. "I speak, or write [a word] down, and at the same time I concentrate my attention on [a] sensation—and so, as it were, point to it inwardly" (*PI*, I § 258). It is in some such way, Cartesians would hold, that words like "pain" are connected with the inner processes of which they are the names.

Such a theory may pass muster, but not inspection. Wittgenstein laid his finger upon its most obvious defect: since words and phrases for sensations belong to common natural languages, their use "stands in need of a justification which everybody [who speaks those languages] understands" (*PI*, I § 261). Such a justification would be impossible if they were names of processes that are essentially incommunicable to others.

Unfortunately, Wittgenstein was not content to press

this criticism, and to inquire into the meanings of expressions for sensations in the natural languages. He also attempted a far more radical proof that not even words or signs in an invented language-game could satisfy the Cartesian theory. This proof has been subjected to justified criticism by Professor Castañeda.[7] I shall therefore pass over it as rapidly as I may, before returning to his principal, and sounder, line of thought.

(a) *The Alleged Impossibility of Cartesian Names of Inner Processes.* As Professor Malcolm has shown,[8] Wittgenstein's more radical argument is a *modus tollens.* It runs as follows. If the Cartesian doctrine is true that there can be a "language which describes my inner experiences and which only I myself can understand" (*PI,* I § 256), then it must be possible to specify a language-game exemplifying it. No game in which words for sensations are "tied up" with natural expressions of sensation will do; for anybody else might understand its words as well as I do (*PI,* I §§ 256, 243). Any game that would do would necessarily be of the same nature as the following one:

> I want to keep a diary about the recurrence of a certain sensation. To this end I associate it with the sign "E" and write this sign in a calendar for every day on which I have the sensation.—I will remark first of all that a definition of the sign cannot be formulated.— But still I can give myself a sort of ostensive definition (*PI,* I § 258).

Let us call the game so specified the "E-game." Is the E-game a *language*-game? If, because of the nature of the E-game, it is not, then no language-game can be specified that would exemplify the private language that the Cartesian doctrine affirms to be possible. But it is not, and because of the nature of the E-game. Therefore, the Cartesian doctrine is false.

[7] Hector-Neri Castañeda, in *Knowledge and Experience,* ed. C. D. Rollins (Pittsburgh, 1964).

[8] Norman Malcolm, *Knowledge and Certainty* (Englewood Cliffs, N.J., 1963), p. 105 [p. 75 of the present volume].

This proof may stand if its cardinal premise is true: that the E-game is not a language-game. Wittgenstein reasonably assumed that the E-game cannot be a language-game unless a player can be said to have written "E" in his calendar either rightly or wrongly. He then argued that, given the E-game as specified, the expressions "right entry" and "wrong entry" can mean nothing, even to the player himself.

> "I impress . . . on myself [the connexion between the sign and the sensation]" can only mean: this process brings it about that I remember the connexion *right* in the future. But in the present case I have no criterion of correctness. One would like to say: whatever is going to seem right to me is right (*PI*, I § 258).

If this is so, it is because of the very nature of the E-game.

Wittgenstein's argument is nevertheless fallacious. He appears to have confounded a player's inability to verify his recollection of the meaning of "E" with inability to understand what it would be for his recollection to be right. The confusion presumably arose from his notion that the phrase "remember the connexion right" is senseless if there is no criterion of correctness. Although what Wittgenstein meant by "criterion" in *Philosophical Investigations* is desperately obscure,[9] in this context it plainly stands for some independent indicator of the accuracy of the player's memory. Yet why should such a criterion be necessary? As any Cartesian imbued with the realist spirit might retort: "A player remembers the connexion right if what he remembers to have been the kind of sensation to which he gave the name 'E' really was that kind of sensation; whether it was or was not is a matter of fact; and it remains a matter of fact even if he has no 'criterion' or independent indicator of whether his recollection is right."

[9] Cf. Rogers Albritton, "On Wittgenstein's Use of the Term 'Criterion'," *Journal of Philosophy* LVI (1959) [reprinted in the present volume]; and the controversy between Newton Garver and Paul Ziff in *Knowledge and Experience*, ed. C. D. Rollins.

Whether it *is* right depends on what the sensation originally named "E" was; whether it *seems* right depends on
how it seems.

This ready and easy way with Wittgenstein's argument
may appear to overlook a point Wittgenstein was fond of
making: if none of our recollections could be independently verified, then it would be pointless to form the concept of true or false recollection (cf. *PI*, I § 265). But
Wittgenstein did not deny that some of the recollections
of players of the E-game can be independently tested. A
Cartesian might therefore argue that nothing prevents a
player of the E-game from forming the general concept of
recollection as true or false, and from applying that concept to his recollection of what sensation he was recording
when he wrote down a particular sign. Wittgenstein would
presumably disagree. But on what ground? The unverifi-
ability of a given recollection does not entail that it is
pointless to think of it as true or false.

There is something wrong with the notion that a player's
claim that his recollection is right is pointless or senseless
unless he can answer the question "What is it for such a
claim to be true?" The question is, of course, unanswerable, except by repeating the claim: it is true if his recollection *is* right; that is, if he originally did mean by "E"
what he recollects he meant by it. The question, "What is
it for the claim that the sky is blue today to be true?" is
equally unanswerable. It is true if the sky is blue today. It
is pointless to ask a question of the form "What is it for
the proposition *p* to be true?" unless the proposition *p* is
in some way suspect. But Wittgenstein has given no reason for suspecting the claim of the E-game player that his
recollection is right, except the invalid one that it is unverifiable.

None of the lesser faults that Wittgenstein detected in
the specification of the E-game entail that it is not a
language-game. It is true that what "E" purports to name
is said to be a sensation, and that sensations are things
with names in our common language, not things nameable

by the player alone (*PI*, I § 261). Nor can the specification of the E-game be improved by describing E as "something" the player "has"; for "something" and "has" are also words in our common language (*PI*, I § 261). Yet it does not follow that the E-game is not a language-game. Certainly, if a player were to identify what he calls "E" as a sensation, or as anything else for which he has an expression in our common language, then "E" would not be a name that only he can understand. But Wittgenstein overlooked the point that the expressions "sensation" and "something he has" were used by him in describing the E-game, not by players in playing it. Players do not identify E: to an outsider, their utterances of "E" are just emissions of "an inarticulate sound" (*PI*, I § 261). Yet that does not show that they articulate nothing to themselves. After all, if the E-game is to satisfy the Cartesian requirement of incommunicability, every utterance in it must appear inarticulate except to the player who makes it.

In examining Wittgenstein's objections to the E-game as a language-game, I have taken it for granted that he conceived its players as already speaking a common language. There are two reasons for doing so: one textual, one not. The textual reason is that, according to the specification of the E-game, a player should "write in a calendar for every day on which [he has] the sensation" (*PI*, I § 258). Only those who command the use of an advanced common language can tell the date of a day.

The non-textual reason is that if Wittgenstein had conceived the E-game as complete in itself, then what he tried to demonstrate about it would have been irrelevant to the truth of Cartesianism. To suppose that the E-game could be a complete, primitive language-game, like the language-games of the builders in *Philosophical Investigations*, I §§ 2–10,[10] would indeed be absurd. But, since Cartesians

[10] Rush Rhees, in "Wittgenstein's Builders" (*Proceedings of the Aristotelian Society*, LX, 1959–60) has questioned whether these games are language-games. If they are complete, they provide for no way of raising the question whether their signs have

need not deny the well-established fact that only in sophisticated languages can there occur names for sensations,
much less for Cartesian inner processes, to show that the
E-game cannot be a complete language-game would not
damage their position at all. In sum: there is textual evidence that Wittgenstein himself did not conceive the
E-game as complete; and, even if he had so conceived it, a
demonstration that the E-game, considered as complete, is
not a language-game, would have been irrelevant to the
question in dispute.

(b) *Names of Sensations Are Not Incommunicable.*
That not only the word "sensation," but all the words and
phrases by which the various kinds of sensation are referred to, belong to "our common language, and not [to]
one intelligible to me alone" (*PI*, I § 261), is a truism.
But in view of the fact that sensations are, in a sense
defined above, private, it is puzzling how this truism can
be true. Wittgenstein only sketched an explanation of it.

His explanation rests on his doctrine that "a great deal
of stage-setting in the language is presupposed if the mere
act of naming is to make sense" (*PI*, I § 257). He made
the following suggestion about the stage-setting in which
it makes sense to name pains.

> Here is one possibility: words are connected with the
> primitive, the natural, expressions of the sensation
> and used in their place. A child has hurt himself and
> cries; and then adults talk to him and teach him ex-
> clamations and, later, sentences. They teach the child
> new pain-behaviour (*PI*, I § 244).

It must be remembered that this does not imply that an
utterance like "I am in pain," which "replaces" crying, is
merely another cry: it can be used to describe a sensation,
a cry cannot (*PI*, II, ix, 189). Wittgenstein elaborated his
suggestion as follows:

---

been rightly or wrongly used (*loc. cit.*, 177–178, 182–183; cf. *PI*,
I §§6, 25, 258).

"What would it be like if human beings showed no outward signs of pain (did not groan, grimace, etc.)? Then it would be impossible to teach a child the use of the word 'tooth-ache'" (*PI*, I § 257).

Although by placing this remark in quotation marks, Wittgenstein assigned it to an imaginary interlocutor, his subsequent remarks *propria persona* show that he accepted it as true. His position, then, was this: Each kind of painful sensation has certain natural physical expressions (cries, grimaces, etc.); and a word is made the name of a specific pain by laying down that it shall stand for whatever has certain specific natural expressions. What has them will, of course, be private.

The natural expressions of a specific pain are neither necessary nor sufficient conditions of its occurrence. A stoical man, who suppresses most of the natural expressions of his pains, does not get rid of the pains themselves; nor does a malingerer who counterfeits the natural expressions of a pain thereby suffer it. If, and only if, everybody who has a certain sensation therefore tends to express it in certain bodily manifestations, then those bodily manifestations are the natural expression of that pain. Such tendencies persist even when they are habitually checked. Thus tears remain a natural expression of grief, even in those who can no longer shed them.

Reference to their natural expressions is not the only stage-setting within which sensations are named. Most visual sensations, and many sensations of hearing, smell, taste, and touch, are caused by physical objects in certain relations to our bodies; and it is by means of such sensations that we discriminate and compare those objects. The name of the colour blue, for example, could not be introduced by reference to the natural expressions of the sensation of seeing blue, because there are no such natural expressions. You can, however, explain to somebody what seeing blue is by telling him that if he looks at the sky on a cloudless day he will see something blue. Just as it would be impossible to teach a child the use of the word "toothache" if human beings did not naturally express toothache in the same ways, so, Wittgenstein held, it would be impossible to teach a child the meaning of "seeing blue" if human beings did not for the most part agree about what things are blue. As he put it:

> If language is to be a means of communication there must be agreement not only in definitions but also (queer as this may sound) in judgements. This seems to abolish logic, but does not do so (*PI*, I § 242).

THE NAMES OF SENSATIONS: WITTGENSTEIN'S THEORY

At this point Wittgenstein's position, as I have represented it, may seem to be merely muddled. Is it not flatly self-contradictory to hold on the one hand that sensations are private and non-dispositional, and on the other that they are named by reference to such external circumstances as their natural expressions? Where, in Wittgenstein's album of reminders, questions, and suggestions is a coherent theory to be found?

It is true that only the materials of a theory have yet been set out. The theory itself Wittgenstein stated tantalizingly and gnomically in *Philosophical Investigations*, I §§ 293–307. The key to understanding it is in § 304:

> "But you will surely admit that there is a difference between pain-behaviour accompanied by pain and pain-behaviour without any pain?"—Admit it? What greater difference could there be?—"And yet you again and again reach the conclusion that the sensation itself is a *nothing*."—Not at all. It is not a *something*, but not a *nothing* either! The conclusion was only that a nothing would serve just as well as a something about which nothing could be said. We have only rejected the grammar which tries to force itself on us here.

Wittgenstein began here by reaffirming that pain is non-behavioural and non-dispositional. There could be no greater difference than that between pain-behaviour accompanied by pain and pain-behaviour not accompanied by it, that is, between the presence of pain and its absence. But he was perplexingly reluctant to draw the tempting conclusion that pain is something that accompanies pain-behaviour: "It is not a *something*, but not a *nothing* either!" The chief problem in expounding Wittgenstein's theory, is to elucidate this verbal contradiction.

In what sense did he think pain not to be a something? His alternative to the Cartesian theory of how sensations are named provides an answer. What accompanies behaviour, inasmuch as it is private, plays no part in determining the meanings of the words and phrases that refer to sensations.

Wittgenstein reconciled the doctrine that unless every normal person had roughly the same natural expressions for pain, a common pain-vocabulary would be impossible, with the apparently incompatible doctrine that there is no greater difference than that between pain-behaviour with the frightful accompaniment of pain, and pain-behaviour without it, by maintaining that that frightful accompaniment only enters our common language as what is naturally expressed by pain-behaviour. He made this point, in another connexion, with a fantastic example:

> "Imagine a person whose memory could not retain *what* the word 'pain' meant—so that he constantly called different things by that name—but nevertheless used the word in a way fitting in with the usual symptoms and presuppositions of pain"—in short he uses it as we all do. Here I should like to say: a wheel that can be turned though nothing else moves with it, is not part of the mechanism (*PI*, I § 271).

Of course if this imaginary person's defective memory had not by its errors compensated for the variations in what accompanied the usual manifestations of pain, he would not have been able to learn the common pain vocabulary. But the crux is that provided what a man truthfully reports as pain is always what he would naturally express by pain-behaviour, it matters not at all what it is that he truthfully reports as pain.

A similar result can be obtained for visual sensation. Suppose that one day a sizeable number of people reported that nearly everything had changed its colour: the sea and cloudless skies had become red, spring grass and summer foliage yellow; ripe wheat had become green, and blood and English pillar-boxes blue. If others saw no difference in the colours of things, for a time there could be no agreed colour vocabulary. But provided the colour judgements of those who reported the change remained constant, since the difference between their colour judgements and those of the majority was systematic, nothing would prevent them from learning once more to employ colour words in the same way as the majority. Whether or not what accompanies the minority's use of colour words is the same as what accompanies the majority's would make no difference to how they spoke. In the mechanism of their use of colour words the character of that internal accompaniment is an idle wheel: it moves nothing.

Yet the accompaniment itself is not a nothing. Why it is not becomes clear upon analysing a passage in which Wittgenstein slipped into dismissing it altogether. Attacking the Cartesian doctrine that it is only from my own case that I know what the word "pain" means, Wittgenstein offered the following parable. If everybody had a box with something in it, nobody being able to look into another's box, and if the word "beetle" were introduced for what is in each person's box, then the meaning of the word "beetle" would not be affected by what was in anybody's box, by whether it changed, or even by whether in some boxes there was nothing at all. "The thing in the box has no place in the language-game at all; not even as a *something*"

(*PI*, I § 293). Wittgenstein applied this parable to the meaning of sensation words as follows:

> No, one can "divide through" by the thing in the box; it cancels out, whatever it is.

> That is to say: if we construe the grammar of the expression of sensation on the model of "object and name" the object drops out of consideration as irrelevant (*PI*, I § 293).

This can only mean: if we construe an expression like "toothache" as the name of the frightful accompaniment of toothache behaviour, then what it names, *or whether it names anything*, is irrelevant to the meaning of "toothache."

That, however, is false. In the language-game of beetles in boxes there is no place for the utterance, "My box has no beetle"; and that is why it does not matter if a box is empty. But in reporting pain there is a place, and a most important place, for the utterance, "I am not in pain"; and one of its uses is to indicate when one's pain-behaviour is not accompanied by pain. The existence of the "object," of that which accompanies natural pain-behaviour, is not only not irrelevant to the meaning of pain words, it is cardinal. What is irrelevant is not the existence of the object, but what it happens to be. You and I could not have a common word for pain unless our natural pain-behaviour was accompanied by something frightful; but whether that accompaniment is the same for both of us or not, or even whether it changes or not (provided we do not notice it) is irrelevant.

THE COMMON ERROR OF CARTESIANISM AND BEHAVIOURISM

If the interpretation I have developed is true, Wittgenstein accepted all three of the propositions Pitcher believes him to have assailed. He did not deny that (1) words like "toothache" and "pain" are the names, in a non-trivial sense, of sensations which people sometimes experience; or that (2) when I say truly "I have toothache" or "I am in pain," I am describing the state of my consciousness; or even that (3) when I say of another person, "He has toothache" or "He is in pain," I claim that he is experiencing the same sort of sensation as I do when I have toothache or am in pain. However, he did think that the phrase "experience the same sort of sensation as I do" conceals a trap. A sensation is that which a normal man naturally expresses in certain ways, or which he naturally has when his body is in a certain kind of state, or stands in a certain kind of relation to certain kinds of physical objects. That is, a sensation is defined by reference to its external circumstances. Yet it is not, according to Wittgenstein, reducible to those external circumstances; for it is defined as their private and non-dispositional accompaniment. It follows that you and I correctly say that we have the same sensation, say toothache, if we both have something frightful that we would naturally express by holding and rubbing our jaws, by certain kinds of grimace, and the like. Whether the internal character of what is expressed in these ways is the same for you as for me is irrelevant to the meaning of the word "toothache."

One misinterpretation of Wittgenstein's position ought to be forestalled. It has been suggested that Wittgenstein professed, like Hegel, to establish necessary connexions between distinct things—in this case, between behaviour and its private accompaniment—but, unlike Hegel, to do it by appealing to implicit rules for the ordinary use of words.[11] Wittgenstein would, I think, have rejected such a description of his theory of sensation. He did not even try to establish a necessary connexion between behaviour and its private accompaniment; for he thought the connexion be-

[11] Cf. Gustav Bergmann, *Logic and Reality* (Madison, Wis., 1964), 239.

tween them to be contingent. He maintained only that the meaning of a sensation word like "pain" is such that if you claim to be in pain then you are claiming to have something that you *in fact* naturally express in certain ways. It is possible that you might not naturally express it in those ways. But if it ceased to be contingently the case that what you spontaneously report as pain coincided with what you naturally express by pain-behaviour, then you would cease to be able to apply the common word "pain" to yourself. It is not very difficult to imagine persons to whom our entire sensation vocabulary would be inapplicable.

That Wittgenstein repudiated behaviourism should now be clear. Since he unequivocally affirmed that sensations are a non-dispositional accompaniment of behaviour and dispositions to behaviour, he necessarily rejected any behaviourist reduction. Less obviously, but demonstrably, he also repudiated Cartesianism; for he rejected the Cartesian doctrine that sensation words are names privately conferred on processes inwardly observed. Since, if he was right, the errors of behaviourism and Cartesianism are opposite and complementary, it should not surprise us that he thought them both to arise from the same fundamental illusion,[12] which he described as follows.

How does the philosophical problem about mental processes and states and about behaviourism arise?— The first step is the one that altogether escapes notice. We talk of processes and states and leave their nature undecided. Sometime perhaps we shall know more about them—we think. But that is just what commits us to a particular way of looking at the matter. For we have a definite concept of what it means to learn to know a process better. (The decisive movement of the conjuring-trick has been made, and it was the very one that we thought quite innocent.) (*PI*, I § 308).

[12] This was pointed out to me, in discussion, by Miss G. E. M. Anscombe.

It is clear from this passage that Wittgenstein considered "the decisive movement of the conjuring-trick" (though here conjuror and audience are one) to have been originally made by the Cartesians. It was they who transformed the grammatical facts which we summed up in the proposition that sensation is non-dispositional and private into the grammatical fiction that sensations are states or processes in a private, and hence non-material, medium. The task of investigating this medium, and the processes that take place in it, was assigned to introspectionist psychology. Some of Wittgenstein's remarks about William James's *Principles of Psychology* indicate that he took James to have been attempting such an investigation (cf. *PI*, I §§ 342, 413, 610).

The behaviourists, whether moved by the barrenness of much introspectionist psychology, by the philosophical difficulties of Cartesianism, or by other considerations, began by denying that the private Cartesian processes in their non-material medium exist at all. This, in itself, Wittgenstein did not consider an error. But the behaviourists shared the Cartesian illusion that the grammatical facts from which Cartesianism springs really do imply the existence of the Cartesian processes and states. Hence they could find no escape from the desperate course of denying the Cartesian grammatical facts.

Wittgenstein's own solution, like the decisive movement of the conjuring-trick itself, was so simple that it is elusive. It was to allow that the Cartesian grammatical facts are facts, that sensations are private non-dispositional accompaniments of the behaviour by which they are naturally expressed, but to refuse to recognize those accompaniments as processes that can be named and investigated independently of the circumstances that produce them, and the behaviour by which they are naturally expressed. Sundered from their external circumstances, such private accompaniments cannot even be named in a common language; *a fortiori*, they cannot be investigated in any way at all. But equally, should an investigation ignore such facts as that something accompanies a cry of pain, something which is important and frightful, then to describe it as an investigation of *sensation* would be preposterous.

CARTESIAN PRIVACY

ANTHONY KENNY

It is frequently said that one of the achievements of
Wittgenstein was to provide a refutation of Cartesian dualism. In this paper I wish to examine such a claim in detail.

Descartes, by making epistemology the centre of philosophical inquiry, created a new philosophy of mind. The
novelty of this philosophy lay less in its explicit theses than
in the whole perspective in which it viewed the relationship between the mental and the physical. Still, Descartes'
epistemological and psychological innovations are well
summed up in his own dictum that mind is better known
than body.

This thesis was novel in two ways.

First, medieval Aristotelians had taught that the human
mind, as we know it, was most at home in the study of the
nature of physical bodies. Intellect is a capacity, so their
theory ran, and capacities are known through their exercise. But the proper exercise of the human intellect as we
know it is the investigation of the physical universe. Knowledge of the human mind, therefore, must be secondary to,
almost parasitic on, knowledge of the external world. For
we can know about the human capacity to know only if we
can see that capacity at work; and that capacity is best
seen at work within the field which is its proper study (cf.
Aquinas, *Summa Theologica*, Ia 87, 1c).

Secondly, the boundaries between mind and body were
redrawn by Descartes. Mind, for him, is *res cogitans*, and
cogitatio includes not only intellectual meditation but also
volition, emotion, pain, pleasure, mental images, and sen-

sations. For Aquinas, by contrast, the boundary between spirit and nature was not between consciousness and clockwork, it was between intellect and sense. It was understanding and judging and willing, not feeling aches or seeing colours or having mental images, which for him set mind apart from matter. The former were possible without a body: God and the angels understand and will and judge no less than men. The latter were inconceivable without a living organism: disembodied spirits neither see nor hear, feel neither joy nor sorrow, have neither imagination nor memory images (*Summa Theologica*, Ia 77, 8). The difference between the two comes out clearly in the case of pain. For Descartes, pain, in the strictest sense, is something spiritual: however much the incautious may confuse the pure sensation of pain with an erroneous judgement about its physical causes, none the less a *res cogitans* can feel pain though he has no body at all. For Aquinas, pain, in the strictest sense, is something physical; the disembodied spirits in hell suffer because of the thwarting of their wills, not through aches or pains (*Summa Theologica*, Ia 64, 3; cited by Geach, *Mental Acts*, 116).

Descartes' innovations influenced philosophers outside the Cartesian tradition. Ideas, impressions, and sense-data are all, by Cartesian standards, mental entities; and for the British empiricists they are all epistemologically prior to the physical substances of the problematic external world. For Locke, Berkeley and Hume, no less than for Descartes, mind is better known than body in the sense that the internal is more certain than the external, the private is prior to the public. The philosophical viability of the Cartesian notion of mind concerns not only the historian of Descartes but anyone interested in epistemology and philosophical psychology. But I propose to approach the question by a study of the text of Descartes. What does Descartes mean by *res cogitans*?

"*Cogitare*" and "*penser*" are naturally translated "think." Descartes, as has been noted, uses the verbs to record many experiences which we would not naturally describe as thoughts. It has been said that the words in the current French and Latin of Descartes' time had a sense wider than that of the modern English equivalent with its predominantly intellectual reference. This may be so. However, French and Latin usage was never as wide as that to be found in Descartes: at no time was it natural to call a headache or a feeling of hunger a *cogitatio* or *pensée*. Moreover, the English use of "thought" is not purely intellectualistic: when a young man's fancy turns to thoughts of love, the thoughts include emotions, desires, and intentions. In fact, it seems that Descartes was consciously extending the use of the words "*cogitare*" and "*penser*." This is brought out by the misunderstandings of his contemporaries. Thus Mersenne objected that if the nature of man consisted solely of thought, then man has no will. "I do not see that this follows," Descartes had to explain, "for willing, understanding, imagining and feeling are simply different ways of thinking, which all belong to the soul" (to Mersenne, 27. 4. 1637, AT I, 366).[1] To another correspondent, a year later, he wrote: "There is nothing entirely in our power except our thoughts; at least if you take the word 'thought' as I do, for all the operations of the soul, in such a way that not only meditations and acts of the will, but even the functions of sight and hearing, and the resolving on one movement rather than another, in so far as they depend on the soul, are all thoughts" (AT II, 36). I shall use the traditional translation "thought" for "*cogitatio*" and "*pensée*." The English word will seem unnatural in some contexts, but no more unnatural than the corresponding words seemed in similar contexts to Descartes' contemporaries.

Descartes extended the concept of *thought* because of a feature which he believed to attach to all the operations of

---

[1] References are given to the volume and page of the standard edition of Descartes' works, *Oeuvres de Descartes*, ed. Ch. Adam et P. Tannery, 12 Vols., Paris, 1897–1910 (henceforth cited as AT). I have made use eclectically of the translations by Haldane and Ross and by Geach and Anscombe.

the soul. "By the noun *thought*," he wrote in the *Principles*, "I understand everything which takes place in us so that we are conscious of it (*nobis consciis*), in so far as it is an object of awareness" (*AT* VIII, 7). When he was setting out his terms *more geometrico* in answer to the Second Objections, he gave a similar definition, adding that the consciousness must be immediate. "Under the term 'thought' I include everything which is in us in such a way that we are immediately conscious of it . . . I added 'immediately' for the purpose of excluding the consequences of thoughts; voluntary movements, for instance, depend upon thoughts but are not themselves thoughts" (*AT* VII, 161).

What is common, then, to all the operations of the mind is consciousness. Consciousness carries with it indubitability, and this is what makes the "*cogito ergo sum*" suitable as a first principle. "*Sum*" is the first indubitable existential judgement; and it is indubitable because the premise on which it is based, "*cogito*," is indubitable. In the *Discourse on Method*, the mental activity referred to by "*je pense*" is the attempt to think everything false; in the *Meditations* the *cogitatio* in question is the thought of Descartes' own existence. But any conscious activity is capable of providing a premise for the cogito, as Descartes explains in the *Principles*. "There is nothing that gives rise to knowledge of any object which does not even more certainly lead us to know our thought. For instance, if I persuade myself that there is an earth because I touch or see it, by that very fact, and for much better reason, I should be persuaded that my thought exists, because it may be that I think I touch the earth even though there is possibly no earth in existence at all, but it is not possible that I—that is my soul—should be non-existent while it has this thought. We can draw the same conclusion from all the other things which come into our thought: namely that we who think them exist" (*AT* VIII, 8).

Sensation, then, as well as intellectual thought, is a thought capable of founding the certainty of one's own

existence. But does not sensation presuppose a body, as
Descartes himself says in the Second Meditation (AT VII,
27): how then can its occurrence be certain while the existence of body is doubtful? Descartes explains that there
are two different ways of taking "sensation." "Suppose I
say I see (or I am walking) therefore I exist. If I take this
to refer to vision (or walking) as a corporeal action, the
conclusion is not absolutely certain; for as often happens
during sleep, I may think I am seeing though I do not
open my eyes (or think I am walking although I do not
change my place); and it may even be that I have no body.
But if I take it to refer to the actual sensation or awareness (*conscientia*) of seeing (or walking) then it is quite
certain; for in that case it has regard to the mind, and it
is the mind alone that has a sense or experience of itself
seeing (or walking)." Sensation so understood, he says, is
thought (AT VIII, 7).

In making this identification Descartes is not so much
extending the sense of *cogitatio* as altering that of *sensus*.
If Macbeth says he sees a dagger where no dagger is, we
may hesitate to say whether he *sees* anything at all; but it
is perfectly natural to say he *thinks* he sees a dagger. Now
this same thought, on Descartes' view, occurs also when
Macbeth really is, in the normal sense, seeing a dagger;
and it is thought of this kind in which sensation strictly
so called consists and which provides a premise for the
cogito. Such thoughts can be mistaken, but their existence
cannot be doubted. "It is I who have sensations, or who
perceive corporeal objects as it were by the senses. Thus,
I am now seeing light, hearing a noise, feeling heat. These
objects are unreal, for I am asleep; but at least I seem to
see, to hear, to be warmed. This cannot be unreal; and this
is what is properly called my sensation; further, sensation,
precisely so regarded, is nothing but an act of thought"
(Second Meditation, AT VII, 29).

In this theory of Descartes there is an unnaturalness and
an ambiguity.

The unnaturalness is this. Comparison of the various

texts of Descartes make clear that what is referred to by "think" in "thinking I am seeing" and by "seem" in "seeming to hear" is to be identified with the consciousness or perception by which Descartes defines the nature of *cogitatio* or thought. (In the passage from the *Principles*, for instance, "*putare me videre*" is used in parallel with "*conscientia videndi*" and with "*mens cogitat se videre*.") But we cannot say that the consciousness, or perception, or awareness of sensation may occur whether or not sensation occurs; "to be conscious of," "to perceive" and "to be aware of" are all success-verbs, so that one can only be conscious of, perceive, and be aware of what is really the case. On the other hand, it is odd to say that "seeming to see" or "thinking that one sees" may occur whether or not seeing occurs; "seeming to see" and "thinking that one sees" seem to be phrases designed to cover just the case in which one *doesn't* see. The cogitatio of seeing is meant to be what is common to the genuine case and the doubtful case. Perhaps it is no accident that there is no natural way of referring to such a common element.

The ambiguity is this. Sometimes, consciousness appears to be something which accompanies thought (as in the Second Replies, quoted above); sometimes it appears to be something which is identical with thought (as in the passage quoted above from the Second Meditation). The ambiguity is multiplied in the two versions of Descartes' reply to Hobbes (AT VII, 176; IX, 137). The Latin version tells us that there are some acts which are called cogitative, such as understanding, willing, imagining, sensing; "these all fall under the common concept of thought, perception or consciousness (*qui omni sub ratione communi cogitationis, sive perceptionis, sive conscientiae conveniunt*)." The authorised French version has: "these all have in common that they cannot occur without thought, or perception, or consciousness and awareness (*tous lesquels conviennent entre eux en ce qu'ils ne peuvent être sans pensée, ou perception, ou conscience et connaissance*)." Both versions here identify thought and consciousness; but

the Latin regards particular mental acts as species of
thought-consciousness, whereas the French regards them as
accompanied by thought-consciousness. We shall later see
reason to believe that this ambiguity is not an accidental
defect in Descartes' terminology, but is the consequence
of an essential element in his system. For the moment it
suffices to note that the ambiguity arises naturally from
the way in which *cogitatio* is introduced. Sensation is a
conscious act in the sense of being itself a mode of consciousness—to see a circle and to feel a circle are two different ways of being conscious of the circle. But willing is
not a conscious act in the same way: to want to be certain
is not to be conscious of being certain; wanting is a conscious act in the different sense that if I want something,
I am conscious that I want it. Equally, it might be said, if
I perceive something, then I am conscious that I perceive
it. But even so, there is the possibility of ambiguity. Willing is conscious in the sense of being an object of consciousness; sensation is conscious not only in this sense but
also in the sense of being a mode of consciousness.

The issue is further complicated because what we do
voluntarily we are normally conscious of doing. Thus, Descartes told the Marquis of Newcastle that there are some
of our actions which are not managed by our thought "for
it often happens that we walk and that we eat without
thinking in any way of what we are doing; likewise, without using our reason, we push away things that are harmful
and parry blows which are aimed at us; and even if we expressly wished not to put our hands in front of our head
when we fall, we could not stop ourselves" (AT IV, 573).
Here Descartes seems to treat as equivalent *attending to*
an action and *intending* an action; we put up our hands
involuntarily but not inadvertently; we eat our food without attention but not without intention. The analogy between sensation and action seems to be merely this: just
as I can think I am seeing without seeing, so I can think I
am breathing without breathing (AT II, 37). As in perception, so in action there is *thought*, in this sense. But it

is not clear what is the relation of this thought to volition.

It would be wrong to identify the thought that I am seeing or the thought that I am walking with the belief that I am seeing or walking in the ordinary sense of "see" and "walk." The occurrence of such a belief is not a necessary condition for the occurrence of the corresponding thought: Descartes, during his period of doubt, has the thought that he is seeing a light—that is, it seems to him that he is seeing a light—but he refrains from believing this. Again, the occurrence of such a belief is not a sufficient condition for the occurrence of the corresponding thought. The intellectual perception of the injury of a limb is not the same as the feeling of pain in that limb (AT VII, 82), and presumably a man whose limbs were anaesthetised and knew that he was moving them only because he was told so would not have the cogitatio of moving his limbs. Rather, to have the thought that *p* is to have an experience similar to the experience I have when we would normally say that *p* is the case. Does the experience have to be so similar as to be indistinguishable, or merely so similar as to be *de facto* not distinguished? This is a question to which we shall have to return.

Two things emerge from the consideration of *cogitatio* in spite of the questions about its nature which we have left, for the moment, unanswered. First, the relation of thought to its bodily causes and expressions is completely contingent. All our thoughts could be just as they are even if no body ever existed: only the veracity of God assures us that this is not in fact the case. Secondly, the occurrence of thoughts themselves is not open to doubt or error. Thoughts cannot occur without our knowing that they occur; and we cannot think that a thought is occurring unless that thought actually is occurring. The first we are told expressly; the second is presupposed by the structure of the *cogito*. Perhaps I only think I see; but that I think I see cannot be doubted. Note that it is not just the occurrence of *thought* that cannot be doubted, but the occurrence of the particular thought in question (AT VII, 29).

We are now in a position to see the precise nature of
Descartes' innovation in philosophy of mind. The introduction of *cogitatio* as the defining characteristic of mind
is tantamount to the substitution of privacy for rationality
as the mark of the mental. For somebody like Aquinas, human beings were distinguished from animals by such things
as their capacity to understand geometry and to desire
riches. Neither the understanding of geometry nor the desire for riches is a specially private state concerning which
the subject is in a position of special authority. I may doubt
whether I understand the proof of a particular theorem,
and a teacher may be able to show me that I was mistaken
about one I believed I understood. I may wonder whether
I am adopting a certain policy out of cupidity; and a perceptive friend may be able to settle the question better
than I can myself. On such topics my sincere statement
is not the last possible word.

On the other hand, if I want to know what sensations
somebody is having, what he seems to see or hear, what
he is imagining or saying to himself, then I have to give his
utterances on the topic a special status. What he says need
not be true—he may be insincere, or misunderstand the
words he is using—but it cannot be erroneous. Experiences
of this kind have the property of indubitability which
Descartes ascribes to thought. They are private to their
owner in the sense that while others can doubt them, he
cannot.

It is clear that privacy, in the sense indicated, is something independent of the rationality discussed above. The
discovery of Pythagoras' theorem was a clearly rational
activity, and to know this we do not need to know whether
Pythagoras worked out the theorem first aloud or in his
head. The production of random grunts is not something
which calls for rationality, whether I produce them aloud,
or in imagination, grunting, as it were, in my mind's
throat.

We can now see in what way Wittgenstein's philosophy
is relevant to Cartesian dualism. If Descartes' innovation

was to identify the mental with the private, Wittgenstein's contribution was to separate the two. Since Wittgenstein, we tend to equate the mental with what is peculiar to language-users; and if Wittgenstein's arguments are valid, languages cannot be private. The cogito and the private language argument each lie at the heart of the epistemology and philosophy of mind of their inventors. The cogito led to the conclusion that mind is better known than body. The private language argument leads, we might say, to the conclusion that body is better known than mind.

I shall examine Wittgenstein's arguments against private language and try to show in detail how they connect with the Cartesian theses. I shall argue that the referents of the words of Wittgenstein's private language correspond to Descartes' *cogitationes*; and that the properties of these entities from which Wittgenstein sought to show the impossibility of a private language are properties from which an argument could also be drawn against Descartes' system of clear and distinct ideas. The comparison of the two arguments is facilitated by the fact that Wittgenstein took the same example, pain, to illustrate his thesis as Descartes had taken to explain the notion of clear and distinct ideas (*Principles of Philosophy*, I, 46 f, 67 ff).

Descartes did not much reflect on the nature of language. When he uttered the words *cogito ergo sum*, he took it for granted that he knew what they meant. Perhaps, as the Sixth Objections said, he should not have done so; perhaps, in accordance with his methodic doubt he should have questioned whether they meant what he thought they meant. Descartes replied that it was enough to know what thought and existence were "by that internal cognition which always precedes reflective knowledge and which, when the object is thought and existence, is innate in all men" (AT VII, 422). In the *Principles* he explained that when he called the *cogito* the first principle, "I was not denying that we must first know what is meant by thought, existence, certainty; again, we must know such things as that it is impossible for that which is thinking to be non-existent; but I thought it needless to enumerate these notions, for they are of the greatest simplicity, and by themselves they can give us no knowledge that anything exists" (AT VIII, 8).

Still, it seems clear that if a Cartesian *res cogitans* uses a language it must be a private language in the sense defined by Wittgenstein (*Philosophical Investigations*, I, secs. 244, 256). If the language contains words for sensations, then the connection between the words and the sensations must be set up without the intermediary of the natural expression of sensation in bodily behaviour; for the words of the language are supposed to have meaning at a stage at which it is doubtful whether there are any bodies at all.

The word "pain" in such a language must refer to what Wittgenstein calls "an immediate private sensation," something which can be known only to the person speaking. For Descartes pain, in the ordinary sense of the word, was something very like perception; whereas taste, say, was a perception of the outer senses, pain was a perception of the inner senses. In this sense, it was subject to deception like the other senses. Thus, in the Sixth Meditation we are told: "[I found error] not only in [judgements] founded on the external senses, but even in those founded on the internal as well; for is there anything more intimate or internal than pain? And yet I have learned from some persons whose arms or legs have been cut off, that they sometimes seemed to feel pain in the part which had been amputated, which made me think that I could not be quite certain that it was a certain member which pained me, even though I felt pain in it" (AT VII, 71). In pain, as in sight, we must distinguish what is strictly *cogitatio*. The indubitable *cogitatio* will be the "immediate private sensation."

In sections 246 and 253 Wittgenstein explains in what sense "private" is to be taken. Pain, in the ordinary sense of the word is private in the sense that it is senseless to say of myself that I doubt whether I am in pain and in the sense that one criterion of identity for pains is the identity of their possessor. "Pain" in the private language is meant to refer to something private in a special sense: a sensation whose existence I can know with certainty and other people cannot.

Now Descartes' *cogitatio* of pain will be private in just this sense. First, it cannot be known with certainty to other people. No bodily manifestation of pain is a sufficient proof of its occurrence; notoriously, Descartes believed that animals displayed all the bodily manifestations of pain without feeling pain itself. Explaining this to the Marquis of Newcastle, Descartes wrote: "There is not one of our exterior actions, which can assure those who examine them that our body is not just a self-moving machine, but also contains a soul which has thoughts, with the exception of the words or other signs deliberately produced in connection with subjects which occur, without having reference to any passion" (AT IV, 574). No bodily behaviour therefore can establish the occurrence of the thought which is pain; even the utterance "I am in pain," would "have reference to a passion," and so be disqualified (AT IV, 573). Secondly, pain, like any other thought, is known with certainty to the sufferer: pain is clearly and distinctly perceived when it is considered merely as a sensation or thought (*Principles*, I, LXVIII. AT VIII, 33).

Wittgenstein objects to the expression "I know I am in pain." He wishes to reserve the use of "know" to cases where deception and doubt are possible, but in fact excluded. In the case of one's own pain the expression of doubt is senseless, so the expression of knowledge rules out nothing. "It can't be said of me at all (except perhaps as a joke) that I *know* I am in pain. What is it supposed to mean—except perhaps that I *am* in pain?" (PI, I, sec. 246).

Here we must return to an ambiguity in Descartes' concept of thought which we left unresolved. Was *cogitatio* identical with *conscientia*, we asked, or was it distinct? If it is identical, then Descartes agrees with Wittgenstein that "I know I am in pain" means nothing more nor less than "I am in pain." Wittgenstein argues in effect that the believer in private sensations must make it both possible and impossible for a sufferer to be mistaken about his pain: possible, if the assertion "I know I am in pain" is to have any content; impossible, if it is to be universally true (*PI*, I, secs. 246, 258, 270).

Descartes' doctrine of pain seems to be open to a very similar objection. He writes thus, to illustrate the doctrine of clear and distinct ideas. "The knowledge upon which a certain and incontrovertible judgement can be formed, should not alone be clear but also distinct. I term that clear which is present and apparent to an attentive mind, in the same way as we assert that we see objects clearly when, being present to the regarding eye, they operate upon it with sufficient strength. But the distinct is that which is so precise and different from all other objects that it contains within itself nothing but what is clear. When, for instance, a severe pain is felt, the perception of this pain may be very clear, and yet for all that not distinct, because it is usually confused by the sufferers with the obscure judgement that they form upon its nature, assuming as they do that something exists in the part affected, similar to the sensation of pain of which they are alone clearly conscious" (*Principles*, I, 45–46. AT VIII, 22). We are told, however, that we may have a clear knowledge of our sensations "if we take care to include in the judgements we form of them that only which we know to be precisely contained in our perception of them, and of which we are intimately conscious" (66). Thus "there is no reason that we should be obliged to believe that the pain, for example, which we feel in our foot, is anything beyond our mind which exists in our foot" (67). We can avoid error if we judge that there is something, of whose nature we are ignorant, which causes the sensation of pain in our minds (cf. the parallel remarks about colour in 70) (AT VIII, 32–33).

Now there seem here to be three separate elements in Descartes' account, namely, the pain, the perception of the pain, and the judgement about the pain. The perception of the pain seems to be something distinct from the pain, for there are properties such as clarity and distinctness which belong to the perception but not to the pain. The perception seems to be something distinct from the judgement; judgement is an act of the will which it is in our power to make or withhold, and we are enjoined to restrict our judgement to what we clearly and distinctly perceive. But it is not at all easy to work out what Descartes considers to be the relationships between these three.

In so far as pain is a *cogitatio*, it would seem that pain cannot occur without being perceived. Can it, however, occur without being perceived clearly? Descartes seems to give two different answers to this. On the one hand, he says "when a man feels great pain, he has a very clear perception of pain" (AT VIII, 22); on the other hand he says that we have a clear perception of our sensations only if we carefully restrict our judgement about them, and this is a condition most difficult to observe. If we ask, however, whether a pain may be perceived clearly without being perceived distinctly, the answer is plain. "A perception may be clear without being distinct, though not distinct without being clear" (AT VIII, 22). Again, Descartes seems explicit enough on the relationship between perception and judgement. Judgement differs from perception in being an act of the will, in being concerned with extramental reality, and in being liable to error. The faculty of perceiving is infallible, that of assenting can err (AT VIII, 21). Judgement may occur without perception; that is precisely the cause of error: "people form judgements about what they do not perceive and thus fall into error" (AT VIII, 21). What of the converse case: can clear and distinct perception occur without judgement? Here there are some puzzles. On the one hand we learn that "we are by nature so disposed to give our assent to things that we clearly perceive, that we cannot possibly doubt of their truth" (AT VIII, 21). Yet on the other hand does not the whole procedure of methodic doubt suppose that one can withhold one's judgement even about what seems most clear?

When we examine Descartes' doctrines closely, the reason for the inconsistencies seems to be this. The clear and distinct perception of pain is not in fact identifiable separately from the occurrence of pain and the judgement about the origin of the pain.

First, to perceive a pain clearly, simply is to have a severe pain. Descartes says: "I call clear that which is present and manifest to an attentive mind; just as we are said to see clearly objects when they are present and operate strongly, and when our eyes are in the right disposition to survey them" (AT VIII, 22). Here there seem to be two elements in clarity: that the object of perception be manifest, and that the perceiving faculty be attentive. In the case of sight, such a distinction is possible; in the case of pain it is illusory. Descartes nowhere suggests what would be the difference between the unclear perception of a manifest pain, and the clear perception of an obscure pain. Yet it must be possible to make out such a difference if the distinction between the occurrence of a pain and the perception of a pain is to be a genuine one.

Secondly, to perceive a pain distinctly is simply to make the correct judgement about one's pain. It is to make the correct, cautious, judgement, "What I feel is caused by I know not what," rather than the incorrect judgement, "What I feel is something in my foot." The difference between a distinct and a confused perception is explained precisely in terms of the nature of the accompanying judgement. When the perception of pain is not distinct, that is because it is "confused by the sufferers with the obscure judgement that they form upon its nature."

The perception of pain, then, is not a genuine intermediary between the occurrence of pain and the judgement on pain. Of the two properties of the perception, one, clarity, is really a property of the pain which occurs, and the other, distinctness, is really a property of the judgement made about it.

The criticism which I have just made of the Cartesian notion of the perception of pain is parallel to that which Wittgenstein makes of the notion of "identifying one's sensations" in the *Philosophical Investigations*. Wittgenstein argues that the expression of doubt has no place in the language-game with "pain"; the utterance, "I doubt whether I have a pain," is senseless. But if we cut out the human behaviour which is the expression of pain, then the doubt becomes permissible, since I need a criterion of identity for the sensation, and it is possible that I might identify the sensation wrongly (*PI*, I, sec. 288). The identification of the sensation as pain thus becomes an intermediate step between the occurrence of the pain and the expression of it in the words "I am in pain." But in fact there is no room for such an intermediate step. We must either in effect identify recognising a sensation with having a sensation (so that "I know I am in pain" means "I am in pain") or else identify the recognition of the sensation with its expression. This last possibility is explored at 270. "I discover that whenever I have a particular sensation a manometer shows that my blood pressure rises. So I shall be able to say that my blood pressure is rising without using any apparatus. This is a useful result. And now it seems quite indifferent whether I have recognised the sensation *right* or not. Let us suppose I regularly identify it wrong, it does not matter in the least." There are in fact only two possibilities of discrepancy between pain and its expression: first, that there should be pain-behaviour without pain (304), second, that there should be pain without pain-behaviour (281). Whereas, if the recognition of pain intervened between pain and its expression, there would seem to be two further possible sources of discrepancy: inaccurate expression of correct recognition, and accurate expression of incorrect recognition. Wittgenstein argues that these are not in fact genuine possibilities. " 'Imagine

a person whose memory could not retain *what* the word
"pain" meant—so that he constantly called different things
by that name—but nevertheless used the word in a way
fitting in with the usual symptoms and presuppositions of
pain'—in short he uses it as we all do. Here I should like
to say: a wheel that can be turned though nothing else
moves with it, is not part of the mechanism" (271).

In general, Wittgenstein advises us, "always get rid of
the idea of the private object in this way: assume that
it constantly changes, but that you do not notice the
change because your memory constantly deceives you" (*PI*,
II, p. 207). If inaccurate recognition and inaccurate
expression were combined, there might in fact be *no* discrepancy between sensation and its expression. In that
case, a man in pain who says, "I am in pain," may be
making two mistakes which cancel each other out. He may
be mistaking his pain for a pleasure, and mistakenly thinking that the word "pain" means pleasure. In fact, Wittgenstein argues, for it to be possible for an utterance to be
mistaken, it must be possible to distinguish the criterion
for the content of an utterance from the criterion for its
truth. But in the case of an utterance in a private language no such distinction is possible. One is forced to say,
"Whatever is going to seem right to me is right." And
"that only means that here we can't talk about 'right'"
(258). In reality, according to Wittgenstein, "what I do
is not . . . to identify my sensation by criteria: but to repeat an expression. But this is not the *end* of the language-
game: it is the beginning" (290).

The parallel with the argument I used against Descartes will now be obvious. The confused judgement about
pain which is made by the man unpurified by Cartesian
doubt corresponds to the use of "I am in pain" in a public
language in connection with bodily causes and manifestations of pain. The Cartesian *cogitatio*, stripped of the obscure judgement, corresponds to the private sensation dis-
connected from bodily expression. The perception of the
cogitatio corresponds to the identification of the sensation

by criteria. The judgement of the purified Cartesian about his clear and distinct perception corresponds to the utterance of the name for the sensation in the private language.

I said earlier that if a Cartesian spirit uses a language at all, it seems that it must be a private language. But, for Descartes, need judgements be made in language at all? Commonly, we gather, they are. "Because we attach all our conceptions to words for the expression of them by speech, and as we commit to memory our thoughts in connection with these words; and as we more easily recall to memory words than things, we can scarcely conceive of anything so distinctly as to be able to separate completely that which we conceive from the words chosen to express the same" (AT VIII, 37). None the less, the philosopher can, and should, separate the conceptions from the words in which it is clothed. It might thus be thought that Descartes could escape the argument derived from Wittgenstein's critique of private language. This, however, would be a mistake. Whether a judgement is made in language or not, there must be some feature of it which makes it the particular judgement that it is. There must be something to distinguish the judgement that p from the judgement that q. And this is enough to let the argument proceed. Wherever Wittgenstein's argument talks of "knowing the meaning of an expression" we can substitute "recognising the judgement for the judgement that it is." Just as Wittgenstein's argument turned on there being no way of recognising the meaning of an utterance in a private language independently of its truth, so the anti-Cartesian argument depended in part on there being no way of recognising the content of a judgement independently of knowing its truth. In each case, the possibility of error gets ruled out and so the supposition of correctness becomes vacuous.

It is sometimes said that all Wittgenstein's argument shows is that it would be impossible to *learn* the words for sensations if sensations had no bodily expression. If that were so, Descartes would seem to be able to avoid criticism by pleading that the knowledge exercised in the perception of sensations was innate. But in fact Wittgenstein's argument seeks to show that it is impossible to give a coherent account of the *exercise* of the knowledge of the meaning of a word in a private language. He does not explicitly consider innate ideas; but in 257 he makes clear that his argument does not depend on considerations about learning when he says: " 'What would it be like if human beings showed no outward signs of pain (did not groan, grimace, etc.)? Then it would be impossible to teach a child the use of the word "tooth-ache".'—Well, let's assume the child is a genius and itself invents a name for the sensation!"

If I am right, neither the postulation of non-linguistic judgements about sensations nor the doctrine of innate ideas can save Descartes from the criticisms suggested by the passages that I have quoted from Wittgenstein. If this is so, then the argument against private languages has an importance which transcends any parochial concerns of ordinary language philosophy and the disputable theories of meaning put forward in the *Philosophical Investigations*.

KNOWLEDGE OF OTHER MINDS

NORMAN MALCOLM

I

I believe that the argument from analogy for the existence of other minds still enjoys more credit than it de-
serves, and my first aim will be to show that it leads
nowhere. J. S. Mill is one of many who have accepted the
argument and I take his statement of it as representative.
He puts to himself the question, "By what evidence do I
know, or by what considerations am I led to believe, that
there exist other sentient creatures; that the walking and
speaking figures which I see and hear, have sensations
and thoughts, or in other words, possess Minds?" His answer is the following:

> I conclude that other human beings have feelings like
> me, because, first, they have bodies like me, which I
> know, in my own case, to be the antecedent condition
> of feelings; and because, secondly, they exhibit the
> acts, and other outward signs, which in my own case I
> know by experience to be caused by feelings. I am con-
> scious in myself of a series of facts connected by an
> uniform sequence, of which the beginning is modifica-
> tions of my body, the middle is feelings, the end is
> outward demeanor. In the case of other human beings
> I have the evidence of my senses for the first and last

From Norman Malcolm, *Knowledge and Certainty: Essays and
Lectures* (Englewood Cliffs, N.J., 1963), © 1963, pp. 130-140.
Reprinted by permission of Prentice-Hall, Inc., Englewood Cliffs,
N.J. This essay originally appeared in *The Journal of Philosophy*,
LV (1958), pp. 969-978.

links of the series, but not for the intermediate link. I
find, however, that the sequence between the first and
last is as regular and constant in those other cases as
it is in mine. In my own case I know that the first
link produces the last through the intermediate link,
and could not produce it without. Experience, therefore, obliges me to conclude that there must be an
intermediate link; which must either be the same in
others as in myself, or a different one: I must either
believe them to be alive, or to be automatons: and
by believing them to be alive, that is, by supposing the
link to be of the same nature as in the case of which
I have experience, and which is in all other respects
similar, I bring other human beings, as phenomena,
under the same generalizations which I know by experience to be the true theory of my own existence.[1]

I shall pass by the possible objection that this would be
very *weak* inductive reasoning, based as it is on the observation of a single instance. More interesting is the following point: Suppose this reasoning could yield a conclusion of the sort "It is probable that that human figure"
(pointing at some person other than oneself) "has
thoughts and feelings." Then there is a question as to
whether this conclusion can *mean* anything to the philosopher who draws it, because there is a question as to
whether the sentence "That human figure has thoughts
and feelings" can mean anything to him. Why should this
be a question? Because the assumption from which Mill
starts is that he has *no criterion* for determining whether
another "walking and speaking figure" does or does not
have thoughts and feelings. If he had a criterion he could
apply it, establishing with certainty that this or that human
figure does or does not have feelings (for the only plausible
criterion would lie in behavior and circumstances that are
open to view), and there would be no call to resort to
tenuous analogical reasoning that yields at best a proba-

---

[1] J. S. Mill, *An Examination of Sir William Hamilton's Philosophy*, 6th ed. (New York, 1889), pp. 243–244.

bility. If Mill has no criterion for the existence of feelings other than his own then in that sense he does not understand the sentence "That human figure has feelings" and therefore does not understand the sentence "It is *probable* that that human figure has feelings."

There is a familiar inclination to make the following reply: "Although I have no criterion of verification still I *understand*, for example, the sentence 'He has a pain.' For I understand the meaning of 'I have a pain,' and 'He has a pain' means that he has the *same* thing I have when I have a pain." But this is a fruitless maneuver. If I do not know how to establish that someone has a pain then I do not know how to establish that he has the *same* as I have when I have a pain.[2] You cannot improve my understanding of "He has a pain" by this recourse to the notion of "the same," unless you give me a criterion for saying that someone *has* the same as I have. If you can do this you will have no use for the argument from analogy: and if you cannot then you do not understand the supposed conclusion of that argument. A philosopher who purports to rely on the analogical argument cannot, I think, escape this dilemma.

There have been various attempts to repair the argument from analogy. Mr. Stuart Hampshire has argued[3] that its validity as a method of inference can be established in the following way: Others sometimes infer that I am feeling giddy from my behavior. Now I have direct, non-inferential knowledge, says Hampshire, of my own feelings. So I can check inferences made about me against the facts, checking thereby the accuracy of the "methods" of inference.

[2] "It is no explanation to say: the supposition that he has a pain is simply the supposition that he has the same as I. For *that* part of the grammar is quite clear to me: that is, that one will say that the stove has the same experience as I, *if* one says: it is in pain and I am in pain" (Ludwig Wittgenstein, *Philosophical Investigations* [New York, 1953], sec. 350).

[3] "The Analogy of Feeling," *Mind*, January 1952, pp. 1–12.

All that is required for testing the validity of any
method of factual inference is that each one of us
should sometimes be in a position to confront the
conclusions of the doubtful method of inference with
what is known by him to be true independently of the
method of inference in question. Each one of us is
certainly in this position in respect of our common
methods of inference about the feelings of persons
other than ourselves, in virtue of the fact that each
one of us is constantly able to compare the results of
this type of inference with what he knows to be true
directly and non-inferentially; each one of us is in the
position to make this testing comparison, whenever he
is the designated subject of a statement about feelings
and sensations. I, Hampshire, know by what sort of
signs I may be misled in inferring Jones's and Smith's
feelings, because I have implicitly noticed (though
probably not formulated) where Jones, Smith and
others generally go wrong in inferring my feelings (*op.
cit.*, pp. 4–5).

Presumably I can also note when the inferences of others
about my feelings do not go wrong. Having ascertained the
reliability of some inference-procedures I can use them
myself, in a guarded way, to draw conclusions about the
feelings of others, with a modest but justified confidence
in the truth of those conclusions.

My first comment is that Hampshire has apparently forgotten the purpose of the argument from analogy, which
is to provide some probability that "the walking and speaking figures which I see and hear, have sensations and
thoughts" (Mill). For the reasoning that he describes involves the assumption that other human figures *do* have
thoughts and sensations: for they are assumed to *make
inferences* about me from *observations* of my behavior.
But the philosophical problem of the existence of other
minds *is* the problem of whether human figures other than
oneself do, among other things, make observations, inferences, and assertions. Hampshire's supposed defense of the
argument from analogy is an *ignoratio elenchi*.

If we struck from the reasoning described by Hampshire all assumption of thoughts and sensations in others we should be left with something roughly like this: "When my behavior is such and such there come from nearby human figures the sounds 'He feels giddy.' And generally I do feel giddy at the time. Therefore when another human figure exhibits the same behavior and I say 'He feels giddy,' it is probable that he does feel giddy." But the reference here to the sentence-like sounds coming from other human bodies is irrelevant, since I must not assume that those sounds express inferences. Thus the reasoning becomes simply the classical argument from analogy: "When my behavior is such and such I feel giddy; so probably when another human figure behaves the same way he feels the same way." This argument, again, is caught in the dilemma about the criterion of the *same*.

The version of analogical reasoning offered by Professor H. H. Price[4] is more interesting. He suggests that "one's evidence for the existence of other minds is derived primarily from the understanding of language" (p. 429). His idea is that if another body gives forth noises one understands, like "There's the bus," and if these noises give one new information, this "provides some evidence that the foreign body which uttered the noises is animated by a mind like one's own. . . . Suppose I am often in its neighborhood, and it repeatedly produces utterances which I can understand, and which I then proceed to verify for myself. And suppose that this happens in many different kinds of situations. I think that my evidence for believing that this body is animated by a mind like my own would then become very strong" (p. 430). The body from which these informative sounds proceed need not be a human body. "If the rustling of the leaves of an oak formed intelligible words conveying new information to me, and if gorse-bushes made intelligible gestures, I should have evidence that the oak or the gorse-bush was animated by

4 "Our Evidence for the Existence of Other Minds," *Philosophy*, XIII (1938), 425–456.

an intelligence like my own" (p. 436). Even if the intelligible and informative sounds did not proceed from a body they would provide evidence for the existence of a (disembodied) mind (p. 435).

Although differing sharply from the classical analogical argument, the reasoning presented by Price is still analogical in form: I know by introspection that when certain combinations of sounds come from me they are "symbols in acts of spontaneous thinking"; therefore similar combinations of sounds, not produced by me, "probably function as instruments to an act of spontaneous thinking, which in this case is not my own" (p. 446). Price says that the reasoning also provides an *explanation* of the otherwise mysterious occurrence of sounds which I understand but did not produce. He anticipates the objection that the hypothesis is nonsensical because unverifiable. "The hypothesis is a perfectly conceivable one," he says, "in the sense that I know very well what the world would have to be like if the hypothesis were true—what sorts of entities there must be in it, and what sorts of events must occur in them. I know from introspection what acts of thinking and perceiving are, and I know what it is for such acts to be combined into the unity of a single mind . . ." (pp. 446–447).

I wish to argue against Price that no amount of intelligible sounds coming from an oak tree or a kitchen table could create any probability that it has sensations and thoughts. The question to be asked is: What would show that a tree or table *understands* the sounds that come from it? We can imagine that useful warnings, true descriptions and predictions, even "replies" to questions, should emanate from a tree, so that it came to be of enormous value to its owner. How should we establish that it understood those sentences? Should we "question" it? Suppose that the tree "said" that there was a vixen in the neighborhood, and we "asked" it "What is a vixen?," and it "replied," "A vixen is a female fox." It might go on to do as well for "female" and "fox." This performance might incline us to say that the tree understood the words, in contrast to the possible case in which it answered "I don't know" or did not answer at all. But would it show that the tree understood the words in the same sense that a person could understand them? With a person such a performance would create a presumption that he could make correct *applications* of the word in question; but not so with a tree. To see this point think of the normal teaching of words (e.g., "spoon," "dog," "red") to a child and how one decides whether he understands them. At a primitive stage of teaching one does not require or expect definitions, but rather that the child should *pick out* reds from blues, dogs from cats, spoons from forks. This involves his looking, pointing, reaching for and going to the right things and not the wrong ones. That a child says "red" when a red thing and "blue" when a blue thing is put before him is indicative of a mastery of those words *only* in conjunction with the other activities of looking, pointing, trying to get, fetching, and carrying. Try to suppose that he says the right words but looks at and reaches for the wrong things. Should we be tempted to say that he has mastered the use of those words? No, indeed. The disparity between words and behavior would make us say that he does not understand the words. In the case of a tree there could be no disparity between its words and its "behavior" because it is logically incapable of behavior of the relevant kind.

Since it has nothing like the human face and body it makes no sense to say of a tree, or an electronic computer, that it is looking or pointing at or fetching something. (Of course one can always *invent* a sense for these expressions.) Therefore it would make no sense to say that it did or did not understand the above words. Trees and computers cannot either pass or fail the tests that a child is put through. They cannot take them. That an object was a source of intelligible sounds or other signs (no matter how sequential) would not be enough by itself to establish that it had thoughts or sensations. How informative sentences and valuable predictions could emanate from a gorse-bush might be a grave scientific problem, but the explanation could never be that the gorse-bush has a mind. Better no explanation than nonsense!

It might be thought that the above difficulty holds only for words whose meaning has a "perceptual content" and that if we imagined, for example, that our gorse-bush produced nothing but pure mathematical propositions we should be justified in attributing thought to it, although not sensation. But suppose there was a remarkable "calculating boy" who could give right answers to arithmetical problems but could not apply numerals to reality in empirical propositions, e.g., he could not *count* any objects. I believe that everyone would be reluctant to say that he *understood* the mathematical signs and truths that he produced. If he could count in the normal way there would not be this reluctance. And "counting in the normal way" involves looking, pointing, reaching, fetching, and so on. That is, it requires the human face and body, and human behavior—or something similar. Things which do not have the human form, or anything like it, not merely do not but *cannot* satisfy the criteria for thinking. I am trying to bring out part of what Wittgenstein meant when he said, "We only say of a human being and what is like one that it thinks" (*Investigations*, sec. 360), and "The human body is the best picture of the human soul" (*ibid.*, p. 178).

I have not yet gone into the most fundamental error of the argument from analogy. It is present whether the argument is the classical one (the analogy between my body and other bodies) or Price's version (the analogy between my language and the noises and signs produced by other things). It is the mistaken assumption that *one learns from one's own case* what thinking, feeling, sensation are. Price gives expression to this assumption when he says: "I know from introspection what acts of thinking and perceiving are . . ." (*op. cit.*, p. 447). It is the most natural assumption for a philosopher to make and indeed seems at first to be the only possibility. Yet Wittgenstein has made us see that it leads first to solipsism and then to nonsense. I shall try to state as briefly as possible how it produces those results.

A philosopher who believes that one must learn what thinking, fear, or pain is "from one's own case," does not believe that the thing to be observed is one's behavior, but rather something "inward." He considers behavior to be related to the inward states and occurrences merely as an accompaniment or possibly an effect. He cannot regard behavior as a *criterion* of psychological phenomena: for if he did he would have no use for the analogical argument (as was said before) and also the priority given to "one's own case" would be pointless. He believes that he notes something in himself that he calls "thinking" or "fear" or "pain," and then he tries to infer the presence of the *same* in others. He should then deal with the question of what his criterion of the *same* in others is. This he cannot do because it is of the essence of his viewpoint to reject circumstances and behavior as a criterion of mental phenomena in others. And what else could serve as a criterion? He ought, therefore, to draw the conclusion that the notion of thinking, fear, or pain in others is in an important sense meaningless. He has no idea of what would count for or against it.[5] "That there should be thinking or pain other than my own is unintelligible," he ought to hold. This would be a rigorous solipsism, and a correct outcome of the assumption that one can know only from one's own case what the mental phenomena are. An equivalent way of putting it would be: "When I say 'I am in pain,' by 'pain' I mean a certain inward state. When I say 'He is in pain,' by 'pain' I mean *behavior*. I cannot attribute pain to others *in the same sense* that I attribute it to myself."

Some philosophers before Wittgenstein may have seen the solipsistic result of starting from "one's own case." But

---

[5] One reason why philosophers have not commonly drawn this conclusion may be, as Wittgenstein acutely suggests, that they assume that they have "an infallible paradigm of identity in the identity of a thing with itself" (*Investigations*, sec. 215).

I believe he is the first to have shown how that starting point destroys itself. This may be presented as follows: One supposes that one inwardly picks out something as thinking or pain and thereafter identifies it whenever it presents itself in the soul. But the question to be pressed is, Does one make *correct* identifications? The proponent of these "private" identifications has nothing to say here. He feels sure that he identifies correctly the occurrences in his soul; but feeling sure is no guarantee of being right. Indeed he has no idea of what being *right* could mean. He does not know how to distinguish between actually making correct identifications and being under the impression that he does. (See *Investigations*, secs. 258–259.) Suppose that he identified the emotion of anxiety as the sensation of pain? Neither he nor anyone else could know about this "mistake." Perhaps he makes a mistake *every* time! Perhaps all of us do! We ought to see now that we are talking nonsense. We do not know what a *mistake* would be. We have no standard, no examples, no customary practice, with which to compare our inner recognitions. The inward identification cannot hit the bull's-eye, or miss it either, because there is no bull's-eye. When we see that the ideas of correct and incorrect have no application to the supposed inner identification, the latter notion loses its appearance of sense. Its collapse brings down both solipsism and the argument from analogy.

II

The destruction of the argument from analogy also destroys the *problem* for which it was supposed to provide a solution. A philosopher feels himself in a difficulty about other minds because he assumes that first of all he is acquainted with mental phenomena "from his own case." What troubles him is how to make the transition from his own case to the case of others. When his thinking is freed of the illusion of the priority of his own case, then he is able to look at the familiar facts and to acknowledge that the circumstances, behavior, and utterances of others actually are his *criteria* (not merely his evidence) for the existence of their mental states. Previously this had seemed impossible.

But now he is in danger of flying to the opposite extreme of behaviorism, which errs by believing that through observation of one's own circumstances, behavior, and utterances one can find out that one is thinking or angry. The philosophy of "from one's own case" and behaviorism, though in a sense opposites, make the common assumption that the first-person, present-tense psychological statements are verified by self-observation. According to the "one's own case" philosophy the self-observation cannot be checked by others; according to behaviorism the self-observation would be by means of outward criteria that are available to all. The first position becomes unintelligible; the second is false for at least many kinds of psychological statements. We are forced to conclude that the first-person psychological statements are not (or hardly ever) verified by self-observation. It follows that they have no verification at all; for if they had a verification it would have to be by self-observation.

But if sentences like "My head aches" or "I wonder where she is" do not express observations then what do they do? What is the relation between my declaration that my head aches and the fact that my head aches, if the former is not the report of an observation? The perplexity about the existence of *other* minds has, as the result of criticism, turned into a perplexity about the meaning of one's own psychological sentences about oneself. At our starting point it was the sentence "*His* head aches" that posed a problem; but now it is the sentence "*My* head aches" that puzzles us.

One way in which this problem can be put is by the question, "How does *one know when to say* the words 'My head aches'?" The inclination to ask this question can be made acute by imagining a fantastic but not impossible

case of a person who has survived to adult years without
ever experiencing pain. He is given various sorts of injec-
tions to correct this condition, and on receiving one of
these one day, he jumps and exclaims, "Now I feel pain!"
One wants to ask, "How did he *recognize* the new sensation as a *pain?*"

Let us note that if the man gives an answer (e.g., "I
knew it must be pain because of the way I jumped") then
he proves by that very fact that he has not mastered the
correct use of the words "I feel pain." They cannot be
used to state a *conclusion*. In telling us *how* he did it he
will convict himself of a misuse. Therefore the question
"How did he recognize his sensation?" requests the impossible. The inclination to ask it is evidence of our inability
to grasp the fact that the use of this psychological sentence has nothing to do with recognizing or identifying or
observing a state of oneself.

The fact that this imagined case produces an especially
strong temptation to ask the "How?" question shows that
we have the idea that it must be more difficult to give the
right name of one's sensation *the first time*. The implication would be that it is not so difficult *after* the first time.
Why should this be? Are we thinking that then the man
would have a paradigm of pain with which he could compare his sensations and so be in a position to know right
off whether a certain sensation was or was not a pain?
But the paradigm would be either something "outer" (behavior) or something "inner" (perhaps a memory impression of the sensation). If the former then he is misusing
the first-person sentence. If the latter then the question of
whether he compared *correctly* the present sensation with
the inner paradigm of pain would be without sense. Thus
the idea that the use of the first-person sentences can be
governed by paradigms must be abandoned. It is another
form of our insistent misconception of the first-person sentence as resting somehow on the identification of a psychological state.

These absurdities prove that we must conceive of the

first-person psychological sentences in some entirely different light. Wittgenstein presents us with the suggestion that the first-person sentences are to be thought of as similar to the natural nonverbal, behavioral expressions of psychological states. "My leg hurts," for example, is to be assimilated to crying, limping, holding one's leg. This is a bewildering comparison and one's first thought is that two sorts of things could not be more unlike. By saying the sentence one can make a *statement*; it has a *contradictory*; it is *true* or *false*; in saying it one *lies* or *tells the truth*; and so on. None of these things, exactly, can be said of crying, limping, holding one's leg. So how can there be any resemblance? But Wittgenstein knew this when he deliberately likened such a sentence to "the primitive, the natural, expressions" of pain, and said that it is "new pain-behavior" (*ibid.*, sec. 244). This analogy has at least two important merits: first, it breaks the hold on us of the question "How does one *know when to say* 'My leg hurts'?", for in the light of the analogy this will be as nonsensical as the question "How does one know when to cry, limp, or hold one's leg?"; second, it explains how the utterance of a first-person psychological sentence by another person can have *importance* for us, although not as an identification—for in the light of the analogy it will have the same importance as the natural behavior which serves as our preverbal criterion of the psychological states of others.

OPERATIONALISM
AND ORDINARY LANGUAGE:
A CRITIQUE OF WITTGENSTEIN

C. S. CHIHARA AND J. A. FODOR[1,2]

INTRODUCTION

This paper explores some lines of argument in Wittgenstein's post-*Tractatus* writings in order to indicate the relations between Wittgenstein's philosophical psychology on the one hand and his philosophy of language, his epistemology, and his doctrines about the nature of philosophical analysis on the other. We shall hold that the later writings of Wittgenstein express a coherent doctrine in which an operationalistic analysis of confirmation and lan-

From *American Philosophical Quarterly*, Vol. II (1965), pp. 281–295. Reprinted with the permission of the authors and editor.

[1] This work was supported in part by the U.S. Army, Navy, and Air Force under Contract DA 36–039–AMC–03200(E); in part by the National Science Foundation (Grant GP–2495), the National Institutes of Health (Grant MH–04737–04), the National Aeronautics and Space Administration (Ns G–496), the U.S. Air Force (ESD Contract AF 19 [628]-2487), the National Institute of Mental Health (Grant MPM 17, 760); and, in addition, by a University of California Faculty Fellowship.

[2] In making references to Part I of Ludwig Wittgenstein's *Philosophical Investigations* (New York, 1953), cited here as PI, we shall give section numbers, e.g. (PI, §13), to Part II, we shall give page numbers, e.g. (PI, p. 220). In referring to his *The Blue and Brown Books* (New York, 1958), cited here as BB, we give page numbers. References to his *Remarks on the Foundations of Mathematics* (New York, 1956), cited here as RFM, will include both part and section numbers, e.g. (RFM, II, §26).

guage supports a philosophical psychology of a type we shall call "logical behaviorism."

We shall also maintain that there are good grounds for rejecting the philosophical theory implicit in Wittgenstein's other works. In particular we shall first argue that Wittgenstein's position leads to some implausible conclusions concerning the nature of language and psychology; second, we shall maintain that the arguments Wittgenstein provides are inconclusive; and third, we shall try to sketch an alternative position which avoids many of the difficulties implicit in Wittgenstein's philosophy. In exposing and rejecting the operationalism which forms the framework of Wittgenstein's later writings, we do not, however, suppose that we have detracted in any way from the importance of the particular analyses of particular philosophical problems which form their primary content.

I

Among the philosophical problems Wittgenstein attempted to dissolve is the "problem of other minds." One aspect of this hoary problem is the question: What justification, if any, can be given for the claim that one can tell, on the basis of someone's behavior, that he is in a certain mental state? To this question, the sceptic answers: No good justification at all. Among the major motivations of the later Wittgenstein's treatment of philosophical psychology is that of showing that this answer rests on a misconception and is *logically* incoherent.

Characteristically, philosophic sceptics have argued in the following way. It is assumed as a premiss that there are no logical or conceptual relations between propositions about mental states and propositions about behavior in virtue of which propositions asserting that a person behaves in a certain way provide support, grounds, or justification for ascribing the mental states to that person. From this, the sceptic deduces that he has no compelling reason for supposing that any person other than himself is ever truly said to feel pains, draw inferences, have motives, etc. For, while his first-hand knowledge of the occurrence of such mental events is of necessity limited to his own case, it is entailed by the premiss just cited that application of mental predicates to others must depend upon logically fallible inferences. Furthermore, attempts to base such inferences on analogies and correlations fall short of convincing justifications.

Various replies have been made to this argument which do not directly depend upon contesting the truth of the premiss. For example, it is sometimes claimed that, at least in some cases, no *inference* from behavior to mental states is at issue in psychological ascriptions. Thus, we sometimes *see* that someone is in pain, and in these cases, we cannot be properly said to *infer* that he is in pain. However, the sceptic might maintain against this argument that it begs the question. For the essential issue is whether anyone is *justified* in claiming to see that another is in pain. Now a physicist, looking at cloud-chamber tracks, may be justified in claiming to see that a charged particle has passed through the chamber. That is because in this case there is justification for the claim that certain sorts of tracks show the presence and motion of particles. The physicist can explain not only how he is able to detect particles, but also why the methods he uses are methods of detecting *particles*. Correspondingly, the sceptic can argue that what is required in the case of another's pain is some justification for the claim that, by observing a person's behavior, one can *see* that he is in *pain*.

Wittgenstein's way of dealing with the sceptic is to attack his premiss by trying to show that there do exist conceptual relations between statements about behavior and statements about mental events, processes, and states. Hence, Wittgenstein argues that in many cases our knowledge of the mental states of some person rests upon something other than an observed empirical correlation or an analogical argument, viz. a conceptual or linguistic connection.

To hold that the sceptical premiss is false is *ipso facto* to commit oneself to some version of *logical behaviorism* where by "logical behaviorism" we mean the doctrine that there are logical or conceptual relations of the sort denied by the sceptical premiss.[3] Which form of logical behaviorism one holds depends on the nature of the logical connection one claims obtains. The strongest form maintains that statements about mental states are translatable into statements about behavior. Wittgenstein, we shall argue, adopts a weaker version.

II

It is well known that Wittgenstein thought that philosophical problems generally arise out of misrepresentations

---

[3] Philosophers of Wittgensteinian persuasion have sometimes heatedly denied that the term "behaviorism" is correctly applied to the view that logical connections of the above sort exist. We do not feel that very much hangs on using the term "behaviorism" as we do, but we are prepared to give some justification for our terminology. "Behaviorism" is, in the first instance, a term applied to a school of psychologists whose interest was in placing constraints upon the conceptual equipment that might be employed in putative psychological explanations, but who were *not* particularly interested in the analysis of the mental vocabulary of ordinary language. The application of this label to a philosopher bent upon this latter task must therefore be, to some extent, analogical. Granted that there has been some tendency for the term "behaviorism" to be pre-empted, even in psychology, for the position held by such *radical* behaviorists as Watson and Skinner, who require that all psychological generalizations be defined over observables, insofar as C. L. Hull can be classified as a behaviorist, there does seem to be grounds for our classification. Hull's view, as we understand it, is that mental predicates are in no sense "eliminable" in favor of behavioral predicates, but that it is a condition upon their coherent employment that they be severally related to behavioral predicates and that some of these relations be logical rather than empirical—a view that is strikingly similar to the one we attribute to Wittgenstein. Cf. C. F. Hull, *Principles of Behavior* (New York, 1943).

and misinterpretations of ordinary language (PI, § 109, § 122, § 194). "Philosophy," he tells us, "is a fight against the fascination which forms of expression exert upon us" (BB, p. 27). Thus, Wittgenstein repeatedly warns us against being misled by superficial similarities between certain forms of expression (BB, p. 16) and tells us that, to avoid philosophical confusions, we must distinguish the "surface grammar" of sentences from their "depth grammar" (PI, § 11, § 664). For example, though the grammar of the sentence "A has a gold tooth" seems to differ in no essential respect from that of "A has a sore tooth," the apparent similarity masks important conceptual differences (BB, pp. 49, 53; PI, § 288–293). Overlooking these differences leads philosophers to suppose that there is a problem about our knowledge of other minds. It is the task of the Wittgensteinian philosopher to dissolve the problem by obtaining a clear view of the workings of pain language in this and other cases.

The Wittgensteinian method of philosophical therapy involves taking a certain view of language and of meaning. Throughout the *Investigations*, Wittgenstein emphasizes that "the speaking of language is part of an activity" (PI, § 23) and that if we are to see the radically different roles superficially similar expressions play, we must keep in mind the countless kinds of language-using activities or "language-games" in which we participate (BB, pp. 67–68).

It is clear that Wittgenstein thought that analyzing the meaning of a word involves exhibiting the role or use of the word in the various language-games in which it occurs. He even suggests that we "think of words as instruments characterized by their use . . ." (BB, p. 67).

This notion of analysis leads rather naturally to an operationalistic view of the meaning of certain sorts of predicates. For, in those cases where it makes sense to say of a predicate that one has determined that it applies, one of the central language-games that the fluent speaker has learned to play is that of making and reporting such determinations. Consider, for example, one of the language-games that imparts meaning to such words as "length," i.e., that of reporting the dimensions of physical objects. To describe this game, one would have to include an account of the procedures involved in measuring lengths; indeed, mastering (at least some of) those procedures would be an essential part of learning this game. "The meaning of the word 'length' is learnt among other things, by learning what it is to determine length" (*PI*, p. 225). As Wittgenstein comments about an analogous case, "Here the teaching of language is not explanation, but training" (*PI*, § 5). For Wittgenstein, "To understand a sentence means to understand a language." "To understand a language means to be master of a technique" (*PI*, § 199).

In short, part of being competent in the language-game played with "length" consists in the ability to arrive at the truth of such statements as "*x* is three feet long" by performing relevant operations with, e.g., rulers, range-finders, etc. A philosophical analysis of "length," insofar as it seeks to articulate the language-game played with that word, must thus refer to the operations which determine the applicability of length predicates. Finally, insofar as the meaning of the word is itself determined by the rules governing the language-games in which it occurs, a reference to these operations will be essential in characterizing the meaning of such predicates as "three feet long." It is in this manner that we are led to the view that the relevant operations for determining the applicability of a predicate are conceptually connected with the predicate.[4]

By parity of reasoning, we can see that to analyze such words as "pain," "motive," "dream," etc., will *inter alia*

---

[4] Cf. "Let us consider what we call an 'exact' explanation in contrast with this one. Perhaps something like drawing a chalk line round an area? Here it strikes us at once that the line has breadth. So a color-edge would be more exact. But has this exactness still got a function here: isn't the engine idling? And remember too that we have not yet defined what is to count as overstepping this exact boundary; *how, with what instruments, it is to be established*" (*PI*, §88, italics ours). Cf., also *RFM*, I, §5.

involve articulating the operations or observations in terms of which we determine that someone is in pain, or that he has such and such a motive, or that he has dreamed, etc. (PI, p. 224). But clearly, such determinations are ultimately made on the basis of the behavior of the individual to whom the predicates are applied (taking behavior in the broad sense in which it includes verbal reports). Hence, for Wittgenstein, reference to the characteristic features of pain behavior on the basis of which we determine that someone is in pain is essential to the philosophical analysis of the word "pain" just as reference to the operations by which we determine the applicability of such predicates as "three feet long" is essential to the philosophical analysis of the word "length." In both cases, the relations are conceptual and the rule of language which articulates them is in that sense a rule of logic.

III

But what, specifically, is this logical connection which, according to Wittgenstein, is supposed to obtain between pain behavior and pain? Obviously, the connection is not that of simple entailment. It is evident that Wittgenstein did not think that some proposition to the effect that a person is screaming, wincing, groaning, or moaning could entail the proposition that the person is in pain. We know that Wittgenstein used the term "criterion" to mark this special connection, but we are in need of an explanation of this term.

We have already remarked that one of the central ideas in Wittgenstein's philosophy is that of a "language-game." Apparently Wittgenstein was passing a field on which a football game was being played when the idea occurred to him that "in language we play *games* with *words*."[5] Since this analogy dominated so much of the later Wittgenstein's

[5] Norman Malcolm, *Ludwig Wittgenstein: a Memoir* (Oxford, 1958), p. 65.

philosophical thinking, perhaps it would be well to begin the intricate task of explicating Wittgenstein's notion of criterion by considering some specific game.

Take basketball as an example. Since the object of the game is to score more points than one's opponents, there must be some way of telling if and when a team scores. Now there are various ways of telling that, say, a field goal has been scored. One might simply keep one's eyes on the scoreboard and wait for two points to be registered. Sometimes one realizes that a field goal has been scored on the basis of the reactions of the crowd. But these are, at best, indirect ways of telling, for if we use them we are relying on someone else: the score-keeper or other spectators. Obviously, not every way of telling is, in that sense, indirect; and anyone who is at all familiar with the game knows that, generally, one *sees* that a field goal has been scored in seeing the ball shot or tipped through the hoop. And if a philosopher asks, "Why does the fact that the ball went through the basket show that a field goal has been scored?" a natural reply would be, "That is what the rules of the game say; that is the way the game is played." The ball going through the basket satisfies a *criterion* for scoring a field goal.

Notice that though the relation between a criterion and that of which it is a criterion is a logical or conceptual one, the fact that the ball goes through the hoop does not entail that a field goal has been scored. First, the ball must be "in play" for it to be possible to score a field goal by tossing the ball through the basket. Second, even if the ball drops through the hoop when "in play," it need not follow that a field goal has been scored, for the rules of basketball do not cover all imaginable situations. Suppose, for example, that a player takes a long two-handed shot and that the ball suddenly reverses its direction, and after soaring and dipping through the air like a swallow in flight, gracefully drops through the player's own basket only to change into a bat, which immediately entangles itself in the net. What do the rules say about that?

An analogous situation would arise, in the case of a "language-game," if what seemed to be a chair suddenly disappeared, reappeared, and, in general, behaved in a fantastic manner. Wittgenstein's comment on this type of situation is:

> Have you rules ready for such cases—rules saying whether one may use the word "chair" to include this kind of thing? But do we miss them when we use the word "chair"; and are we to say that we do not really attach any meaning to this word, because we are not equipped with rules for every possible application of it? (*PI*, § 80).

For Wittgenstein, a sign "is in order—if, under normal circumstances it fulfils its purpose" (*PI*, § 87).

> It is only in normal cases that the use of a word is clearly prescribed; we know, are in no doubt, what to say in this or that case. The more abnormal the case, the more doubtful it becomes what we are to say (*PI*, § 142).

Let us now try to make out Wittgenstein's distinction between *criterion* and *symptom*, again utilizing the example of basketball. Suppose that, while a game is in progress, a spectator leaves his seat. Though he is unable to see the playing court, he might realize that the home team had scored a field goal on the basis of a symptom—say, the distinctive roar of the crowd—which he had observed to be correlated with home-team field goals. This correlation, according to Wittgenstein, would have to be established *via* criteria, say, by noting the sound of the cheering when the home team shot the ball through the basket. Thus, a symptom is "a phenomenon of which experience has taught us that it coincided, in some way or other, with the phenomenon which is our defining criterion" (*BB*, p. 25). Though both symptoms and criteria are cited in answer to the question, "How do you know that so-and-so is the case?" (*BB*, p. 24), symptoms, unlike criteria, are discovered through experience or observation: that something is a symptom is not given by the rules of the "language-game" (not deducible from the rules alone). However, to say of a statement that it expresses a symptom is to say something about the relation between the statement and the rules, viz., that it is not derivable from them. Hence, Wittgenstein once claimed that "whereas 'When it rains the pavement gets wet' is not a grammatical statement at all, if we say 'The fact that the pavement is wet is a *symptom* that it has been raining' this statement is 'a matter of grammar'."[6] Furthermore, giving the criterion for (e.g.) another's having a toothache "is to give a grammatical explanation about the word 'toothache' and, in this sense, an explanation concerning the meaning of the word 'toothache'" (*BB*, p. 24). However, given that there is this important difference between criteria and symptoms, the fact remains that Wittgenstein considered both symptoms and criteria as "evidences" (*BB*, p. 51).

Other salient features of criteria can be illuminated by exploiting our illustrative example. Consider Wittgenstein's claim that "in different circumstances we apply different criteria for a person's reading" (*PI*, § 164). It is clear that in different circumstances we apply different criteria for a person's scoring a field goal. For example, the question whether a player scored a field goal may arise even though the ball went nowhere near the basket: in a "goal-tending" situation, the question will have to be decided on the basis of whether the ball had started its descent before the defensive player had deflected it. According to the rules it would be a decisive reason for not awarding a field goal that the ball had not reached its apogee when it was blocked.

One can now see that to claim that X is a criterion of Y is not to claim that the presence, occurrence, existence, etc., of X is a necessary condition of the applicability of 'Y,' and it is not to claim that the presence, occurrence,

---

[6] G. E. Moore, "Wittgenstein's Lectures in 1930–33," *Philosophical Papers* (London, 1959), pp. 266–267.

existence, etc., of X is a sufficient condition of Y, although if X is a criterion of Y, it may be the case that X is a necessary or a sufficient condition of Y.

Again, consider the tendency of Wittgenstein, noted by Albritton,[7] to write as if X (a criterion of Y) just *is* Y or is what is called 'Y' in certain circumstances. We can understand a philosopher's wanting to say that shooting the ball through the basket in the appropriate situation just *is* scoring a field goal or is what we call "scoring a field goal."

Consider now the following passage from the *Investigations* (§ 376) which suggests a kind of test for "non-criterionhood":

> When I say the ABC to myself, what is the criterion of my doing the same as someone else who silently repeats it to himself? It might be found that the same thing took place in my larynx and in his. (And similarly when we both think of the same thing, wish the same, and so on.) But then did we learn the use of the words: "to say such-and-such to oneself" by someone's pointing to a process in the larynx or the brain?

Obviously not. Hence, Wittgenstein suggests, something taking place in the larynx cannot be the criterion. The rationale behind this "test" seems to be this: For the teaching of a particular predicate 'Y' to be successful, the pupil must learn the rules for the use of 'Y' and hence must learn the criteria for 'Y' if there are such criteria. Thus, if the teaching could be entirely successful without one learning that X is something on the basis of which one tells that 'Y' applies, X cannot be a criterion of Y. For example, since a person could be taught what "field goal" means without learning that one can generally tell that the home team has scored a field goal by noting the roar of the home crowd, the roar of the home crowd cannot be a criterion of field goals.

[7] Rogers Albritton, "On Wittgenstein's Use of the Term 'Criterion'," *Journal of Philosophy*, LVI (1959), pp. 851–854 [reprinted in the present volume].

Finally, let us examine the principle, which Wittgenstein appears to maintain, that any change of criteria of X involves changing the concept of X. In the *Investigations*, Wittgenstein makes the puzzling claim:

> There is *one* thing of which one can say neither that it is one metre long, nor that it is not one metre long, and that is the standard metre in Paris.—But this is, of course, not to ascribe any extraordinary property to it, but only to mark its peculiar role in the language-game of measuring with a metre-rule.—Let us imagine samples of colour being preserved in Paris like the standard metre. We define: "Sepia" means the colour of the standard sepia which is there kept hermetically sealed. Then it will make no sense to say of this sample either that it is of this colour or that it is not (*PI*, § 50).

Wittgenstein evidently is maintaining not only that the senses of the predicates "x is one meter long" and "x is sepia" are given by the operations which determine the applicability of the respective predicates (the operations of comparing objects in certain ways with the respective standards),[8] but also that these operations cannot be performed on the standards themselves and hence neither standard can be said to be an instance of either the *predicate* for which it is a standard or of its negation. (Cf., "A thing cannot be at the same time the measure and the thing measured" [*RFM*, I, § 40, notes].)

Wittgenstein would undoubtedly allow that we might introduce a new language-game in which "meter" is defined in terms of the wave length of the spectral line of

---

[8] Note Wittgenstein's suggestion that we can "give the phrase 'unconscious pain' sense by fixing experiential criteria for the case in which a man has pain and doesn't know it" (*BB*, p. 55). Cf., also: "If however we do use the expression 'the thought takes place in the head,' we have given this expression its meaning by describing the experience which would justify the *hypothesis* that the thought takes place in our heads, by describing the experience which we wish to call observing thought in our brain" (*BB*, p. 8).

the element krypton of atomic weight 86.[9] In this
language-game, where such highly accurate and complex
measuring devices as the interferometer are required, the
standard meter does not have any privileged position: it,
too, can be measured and "represented." In this language-
game, the standard meter is or is not a meter. But here,
Wittgenstein would evidently distinguish two senses of the
term "meter." Obviously what is a meter in one language-
game need not be a meter in the other. Thus, Wittgenstein's view seems to be that by introducing a new
criterion for something's being a meter long, we have introduced a new language-game, a new sense of the term
"meter," and a new concept of meter. Such a position is
indicated by Wittgenstein's comment:

> We can speak of measurements of time in which there
> is a different, and as we should say a greater, exact-
> ness than in the measurement of time by a pocket-
> watch; in which the words "to set the clock to the
> exact time" have a different, though related mean-
> ing . . . (PI, § 88).

Returning to our basketball analogy, suppose that the
National Collegiate Athletic Association ruled that, henceforth, a player can score a field goal by pushing the ball
upward through the basket. Obviously, this would involve
changing the rules of basketball. And to some extent, by
introducing this new criterion, the rules governing the use
or "grammar" of the term "field goal" would be altered.
To put it somewhat dramatically (in the Wittgensteinian
style), a new *essence* of field goal would be created. (Cf.
"The mathematician creates *essence*" [RFM, I, § 32].)
For Wittgenstein, not only is it the case that the criteria
we use "give our words their common meanings" (BB, p.
57) and that to explain the criteria we use is to explain
the meanings of words (BB, p. 24), but also it is the case

[9] Adopted by the eleventh General International Conference
on Weights and Measures in the fall of 1960.

that to introduce a new criterion of Y is to define a new concept of Y.[10]

In summary, we can roughly and schematically characterize Wittgenstein's notion of criterion in the following way: X is a criterion of Y in situations of type S if the very meaning or definition of 'Y' (or, as Wittgenstein might have put it, if the "grammatical" rules for the use of 'Y')[11] justify the claim that one can recognize, see, detect, or determine the applicability of 'Y' on the basis of X in *normal* situations of type S. Hence, if the above relation obtains between X and Y, and if someone admits that X but denies Y, the burden of proof is upon him to show that something is abnormal in the situation. In a normal situation, the problem of gathering evidence which justifies concluding Y from X simply does not arise.

IV

The following passage occurs in the *Blue Book* (p. 24):

When we learnt the use of the phrase "so-and-so has toothache" we were pointed out certain kinds of behavior of those who were said to have toothache. As an instance of these kinds of behavior let us take holding your cheek. Suppose that by observation I found that in certain cases whenever these first criteria told me a person had toothache, a red patch appeared on the person's cheek. Supposing I now said to someone "I see A has toothache, he's got a red patch on his cheek." He may ask me "How do you know A has toothache when you see a red patch?" I would then

[10] *RFM*, II, §24; III, §29; and I, Appendix I, §15–16. See also C. S. Chihara "Mathematical Discovery and Concept Formation," *The Philosophical Review*, LXXII (1963), pp. 17–34 [reprinted in the present volume].

[11] Cf. "The person of whom we say 'he has pain' is, *by the rules of the game*, the person who cries, contorts his face, etc." (*BB*, p. 68, italics ours).

point out that certain phenomena had always coincided with the appearance of the red patch.

Now one may go on and ask: "How do you know
that he has got toothache when he holds his cheek?"
The answer to this might be, "I say, *he* has toothache
when he holds his cheek because I hold my cheek
when I have toothache." But what if we went on asking:—"And why do you suppose that toothache corresponds to his holding his cheek just because your
toothache corresponds to your holding your cheek?"
You will be at a loss to answer this question, and find
that here we strike rock bottom, that is we have come
down to conventions.

It would seem that, on Wittgenstein's view, empirical
justification of the claim to see, recognize, or know that
such and such is the case *on the basis of some observable
feature or state of affairs*, would have to rest upon induc-
tions from observed correlations, so that, if a person claims
that Y is the case on the grounds that X is the case, in answer to the question "Why does the fact that X show that
Y?" he would have to cite either conventions or observed
correlations linking X and Y. Thus, Wittgenstein appears
to be arguing that the possibility of ever inferring a person's toothache from his behavior requires the existence of
a criterion of toothache that can sometimes be observed to
obtain. A generalized form of this argument leads to the
conclusion that "an 'inner process' stands in need of outward criteria" (*PI*, § 580).

As an illustration of Wittgenstein's reasoning, consider
the following example: It appears to be the case that the
measurement of the alcohol content of the blood affords a
reasonably reliable index of intoxication. On the basis of
this empirical information, we may sometimes justify the
claim that X is intoxicated by showing that the alcohol
content of his blood is higher than some specified per-
centage. But now consider the justification of the claim
that blood-alcohol is in fact an index of intoxication. On
Wittgenstein's view, the justification of *this* claim must

rest ultimately upon correlating cases of intoxication with determinations of high blood-alcohol content. But, the observations required for this correlation could be made only if there exist independent techniques for identifying each of the correlated items. In any particular case, these independent techniques may themselves be based upon further empirical correlations; we might justify the claim that the blood-alcohol content is high by appealing to some previously established correlation between the presence of blood-alcohol and some test result. But ultimately according to Wittgenstein, we must come upon identifying techniques based not upon further empirical correlations, but rather upon definitions or conventions which determine criteria for applying the relevant predicates. This is why Wittgenstein can say that a symptom is "a phenomenon of which experience has taught us that it coincided, in some way or other with the phenomenon which is our defining criterion" (*BB*, p. 25).

A similar argument has recently been given by Sidney Shoemaker who writes:

If we know psychological facts about other persons at all, we know them on the basis of their behavior (including, of course, their verbal behavior). Sometimes we make psychological statements about other persons on the basis of bodily or behavioral facts that are only contingently related to the psychological facts for which we accept them as evidence. But we do this only because we have discovered, or think we have discovered, empirical correlations between physical (bodily and behavioral) facts of a certain kind and psychological facts of a certain kind. And if *all* relations between physical and psychological facts were contingent, it would be impossible for us to discover such correlations. . . . Unless some relationships between physical and psychological states are not contingent, and can be known prior to the discovery of empirical correlations, we cannot have even indirect inductive evidence for the truth of psychological

statements about other persons, and cannot know such
statements to be true or even probably true.[12]

Malcolm argues in a similar manner in *Dreaming*.[13]

Of course, Wittgenstein did not claim that all predicates
presuppose criteria of applicability. For example, Wittgenstein probably did not think that we, in general, see, tell,
determine, or know that something is red on the basis of
either a criterion or a symptom. The relevant difference
between ascriptions of "red" and third-person ascriptions
of "pain" is that we generally see, recognize, determine, or
know that another is in pain on the basis of something
which is not the pain itself (as for example, behavior and
circumstances) whereas, if it made any sense at all to say
we generally see, recognize, etc., that an object is red on
the basis of something, what could this something be other
than just the object's redness? But Wittgenstein's use of
the term "criterion" seems to preclude redness being a
criterion of redness. If someone asks "How do you know or
tell that an object is red?" it would not, in general, do to
answer "By its redness." (Cf. Wittgenstein's comment
"How do I know that this color is red?—It would be an
answer to say: 'I have learnt English'" [PI, § 381].)
Evidently, some color predicates and, more generally, what
are sometimes called "sense datum" predicates (those that
can be known to apply—as some philosophers put it—*immediately*), do not fall within the domain of arguments of
the above type. But the predicates with which we assign
"inner states" to another person are not of this sort. One
recognizes that another is in a certain mental state, Y, on
the basis of something, say, X. Now it is assumed that X
must be either a criterion or symptom of Y. If X is a symptom, X must be known to be correlated with Y, and we
may then inquire into the way in which this correlation
was established. Again, X must have been observed to be

[12] Sidney Shoemaker, *Self-knowledge and Self-identity* (Ithaca,
1963), pp. 167–168.
[13] Norman Malcolm, *Dreaming* (London, 1959), pp. 60–61.

correlated with a criterion of Y or with a symptom, X_1, of
Y. On the second alternative, we may inquire into the basis
for holding that X_1 is a symptom of Y. . . . Such a chain
may go on for any distance you like, but it cannot go on
indefinitely. That is, at some point, we must come to a
criterion of Y. But once this conclusion has been accepted,
there appears to be no reasonable non-sceptical alternative
to Wittgenstein's logical behaviorism, for if "inner" states
require "outward" criteria, behavioral criteria are the only
plausible candidates.

V

As a refutation of scepticism, the above argument certainly will not do; for, at best, it supports Wittgenstein's
position only on the assumption that the sceptic is not
right. That is, it demonstrates that there must be criteria
for psychological predicates by assuming that such predicates are sometimes applied justifiably. A sceptic who accepts the argument of Section IV could maintain his position only by allowing that no one could have any idea of
what would show or even indicate that another is in pain,
having a dream, thinking, etc. In this section we shall
show how Wittgenstein argues that that move would lead
the sceptic to the absurd conclusion that it must be impossible to teach the meaning of these psychological predicates.

"What would it be like if human beings showed no outward signs of pain (did not groan, grimace, etc.)? Then it
would be impossible to teach a child the use of the word
'toothache'" (*PI*, § 257). For just imagine trying to teach
a child the meaning of the term "toothache," say, on the
supposition that there is absolutely no way of telling
whether the child—or anyone else for that matter—is actually in pain. How would one go about it, if one had no
reason for believing that gross damage to the body causes
pain or that crying out, wincing, and the like indicate pain?

("How could I even have come by the idea of another's experience if there is no possibility of any evidence for it?" [*BB*, p. 46; cf. also *BB*, p. 48].)

Again, what would show us that the child had grasped the teaching? If anything would, the argument of Section IV requires that there be a criterion of having succeeded in teaching the child. (As Wittgenstein says of an analogous case, "If I speak of communicating a feeling to someone else, mustn't I in order to understand what I say know what I shall call the criterion of having succeeded in communicating?" [*BB*, p. 185].) But the only plausible criterion of this would be that the child applies the psychological predicates correctly (cf. *PI*, § 146); and since the sceptical position implies that there is no way of knowing if the child correctly applies such predicates, it would seem to follow that nothing could show or indicate that the child had learned what these terms mean.

We now have a basis for explicating the sense of "logical" which is involved in the claim that scepticism is a logically incoherent doctrine. What Wittgenstein holds is not that "*P* and not-*P*" are strictly deducible from the sceptic's position, but rather that the sceptic's view presupposes a deviation from the rules for the use of key terms. In particular, Wittgenstein holds that if the sceptic were right, the preconditions for teaching the meaning of the mental predicates of our ordinary language could not be satisfied.[14]

We now see too the point to the insistence that the sceptic's position must incorporate an extraordinary and misleading use of mental predicates. The sceptic's view is logically incompatible with the operation of the ordinary language rules for the application of these terms, and these

---

[14] Cf. " 'Before I judge that two images which I have are the same, I must recognize them as the same.' And . . . how am I to know that the word 'same' describes what I recognize? Only if I can express my recognition in some other way, and if it is possible for someone else to teach me that 'same' is the correct word here" (*PI*, §378).

rules determine their meanings. (Cf. "What *we* do is to bring words back from their metaphysical to their everyday use" [*PI*, § 116].) As Wittgenstein diagnoses the sceptic's view, the sceptic does not have in mind any criteria of third person ascriptions when he denies that he can know if anyone else has pains (cf. *PI*, § 272). The sceptic tempts us to picture the situation as involving "a barrier which doesn't allow one person to come closer to another's experience than to the point of observing his behavior"; but, according to Wittgenstein, "on looking closer we find that we can't apply the picture" (*BB*, p. 56); no clear meaning can be attached to the sceptic's claim: no sense can even be given the hypothesis that other people feel "pains," as the sceptic uses the term "pain." ("For how can I even make the hypothesis if it transcends all possible experience?" [*BB*, p. 48].) And if the sceptic says, "But if I suppose that someone has a pain, then I am simply supposing that he has just the same as I have so often had." Wittgenstein can reply:

> That gets us no further. It is as if I were to say: "You surely know what 'It is 5 o'clock here' means; so you also know what 'It's 5 o'clock on the sun' means. It means simply that it is just the same time there as it is here when it is 5 o'clock."—The explanation by means of *identity* does not work here. For I know well enough that one can call 5 o'clock here and 5 o'clock there "the same time," but what I do not know is in what cases one is to speak of its being the same time here and there (*PI*, § 350).

Thus, we can see how Wittgenstein supports his logical behaviorism: the argument in Section IV purports to show that the only plausible alternative to Wittgenstein's philosophical psychology is radical scepticism; and the argument in the present section rules out this alternative. For Wittgenstein, then, "the person of whom we say 'he has pains' is, by the rules of the game, the person who cries, contorts his face, etc.," (*BB*, p. 68).

Undoubtedly, there is much that philosophers find comforting and attractive in Wittgenstein's philosophical psychology, but there are also difficulties in the doctrine which mar its attractiveness. To some of these difficulties, we shall now turn.

VI

In this section, we shall consider some consequences of applying the views just discussed to the analysis of dreaming, and we shall attempt to show that the conclusions to which these views lead are counter-intuitive.

According to Wittgenstein, we are to understand the concept of dreaming in terms of the language-game(s) in which "dream" plays a role and, in particular, in terms of the language-game of dream telling. For, to master the use of the word "dream" is precisely to learn what it is to find out that someone has dreamed, to tell what someone has dreamed, to report one's own dreams, and so on. Passages in the *Investigations* (e.g., *PI*, pp. 184, 222–223) indicate that, for Wittgenstein, a criterion of someone's having dreamed is the dream report. On this analysis, sceptical doubts about dreams arise when we fail to appreciate the logical bond between statements about dreams and statements about dream reports. The sceptic treats the dream report as, at best, an empirical correlate of the occurrence of a dream: a symptom that is, at any event, no more reliable than the memory of the subject who reports the dream. But, according to Wittgenstein, once we have understood the criterial relation between dream reporting and dreaming, we see that "the question whether the dreamer's memory deceives him when he reports the dream after waking cannot arise . . ." (*PI*, p. 222). (Compare: "Once we understand the rules for playing chess, the question whether a player has won when he has achieved check-mate cannot arise.")

The rules articulating the criteria for applying the word

"dream" determine a logical relation between dreaming
and reporting dreams. Moreover, the set of such rules fixes
the language-game in which "dream" has its role and hence
determines the meaning of the word.

It is important to notice that there are a number of
prima facie objections to this analysis which, though perhaps not conclusive, supply grounds for questioning the
doctrines which lead to it. Though we could perhaps learn
to live with these objections were no other analyses available, when seen from the vantage point of an alternative
theory they indicate deep troubles with Wittgenstein's
views.

(1) Given that there exist no criteria for first person
applications of many psychological predicates ("pain,"
"wish," or the like) it is unclear how the first person aspects of the game played with these predicates are to be
described. Wittgenstein does not appear to present a coherent account of the behavior of predicates whose applicability is not determined by criteria. On the other
hand, the attempt to characterize "I dreamt" as criterion-
governed leads immediately to absurdities. Thus, in Malcolm's *Dreaming* it is suggested that:

> If a man wakes up with the impression of having seen
> and done various things, and if it is known that he did
> not see and do those things, then it is known that he
> dreamt them. . . . When he says "I dreamt so and so"
> he implies, first, that it seemed to him on waking up
> as if the so and so had occurred and second, that the
> so and so did not occur (p. 66).

That this is an incredibly counter-intuitive analysis of our
concept of dreaming hardly needs mentioning. We ask the
reader to consider the following example: A person, from
time to time, gets the strange feeling that, shortly before,
he had seen and heard his father commanding him to come
home. One morning he wakes with this feeling, knowing
full well that his father is dead. Now we are asked by Malcolm to believe that the person *must have dreamt* that he
saw and heard his father: supposedly, it would be logically

absurd for the person to claim to have this feeling and deny that he had dreamt it!

(2) Wittgenstein's view appears to entail that no sense can be made of such statements as "Jones totally forgot the dream he had last night," since we seem to have no criteria for determining the truth of such a statement. (We have in mind the case in which Jones is totally unable to remember having dreamed and no behavioral manifestations of dreaming were exhibited.) It is sometimes denied that observations of what people ordinarily say are relevant to a description of ordinary language. But, insofar as statements about what we would say are susceptible to empirical disconfirmation, the claim that we would feel hesitation about saying that someone completely forgot his dream appears to be just false.[15]

(3) The Wittgensteinian method of counting concepts is certainly not an intuitive one. Consider Malcolm's analysis of dreaming again. Malcolm realizes that sometimes, on the basis of a person's behavior during sleep, we say that he had a dream, even though he is unable to recall a dream upon awaking. But, in such cases, Malcolm claims, "our words . . . have no clear sense" (*Dreaming*, p. 62). On the other hand, Malcolm admits that there is a *sense* of the term "nightmare" where behavior during sleep is the criterion. However, a different concept of dreaming is supposedly involved in this case. An analogous situation is treated in the *Blue Book* (p. 63), where Wittgenstein writes:

If a man tries to obey the order "Point to your eye," he may do many different things, and there are many

15 Thus consider the following: "Up until the night I opened the door, I remembered my dreams. Soon after, I ceased to recall them. I still dreamed, but my waking consciousness concealed from itself what sleep revealed. If the recurrent nightmare of the iron fence awoke me, I recognized it. But if any other nightmare broke my sleep, I forgot what it was about by morning. And of all the other dreams I had during the night I remembered nothing" (Windham, D., "Myopia," *The New Yorker*, July 13, 1963).

different criteria which he will accept for having pointed to his eye. If these criteria, as they usually do, coincide, I may use them alternately and in different combinations to show me that I have touched my eye. If they don't coincide, I shall have to distinguish between different senses of the phrase "I touch my eye" or "I move my finger towards my eye."

Following this suggestion of Wittgenstein, Malcolm distinguishes not only different senses of the term "dream," but also different concepts of sleep—one based upon report, one based upon nonverbal behavior. But surely, this is an unnatural way of counting concepts. Compare Malcolm's two concepts of sleep with a case where it really does seem natural to say that a special concept of sleep has been employed, viz., where we say of a hibernating bear that it sleeps through the winter.

(4) As Malcolm points out, the language-game *now* played with "dream" seems to exhibit no criteria which would enable one to determine the precise duration of dreams. Hence, it would seem to follow (as Malcolm has noticed) that scientists who have attempted to answer such questions as, "How long do dreams last?" are involved in conceptual confusions rather than empirical determinations. For such questions cannot be answered without adopting criteria for ascribing the relevant properties to dreams. But since, on Wittgenstein's view, to adopt such new criteria for the use of a word is, to that extent, to change its meaning, it follows that the concept of "dream" that such researchers employ is not the ordinary concept and hence that the measurements they effect are not, strictly speaking, measurements of *dreams*.[16] The notion

[16] In *Dreaming*, Malcolm gives a number of arguments, not to be found in Wittgenstein's published writings, for the position that psychologists attempting to discover methods of measuring the duration of dreams must be using the term "dream" in a misleading and extraordinary way. For a reply to these arguments, see C. S. Chihara "What Dreams are Made On," *Theoria*, XXXI (1965), pp. 145–158. See also H. Putnam's criticism of

that adopting any test for dreaming which arrives at features of dreams not determinable from the dream report thereby alters the concept of a dream seems to run counter to our intuitions about the goals of psychological research. It is not immediately obvious that the psychologist who says he has found a method of measuring the duration of dreams *ipso facto* commits the fallacy of ambiguity.[17]

(5) Consider the fact that such measures as EEG, eye-movements and "dream-behavior" (murmuring, tossing, etc., during sleep) correlate reasonably reliably with one another and dream reports. The relation between, say, EEG and dream reports is clearly not criterial; no one holds that EEG is a criterion of dream reports. It would seem then that, on Wittgenstein's view, EEG provides us with, at best, a symptom of positive dream reports; and symptoms are supposedly discovered by observing co-occurrences. The difficulty, however, is that this makes it unclear how the expectation that such a correlation must obtain could have been a rational expectation even *before* the correlation was experimentally confirmed. One cannot have an inductive generalization over no observations; nor, in this case, was any higher level "covering law" used to infer the probability of a correlation between EEG and dream reports. Given Wittgenstein's analysis of the concept of dreaming, not only do the researches of psychologists into the nature of dreams appear mysterious, but even the expectations, based upon these researches, seem somewhat irrational.

The difficulties we have mentioned are not peculiar to

Malcolm, "Dreaming and 'Depth Grammar'," *Analytical Philosophy*, ed. by R. J. Butler (Oxford, 1962), pp. 211–235.

[17] The implausibility of this view is even more striking when Wittgenstein applies it in his philosophy of mathematics to arrive at the conclusion that every new theorem about a concept alters the concept or introduces a new concept. When the notion of conceptual change is allowed to degenerate this far, it is not easy to see that anything rides on the claim that a conceptual change has taken place. Cf. C. S. Chihara, "Mathematical Discovery and Concept Formation."

the Wittgensteinian analysis of dreams. Most of them have counterparts in the analyses of sensation, perception, intention, etc. Whether or not these difficulties can be obviated, in some way, noticing them provides a motive for re-examining the deeper doctrines upon which Wittgensteinian analyses of psychological terms are based.

VIII

The Wittgensteinian argument of Section IV rests on the premiss that if we are justified in claiming that one can tell, recognize, see, or determine that 'Y' applies on the basis of the presence of X, then either X is a criterion of Y or observations have shown that X is correlated with Y. Wittgenstein does not present any justification for this premiss in his published writings. Evidently, some philosophers find it self-evident and hence in need of no justification. We, on the other hand, far from finding this premiss self-evident, believe it to be false. Consider: one standard instrument used in the detection of high-speed, charged particles is the Wilson cloud-chamber. According to present scientific theories, the formation of tiny, thin bands of fog on the glass surface of the instrument indicates the passage of charged particles through the chamber. It is obvious that the formation of these streaks is not a Wittgensteinian criterion of the presence and motion of these particles in the apparatus. That one can detect these charged particles and determine their paths by means of such devices is surely not, by any stretch of the imagination, a *conceptual* truth. C. T. R. Wilson did not learn what "path of a charged particle" means by having the cloud-chamber explained to him: he *discovered* the method, and the discovery was contingent upon recognizing the empirical fact that ions could act as centers of condensation in a supersaturated vapor. Hence, applying Wittgenstein's own test for non-criterionhood (see above), the formation of a cloud-chamber track cannot be a criterion of the presence and motion of charged particles.

It is equally clear that the basis for taking these streaks as indicators of the paths of the particles is not observed *correlations* between streaks and some criterion of motion of charged particles. (What criterion for determining the path of an electron could Wilson have used to establish such correlations?) Rather, scientists were able to give compelling explanations of the formation of the streaks on the hypothesis that high-velocity, charged particles were passing through the chamber; on this hypothesis, further predictions were made, tested, and confirmed; no other equally plausible explanation is available; and so forth.

Such cases suggest that Wittgenstein failed to consider all the possible types of answers to the question, "What is the justification for the claim that one can tell, recognize, or determine that Y applies on the basis of the presence of X?" For, where Y is the predicate "is the path of a high-velocity particle," X need not have the form of either a criterion or a correlate.

Wittgensteinians may be tempted to argue that cloud-chamber tracks really are criteria, or symptoms observed to be correlated with criteria, of the paths of charged particles. To obviate this type of counter, we wish to stress that the example just given is by no means idiosyncratic. The reader who is not satisfied with it will easily construct others from the history of science. What is at issue is the possibility of a type of justification which consists in neither the appeal to criteria nor the appeal to observed correlations. If the Wittgensteinian argument we have been considering is to be compelling, some grounds must be given for the exhaustiveness of these types of justification. This, it would seem, Wittgenstein has failed to do.

It is worth noticing that a plausible solution to the problem raised in VI. 5 can be given if we consider experiments with dreams and EEG to be analogous to the cloud-chamber case. That is, we can see how it could be the case that the correlation of EEG with dream reports was anticipated prior to observation. The dream report was taken by the experiments to be an indicator of a psychological event occurring prior to it. Given considerations about the relation of cortical to psychological events, and given also the theory of EEG, it was predicted that the EEG should provide an index of the occurrence of dreams. From the hypothesis that dream reports and EEG readings are both indices of the same psychological events, it could be deduced that they ought to be reliably correlated with one another, and this deduction in fact proved to be correct.

This situation is not at all unusual in the case of explanations based upon theoretical inferences to events underlying observable syndromes. As Meehl and Cronbach have pointed out, in such cases the validity of the "criterion" is often nearly as much at issue as the validity of the indices to be correlated with it.[18] The successful prediction of the correlation on the basis of the postulation of a common etiology is taken both as evidence for the existence of the cause and as indicating the validity of each of the correlates as an index of its presence.

In this kind of case, the justification of existential statements is thus identical neither with an appeal to criteria nor with an appeal to symptoms. Such justifications depend rather on appeals to the simplicity, plausibility, and predictive adequacy of an explanatory system as a whole, so that it is incorrect to say that relations between statements which are mediated by such explanations are either logical in Wittgenstein's sense or contingent in the sense in which this term suggests simple correlation.

It cannot be stressed too often that there exist patterns of justificatory argument which are not happily identified

[18] P. M. Meehl and H. J. Cronbach, "Construct Validity in Psychological Tests," *Minnesota Studies in the Philosophy of Science*, Vol. I, ed. by H. Feigl and M. Scriven (Minneapolis, 1956), pp. 174–204. We have followed Meehl and Cronbach's usage of the terms "reliability" and "validity" so that *reliability* is a measure of the correlation between criteria while *validity* is a measure of the correlation between a criterion and the construct whose presence it is supposed to indicate.

either with appeals to symptoms or with appeals to criteria, and which do not in any obvious way rest upon such appeals. In these arguments, existential claims about states, events, and processes, which are *not* directly observable are susceptible of justification despite the fact that no *logical* relation obtains between the predicates ascribing such states and predicates whose applicability *can* be directly observed. There is a temptation to hold that in such cases there *must* be a criterion, that there must be some set of possible observations which would settle *for sure* whether the theoretical predicate applies. But we succumb to this temptation at the price of postulating stipulative definitions and conceptual alterations which fail to correspond to anything we can discover in the course of empirical arguments. The counter-intuitive features of philosophic analyses based on the assumption that there must be criteria are thus not the consequences of a profound methodological insight, but rather a projection of an inadequate philosophical theory of justification.

IX

It might be replied that the above examples do not constitute counter-instances to Wittgenstein's criterion-correlation premiss since Wittgenstein may have intended his principle to be applicable only in the case of ordinary language terms which, so it might seem, do not function within the framework of a theory. It is perhaps possible to have indicators that are neither criteria nor symptoms of such highly theoretical entities as electrons and positrons, but the terms used by ordinary people in everyday life are obviously (?) in a different category. (Notice that Wittgenstein considers "making scientific hypotheses and theories" a different "game" from such "language-games" as "describing an event" and "describing an immediate experience" [BB, pp. 67–68; cf. PI, § 23]). Hence, Wittgenstein might argue, it is only in the case of ordinary language terms that the demand for criteria is necessary.

Once one perceives the presuppositions of Wittgenstein's demand for criteria, however, it becomes evident that alternatives to Wittgenstein's analyses of ordinary language mental terms should at least be explored. Perhaps, what we all learn in learning what such terms as "pain" and "dream" mean are not criterial connections which map these terms severally onto characteristic patterns of behavior. We may instead form complex conceptual connections which interrelate a wide variety of mental states. It is to such a conceptual system that we appeal when we attempt to explain someone's behavior by reference to his motives, intentions, beliefs, desires, or sensations. In other words, in learning the language, we develop a number of intricately interrelated "mental concepts" which we use in dealing with, coming to terms with, understanding, explaining, interpreting, etc., the behavior of other human beings (as well as our own). In the course of acquiring these mental concepts we develop a variety of beliefs involving them. Such beliefs result in a wide range of expectations about how people are likely to behave. Since only a portion of these beliefs are confirmed in the normal course, these beliefs and the conceptual systems which they articulate are both subject to correction and alteration as the consequence of our constant interaction with other people.

On this view, our success in accounting for the behavior on the basis of which mental predicates are applied might properly be thought of as supplying *evidence* for the existence of the mental processes we postulate. It does so by attesting to the adequacy of the conceptual system in terms of which the processes are understood. The behavior would be, in that sense, analogous to the cloud-chamber track on the basis of which we detect the presence and motion of charged particles. Correspondingly, the conceptual system is analogous to the physical *theory* in which the properties of these particles are formulated.

If something like this should be correct, it would be possible, at least in theory, to reconstruct and describe the conceptual system involved and then to obtain some confirmation that the putative system is in fact employed by English speakers. For example, confirmation might come *via* the usual methods of "reading off" the conceptual relation in the putative system and *matching them* against the linguistic intuitions of native speakers. Thus, given that a particular conceptual system is being employed, certain statements should strike native speakers as nonsensical, others should seem necessarily true, others should seem ambiguous, others empirically false, and so on, all of which would be testable.

To maintain that there are no criterial connections between pains and behavior does not commit us to holding that the fact that people often feel *pains* when they cry out is *just* a contingent fact (in the sense in which it is just a contingent fact that most of the books in my library are unread). The belief that other people feel pains is not gratuitous even on the view that there are no criteria of pains. On the contrary, it provides the only plausible explanation of the facts I know about the way that they behave in and *vis à vis* the sorts of situations I find painful. These facts are, of course, enormously complex. The "pain syndrome" includes not only correlations between varieties of overt behaviors but also more subtle relations between pain and motivations, utilities, desires, and so on. Moreover, I confidently expect that there must exist reliable members of this syndrome other than the ones with which I am currently familiar. I am in need of an explanation of the reliability and fruitfulness of this syndrome, an explanation which reference to the occurrence of pains supplies. Here, as elsewhere, an "outer" syndrome stands in need of an inner process.

Thus, it is at least conceivable that a non-Wittgensteinian account ought to be given of the way children learn the mental predicates. (It is, at any event, sufficient to notice that such an account *could* be given, that there exist alternatives to Wittgenstein's doctrine.) For example, if the concept of dreaming is *inter alia* that of an inner event which takes place during a definite stretch of "real" time, which causes such involuntary behavior as moaning and murmuring in one's sleep, tossing about, etc., and which is remembered when one correctly reports a dream, then there are a number of ways in which a child might be supposed to "get" this concept other than by learning criteria for the application of the word "dream." Perhaps it is true of many children that they learn what a dream is by being told that what they have just experienced was a dream. Perhaps it was also true of many children that, having grasped the notions of *imagining* and *sleep*, they learn what a dream is when they are told that dreaming is something like imagining in your sleep.

But does this imply that children learn what a dream is "from their own case"? If this is a logical rather than psychological question, the answer is "Not necessarily": a child who never dreamed, but who was very clever, might arrive at an understanding of what dreams are just on the basis of the sort of theoretical inference we have described above. For our notion of a dream is that of a mental event having various properties that are required in order to explain the characteristic features of the dream-behavior syndrome. For example, dreams occur during sleep, have duration, sometimes cause people who are sleeping to murmur or to toss, can be described in visual, auditory, or tactile terms, are sometimes remembered and sometimes not, are sometimes reported and sometimes not, sometimes prove frightening, sometimes are interrupted before they are finished, etc. But if these are the sorts of facts that characterize our concept of dream, then there seems to be nothing which would, in principle, prevent a child who never dreamed from arriving at this notion.

A similar story might be told about how such sensation terms as "pain" are learned and about the learning of such quasi-dispositionals as "having a motive." In each case, since the features that we in fact attribute to these states, processes, or dispositions are just those features we know they must have if they are to fulfill their role in explanations of behavior, etiology, personality, etc., it would seem that there is nothing about them the child could not in principle learn by employing the pattern of inference we have described above, and hence nothing that he could in principle learn *only* by an analogy to his own case.

Now it might be argued that the alternative to Wittgenstein's position we have been sketching is highly implausible. For, if children do have to acquire the complicated conceptual system our theory requires to understand and use mental predicates, surely they would have to be taught this system. And the teaching would surely have to be terribly involved and complex. But as a matter of fact, children do not require any such teaching at all, and hence we should conclude that our alternative to Wittgenstein's criterion view is untenable.

The force of this argument, however, can to some extent be dispelled if we consider the child's acquisition of, e.g., the grammar of a natural language. It is clear that, by some process we are only now beginning to understand, a child, on the basis of a relatively short "exposure" to utterances in his language, develops capacities for producing and understanding "novel" sentences (sentences which he has never previously heard or seen). The exercise of these capacities, so far as we can tell, "involves" the use of an intricate system of linguistic rules of very considerable generality and complexity.[19] That the child is not taught (in any ordinary sense) any such system of rules is undeniable. These capacities seem to develop naturally in the child in response to little more than contact with a relatively small number of sentences uttered in ordinary con-

[19] This point is susceptible of direct empirical ratification, for it can be demonstrated that in perceptual analysis, speech is analyzed into segments which correspond precisely to the segmentation assigned by a grammar.

texts in everyday life.[20] Granting for the moment that the apparent complexity of such systems of rules is not somehow an artifact of an unsatisfactory theory of language, the fact that the child develops these linguistic capacities shows that a corresponding "natural" development of a system of mental concepts may not, as a matter of brute fact, require the sort of explicit teaching a person needs to master, say, calculus or quantum physics.

X

It is easily seen that this unabashedly non-behavioristic view avoids each of the difficulties we raised regarding Wittgenstein's analyses of mental predicates. Thus, the asymmetry between first and third person uses of "dream" discussed in Section VI need not arise since there need be no criteria for "X dreamed," *whatever* value X takes: we do not have the special problem of characterizing the meaning of "I dreamed" since "dream" in this context means just what it means in third person contexts, viz., "a series of thoughts, images, or emotions occurring during sleep." Again, it is now clear why people find such remarks as "Jones totally forgot what and that he dreamed last night" perfectly sensible. It is even clear how such assertions might be confirmed. Suppose, for example, that there exists a neurological state α such that there is a very high correlation between the presence of α and such dream behavior as tossing in one's sleep, crying out in one's sleep, reporting dreams, and so on. Suppose, too that there exists some neurological state β such that whenever β occurs, experiences that the subject has had just prior to β are forgotten. Suppose, finally, that sometimes we observe sequences, α, β, and that such sequences are not followed by dream reports though the occurrences of α are accom-

---

[20] Cf. N. Chomsky's "A Review of Skinner's *Verbal Behavior*," reprinted in J. Fodor and J. Katz, *The Structure of Language* (Englewood Cliffs, 1964).

panied by other characteristic dream behaviors. It seems clear that the reasonable thing to say in such a case is that the subject has dreamed and forgotten his dream. And since we have postulated no criterion for dreaming, but only a syndrome of dream behaviors each related to some inner psychological event, we need have no fear that, in saying what it is reasonable to say, we have changed the meaning of "dream." We leave it to the reader to verify that the other objections we raised against the Wittgensteinian analysis of "dream" also fail to apply to the present doctrine.

Thus, once we have abandoned the arguments for a criterial connection between statements about behavior and statements about psychological states, the question remains open whether applications of ordinary language psychological terms on the basis of observations of behavior ought not themselves be treated as theoretical inferences to underlying mental occurrences. The question whether such statements as "He moaned because he was in pain" function to explain behavior by relating it to an assumed mental event cannot be settled simply by reference to ordinary linguistic usage. Answering this question requires broadly empirical investigations into the nature of thought and concept formation in normal human beings. What is at issue is the question of the role of theory construction and theoretical inference in thought and argument outside pure science. Psychological investigations indicate that much everyday conceptualization depends on the exploitation of theories and explanatory models in terms of which experience is integrated and understood.[21] Such prescientific theories, far from being mere functionless "pic-

---

[21] Among the many psychological studies relevant to this point, the following are of special importance: F. Bartlett, *Remembering, A Study in Experimental and Social Psychology* (Cambridge, 1932); J. Piaget, *The Child's Conception of the World* (London, 1928); J. Bruner, "On Perceptual Readiness," reprinted in *Readings in Perception*, ed. M. Wertheimer and D. Beardslee (Princeton, 1958), pp. 686–729.

tures," play an essential role in determining the sorts of perceptual and inductive expectations we form and the kind of arguments and explanations we accept. It thus seems *possible* that the correct view of the functioning of ordinary language mental predicates would assimilate applying them to the sorts of processes of theoretical inference operative in scientific psychological explanation. If this is correct, the primary difference between ordinary and scientific uses of psychological predicates would be just that the processes of inference which are made explicit in the latter case remain implicit in the former.

We can now see what should be said in reply to Wittgenstein's argument that the possibility of teaching a language rests upon the existence of criteria. Perhaps teaching a word would be impossible if it could not sometimes be determined that the student has mastered the use of the word. But this does not entail that there need be *criteria* for "X learned the word *w*." All that is required is that we must sometimes have good reasons for saying that the word has been mastered; and this condition is satisfied when, for example, the simplest and most plausible explanation available of the verbal behavior of the student is that he has learned the use of the word.

WITTGENSTEIN'S PHILOSOPHY
OF MATHEMATICS

MICHAEL DUMMETT

From time to time Wittgenstein recorded in separate
notebooks thoughts that occurred to him about the philosophy of mathematics. His recently published *Bemerkungen über die Grundlagen der Mathematik*[1] consists of ex-
tracts made by the editors from five of these. Neither it
nor any of these notebooks was intended by its author as a
book. That it cannot be considered, and ought not to be
criticized, as such is therefore unsurprising, though disap-
pointing. Many of the thoughts are expressed in a manner
which the author recognized as inaccurate or obscure; some
passages contradict others; some are quite inconclusive;
some raise objections to ideas which Wittgenstein held or
had held which are not themselves stated clearly in the
volume; other passages again, particularly those on consistency and on Gödel's theorem, are of poor quality or
contain definite errors. This being so, the book has to be
treated as what it is—a selection from the jottings of a
great philosopher. As Frege said of his unpublished writings, they are not all gold but there is gold in them. One
of the tasks of the reader is therefore to extract the gold.

From *The Philosophical Review*, Vol. LXVIII (1959), pp.
324–348. Reprinted with the permission of the author and
editors.

[1] *Bemerkungen über die Grundlagen der Mathematik.* By Ludwig Wittgenstein. Edited by G. H. von Wright, R. Rhees, and
G. E. M. Anscombe. With English translation (*Remarks on the
Foundations of Mathematics*) by G. E. M. Anscombe, on facing
pages. Oxford, 1956. Pp. xix, 196, each version.

I encounter frequently in conversation the impression that this is typical of Wittgenstein's work in general; I have often heard the *Investigations* characterized as evasive and inconclusive. This seems to me a travesty of the truth; the book expresses with great clarity many forceful, profound, and quite definite ideas—though it is true that a hasty reader may sometimes be bewildered by the complexity of some of the thoughts. The contrast with the present volume is marked, and is due entirely to the different origins of the two books.

In the philosophy of mathematics, Platonism stands opposed to various degrees of constructivism. According to Platonism, mathematical objects are there and stand in certain relations to one another, independently of us, and what we do is to discover these objects and their relations to one another. The constructivist usually opposes to this the picture of our making, constructing, the mathematical entities as we go along. For the Platonist, the meaning of a mathematical statement is to be explained in terms of its truth-conditions; for each statement, there is something in mathematical reality in virtue of which it is either true or false. An example of the explanation of meaning in terms of truth and falsity is the truth-table explanation of the sentential connectives. For the constructivist, the general form of an explanation of meaning must be in terms of the conditions under which we regard ourselves as justified in asserting a statement, that is, the circumstances in which we are in possession of a proof. For instance, a statement made up of two statements joined by a connective is to be explained by explaining a claim to have proved the complex statement in terms of what a claim to have proved the constituent statements consists in; thus a claim to have proved ⌜A or B⌝ will be a claim to have a method leading either to a proof of A or to a proof of B. What in practice this will lead to will depend upon the degree of constructivism adopted; for example, if we confine ourselves to decidable statements, then the truth-tables will receive an acceptable interpretation and the whole classical logic will be applicable; if, on the other hand, we allow with the intuitionists a much wider range of mathematical statements to be considered as intelligible, then the law of excluded middle and many other classically valid laws will cease to hold generally. But in either case it is the notion of proof and not the notions of truth and falsity which is for the constructivist central to the account of the meaning of mathematical statements.

We may regard Platonism and the various varieties of constructivism not as rivals but merely as means of demarcating different areas of mathematics with respect not to subject matter but to methods of proof. In this case there are only the essentially mathematical problems of formulating clearly the different conceptions and investigating in detail the mathematical consequences of each. If, on the other hand, one regards the different schools as rivals, there remains the philosophical problem of deciding which of the various accounts is correct. Wittgenstein's book is intended as a contribution to the latter task only. It seems natural to suppose that the philosophical task and the mathematical go hand in hand, for the precise formulation of a conception is not irrelevant to deciding on its correctness, and unexpected consequences of adopting it may lead one to revise one's opinion as to its value. Wittgenstein will have none of this: for him philosophy and mathematics have nothing to say to one another; no mathematical discovery can have any bearing on the philosophy of mathematics.[2] It would seem that he is theoretically committed also to the converse, that no philosophical opinion could, or at least ought to, affect the procedure of the mathematician. This comes out to some extent in his discussion of the law of excluded middle in mathematics. Against one who insisted that either the sequence "77777" occurs in the development of π or it does not, he employs arguments similar to those of the intuitionists; and yet it appears that he is not wishing to question the validity in a

[2] Cf. V, 13, 19; IV, 52; also *Investigations*, II, xiv; I, 124.

mathematical proof of, for example, argument by cases, but only to reprove someone who in the course of philosophical reflection wishes to insist on the law of excluded middle.[3] Yet this is not to be taken too seriously, for Wittgenstein would always be able to claim that, while he had not shown that certain mathematical procedures were *wrong*, still he had shown them not to have the interest we were inclined to attach to them. Certainly in his discussion of Cantor he displays no timidity about "interfering with the mathematicians."[4] I think that there is no ground for Wittgenstein's segregation of philosophy from mathematics but that this springs only from a general tendency of his to regard discourse as split up into a number of distinct islands with no communication between them (statements of natural science, of philosophy, of mathematics, of religion).

As Frege showed, the nominalist objection to Platonism —that talk about "abstract entities" is unintelligible—is illtaken; if we believe in the objectivity of mathematics, then there is no objection to our thinking in terms of mathematical objects, nor to the picture of them as already there waiting to be discovered that goes with it. Nor is formalism a real alternative. The formalist insists that the content of a mathematical theorem is simply that *if* there is any domain for which the axioms hold good, then the theorem will also hold good for that domain; and he will add that so long as we do not know the axioms to be categorical, a statement of the theory need not be either true or false. But he will not reject the classical logic, since he will agree that in any particular domain for which the axioms hold, the statement will be either true or false; and furthermore, he will allow that any given statement either does or does not follow from the axioms. Since the statement that there exists a proof of a given statement from given axioms is in exactly the same position as, say, an existence-statement in number theory for which we have neither proof nor

[3] IV, 10.
[4] I, App. II.

disproof, the formalist has gained no advantage; he has merely switched from one kind of mathematical object— numbers—to another—formal proofs.

Wittgenstein adopts a version (as we shall see, an extreme version) of constructivism; for him it is of the essence of a mathematical statement that it is asserted as the conclusion of a *proof*, whereas I suppose that for a Platonist a being who had *direct* apprehension of mathematical truth, not mediated by inferences, would not be a complete absurdity. There are many different lines of thought converging upon Wittgenstein's constructivism; I shall deal first with his conception of logical necessity.

A great many philosophers nowadays subscribe to some form of conventionalist account of logical necessity, and it is perhaps difficult to realize what a liberation was effected by this theory. The philosophical problem of necessity is twofold: what is its source, and how do we recognize it? God can ordain that something shall hold good of the actual world; but how can even God ordain that something is to hold good in all possible worlds? We know what it is to set about finding out if something *is* true; but what account can we give of the process of discovering whether it *must* be true? According to conventionalism, all necessity is imposed by us not on reality, but upon our language; a statement is necessary by virtue of our having chosen not to count anything as falsifying it. Our recognition of logical necessity thus becomes a particular case of our knowledge of our own intentions.

The conventionalism that is so widespread is, however, a modified conventionalism. On this view, although all necessity derives from linguistic conventions that we have adopted, the derivation is not always direct. Some necessary statements are straightforwardly registers of conventions we have laid down; others are more or less remote *consequences* of conventions. Thus "Nothing can at the same time be green and blue all over" is a direct register of a convention, since there is nothing in the ostensive training we give in the use of color-words which shows that we are not to call something on the borderline between green and blue "both green and blue." "Nothing can be both green and red," on the other hand, is necessary in consequence of the meanings of "green" and "red" as shown in the ostensive training. We did not need to adopt a special convention excluding the expression "both green and red" from our language, since the use by someone of this expression would already show that he had not learned what he was supposed to have learned from the ostensive training.

When applied to mathematics, this modified conventionalism results in the sort of account of mathematical truth with which we are so familiar from logical positivist writings. The axioms of a mathematical theory are necessary in virtue of their being direct registers of certain conventions we have adopted about the use of the terms of the theory; it is the job of the mathematician to discover the more or less remote consequences of our having adopted these conventions, which consequences are epitomized in the theorems. If it is inquired what is the status of the logical principles in accordance with which we pass from axioms to theorems, the reply is that to subscribe to these principles is again the expression of the adoption of linguistic conventions, in this case conventions about the use of "if," "all," and so forth. This account is entirely superficial and throws away all the advantages of conventionalism, since it leaves unexplained the status of the assertion that certain conventions have certain consequences. It appears that if we adopt the conventions registered by the axioms, together with those registered by the principles of inference, then we *must* adhere to the way of talking embodied in the theorem; and *this* necessity must be one imposed upon us, one that we meet with. It cannot itself express the adoption of a convention; the account leaves no room for any further such convention.

Wittgenstein goes in for a full-blooded conventionalism; for him the logical necessity of any statement is always the *direct* expression of a linguistic convention. That a given statement is necessary consists always in our having expressly decided to treat that very statement as unassailable; it cannot rest on our having adopted certain other conventions which are found to involve our treating it so. This account is applied alike to deep theorems and to elementary computations. To give an example of the latter, the criterion which we adopt in the first place for saying that there are *n* things of a certain kind is to be explained by describing the procedure of counting. But when we find that there are five boys and seven girls in a room, we say that there are twelve children altogether, without counting them all together. The fact that we are justified in doing this is not, as it were, implicit in the procedure of counting itself; rather, we have chosen to adopt a *new* criterion for saying that there are twelve children, different from the criterion of counting up all the children together. It would seem that, if we have genuinely distinct criteria for the same statement, they may clash. But the necessity of "5 + 7 = 12" consists just in this, that we do not count anything as a clash; if we count the children all together and get eleven, we say, "We must have miscounted."

This account is very difficult to accept, since it appears that the mathematical proof drives us along willy-nilly until we arrive at the theorem. (Of course, we learned "5 + 7 = 12" by rote; but we could produce an argument to prove it if the need arose.) But here Wittgenstein brings in the considerations about rules presented in the *Investigations* and elsewhere. A proof proceeds according to certain logical principles or rules of inference. We are inclined to suppose that once we have accepted the axioms from which the proof starts, we have, as it were, no further active part to play; when the proof is shown us, we are mere passive spectators. But in order to follow the proof, we have to recognize various transitions as applications of the general rules of inference. Now even if these rules had been explicitly formulated at the start, and we had given our assent to them, our doing so would not in itself constitute recognition of each transition as a correct application of the rules. Once we have the proof, we shall indeed say that anyone who does not accept it either cannot really have understood or cannot really have accepted the rules of inference; but it does not have to be the case that there was anything in what he said or did before he rejected the proof which revealed such a misunderstanding or rejection of the rules of inference. Hence at each step we are free to choose to accept or reject the proof; there is nothing in our formulation of the axioms and of the rules of inference, and nothing in our minds when we accepted these before the proof was given, which of itself shows whether we shall accept the proof or not; and hence there is nothing which *forces* us to accept the proof. If we accept the proof, we confer necessity on the theorem proved; we "put it in the archives" and will count nothing as telling against it. In doing this we are making a new decision, and not merely making explicit a decision we had already made implicitly.

A natural reaction to this is to say that it is true enough when we have not formulated our principles of inference, or have formulated them only in an imprecise form, but that it does not apply at all when we have achieved a strict formalization. Wittgenstein's hostility to mathematical logic is great; he says that it has completely distorted the thinking of philosophers.[5] Because this remark as it stands is so plainly silly, it is difficult to get a clear view of the matter. Consider a favorite example of Wittgenstein's: you train someone to obey orders of the form "Add *n*" with examples taken from fairly small numbers, then give him the order "Add one" and find that he adds two for numbers from 100 to 199, three for numbers from 200 to 299, and so forth. Wittgenstein says that there need have been nothing either in what you said to him during the training or in what "went on in your mind" then which of itself showed that this was not what you intended. This is certainly true, and shows something important about the con-

[5] IV, 48.

cept of intention (it is a very striking case of what Wittgenstein means when he says in the *Investigations* that if God had looked into my mind, he would not have been able to see there whom I meant). But suppose the training was not given only by example, but made use also of an explicit formulation of the rule for forming from an Arabic numeral its successor. A machine can follow this rule; whence does a human being gain a freedom of choice in this matter which the machine does not possess?

It would of course be possible to argue that someone might appear to understand a rule of inference in a formal system—a substitution rule, say—and yet later reject a correct application of it; but it remains that we can see *in* the precise wording of the rule that that application was warranted. It might be replied that this is to take for granted the ordinary understanding of the words or symbols in terms of which the rule is framed; an explanation of these words or symbols would be something like Wittgenstein's idea of a rule for interpreting the rule. It is undoubtedly true and important that, while in using a word or symbol we are in some sense following a rule, this rule cannot in its turn be formulated in such a way as to leave no latitude in its interpretation, or if it can, the rules for using the words in terms of which this rule is formulated cannot in their turn be so formulated. But such considerations seem to belong to the theory of meaning in general, rather than having any particular relevance to the philosophy of mathematics. Rather, it seems that to someone who suggests that Wittgenstein's point about the scope left in deciding on the correctness of an application of a rule of inference is to be countered by concentrating on rules of inference in formal systems we ought to reply by referring to what Wittgenstein calls the "motley" of mathematics.[6] He wishes, like the intuitionists, to insist that we cannot draw a line in advance round the possible forms of argument that may be used in

[6] II, 46, 48.

mathematical proofs. Furthermore, it might be pointed out that a formal system does not *replace* the intuitive proofs as, frequently, a precise concept replaces a vague intuitive one; the formal system remains, as it were, answerable to the intuitive conception, and remains of interest only so long as it does not reveal undesirable features which the intuitive idea does not possess. An example would be Gödel's theorem, which shows that provability in a formal system cannot do duty as a substitute for the intuitive idea of arithmetical truth.

Suppose we are considering a statement of some mathematical theory. To avoid complications, assume that the theory is complete, that is, that it can be completely formalized, but that we are not thinking of any particular formal system. Then a Platonist will say that there exists either a proof or a disproof of the statement; the fact that the statement is true, if it is true, consists in the existence of such a proof even though we have not yet discovered it. Now if there exists a proof, let us suppose that there is somewhere an actual document, as yet unseen by human eyes, on which is written what purports to be a proof of the statement. Then Wittgenstein will reply that all the same there does not yet exist a proof, since when we discover the document it is still up to us to decide whether or not we wish to count it as a proof. It is evident that, if this is correct, then all motive for saying with the Platonist that there either *is* or *is not* a proof, that the statement must be either true or false, and so forth, has gone. What is not clear to me is that rejecting the Platonist's conception involves adopting this line about proofs; it seems to me that a man might hold that, once the proof was discovered, we had no choice but to follow it, without allowing the correctness of saying, before the proof was discovered, that either there is a proof or there is not. I will return to this later.

Wittgenstein's conception is extremely hard to swallow, even though it is not clear what one wishes to oppose to it. The proof is supposed to have the effect of persuading us, inducing us, to count such-and-such a form of words as unassailably true, or to exclude such-and-such a form of words from our language. It seems quite unclear how the proof accomplishes this remarkable feat. Another difficulty is the scarcity of examples. We naturally think that, face to face with a proof, we have no alternative but to accept the proof if we are to remain faithful to the understanding we already had of the expressions contained in it. For Wittgenstein, accepting the theorem is adopting a new rule of language, and hence our concepts cannot remain unchanged at the end of the proof. But we could have rejected the proof without doing any more violence to our concepts than is done by accepting it; in rejecting it we could have remained equally faithful to the concepts with which we started out. It seems extraordinarily difficult to take this idea seriously when we think of some particular actual proof. It may of course be said that this is because we have already accepted the proof and thereby subjected our concepts to the modification which acceptance of the proof involved; but the difficulty of believing Wittgenstein's account of the matter while reading the proof of some theorem with which one was not previously familiar is just as great. We want to say that we do not know what it would be like for someone who, by ordinary criteria, already understood the concepts employed, to reject this proof. Of course we are familiar with someone's simply not following a proof, but we are also familiar with the remedy, namely to interpolate simpler steps between each line of the proof. The examples given in Wittgenstein's book are—amazingly for him—thin and unconvincing. I think that this is a fairly sure sign that there is something wrong with Wittgenstein's account.

Consider the case of an elementary computation, for example "$5 + 7 = 12$." There might be people who counted as we do but did not have the concept of addition. If such a person had found out by counting that there were five boys and seven girls in a classroom, and were then asked how many children were present, he would proceed to count all the children together to discover the answer. Thus he would be quite prepared to say that on one occasion there were five boys, seven girls, and twelve children altogether, but on another occasion five boys, seven girls, and thirteen children altogether. Now if we came across such a person, we should know what kind of arguments to bring to show him that in such circumstances he must have miscounted on one occasion, and that whenever there are five boys and seven girls there are twelve children. If he accepts these arguments it will be quite true that he will have adopted a new criterion for saying that there are twelve children present, and again a new criterion for saying, "I must have miscounted." Before, he would say, "I miscounted," only when he noticed that he had, for example, counted one of the children twice over; now he will say, "I miscounted," when he has not observed anything of this kind, simply on the ground that he got the result that there were five boys, seven girls, and thirteen children. But we wish to say that even before we met this person and taught him the principles of addition, it would have been true that if he had counted five boys, seven girls, and thirteen children, he would have been wrong even according to the criteria he himself then acknowledged. That is, he must have made a mistake in counting; and if he made a mistake, then there must have been something that he did which, if he had noticed it, he himself would then have allowed as showing that he had miscounted.

If we say that if he counted five boys, seven girls, and thirteen children, then there must have been something which, if he had noticed it, he would have regarded as a criterion for having miscounted, then the effect of introducing him to the concept of addition is not to be simply described as persuading him to adopt a new criterion for having miscounted; rather, he has been induced to recognize getting additively discordant results as a *symptom* of the presence of something he already accepted as a criterion for having miscounted. That is, learning about addition leads him to say, "I miscounted," in circumstances where he would not before have said it; but if, before he had learned, he had said, "I miscounted," in those circumstances, he would have been right by the criteria he then possessed. Hence the necessity for his having miscounted when he gets additively discordant results does not, as it were, get its whole being from his now recognizing such results as a criterion for having miscounted.

If on the other hand we say that it is possible to count five boys, seven girls, and thirteen children without there being anything other than the fact of getting these results such that, if we had noticed it, we should have regarded it as a ground for saying that we had miscounted, then it appears to follow that one can make a mistake in counting (according to the criteria *we* recognize for having miscounted) without having made any particular mistake; that is, one cannot say that if one has miscounted, then either one counted this boy twice, or one counted that girl twice, or . . . . But this is absurd: one cannot make some mistake without there having been some particular mistake which one has made. It might be replied that we can choose to say that if one has miscounted, then either . . . , and that that is in fact what we do choose to say. But if a disjunction is true, then at least one of its limbs must be true; and if a statement is true, there must be something such that if we knew of it, we would regard it as a criterion for the truth of the statement. Yet the assumption from which we started is that someone counts five boys, seven girls, and thirteen children (and hence says that he must have miscounted) and that there is nevertheless nothing apart from his having got these results which (if he knew of it) he would regard as showing that he had miscounted; and hence there can be nothing which (if he knew of it) would show the truth of any one of the disjuncts of the form "He counted that boy twice," and so forth. One might put it by saying that if a disjunction is true, God must know which of the disjuncts is true; hence it cannot be right to count something as a criterion for the truth of the disjunction whose presence does not guarantee the existence of something which would show the truth of some one particular disjunct. For example, it would be wrong to regard ⌜Either if it had been the case that P, it would have been the case that Q, or if it had been the case that P, it would have been the case that not Q⌝ as a logical law, since it is perfectly possible to suppose that however much we knew about the kind of fact which we should regard as bearing on the truth of the disjunct counterfactuals, we should still know nothing which we should count as a reason for accepting either the one or the other.

It is certainly part of the meaning of the word "true" that if a statement is true, there must be something in virtue of which it is true. "There is something in virtue of which it is true" means: there is something such that if we knew of it we should regard it as a criterion (or at least as a ground) for asserting the statement. The essence of realism is this: for any statement which has a definite sense, there must be something in virtue of which either it or its negation is true. (Realism about the realm of mathematics is what we call Platonism.) Intuitionists do not at all deny the first thesis; for them one is justified in asserting a disjunction only when one has a method for arriving at something which would justify the assertion of some one particular limb of the disjunction. Rather, they deny the second thesis: there is no reason for supposing in general that, just because a statement has a quite definite use, there must be something in virtue of which either it is true or it is false. One must beware of saying that logical truths are an exception, that there is nothing in virtue of which they are true; on the contrary, for the realist we are justified in asserting ⌜P or not P⌝ because there must be something in virtue of which either P or ⌜Not P⌝ is true, and hence in any case there must be something in virtue of which ⌜P or not P⌝ is true.

Now there seems here to be one of the big differences between Wittgenstein and the intuitionists. He appears to hold that it is up to us to decide to regard any statement we happen to pick on as holding necessarily, if we choose to do so.[7] The idea behind this appears to be that, by laying down that something is to be regarded as holding necessarily, we thereby in part determine the sense of the words it contains; since we have the right to attach what sense we choose to the words we employ, we have the right to lay down as necessary any statement we choose to regard as such. Against this one would like to say that the senses of the words in the statement may have already been fully determined, so that there is no room for any further determination. Thus, if one takes a classical (realist) view, the general form of explanation of the sense of a statement consists in the stipulation of its truth-conditions (this is the view taken by Wittgenstein in the *Tractatus* and also the view of Frege). Thus the sense of the sentential operators is to be explained by means of truth-tables; it is by reference to the truth-tables that one justifies taking certain forms as logically true.

Since the intuitionist rejects the conception according to which there must be for every statement something in virtue of which either it is true or it is false (and does not regard it as possible to remedy the situation by the introduction of further truth-values), for him the fundamental form of an explanation of a statement's meaning consists in stating the criteria we recognize as justifying the assertion of the statement (in mathematics, this is in general the possession of a proof). We thus specify the sense of the sentential operators, of "or," for example, by explaining the criteria for asserting the complex statement in terms of the criteria for asserting the constituents; hence, roughly speaking, we are justified in asserting $\ulcorner P$ or $Q \urcorner$ only when we are justified either in asserting P or in asserting Q. A logical law holds in virtue of these explanations; by reference to them we see that we shall *always* be justified in asserting a statement of this form.

Wittgenstein's quite different idea, that one has the right simply to *lay down* that the assertion of a statement

[7] Cf. V, 23, last par. on p. 179.

of a given form is to be regarded as always justified, without regard to the use that has already been given to the words contained in the statement, seems to me mistaken. If Wittgenstein were right, it appears to me that communication would be in constant danger of simply breaking down. The decision to count a particular form of statement as logically true does not affect only the sense of statements of that form; the senses of all sorts of other statements will be infected, and in a way that we shall be unable to give a direct account of, without reference to our taking the form of statement in question as logically true. Thus it will become impossible to give an account of the sense of any statement without giving an account of the sense of every statement, and since it is of the essence of language that we understand *new* statements, this means that it will be impossible to give an account of the use of our language at all. To give an example: suppose someone were to choose to regard as a logical law the counterfactual disjunction I mentioned above. We try to object to his claim that this is logically valid by observing that either he must admit that a disjunction may be true when neither limb is true, or that a counterfactual may be true when there is nothing in virtue of which it is true, that is, nothing such that if we knew of it we should regard it as a ground for asserting the counterfactual. But he may respond by denying that these consequences follow; rather, he adduces it as a consequence of the validity of the law that there must be something such that if we knew of it we should ⌜count it as a ground either for asserting ⌜If it had been the case that P, then it would have been the case that Q⌝ or for asserting ⌜If it had been the case that P, then it would have been the case that not Q⌝. For example, he will say that there must be something in which either the bravery or the cowardice of a man consisted, even if that man had never encountered danger and hence had never had an opportunity to display either courage or cowardice. If we hold that he is entitled to regard anything as a logical law which he chooses so to regard, then we

cannot deny him the right to draw this conclusion. The
conclusion follows from the disjunction of counterfactuals
which he elected to regard as logically true in the first
place, together with statements we should all regard as
logically true; and in any case, he must have the right to
regard the conclusion itself as logically true if he so
chooses. He will thus conclude that either a man must
reveal in his behavior how he would behave in all possible
circumstances, or else that there is inside him a sort of
spiritual mechanism determining how he behaves in each
situation.

Now we know from the rest of Wittgenstein's philosophy how repugnant such a conclusion would be to him;
but what right would he have, on his own account of the
matter, to object to this man's reaching this conclusion? It
is all very well to say, "Say what you like once you know
what the facts are"; but how are we to be sure that we can
tell anyone what the facts are if it may be that the form
of words we use to tell him the facts has for him a different
sense as a result of his having adopted some logical law
which we do not accept? It might be said that once we discover this difference in the understanding of a certain form
of words, we must select another form of words which he
does understand as we do and which expresses what we
wanted to say; but how are we to know that there is a form
of words which does the trick? If we ask him how he
understands a certain statement, and he gives the same
explanation of it that we should give, this is no guarantee
that he in fact understands it as we do; for the mere fact
that he recognizes certain forms as logically true which we
do not recognize means that he may be able to construct
arguments leading to the given statement as a conclusion
and with premises that we accept, although we should not
accept the argument; that is, he will regard himself as
entitled to assert the statement in circumstances in which
we should not regard ourselves as entitled to assert it.
(An analogy, *not* strictly parallel, is this: we might imagine a classicist and an intuitionist giving explanations of

the meaning of the existential quantifier which sounded exactly the same. Yet for all that the classicist will make existential assertions in cases in which the intuitionist will not, since he has been able to arrive at them by means of arguments which the intuitionist will not accept.) Now in the case we are imagining, it is essential to suppose that our man is not capable of giving any general kind of explanation of the words he uses such that we can, from this explanation, derive directly the meaning he attaches to any sentence composed of these words. For if he could give such an explanation, we could see from the explanation why the logical law which he accepts but we do not *is* necessary if the words in it are understood as he understands them. We should thus have a justification for taking statements of that form to be logical laws parallel to the justification of the laws of classical logic in terms of an explanation of meaning by reference to truth-conditions and the justification of intuitionist logic in terms of the explanation by reference to assertibility-conditions. But the whole point of the example was that this was a case of simply laying down a certain form of statement as logically true without the requirement of a justification of this kind.

This attitude of Wittgenstein's to logical necessity may in part explain his ambivalence about the law of excluded middle in mathematics. If a philosopher insists on the law of excluded middle, this is probably the expression of a realist (Platonist) conception of mathematics which Wittgenstein rejects: he insists that ⌜P or not P⌝ is true because he thinks that the general form of explanation of meaning is in terms of truth-conditions, and that for any mathematical statement possessing a definite sense there must be something in virtue of which either it is true or it is false. On the other hand, if a mathematician wishes to use a form of argument depending upon the law of excluded middle (for example, ⌜If P, then Q⌝; ⌜If not P, then Q⌝; therefore, Q), Wittgenstein will not object, since the mathematician has the right to regard the form of words ⌐P or not P⌐ as holding necessarily if he chooses to do so.

To return to the example of the people who counted but did not have addition, it seems likely that someone who accepted Wittgenstein's viewpoint would wish to reject the alternative: either when one of these people counted five boys, seven girls, and thirteen children there must have been something which, if he had noticed it, would have been for him evidence of his having miscounted, or else he could have done so when there was nothing which would have shown him he had miscounted. He would reject it on the ground that it is unclear whether the alternative is being posed in *our* language or in the language of the people in question. We say that he must have miscounted, and hence that he must either have counted this boy twice, or . . . , and hence that there was something which if he had noticed it would have shown him that he had miscounted, and we say this just on the ground that his figures do not add up. But he would have no reason for saying it, and would assert that he had probably counted correctly. Now we must not ask whether what we say or what he says is *true*, as if we could stand outside both languages; we just *say* this, that is, we count his having got discordant results as a criterion for saying it, and he does not. Against this I wish, for the reasons I have stated, to set the conventional view that in deciding to regard a form of words as necessary, or to count such-and-such as a criterion for making a statement of a certain kind, we have a responsibility to the sense we have already given to the words of which the statement is composed.

It is easy to see from this why Wittgenstein is so obsessed in this book with an empiricist philosophy of mathematics. He does not wish to accept the empiricist account, but it has a strong allure for him; again and again he comes back to the question, "What is the difference between a calculation and an experiment?". The fact is that even if we decide to *say* that we must have made a mistake in counting when we count five boys, seven girls, and thirteen children, our mere decision to treat this result as a criterion for having made a mistake cannot of itself make it probable that in such circumstances we shall be able to find a mistake; that is, if Wittgenstein's account of the matter is correct. Nevertheless, getting such a discrepancy in counting is a very sure sign in practice that we shall be able to find a mistake, or that if we count again we shall get results that agree. It is because it is such a sure sign in practice that it is possible—or useful—for us to put "5 + 7 = 12" in the archives. Thus for Wittgenstein an empirical regularity lies behind a mathematical law.[8] The mathematical law does not *assert* that the regularity obtains, because we do not treat it as we treat an assertion of empirical fact, but as a necessary statement; all the same, what leads us to treat it in this way is the empirical regularity, since it is only because the regularity obtains that the law has a useful application.[9] What the relation is between the regularity and the proof which induces us to put the law in the archives Wittgenstein does not succeed in explaining.

To avoid misunderstanding, I must emphasize that I am not proposing an alternative account of the necessity of mathematical theorems, and I do not know what account should be given. I have merely attempted to give reasons for the natural resistance one feels to Wittgenstein's account, reasons for thinking that it must be wrong. But I believe that whether one accepts Wittgenstein's account or rejects it, one could not after reflecting on it remain content with the standard view which I have called modified conventionalism.

Wittgenstein's constructivism is of a much more extreme kind than that of the intuitionists. For an intuitionist, we may say that every natural number is either prime or composite because we have a method for deciding, for each natural number, whether it is prime or not. Wittgen-

---

[8] III, 44.
[9] E.g., II, 73, 75.

stein would deny that we have such a method. Normally one would say that the sieve of Eratosthenes was such a method; but with a large number one would not—*could not*—use the sieve, but would resort to some more powerful criterion. It will be said that this is a mere practical, not a theoretical, matter, due to the comparative shortness of our lives. But if some fanatic devoted his life to computing, by means of the sieve, the primality of some very large number proved to be prime by more powerful means, and arrived at the conclusion that it was composite, we should not abandon our proof but say that there must be some error in his computations. This shows that we are taking the "advanced" test, and not the sieve, as the *criterion* for primality here: we use the theorem as the standard whereby we judge the computation, and not conversely. The computation is of no use to us because it is not *surveyable*. A mathematical proof, of which computations are a special case, is a proof in virtue of our using it to serve a certain purpose; namely, we put the conclusion or result in the archives, that is, treat it as unassailable and use it as a standard whereby to judge other results. Now something cannot serve this purpose, and hence is not a mathematical proof, unless we are able to exclude the possibility of a mistake's having occurred in it. We must be able to "take in" a proof, and this means that we must be certain of being able to reproduce the *same* proof. We cannot in general *guarantee* that we shall be able to repeat an experiment and get the same result as before. Admittedly, if we get a different result, we shall look for a relevant difference in the conditions of the experiment; but we did not have in advance a clear conception of just what was to count as a relevant difference. (It is not quite clear whether in saying that we must be able to reproduce a proof Wittgenstein means that one must be able to copy from the written proof before one and be certain that one has copied without error, or that one must be able to read the proof and understand it so that one could write it down without referring to the original written proof, so that the possibility of a misprint becomes more or less irrelevant. It does not seem to affect the argument which interpretation is adopted.)

Thus the computation, for a very large number proved prime by other means, of its primality by means of Eratosthenes' sieve would not be a mathematical proof but an experiment to see whether one could do such enormous computations correctly; for the computation would be unsurveyable in the sense explained. Now what the word "prime" means as applied to large numbers is shown by what we accept as the *criterion* for primality, what we take as the standard whereby to assess claims that a number is prime or is composite. The sense of the word "prime" is not therefore given once for all by the sieve of Eratosthenes. Hence we should have no right to assert that every number is either prime or composite, since for any criterion we may adopt there will be a number so large that the application of the criterion to it will not be surveyable. This throws light on Wittgenstein's insistence that the sense of a mathematical statement is determined by its proof (or disproof),[10] that finding a proof alters the concept. One is inclined to think that such a statement as "There is an odd perfect number" is fixed quite definitely in advance, and that our finding a proof or a disproof cannot alter that already determinate sense. We think this on the ground that we are in possession of a method for determining, for *any* number, whether or not it is odd and whether or not it is perfect. But suppose that the statement were to be proved, say by exhibiting a particular odd perfect number. This number would have to be very large, and it is unthinkable that it should be proved to be perfect by the simple method of computing its factors by means of the sieve and adding them all up. The proof would probably proceed by giving a new method for determining perfection, and this method would then have been adopted as our *criterion* for saying of numbers within this range

[10] But cf., e.g., V, 7.

whether or not they are perfect. Thus the proof determines, for numbers of this size, what the *sense* of the predicate "perfect" is to be.

This constructivism, more severe than any version yet proposed, has been called "strict finitism" by Mr. G. Kreisel and "anthropologism" by Dr. Hao Wang. It was adumbrated by Professor Paul Bernays in his *Sur le platonisme dans les mathématiques*.[11] As presented by Bernays, it would consist in concentrating on practical rather than on theoretical possibility. I have tried to explain how for Wittgenstein this is not the correct way in which to draw the contrast.

It is a matter of some difficulty to consider just what our mathematics would look like if we adopted this "anthropologistic" standpoint. Would the Peano axioms survive unaltered? "Every number has a successor" would mean, in this mathematics, that if a number is accessible (that is, if we have a notation in which it can be surveyably represented) then its successor is accessible, and this at first seems reasonable. On the other hand, it seems to lead to the conclusion that *every* number is accessible, and it is clear that, whatever notation we have, there will be numbers for which there will not be a surveyable symbol in that notation. The problem seems similar to the Greek problem of the heap: if I have something that is not a heap of sand, I cannot turn it into a heap by adding one grain of sand to it. One might solve the present difficulty by arguing as follows. Let us say that we "get to" a number if we actually write down a surveyable symbol for it. Then we may say: if I get to a number, I can get to its successor. From this it follows that if I *can* get to a number, then it is possible that I can get to its successor; that is, if a number is accessible, then its successor is possibly accessible. Unless we think that "possibly possibly p" implies "possibly p" it does not follow that if a number is accessible, its successor is accessible. We should thus have to

11 *L'enseignement mathématique*, XXXIV (1935), 52–69.

adopt a modal logic like S2 or M which does not contain
the law (in Polish notation) "CMMpMp." Another consideration pointing in the same direction is the following.
"Surveyable," "accessible," and so forth, are *vague* concepts.
It is often profitable to substitute for a vague concept a
precise one, but that would be quite out of place here;
we do not want to fix on some definite number as the last
accessible number, all bigger numbers being definitely
inaccessible. Now the vagueness of a vague predicate is in-
eradicable. Thus "hill" is a vague predicate, in that there is
no definite line between hills and mountains. But we
could not eliminate this vagueness by introducing a new
predicate, say "eminence," to apply to those things which
are neither definitely hills nor definitely mountains, since
there would still remain things which were neither definitely hills nor definitely eminences, and so ad infinitum.
Hence if we are looking for a logical theory suitable for
sentences containing vague predicates, it would be natural
to select a modal logic like S2 or M with infinitely many
modalities (interpreting the necessity-operator as meaning
"definitely"). Thus a suggestion for a propositional calculus appropriate to an anthropologistic mathematics would
be one bearing to the modal system M the same relation
as intuitionistic propositional calculus bears to S4. (This
system would probably have to have axioms of a similar
form to those originally given by Heyting, namely, they
would frequently be implications whose antecedent was a
conjunction, and would have a rule of adjunction as primitive; for, as has been pointed out to me by Mr. E. J. Lem-
mon, under Tarski's or Gödel's translation an implication
whose consequent contains implication reiterated more
often than does the antecedent does not usually go over
into a valid formula of M, precisely because we do not
have in M "CLpLLp.") Another suggestion, made by Dr.
Wang, is that anthropologistic logic would coincide with
intuitionist, but that the number theory would be weaker.

Wittgenstein uses these ideas to cast doubt upon the
significance attached by some philosophers to the reduc-

tionist programs of Frege and Russell. We may think that
the real meaning of and justification for such an equation
as "$5 + 7 = 12$" has been attained if we interpret it as a
statement in set theory or in a higher-order predicate calculus; but the fact is that not only the proof but the statement of the proposition in the primitive notation of these
theories would be so enormously long as to be quite unsurveyable. It might be replied that we can shorten both
the proof and the statement by using defined symbols; but
then the definitions play an essential role, whereas for
Russell definitions are *mere* abbreviations, so that the real
formal statement and formal proof are those in primitive
notation. For Wittgenstein notation is not a mere outward
covering for a thought which is in itself indifferent to the
notation adopted. The proof in primitive notation is not
what "really" justifies us in asserting "$5 + 7 = 12$" since
we never do write down this proof; if someone were to
write it down and obtain the result "$5 + 7 = 11$," we
should—appealing to schoolroom addition as a standard—
say that he must have made a mistake; we do not even
write down the proof with defined symbols; what, if anything, could be called the justification of "$5 + 7 = 12$"
would be the proof that we actually do carry out that
every addition sum "could" be formulated and proved
within our formal logical system, and this proof uses methods far more powerful than the rules for ordinary schoolroom addition.

I now revert to the opposing *pictures* used by Platonists
and constructivists—the picture of our making discoveries
within an already existing mathematical reality and the
picture of our constructing mathematics as we go along.
Sometimes people — including intuitionists — argue as
though it were a matter of first deciding which of these
pictures is correct and then drawing conclusions from this
decision. But it is clear that these are only pictures, that is,
that the dispute as to which is correct must find its substance elsewhere—that such a dispute ought to be capable

of being expressed without reference to these pictures. On the other hand, such pictures have an enormous influence over us, and the desire to be able to form an appropriate picture is almost irresistible. If one does not believe in the objectivity of mathematical truth, one cannot accept the Platonist picture. Wittgenstein's main reason for denying the objectivity of mathematical truth is his denial of the objectivity of *proof* in mathematics, his idea that a proof does not *compel* acceptance; and what fits this conception is obviously the picture of our constructing mathematics as we go along. Now suppose that someone disagrees with Wittgenstein over this and holds that a good proof is precisely one which imposes itself upon us, not only in the sense that once we have accepted the proof we use rejection of it as a criterion for not having understood the terms in which it is expressed, but in the sense that it can be put in such a form that no one could reject it without saying something which would have been recognized before the proof was given as going back on what he had previously agreed to. Is such a person bound to adopt the Platonist picture of mathematics? Clearly not; he can accept the objectivity of mathematical proof without having to believe also in the objectivity of mathematical truth. The intuitionists, for example, usually speak as though they believed in the former without believing in the latter. It is true that A. Heyting, for instance, writes, "As the meaning of a word can never be fixed precisely enough to exclude every possibility of misunderstanding, we can never be mathematically sure that [a] formal system expresses correctly our mathematical thoughts."[12] But intuitionists incline to write as though, while we cannot delimit in advance the realm of all possible intuitionistically valid proofs, still we can be certain for particular proofs given, and particular principles of proof enunciated, that they are intuitionistically correct. That is to say, the point involved here concerns what Wittgenstein calls the

[12] *Intuitionism, an Introduction* (Amsterdam, 1956), p. 4.

motley of mathematics; the question whether a certain statement is provable cannot be given a mathematically definite formulation since we cannot foresee in advance all possible forms of argument that might be used in mathematics. Still, I suppose that someone might deny even this, in the sense that he claimed for some particular logical framework that every theorem that could be proved intuitionistically could be proved within this framework (though perhaps the proof given might not be reproducible within the framework), and yet remain essentially an intuitionist. For the strongest arguments for intuitionism seem to be quite independent of the question of the objectivity of mathematical proof—whether the proof once given compels acceptance, and whether the concept of valid proof can be made precise. The strongest arguments come from the insistence that the general form of explanation of meaning, and hence of the logical operators in particular, is a statement not of the truth-conditions but of the assertibility-conditions. We learn the meaning of the logical operators by being *trained* in their use, and this means being trained to assert complex statements in certain kinds of situation. We cannot, as it were, extract from this training more than was put into it, and unless we are concerned with a class of decidable statements the notions of truth and falsity cannot be used to give a description of the training we receive. Hence a general account of meaning which makes essential use of the notions of truth and falsity (or of any other number of truth-values) is not of the right form for an explanation of meaning.

It is clear that considerations of this kind have nothing to do with mathematics in particular, but are of quite general application. They also have a close connection with Wittgenstein's doctrine that the meaning is the use; and I believe that the *Investigations* contains implicitly a rejection of the classical (realist) Frege-*Tractatus* view that the general form of explanation of meaning is a statement of the truth-conditions.[13] This provides a motive for the rejection by Wittgenstein and the intuitionists of the Platonist picture quite independent of any considerations about the non-objective character of mathematical proof and the motley of mathematics. On the other hand, it is not clear that someone such as I have described, who accepted the considerations about meaning but rejected the considerations about proof, would be happy with the usual constructivist picture of our making up our mathematics. After all, the considerations about meaning do not apply only to mathematics but to all discourse; and while they certainly show something mistaken in the realist conception of thought and reality, they surely do not imply outside mathematics the extreme of subjective idealism—that we *create* the world. But it seems that we ought to interpose between the Platonist and the constructivist picture an intermediate picture, say of objects springing into being in response to our probing. We do not *make* the objects but must accept them as we find them (this corresponds to the proof imposing itself on us); but they were not already there for our statements to be true or false of before we carried out the investigations which brought them into being. (This is of course intended only as a picture; but its point is to break what seems to me the false dichotomy between the Platonist and the constructivist pictures which surreptitiously dominates our thinking about the philosophy of mathematics.)

13 Cf. also *Remarks*, I, App. I, 6.

MATHEMATICAL DISCOVERY AND CONCEPT FORMATION

CHARLES S. CHIHARA

It has recently been claimed that in the philosophy of mathematics, Platonists, who hold among other things that the mathematician is primarily a discoverer of truths which are in some sense independent of us, stand opposed to constructivists who claim that the activity of the mathematician is essentially one of creating rather than finding.[1] Now, is the mathematician a discoverer or a creator? Compare:

> The discovery of the proof that π is transcendental did not create any logical relations but showed us what the relation always has been.[2]

> [A proof] makes new connexions, and it creates the concept of these connexions. (It does not establish that they are there; they do not exist until it makes them.)[3]

Here, we certainly seem to have completely opposed views of mathematics, and in this paper I shall examine

From *The Philosophical Review*, Vol. LXXII (1963), pp. 17-34. Reprinted with the permission of the author and editors.

[1] Michael Dummett, "Wittgenstein's Philosophy of Mathematics," *Philosophical Review*, LXVIII (1959), 324-325 [421-422 in the present volume].

[2] Morris Cohen, *Reason and Nature*, (Glencoe, Ill., 1953), p. 193.

[3] Ludwig Wittgenstein, *Remarks on the Foundations of Mathematics* (New York, 1956), II, 31. Cited here as *RFM*.

the nature of this opposition. I shall consider the question: Is the mathematician a discoverer or a creator? not with a view to answering it, but in order to bring out some of the considerations that have led various philosophers to take one side or the other; to point out mistakes and confusions that have muddied up the issue, and to indicate a few regions that require clarification before any sound answer can be given.

I

When Wittgenstein claimed that the mathematician creates rather than discovers, he was writing in opposition to the view of many realists who held that the mathematician is essentially one whose business is to apprehend and describe "internal relations" between certain things called "universals," "concepts," or "ideas." In recent years, traditional realists have been charged with committing such outrageous logical fallacies that it might appear no sensible philosopher could have held such a position. For example, in his article "Properties and Classes" Anthony Quinton presents us with the following argument:

"We are able to classify these things together because we apprehend the universal of which they are instances" looks fairly substantial, until you ask what else can be meant by the apprehension of universals beyond the ability to classify. I am not objecting to the intermediary theories interpreted in this way just because they are repetitious. . . . But this repetition is both unilluminating and misleading; it casts no light and a good deal of darkness. It is unilluminating because the use of a re-applicable word is something more concrete and definite than the apprehension of a universal and it is misleading in its suggestion that these are quite different things, and in particular that there is some other way of finding out about universals than that of inspecting concrete activities of classification.[4]

I do not know what traditional philosophers Quinton has in mind, but it does seem clear that few, if any, identified the "apprehension of a universal" with "having the ability to classify in a certain way." Most traditional realists would claim that apprehending a universal is something one does—having an ability is not. Again, when one apprehends a universal, one must in some sense be aware of the universal, whereas one can have an ability though one is not aware of anything. The early Russell, it should be recalled, claimed, in his well-known article, "Knowledge by Acquaintance and Knowledge by Description," that we have direct acquaintance with universals and defined acquaintance in the following way: "I say that I am *acquainted* with an object when I have a direct cognitive relation to that object, i.e. when I am directly aware of the object itself."[5]

Of course, many realists did think that our apprehension of a universal, in some sense, explained our ability to classify, but I think many realists thought this apprehension explained much more. Some realists have held it explained how we discover certain necessary relations between universals. For example, Russell writes in *The Problems of Philosophy*:

> The statement "two and two are four" deals exclusively with universals, and therefore may be known by anybody who is acquainted with the universals concerned and can perceive the relation between them which the statement asserts. It must be taken as a fact, discovered by reflecting upon our knowledge, that we can have the power of sometimes perceiving such relations between universals.[6]

[4] *Proceedings of the Aristotelian Society*, LVIII (1957–58), 39–40.

[5] Bertrand Russell, *Mysticism and Logic* (New York, 1918), p. 202.

[6] Oxford, 1912, p. 105.

Quinton might argue that the realist is merely using the misleading expression "perceiving such a relation between universals" to mean simply "coming to know one classifies in such a way that whenever one can say there are two and two things that have a certain property, one can also say there are four things that have a certain property; and conversely, when one can say there are four things that have a certain property, one can also say there are two and two things that have the property." I do not think, however, this is what the realist means. Coming to know that such a relation obtains is not the same as perceiving or apprehending the relation, according to some realists; for one might come to maintain that a certain relation holds between universals not on the basis of an apprehension of the relation but on the basis of induction.

As Russell puts it,

> Our general proposition may be arrived at in the first instance by induction, and the connexion of universals may be only subsequently perceived. For example, it is known that if we draw perpendiculars to the sides of a triangle from the opposite angles, all three perpendiculars meet in a point. It would be quite possible to be first led to this proposition by actually drawing perpendiculars in many cases, and finding that they always met in a point; this experience might lead us to look for the general proof and find it. Such cases are common in the experience of every mathematician.[7]

Now someone might fail to perceive this connection of universals but be certain on the basis of examining particular instances that the connection holds. He might even claim to know, saying, "I know that this is true but I can't see why"—his not seeing why is perhaps what Russell would call "his not perceiving the connexion." One could, of course, argue that such a person would not really know that the connection holds, but I shall not go into that here. It would seem at any rate, that he does have true belief

[7] *Ibid.*, p. 107.

and that he does have grounds for his belief. Thus, we might speak of two reasons for holding that a certain relation holds between universals: (1) the direct apprehension of the relation, and (2) induction. There are also other reasons. One might do so on the basis of being informed of the fact by some authoritative source or by a reliable person who is in a position to know. For instance, a mathematician, say an analyst, might use a theorem of algebra in one of his proofs even though he had never actually gone through the proof of the theorem, and, if asked if he knew whether or not the algebraic statement is a true one, he might very well, and with some justification reply, "Oh yes—it's a well-known theorem of algebra."

It would seem then that the realist has grounds for denying Quinton's implication that there is no other way of "finding out about universals . . . [except by] inspecting concrete activities of classification." Indeed, none of the three ways noted above could be described as "inspecting concrete activities of classification."

This claim of Quinton is similar to a claim made by Norman Malcolm in an early article entitled, "Are Necessary Propositions Really Verbal?"[8] Malcolm, in attempting to dispel the metaphysical mystery from the discovery of necessary truths, argued that "the question as to whether one proposition entails another is a question as to how certain words are used."[9] And to find out how words are being used requires no intellectual vision or intuition; for, as Malcolm puts it, "we find out necessary truths in the same way we find out the empirical truth that if you suddenly jab a man with a pin he will jump . . . it is by observing how people use expressions in certain circumstances that we learn necessary truths."[10]

Malcolm's view, however, suffers from a serious defect —it makes a complete mystery of mathematical discovery; for if the discovery of necessary truths is simply a matter

[8] *Mind*, XLIX (1940), 189–203.
[9] *Ibid.*, p. 193.
[10] *Ibid.*, p. 192.

of observing people use expressions, mathematics should be, it would seem, an empirical science. There then should be a way of finding out whether or not Fermat's "last theorem" is true by observing the way people use symbols. That this absurdity is not implied by Malcolm's thesis certainly needs to be shown. Furthermore, what in the world is the mathematician doing when he sits locked in his room proving theorems that have hitherto been unknown? According to Malcolm's analysis, he cannot be discovering necessary truths. Yet to deny that the mathematician is making discoveries is paradoxical and surely requires justification. But aside from these difficulties, is it as a matter of fact true that we always discover necessary truths by simply observing the way people react in certain situations? This is surely not a point for argument—we need simply recall that there are countless occasions on which we discover necessary truths without observing the way people use symbols.

Both Malcolm and Quinton, then, seem to overlook the obvious and common phenomenon of seeing conceptual connections—something that realists are not likely to overlook. Thus, the well-known mathematician, G. H. Hardy, unblushingly suggests that "mathematical reality lies outside us, that our function is to discover or to *observe* it, and that the theorems which we prove and which we describe grandiloquently as our 'creation,' are simply our notes of our observations."[11] Realists on the whole, I think, have been struck by certain similarities between our knowledge of the physical world and our "knowledge of universals." I know certain things about J. F. Kennedy secondhand, so to speak, from newspaper accounts, magazine articles, and the like. Other facts about Kennedy, I know firsthand from actually seeing and hearing him. Analogously a realist might claim that I know certain things about the number π secondhand from reading about it in books on mathematics; other things, firsthand from actu-

[11] *A Mathematician's Apology* (Cambridge, 1941), pp. 63–64.

ally seeing that π must have certain mathematical properties and relations to other numbers. And just as one can
make conjectures about the physical world, form hypotheses on the basis of observations and experiments, test and
confirm them, so in the case of mathematics, one can make
conjectures about mathematical relations, form hypotheses
on the basis of the results obtained by a number of operations or computations, test the hypotheses, and finally
prove some of the hypotheses to be true.[12]

For many realists, then, the essential difference between
mathematics and the natural sciences is to be found in the
peculiar "sphere of reality" which is the object of mathematical explorations.[13] It is not my purpose in this paper,
however, to discuss or defend the details of this aspect of
realism. I do wish to point out that traditional realists, in
attempting to explain our knowledge of necessary truths
and to clarify the nature of proof and mathematical dis-

[12] Consider the following example from G. Polya's *Mathematics and Plausible Reasoning* (Princeton, 1954), I, 108–109.
The quotient $\dfrac{1^2 + 2^2 + \ldots + n^2}{1 + 2 + \ldots + n}$ takes on the following val-
ues for $n = 1$, 2, 3, 4, 5, 6: $\frac{3}{3}$, $\frac{5}{3}$, $\frac{7}{3}$, $\frac{9}{3}$, $\frac{11}{3}$, $\frac{13}{3}$. Upon
examining these values, one might plausibly conjecture that
$\dfrac{1^2 + 2^2 + \ldots + n^2}{1 + 2 + \ldots + n} = \dfrac{2n + 1}{3}$, and one might then verify that
the formula is true for $n = 7$, 8, 9, 10, etc. Indeed, as a result
of testing the formula for a large number of cases, one might
become convinced that the formula is true for all natural
numbers, though of course, one would still lack the proof and,
in this sense, not know why the formula is true. Later, one might
find a proof using mathematical induction. Polya, in his book,
masterfully brings out many striking similarities between the way
mathematicians and the way natural scientists discover truths.

[13] Cf. Russell's claim that "mathematics takes us . . . from
what is human, into the region of absolute necessity, to which
not only the actual world, but every possible world, must con-
form; and even here it builds a habitation, or rather finds a habitation eternally standing, where our ideals are fully satisfied and
our best hopes are not thwarted" (*Mysticism and Logic*, p. 65).
Cf. also E. W. Beth's talk about "spheres of reality" in *The
Foundation of Mathematics* (Amsterdam, 1959), pp. 644–645.

covery, have taken into account certain facts about the activity of mathematicians that are frequently overlooked by philosophers overzealously attempting to sweep away metaphysical explanations.

II

But is not this talk about "mathematical reality" obscure, misleading and, in some ways, an obstacle to obtaining a clear understanding of the nature of mathematics? Wittgenstein, reacting against such a platonic view, wrote, "The mathematician creates *essence*" (RFM, I, 32). To see what is behind Wittgenstein's claim, imagine that we are trying to teach a young person named John the meaning of such words as "circle," "triangle" and "square." We show John many cardboard cutouts, telling him that these objects are all circular, those are triangular, and these are square. Perhaps we also draw a number of figures for him telling him which ones are circular, and so on. Let us suppose that after a while John catches on. He learns to distinguish figures as being circles, triangles, or squares. If you ask him to pick out those figures on the blackboard that are circles, he is able to do so. He also learns to characterize particular figures as being circles, squares, or triangles.

Russell would have claimed, I think, that John must have apprehended the relevant universals. He seems to have thought it obvious that if one understands the meaning of a term one must be acquainted with something for which the term stands. Of course, John does not fully understand the meaning of these shape-terms, since he has not yet learned to refer to these shapes and talk about the shapes; he is able to pick out squares, but he has not yet learned to talk about the property of being square. He has not learned to characterize the property or discuss its relation to other properties. Russell might have claimed that John only dimly apprehended the universal. I shall not criticize this view.

Suppose that a little later John is taught various referring uses of these shape expressions. I do not mean he merely learns to refer to particular figures by means of these shape expressions ("That square is larger than this one"). I mean he also learns to refer to the shape *qua* shape ("Being square differs from being rectangular in that squares must have sides all of which are equal in length"). To use the language of the realist, he learns to refer to the *universal*. At this point, there is little temptation to explain John's newly acquired skills in terms of a clearer intellectual apprehension of the shape universals. Someone might suggest that John has apprehended instead a bit more of the "workings of language," but this does not seem especially apt nor will it do as an explanation. Of course, it is not clear in what respect the acquiring of an intellectual ability requires explanation. But this is another matter.

Imagine now that we show John various connections between squares, angles, sides, and triangles. We show him, for example, that the angles formed by the sides of a square are all equal, not only to each other, but to any angle of any square. He is also brought to see that a diagonal joining opposite vertices of any square must divide the figure into two congruent isosceles triangles. Russell, in "Knowledge by Acquaintance and Knowledge by Description," stated that he did not know how we could know such facts unless we were acquainted with the relevant universals.[14]

But what did take place in John's mind when he perceived these "internal" relations? Or is that important? What I am interested in is what this perceiving amounts to.[15] Perhaps we should ask: In virtue of what do we say John has perceived these "internal" relations? Surely not merely his saying that he sees.

[14] *Mysticism and Logic*, p. 206.

[15] Cf. Wittgenstein's comment: "The proof convinces us of something—though what interests us is, not the mental state of conviction, but the applications attaching to this conviction" (*RFM*, II, 25).

Let us start with the first example. John claims to see that the angles of a square must all be equal. But suppose we show him a figure which at first glance seems to be square but whose angles when measured turn out to be clearly unequal in magnitude, and John does not see that this fact has any relevance to the claim that the figure is a square. I think this would be grounds for thinking John had not really seen the connection between squares and angles.

What I am driving at is this: what is called "apprehending an internal relation" or "seeing a conceptual connection" seems to affect, in one way or another, the way one applies the relevant terms. One might be tempted to say that seeing that the angles of a square must all be equal involves, as Wittgenstein would have put it, "accepting a new criterion" for the application of the term "square," and with this "acceptance," a combination of words would become for John senseless. For if John "accepts" the equal angle criterion for determining squareness, then it would not make sense to him to describe a figure as being a square with angles that are not equal in magnitude. Perhaps one can see now a bit of what lies behind Wittgenstein's statements:

> The mathematical proposition is to show us what it makes *sense* to say.

> The proof constructs a proposition. . . . When we say that the construction must *convince* us of the proposition, that means that it must lead us to apply this in such-and-such a way. That it must determine us to accept this as sense, that not [*RFM*, II, 28].

Assuming that John sees the connection between squares and their angles, we might wonder if John has the same concept of square after this apprehension. It is easy to see that John might now refuse to characterize certain figures as being square which he previously would have so characterized, and this, taken with the consideration above, might lead one, as I think it led Wittgenstein, to claim that seeing a conceptual connection of this sort involves altering one's concepts.[16] One must keep it in mind, however, that John might insist that he means now by "square" the very same thing he meant before being shown this "internal" relation. John might claim that he means the same thing though he now knows a bit more about the nature of squares. In spite of this, according to Wittgenstein, what we have here is a case of concept formation, which brings out an essential role of an informal proof.

Let us start at the beginning with the educating process of John. At first John has, one might say, a primitive concept of square. He is able to do such things as pick out square figures simply by the "look" of the figures, though he has not yet learned to do so by measuring the magnitude of angles and sides. We now show him that squares must have equal angles by showing him, for example, the way various figures which he calls non-square differ from those that he calls square. As a result, he applies the term "square," so Wittgenstein would have put it, in a new way, which shows that he has formed a new concept of square.

The thesis that the role of mathematical proofs is to be understood in terms of the application of mathematical propositions and concept formation explains to some extent Wittgenstein's wanting to say:

> It is essential to mathematics that its signs should also be used in civil life.
>
> It is their use outside mathematics, in other words the *meaning* of the signs, that makes the sign-game mathematics.
>
> Just as it is not a logical conclusion if I change one configuration into another (say one arrangement of chairs into another) unless these configurations have some use in language *besides* the making of these transformations.[17]

---

[16] "The proof changes the grammar of our language, changes our concepts" (RFM, II, 31).

[17] RFM, IV, 2. I use R. Rhees's translation, in "Wittgenstein's Builders," *Proceedings of the Aristotelian Society*, IX (1959–60), 179. Cf. Frege's statement: "It is applicability alone

And this thesis perhaps lies behind Wittgenstein's extreme claim regarding a proved mathematical proposition that "you do not understand the proposition so long as you have not found the application."[18]

Now consider John again. He sees that one of the diagonals of a square divides the square into two congruent isosceles triangles. How is there concept formation in this case? In the light of Wittgenstein's thesis, one might suggest the following considerations. John has a piece of paper which appears to be square. He folds the square along a diagonal by bringing opposite vertices together, but the triangles formed are clearly not congruent. This would show him that the piece of paper was not square. John would be "utilizing a new criterion" for determining squareness which he had "adopted" as a result of being shown the proof.

Suppose that prior to seeing the proof above, John had been trying to construct a square with diagonals dividing the figures into triangles that are not congruent. Of course, after seeing the proof, he would see that there are no squares of this sort, but his seeing this, Wittgenstein argued, is in important respects different from his seeing, say, that there are no unicorns. For though realists like Hardy

---

which elevates arithmetic from a game to the rank of a science. So applicability necessarily belongs to it" (*Translations from the Philosophical Writings of Gottlob Frege*, ed. by P. T. Geach and Max Black [Oxford, 1952] p. 187). In "Wittgenstein's Builders," Rhees makes the interesting comment on Wittgenstein's wondering whether there might be a society in which there was no pure mathematics but only applied mathematics: "Could we still say that they calculated and had proofs[?] . . . These proofs would have nothing to do with 'concept formation,' as the proofs of pure mathematics do. . . . But just for this reason their whole position or rôle as proofs would become obscure. 'What puzzles me,' Wittgenstein said, 'Is how these proofs are *kept*'" (pp. 178–179).

[18] *RFM*, IV, 25. But the concept of applying mathematical propositions, especially when one is dealing with highly abstract mathematical systems, is hardly clear and precise; and this gave Wittgenstein trouble.

and the early Russell would have emphasized the similarities by describing John as exploring the mathematical realm in an attempt to find a certain geometric construction, Wittgenstein continually emphasized the differences and, indeed, felt that such "exploration-discovery" talk obscured the differences. According to Wittgenstein, the discovery that there is no geometric construction of a certain sort involves concept formation, unlike the discovery that there are no unicorns.[19] And in this connection Wittgenstein is reported by Moore to have said:

> "Looking for" a trisection by rule and compasses is not like "looking for" a unicorn, since "There are unicorns" has sense, although in fact there are no unicorns, whereas "There are animals which show on their foreheads a construction by rule and compasses of the trisection of an angle" is just nonsense like "There are animals with three horns, but also with only one horn" . . . by proving that it is impossible to trisect an angle by rule and compasses "we change a man's idea of trisection of an angle" but . . . we should say that what has been proved impossible is the very thing he had been trying to do, because "we are willingly led in this case to identify two different things."[20]

But what two different things do we identify? According to Wittgenstein, as a result of seeing the proof, the person forms a new concept, and we identify the new concept with

[19] Cf. "What I always do seems to be—to emphasize a distinction between the determination of a sense and the employment of a sense" (*RFM*, II, 37).

[20] G. E. Moore, "Wittgenstein's Lectures in 1930–33," *Philosophical Papers* (London, 1959), pp. 304–305. Moore also indicates the kind of view Wittgenstein held at this time concerning arithmetic and concept formation. In this regard, Wittgenstein says of a proof that 200 and 200 added together yield 400: "It defines a new concept: 'the counting of 200 and 200 objects together.' Or, as we could also say: 'A new criterion for nothing's having been lost or added'" (*RFM*, II, 24). We see the stresses and strains on Wittgenstein's thesis as he tries to account for the "motley" of mathematics.

the one he had prior to seeing the proof, though "the old concept is still there in the background" (*RFM*, III, 30).

III

Wittgenstein's construction view of mathematics is perhaps least persuasive when one considers simple calculating examples. One can, of course, *discover* that there is a 9 in the decimal expansion of π by simply calculating. Indeed, one can discover an indefinite number of "mathematical truths" by simply calculating more and more places of the expansion; and the platonic picture of all the digits in the decimal expansion spread out, so to speak, in "mathematical space" comes readily to mind. But for Wittgenstein, "we learn an endless technique . . . what is in question here is not some gigantic extension" (*RFM*, IV, 19), and in exercising my mastery of the technique by calculating, I form new concepts.

Part of the difficulty one finds in trying to understand Wittgenstein's constructivism is generated by his murky use of the term "concept" which for some reason he does not bother to define. Unlike his use of the term "criterion," it has been given little attention despite the intimate connection between *criterion* and *concept*, and despite the prominent role *concept* plays in Wittgenstein's philosophy of mathematics.[21] It is, of course, paradoxical to claim that the proving of a new theorem of mathematics results in new concepts being formed, but perhaps we should consider how Wittgenstein is using the term "concept" ("*Begriff*") in those passages where he discusses proof and concept formation. Unfortunately this is not very clear from

[21] For discussion of what Wittgenstein means (or may have meant) by "criterion," see Norman Malcolm, "Wittgenstein's *Philosophical Investigations*," *Philosophical Review*, LXIII (1954), 530–559; also Rogers Albritton, "On Wittgenstein's Use of the Term 'Criterion,'" *Journal of Philosophy*, LVI (1959), 845–857. [Both articles are reprinted in the present volume.]

the fragmentary notes which comprise the *Remarks on the Foundations of Mathematics*. He does tell us, bringing to mind his early *Tractatus* view, that " 'concept' is something like a picture with which one compares objects" (*RFM*, V, 50). And since the picture analogy seems to have dominated so much of Wittgenstein's thinking on the subject, I shall put the analogy to work in an attempt to clarify a little Wittgenstein's peculiar constructivistic doctrine as it is applied to the case of the expansion of irrational numbers.

In the *Brown Book*, Wittgenstein describes a "language game" involving the use of a table consisting of pictures of objects (a chair, a cup, etc.) with written signs opposite each picture, the table being used in the following way: one person writes one of the signs, and the other, after locating the sign in the table, fetches the object represented in the picture opposite the sign in the table.[22] This language game can be extended, I imagine, so that the tables would be used for actions analogous to, say, referring to objects or describing things. Interestingly enough, Wittgenstein classifies the pictures of this language game among the "instruments of language" and calls "instruments" which are similar in function to the pictures, as for example color samples in a color chart, "patterns" (*BB*, p. 84). This explanation of what he means by "pattern," he admits, is vague. Still, one can understand the transition he makes from these simple pictures and color-chart examples to the claim that in the sentence "He said 'Go to Hell,' " "Go to Hell" is a pattern also (*BB*, p. 84). And from examples of this sort, it is only a short step to "numeral-patterns" like "3.14159265."

Thus, one can see why Wittgenstein might claim that by actually calculating the expansion of π, one can produce new "patterns"—new "instruments of language"—which can be used as objects of comparison to determine, say, whether someone else is correctly expanding π. And notice for Witt-

22 Ludwig Wittgenstein, *The Blue and Brown Books* (Oxford, 1958), p. 82. Cited here as *BB*.

genstein, "the concepts of infinite decimals in mathematical propositions are not concepts of series, but of the unlimited technique of expansion of series" (*RFM*, IV, 19). These "patterns," then, that are constructed and accepted as correct patterns, provide us, according to Wittgenstein, with criteria for recognizing correct expansions.

Let us say that when π was first defined for me, I was given only a rule for calculating the decimal expansion. At that point, I had no "numeral-pattern" to use as a standard of comparison for recognizing correct expansions. Later, by calculating the first four places of the expansion, I produced a "numeral-pattern" which I accepted as correct. Since this provides me with a new criterion for recognizing correct expansion, I would have, on Wittgenstein's view, a new concept of π. However, there is no reason why I must have calculated the "numeral-pattern" in order for this sort of concept formation to occur. A pattern produced by a calculating machine would do just as well. In fact, sequences of numerals produced by machines, copied and printed in mathematical tables are, as I interpret Wittgenstein, concept-forming "patterns" which we frequently do use.[23] Furthermore, there is no reason why one would have to carry such "patterns" around as long as one is able to memorize them.[24] Thus, in discussing calculations, Wittgenstein writes:

> You *find* a new physiognomy. Now you can e.g. memorize or copy it.

> A *new* form has been found, constructed. But it is used to give a new concept together with the old one [*RFM*, III, 47].

[23] Wittgenstein implies, however, that he does not think it is necessary that such machine-calculated results form concepts: people might have adopted a quite different attitude toward machines, not trusting them for calculation purposes (*RFM*, II, 81).

[24] It should be recalled that in the *Brown Book* Wittgenstein considers various cases in which persons compare objects with patterns "from memory" (*BB*, p. 85).

Logicians frequently define a *proof in a formal system* to be a finite sequence of well-formed formulas each of which is one of the axioms or derived according to one of the transformation rules of the system from one or more of the well-formed formulas which precede it in the sequence, calling a proof of this sort the proof *of* the last well-formed formula in the sequence.[25] If we look at proofs in this way,[26] there is a striking similarity between producing such proofs and calculating the expansion of irrational numbers, and this sheds light, I think, on Wittgenstein's comment: "When I said that a proof introduces a new concept, I meant something like: the proof puts a new paradigm among the paradigms of the language" (*RFM*, II, 31).

Wittgenstein's use of the term "rule" is notoriously eccentric, and it is rather surprising to find him claiming that it is in accordance with *ordinary usage* that he applies the term "rule" to the tables of his "language games," ostensive definitions, and similar "instruments" (*BB*, p. 91). (Is Wittgenstein really an "ordinary language philosopher"?) In view of this, however, it should not surprise us that he would call such things as "numeral-patterns" rules also, which gives us an indication of what lies behind his paradoxical claims that, "when I calculate the expansion further, I am deriving new rules which the series obeys" (*RFM*, IV, 11). And in view of the considerations above, perhaps one can get some rough idea of what led Wittgenstein to say, "However queer it sounds, the further expansion of an irrational number is a further expansion of mathematics" (*RFM*, IV, 9).

There is a great deal that is obscure in Wittgenstein's constructivistic talk, however, and some of the obscurity is due to Wittgenstein's imprecise and confusing use of such crucial terms as "concept," "criterion," and "use." Even

25 Cf. A. Church, *Introduction to Mathematical Logic* (Princeton, 1956), I, 49.

26 Cf. "A proof—I might say—is a *single* pattern, at one end of which are written certain sentences and at the other end a sentence (which we call the 'proved proposition')" (*RFM*, I, 28).

Wittgenstein has to admit, at one point, that the meaning of the term "concept" is "by far too vague" (RFM, V, 38). And the vagueness here is not simply a matter of the existence of a vague boundary—there seems to be a great deal in Wittgenstein's use of the term that is unspecified and indeterminate. One wonders, for example, when it would be correct to say, "John and Mary have the *same* concept of square." When John and Mary know precisely the same theorems about squares? In that case, it would be a rather remarkable coincidence if two mathematicians, picked at random, happen to have the same concept of square. And does the fact that two persons have different concepts of π imply that they mean different things by "π"? If this is so, Wittgenstein's doctrine would have the strange consequence that two persons mean different things by "π" simply because one has calculated the decimal expansion to more places than the other.

I do not think that Wittgenstein's thoughts on the subject at this time were especially precise or clear. Very probably, *he* was not satisfied with much of his work in this area, and it is significant that he included so little of this work in his *Philosophical Investigations*.

IV

Michael Dummett contends that to adopt the picture of our creating mathematics as we go along "involves thinking with Wittgenstein that we are *free* in mathematics at every point; no step we take has been forced on us by a necessity external to us, but has been freely chosen."[27] Now what has being free or not free to do with the construction notion of mathematics? Indeed, what does it even mean to say that we are or are not free in mathematics or that some step in a proof has been forced on us? For

[27] Michael Dummett, "Truth," *Proceedings of the Aristotelian Society*, LIX (1958–59), 162.

Wittgenstein did not deny that, in some sense, we are compelled to accept the results of certain proofs.[28]

Suppose, to use Dummett's own example,[29] that we humans are like calculating machines when it comes to doing such things as calculating the decimal expansion of π—we are, so to speak, "compelled" by some mechanism to get certain results. Would this preclude concept formation and the construction model of mathematics? I do not think it is obviously so at all. Wittgenstein himself, it should be noted, considered this analogy, remarking, "If calculating looks to us like the action of a machine, it is *the human being* doing the calculation that is the machine" (*RFM*, III, 20), and, as we have already seen, there are indications that Wittgenstein allowed that calculating machines play a part in concept formation.

When one calculates and gets a certain result, it might appear that one is, in some sense, *compelled* to get the result one gets. Yet Wittgenstein frequently writes as if one were not compelled—at least not "logically compelled" —to get the result one does get. But what is "logical compulsion"? Wittgenstein's discussions on the topic are, for the most part, in terms of metaphors, analogies, and models, again making it difficult to get a precise idea of Wittgenstein's own position. But since I have discussed this aspect of Wittgenstein's philosophy of mathematics elsewhere,[30] I shall pass over it, though a great deal more needs to be said on the topic.

[28] Cf. "And although . . . . proof is something that must be capable of being reproduced *in toto* automatically, still every such production must contain the force of proof, which compels acceptance of the result" (*RFM*, II, 55).

[29] Dummett, "Wittgenstein's Philosophy of Mathematics," p. 331 [p. 420 of the present volume].

[30] C. S. Chihara, "Wittgenstein and Logical Compulsion," *Analysis*, XXI (1961), 136–140 [reprinted in the present volume]. See also in this regard, Dummett, "Truth"; also the symposium in which J. F. Bennett and O. P. Wood discuss "On Being Forced to a Conclusion," *Proceedings of the Aristotelian Society*, Sup. Vol. XXXV (1961), 15–44. I do not think, however, that the position in this symposium criticized by Bennett should be

V

Does accepting Wittgenstein's construction view of mathematics commit one to a rejection of the realist's discovery view? This is not clearly so. Even if one grants the soundness of Wittgenstein's construction doctrine, additional consideration, I think, would have to be brought to bear on the problem to refute the realist's view. Could not a realist allow, without inconsistency, that in calculating decimal expansions one constructs "patterns" which serve as new "instruments of language"? And could not a realist hold that one's "concepts" (in Wittgenstein's sense, whatever that is) may undergo a change as a result of being shown a proof without giving up the notion of a "mathematical reality" awaiting exploration? These questions are difficult to answer, for one thing, because the realist's "mathematical reality" doctrine is so vague and obscure. But then there is a great deal that is obscure on both sides of the issue, for what Wittgenstein says about concepts and mathematical discovery is hardly a model of clarity. And although both sides are able to generate a certain amount of sympathy for their positions by emphasizing

---

identified with Wittgenstein's. In this regard, too, Joseph L. Cowan recently has given a radical interpretation of Wittgenstein's philosophy of logic in suggesting that Wittgenstein claimed "that (in a sense) *there is no such thing as a rule*. There is no such thing as (or state or condition of) understanding a rule, or knowing a rule, or meaning of a rule. There is no such thing as behavior guided by, or even according to, a rule" ("Wittgenstein's Philosophy of Logic," *Philosophical Review*, LXX [1961], 364). Cowan does not cite passages which really support this remarkable interpretation, and I am at a loss to explain how he came to it. But regardless of whether or not Wittgenstein held such a position (and I doubt that he did), I do not understand how Cowan can think sufficient grounds for accepting such a paradoxical metaphysical position have been provided by the considerations that he brings to bear on the question in his article.

particular aspects of "mathematical discovery," the opposition between the sides is much too vague and uncertain for me to make any clear-cut and confident judgment about the matter. I suggest, however, that both sides have exaggerated certain features of our activities at the expense of overlooking other important features, yielding incomplete and distorted philosophical accounts.

WITTGENSTEIN AND
LOGICAL COMPULSION

CHARLES S. CHIHARA

'But am I not compelled, then, to go the way I do
in a chain of inferences?'—Compelled? After all I can
presumably go as I choose!—'But if you want to remain in accord with the rules you *must* go this way.'
—Not at all, I call *this* "accord".—'Then you have
changed the meaning of the word "accord", or the
meaning of the rule.'—No;—who says what "change"
and "remaining the same" mean here? . . . 'But you
surely can't suddenly make a different application of
the law now!' . . . But if I simply reply: 'Different?
—But this surely *isn't* different!'—what will you do?
That is: somebody may reply like a rational person
and yet not be playing our game.

WITTGENSTEIN, *Remarks on the Foundations
of Mathematics*, I, 113, 115

In "The Hardness of the Logical Must,"[1] Edward J.
Nell takes Wittgenstein to be claiming in the above passages that someone might reject outright our ideas of what
constitutes identity, difference, and correctness of inference, and simply refuse to play "the language-game of
logic" as we know it. He then goes on to criticize Wittgenstein, arguing that if a person did not see identity and dif-

From *Analysis*, Vol. XXI (1960–61), pp. 136–140. Reprinted,
in slightly modified form, with the permission of the author and
publisher.

[1] *Analysis*, XXI (1960–61).

ference as we do, a conversation of the sort presented by Wittgenstein could not take place, "for such a person could not *recognize* disagreement."[2]

But what does it mean to say of someone 'He does not see identity and difference as we do'? This question is extremely difficult to answer from the information Nell gives us. We are told not only that the person could not recognize disagreement, but also that he would be unable to "remain either human or alive."[3] I am afraid these hints only make the expression more puzzling.

Did Wittgenstein think that there could be a society with entirely different concepts of "identity" and "difference" from us? What would that be like? In the *Investigations*,[4] he wrote: "The common behaviour of mankind is the system of reference by means of which we interpret an unknown language." But how could we compare a completely different notion of "sameness" with ours? What could we point to as "their concept of sameness"? Why call it "sameness"? We seem to run into insuperable difficulties if we take this line, and the issues become exceedingly murky.

However, I do think Wittgenstein is saying something intelligible in these sections, which at least merits consideration. Many of us are inclined to think we are logically compelled to do certain things, without being at all clear about the nature of this compulsion. If we begin to develop a sequence according to a particular rule, it does seem that we are compelled by the rule to put down a certain number at a particular place in the sequence. As against this, Wittgenstein writes: "—Compelled? After all I can presumably go as I choose!" Here, he is simply pointing out that, in one sense at least, we certainly are not compelled to write down any particular number at a par-

---

[2] *Analysis*, XXI (1960–61), p. 70.
[3] *Ibid.*, p. 71.
[4] I, 206.

ticular place in the sequence, since we are not compelled to write anything: one might just put down one's pencil.

A natural reply to this, which Wittgenstein considers, is: "—But if you want to remain in accord with the rules you *must* go this way." Still, if we are not compelled to take this rather than that as being in accord with the rule, how can we be said to be compelled to get this at all? But if I am compelled to take this and only this as being in accord with the rule, what compels me? Does the meaning of the rule compel? How can the meaning compel me to take this as the meaning? Where is the compulsion to take this as being in accord with the rule? It now seems somewhat difficult to specify just what the compulsion is.

Suppose, in answer to the assertion 'If you want to remain in accord with the rules you *must* go this way,' someone replies as suggested by Wittgenstein: '—Not at all, I call *this* "accord."' Perhaps we would retort 'You can *say* that is in accord with the rules; you can say anything you please; but you surely can't *think* it.' Wittgenstein considers such a reply in section 116 where he writes:

> . . . I am only saying that that means, not: try as he may he can't think, it, but: it is for us an essential part of 'thinking' that—in talking, writing, etc.—he makes *this sort* of transitions. And I say further that the line between what we include in 'thinking' and what we no longer include in 'thinking' is no more a hard and fast one than the line between what is still and what is no longer called "regularity."

Is the real question here what is the meaning of the expression 'being in accord'? For Wittgenstein, such terms as 'accord,' 'agreement' and 'same' are intertwined with 'rule'—"they are cousins."[5]

The point Wittgenstein is making can perhaps be seen in terms of the following example. Suppose you write

[5] *Philosophical Investigations*, I, 224.

down the sequence 3, 6, 9, and say to a person: 'Now continue the sequence doing the same thing as I did in obtaining each term from its preceding term.' Imagine however that the person puts down 13, 17, 21. You immediately interrupt him saying: 'That's not right—you are not doing the same thing as I did.' If, after checking what had been done, he asks 'But what is "doing the same thing"?', it would probably do no good to explain the meaning of the word 'same.' Might there not be various things he could do which could be correctly described as "doing the same thing as you"? And could he not also say 'But I am doing the same thing as you did'? That is, could he not reply like a rational person, and yet not be playing your game? (Here, I take it, not even Mr. Nell would be tempted to interpret 'game' as referring to some "language-game of logic.")

And suppose you then say 'Look—just continue in the obvious way.' Would it not be possible for someone to take it as obvious that since one began the sequence from 0 by adding 3 three times to get the first three terms, one should continue the sequence by adding 4 four times, 5 five times, 6 six times, and so on? Of course, a child who proceeded in this manner on an I.Q. test would probably be marked down for it. But if children were only taught to develop sequences of natural numbers according to rules like: 'add 1 once, add 2 twice, and 3 thrice, etc.,' we would consider continuations of 3, 6, 9, in the above manner to be quite proper.

Imagine there are people, living in a far-away land called Myo, who consider sequences of the above sort to be fundamental and primary. If you asked one of the Myonese to continue the sequence 3, 6, 9, by doing the same thing as you in deriving each term from its preceding term, might he not think that you were following the procedure which we would describe as 'adding 3 three times, 4 four times, etc.'?

Mr. Nell argues: "When one proposes a new or different interpretation, or challenges that of another, one must justify oneself, one must present reasons for one's views. . . ."[6] Now what reasons can we give for saying 3, 6, 9, is obviously to be continued 12, 15, 18, . . . ? I am tempted to say 'It strikes me that way,' but this does not *justify* my interpretation. I suppose if I had to give a reason, I would say to the Myonese something like this: 'As you continue the sequence, you must do something *different*, for the operation of adding 4 was not performed in deriving the second term from the first, or the third from the second. Furthermore, my way of continuing the sequence is clearly the simpler.'

Suppose however that the Myonese, for some reason, very easily learn the operation which we would describe as adding 1 once, adding 2 twice, adding 3 three times, etc. They use the notation "$\overset{n}{\underset{j=a}{*}} j$" for operations of this sort where we would define $\overset{n}{\underset{j=a}{*}} j$ as the operation of adding a a times, adding $(a + 1)(a + 1)$ times, $(a + 2)(a + 2)$ times, ... , n n times. The Myonese use this operation to define sequences of natural numbers, it being understood that one obtains the first term in the sequence by adding to 0 and that successive additions yield successive terms.[7]

Now though $*j$ operations come easily to the Myonese, the operation which we describe as 'adding 3 continually' is extremely difficult for them to master: they have a strong tendency to stop adding 3 after the third time. The opera-

---

[6] Nell, *op. cit.*, p. 68.

[7] The Myonese "$*j$" notation is obviously similar to our "Σj" notation. Of course '$\underset{j=a}{\Sigma} j$' is our symbol for the *sum* $a + (a+1) + (a+2) + . . . + n$, whereas $\overset{n}{\underset{j=a}{*}} j$ stands for either an operation or a sequence.

tion which we describe as 'adding 3 continually' the Myonese see as:

When it comes to developing sequences of natural numbers, *j operations are considered fundamental. The Myonese would not think they were doing anything different in continuing the *same* *j operation, which (they thought) we were performing in putting down 3, 6, 9; and they would not dream that we expected them to perform a very "complicated" operation in which one breaks off the *j operation for j = 3 and begins a "new" *j operation for j = 3.

We are inclined to think situations of the above sort could not arise if a precise mathematical definition of the sequence were given. If we had precisely defined the rule we were following in developing the first three terms of the sequence, there could be no question, it would seem, as to what "doing the same thing" would be. Wittgenstein, rightly or wrongly, assimilated even cases involving precise definitions to the above type of case; and I think it is in connection with such thoughts that Wittgenstein considers the example of the person being taught to develop the sequence of even natural numbers.[9] In explaining the sequence to someone, we might give him the formula '2n: n = 1, 2, 3, . . .' But to be of any use, the pupil would have to know how to apply the formula. And how would we teach him that? Well, we might explain the formula

---

[8] The reader may wonder why the Myonese use the symbol "➘" since it may seem easier to describe the operation as $\overset{3}{\underset{j=3}{*j}}, \overset{3}{\underset{j=3}{*j}}, \overset{3}{\underset{j=3}{*j}}, \ldots$ The Myonese, however, reserve "$\overset{3}{\underset{j=3}{*j}}, \overset{3}{\underset{j=3}{*j}}, \overset{3}{\underset{j=3}{*j}},$ . . ." for the infinite sequence of finite sequences: (3, 6, 9), (3, 6, 9), . . . The arrow also serves to remind the Myonese that they are not to continue the *j operation beyond j=3 but must begin a "new" *j operation for j=3.

[9] *Philosophical Investigations*, I, 185.

in terms of the recursive formula '$A_{n+1} = A_n + 2$: $n = 1, 2, 3, \ldots$' But how would we teach him to apply the latter? Ultimately we come to a situation very much like the one we started with: we give him various examples of applying the formula; we start him off and encourage him to continue; we correct his mistakes, etc. Now isn't it possible that after apparently learning how to apply the formulas, the pupil may suddenly, after reaching, say, 1000, begin to do what *we* would describe as 'adding 4 to the preceding term'? And if we say 'Look—you are making a different application of the formula' is it not possible that he might sincerely reply, 'Different?—But this surely *isn't* different!'? This will probably seem incredible to some people. One may want to ask 'How could anyone think that?' And here, Wittgenstein's comment in section 116, which Mr. Nell so badly misconstrues,[10] does make sense, for there is "something in saying: he can't *think* it. One is trying e.g. to say: he can't fill it with personal content; he can't really go *along with it*—personally, with his intelligence." It strikes us as incredible that anyone should take the explanations in such an odd way; that way of taking the explanations makes no sense to us.[11] "It is like when one says: this sequence of notes makes no sense, I can't sing it with expression. I cannot *respond* to it. Or, what comes to the same thing here: I don't respond to it."[12]

Of course, cases of such deviant reactions to explanations and training are necessarily rare; but they are not impossible. And a person who frequently took our utterances, signs, explanations and the like so differently from the rest of us would most certainly "get into conflict, e.g. with society; and also with other practical consequences."[13]

That these considerations by no means settle the issue

[10] Nell, *op. cit.*, p. 72.
[11] It is not difficult, however, to fill in the example, as in the previous case, in such a way that this way of taking the explanations would not strike us as being so unintelligible.
[12] *Remarks on the Foundations of Mathematics*, I, 116.
[13] *Ibid.*

Wittgenstein certainly realized (as can be seen from the fact that he returned again and again to this puzzling notion of logical compulsion). Still, what he says in these sections of the *Remarks* throws much light on many of his paradoxical statements about the nature of logic and mathematics. And whether Wittgenstein is right or wrong, I think what he says here is worth serious examination and should not be set aside as the utter nonsense Mr. Nell would have us believe it to be.

WITTGENSTEIN AND
LOGICAL NECESSITY

BARRY STROUD

Michael Dummett has described Wittgenstein's account of logical necessity as a "full-blooded conventionalism."[1] On this view, the source of the necessity of any necessary statement is "our having expressly decided to treat that very statement as unassailable" (p. 329 [p. 426 above]). Even faced with a rigorous mathematical proof:

> at each step we are free to choose to accept or reject the proof; there is nothing in our formulation of the axioms and of the rules of inference, and nothing in our minds when we accepted these before the proof was given, which of itself shows whether we shall accept the proof or not; and hence there is nothing which *forces* us to accept the proof. If we accept the proof, we confer necessity on the theorem proved; we "put it in the archives" and will count nothing as telling against it. In doing this we are making a new decision, and not merely making explicit a decision we had already made implicitly (p. 330 [p. 427]).

From *The Philosophical Review*, Vol. LXXIV (1965), pp. 504–518. Reprinted with the permission of the author and editors.
[1] Michael Dummett, "Wittgenstein's Philosophy of Mathematics," *Philosophical Review*, LXVIII (1959), 324 ff [pp. 420–447 of the present volume]. Page numbers alone in parentheses in the text always refer to this article. References to Wittgenstein's writings always contain an abbreviation of the title of the book in question. "PI" will refer to Wittgenstein's *Philosophical Investigations* (New York, 1953), and unless otherwise indicated, parenthetical references will be to the numbered sections of Pt. I. "RFM" will refer to *Remarks on the Foundations of Mathematics* (Oxford, 1956).

This implies that it is possible for someone to accept the axioms and the rules of inference and yet to reject the proof, without having failed to understand those axioms or rules. But, Dummett objects:

> We want to say that we do not know what it would be like for someone who, by ordinary criteria, already understood the concepts employed, to reject this proof . . . . The examples given in Wittgenstein's book are—amazingly for him—thin and unconvincing. I think that this is a fairly sure sign that there is something wrong with Wittgenstein's account (p. 333 [p. 430]).

Dummett is obviously on strong ground here—it seems impossible to understand this alleged possibility—but I think Wittgenstein would agree. His examples are not designed to show that we do understand this. What is important for the problem of logical necessity is to explain what makes the denial of a necessary truth "impossible" or "unintelligible." It is not enough to say that it is "logically impossible," since an explanation of logical necessity is just what is in question. Dummett appears to agree with this (pp. 328–329 [pp. 424–426 above]). In the rest of this paper I shall try to say what, according to Wittgenstein, is responsible for the unintelligibility in such cases.

In defending the claim that he is not committed to saying that everybody could infer in any way at all, Wittgenstein points out that it is essential to inferring, calculating, counting, and so forth, that not just any result is allowed as correct. If everybody continues the series as he likes, or infers just any way at all, then "we shan't call it 'continuing the series' and also presumably not 'inference'" (*RFM*, I, 116). General agreement among people as to the correct results of inferences or calculations and general agreement in the results that one gets oneself at different times are both necessary in order for there to be inferring or calculating at all (*RFM*, II, 66, 73). The same holds for counting, continuing a series, and so on. These are all activities in which the possibility of different results at different times and places is not left open. It is just here that a calculation differs from an experiment, where people at different times and places can get different results.

These remarks suggest that the source of necessity in inferring or calculating is simply that any activity in which just any results were allowed would not be *called* "inferring," "calculating," and so forth. In the case of drawing logical conclusions:

> The steps which are not brought in question are logical inferences. But the reason why they are not brought in question is not that they "certainly correspond to the truth"—or something of the sort—no, it is just this that is called "thinking," "speaking," "inferring," "arguing" [*RFM*, I, 155].

This looks like the standard claim that all necessity finds its source in definitions or in the meanings of words. In inferring, one must write down "q" after "$p \supset q$" and "p" because to do otherwise is to cease to infer correctly, and correct inference is just "defined" by the laws of logic. That is what we call correct inference. This would presumably mean that, since it is possible for something else to be meant by "correct inference," it would also be possible for something else to be the conclusion. Despite suggestions of this "standard conventionalism" in Wittgenstein, I agree with Dummett that he does not hold such a view, although it is not always easy to see how what he says differs from it.

The main target of Wittgenstein's writings on necessity is the Platonism of Frege and the early Russell. In this respect he and the logical positivists are alike. According to Platonism it would be impossible for someone, when given the order "Add 2," to write down all the same numerals as we do up to "1000" and then to go on "1004, 1008, . . . ," and still be able to justify his going on in that way. It would be impossible because it is simply wrong, in continuing the series "+ 2," to write down "1004" right after "1000"; that is not, in fact, the next

member of the series. So the pupil must either have misunderstood the instructions or have made a mistake. Anyone who puts anything other than "1002" is wrong and
should be declared an idiot or an incorrigible if he persists
in his perversity. As Frege puts it: "here we have a hitherto
unknown kind of insanity."[2]

The conventionalist's opposition to Platonism consists
primarily in showing that our present ways of inferring,
counting, calculating, and so forth, are not the only possible ones. But the standard conventionalist would also reject the alleged possibility on the grounds that the description of such a state of affairs is contradictory. If the person
has understood the instructions, if he has just written
down "1000," and if he is to continue following the instructions, then he *must* write down "1002." Of course, he
is free not to continue the series at all, or to claim that he
has been following instructions like "Add 2 up to 1000, 4
up to 2000," and so forth, but it is logically impossible
(involves a contradiction) for him to have understood the
instructions correctly and to write down "1004" right after
"1000." His claiming that "1004" is the correct step is a
sufficient condition of his having abandoned the ordinary
sense attached to the order "Add 2." That it is correct to
write "1002" is already contained in the meaning of those
instructions, and once one has agreed to follow them, then
because they mean what they do there are certain steps
which one logically must take.

The crucial notion in this conventionalistic theory is
that of understanding the meaning of a word or a rule,
and this is something to which Wittgenstein devotes a
great deal of attention. Part of his interest in it is in the
sense, if any, in which someone's having understood the
instructions somehow logically guarantees that he will
write down "1002" right after "1000." If this is logically
guaranteed, then it would seem that his going on "1004,
1008, . . ." could be due only to misunderstanding or to

2 G. Frege, *Grundgesetze der Arithmetik* (Jena, 1903), p. xvi.

a mistake; in any event, he could not have understood correctly. But what is it to understand correctly? What determines which move is the correct one at a given point? The answer would appear to be that the way the order was meant, or what was meant by the person giving the order, determines which steps are correct. But again, Wittgenstein asks, what shows which way the order was meant? It is not the case that the teacher very quickly thought of each particular step which he wanted the pupil to take, and even if he did, that would not show that "meaning 1002, 1004, . . ." meant "thinking of 1002, 1004, . . ." (*PI*, 692). Rather, what the order means will be shown in the ways we use it, in what we do in following it, in the ways we are taught to use it, and so on (*RFM*, I, 2).

If someone who had learned to continue various series just as we do began to differ from us when he went beyond any point he had reached in his training, would it follow that he simply had not understood the instructions? If he continued to do this, must we say that he is unintelligent, perhaps idiotic? Wittgenstein tries as follows to suggest negative answers to these questions:

> If my reply is: "Oh yes of course, *that* is how I was applying it!" or: "Oh! That's how I ought to have applied it—!"; then I am playing your game. But if I simply reply: "Different?—But this surely *isn't* different!"—what will you do? That is: somebody may reply like a rational person and yet not be playing our game [*RFM*, I, 115].

He tries to show that not all cases of deviating from what we expect or from what we all do in continuing the series can be put down to simple misunderstanding, stupidity, or deliberate perversity on the part of the pupil. It is almost certain in any particular case we come across that some discoverable mistake has occurred, and that the pupil will come to recognize this. But *must* he do so? Is there no possibility other than those mentioned above? The example is intended to suggest that there is. But the important, and difficult, problem is to say exactly what this alleged possibility comes to. Although Frege said it would be a new kind of insanity, "he never said what this 'insanity' would really be like" (*RFM*, I, 151). To see what it would be like is to understand on what our being compelled in inferring, calculating, counting, and so forth, rests.

The person who continues the series "1004, 1008, . . ." is described as "finding it natural" to go on in that way; it "strikes him as the same" as he has done earlier. In trying to get such a person to continue the series as we do it would no longer be useful for us to go through the training and give him the old explanations over again. And providing him with a rule precisely formulated in mathematical terms would not avoid the difficulties, since it is just the possibility of his understanding such a rule that is in question.

> In such a case we might say, perhaps: It comes natural to this person to understand our order with our explanations as *we* should understand the order: "Add 2 up to 1000, 4 up to 2000, 6 up to 3000, and so on."

> Such a case would present similarities with one in which a person naturally reacted to the gesture of pointing with the hand by looking in the direction of the line from finger-tip to wrist, not from wrist to finger-tip [*PI*, 185].

For Wittgenstein, it will not be enough to object that, if we are patient and careful, surely we could eventually get the pupil to see that he is to make the same move after "1000" as before—that he is not to change the size of the steps. He is convinced that he is making the same move, and "who says what 'change' and 'remaining the same' mean here" (*RFM*, I, 113)? One is inclined to reply, I think, that nobody *says* what is the same and what is different; it is just a fact that the pupil is wrong in supposing that going on "1004, 1008, . . ." is doing the same as he was in writing down "2, 4, 6, ..." But is there some discoverable fact of which we are aware, and which he is missing? What sort of fact is it, and how could he be brought to acknowledge it? Trying to explain to him that he has not gone on in the same way would be like trying to teach someone how to carry out the order "Go this way" when I point in a particular direction. If that person naturally reacted to the gesture of pointing by looking in the direction of the line from fingertip to wrist, it would not be enough to say to him, "If I point this way (pointing with my right hand) I mean that you should go *this* way (pointing with my left hand in the same direction)." Isn't every explanation of how someone should follow an arrow in the position of another arrow (*BB*, p. 97)?

Or, to choose another example, suppose we come across some people who find it natural to sell wood, not by cubic measure or board feet as we do, but at a price proportionate to the area covered by the pile of wood, and they pay no attention to the height of the pile.

> How could I show them that—as I should say—you don't really buy more wood if you buy a pile covering a bigger area?—I should, for instance, take a pile which was small by their ideas and, by laying the logs around, change it into a "big" one. This *might* convince them—but perhaps they would say: "Yes, now it's a *lot* of wood and costs more"—and that would be the end of the matter [*RFM*, I, 149].

This case is analogous to that of trying to get the deviant pupil to see that the next step after "1000" is really "1002."[3] But can we describe what these people do as

---

[3] There are some important features of the two cases as presented which are not analogous. We are imagining a single pupil who makes a single deviant move after having done exactly as we had expected up till now, whereas the example of the wood-sellers is presented from the outset as one in which we come across a whole, flourishing society. Consequently, what appears to be a sudden and inexplicable change, or an individual aberration, in the former case is not present in the latter. Furthermore, and crucially, the society of wood-sellers is not our own, but the

"selling wood the wrong way"? Is it a way whose "incorrectness" we could point out to them? And surely it is not
logically impossible for there to be such people: the example does not contain a hidden contradiction.

The natural reply to this example is that it shows only
that such people mean by "a lot of wood" and "a little
wood" something different from what we mean by it, and
similarly, as Dummett suggests, anyone who agrees with
us in accepting all the steps in a proof but who then re-
fuses to accept what we all accept as the conclusion must
be blind to the meaning that has already been given to
the words in the premises or in previous proofs. It seems
as if he could not remain faithful to the meanings of
those words and still reject the conclusion. Dummett concludes from this that he is simply *deciding* to accept some
particular statement as necessary in complete isolation
from everything else he has accepted. This is why Wittgenstein is called a "full-blooded" conventionalist. The
strange people Wittgenstein describes differ from us only
in having "adopted different conventions." But does it follow from the case which Wittgenstein tries to construct
that the deviant pupil simply chooses to write "1004" and
that his choice makes that the correct step? Can the people
in Wittgenstein's examples properly be said to differ from
us only in having adopted different conventions? I think
the answer is "No." One thing implied by saying that we
have adopted, or are following, a convention is that there
are alternatives which we could adopt in its place. But in
the case of writing "1002" right after "1000" there appear
to be no alternatives open to us. It seems impossible to
understand how we could "adopt the convention" that
writing "998, 1000, 1004, . . ." is going on in the same

strange pupil has apparently sprung up right in our midst. I think
that these and other disanalogies can be avoided by presenting
both cases in the same way from the beginning, although Wittgenstein never does this. (Some of the difficulties which these
differences appear to create for the later stages of my argument
were pointed out to me by Professor Stanley Cavell.)

way, or taking steps of the same size. Surely if writing "998, 1000, 1002, . . ." is not taking steps of the same size, then nothing is.

I have been trying to suggest so far that for Wittgenstein such "alternatives" are not inconceivable or unimaginable because they involve or lead to a logical contradiction. Just as there is no logical contradiction involved in the supposition that people might sell wood, and defend their doing so, in the way described earlier, so there is no logical contradiction involved in supposing that someone might agree with us in all uses of words or in all steps of a proof up to the present, and that he should now accept something different from what we all accept as the conclusion, without being simply idiotic or deliberately perverse. Wittgenstein's examples are designed to show this; it is part of the attack on Platonism. But as long as such alternatives are inconceivable in whatever sense, it looks as if Dummett is right in pointing out that "we do not know what it would be like for someone who, by ordinary criteria, already understood the concepts employed, to reject the proof." And if we do not know what this would be like, how can we find at all plausible Wittgenstein's purported examples of someone who "replies like a rational person" and yet is not "playing our game"? So it appears that, as Dummett says, Wittgenstein's examples are "thin and unconvincing," as they presumably must be if they are supposed to be examples of something that is unimaginable or inconceivable.

This seems to present the interpreter of Wittgenstein with a choice between two alternatives. Either Wittgenstein has not succeeded in giving any clear or intelligible examples of people whose ways of calculating, and so forth, are radically different from ours, and therefore he has not begun to support his anti-Platonistic account of logical necessity; or else he has succeeded in giving intelligible, perhaps even convincing, examples which commit him to a "full-blooded conventionalism." And if the latter is the case, then Dummett's successful attack on radical conven-

tionalism will be equally successful against Wittgenstein.
But this choice is not an exhaustive one. There can be
plausible examples to show the possibility of ways of
counting, inferring, calculating, and so forth, different from
ours, but which do not imply that our doing these things
as we do is solely a result of our abiding by, or having
adopted, certain more or less arbitrary conventions to
which there are clear and intelligible alternatives. Nor do
such examples imply that "at each step we are free to
accept or reject the proof" or that "a statement's being
necessarily true is solely a result of our having decided to
treat that very statement as unassailable." But at one point
Wittgenstein says:

> So much is clear: when someone says: "If you follow
> the rule, it *must* be like this," he has not any *clear*
> concept of what experience would correspond to the
> opposite.
>
> Or again: he has not any clear concept of what it
> would be like for it to be otherwise. And this is very
> important [*RFM*, III, 29].

If this is true, how can he hope to be successful in giving
examples of what it would be like for it to be otherwise,
while still maintaining that there is logical necessity in
such cases? How can he have it both ways? The solution to
this dilemma is to be found in the explanation of why we
do not have any clear concept of the opposite in the case
of logical necessity, and why Wittgenstein speaks of our
not having a *clear* concept here. How could we have any
concept at all?

Wittgenstein gives many examples of people whose ways
of inferring, counting, calculating, and so forth, are different in significant ways from ours. As well as the wood-
sellers mentioned earlier, there might be others who sell
wood at a price equal to the labor of felling the timber,
measured by the age and strength of the woodsman. Or
perhaps each buyer pays the same however much he takes
(*RFM*, I, 147). Also, there might be people who measured

with soft rubber rulers, or with rulers which expanded to
an extraordinary extent when slightly heated (*RFM*, I,
5). Or suppose that people in their calculations sometimes
divided by "(n-n)" and yet were not bothered by the results. They would be like people who did not prepare lists
of names systematically (for example, alphabetically), and
so in some lists some names would appear more than once,
but they accept this without worrying (*RFM*, V, 8). Or
there might be people who count, but when they want to
know numbers for various practical purposes ask certain
other people who, having had the practical problem explained to them, shut their eyes and let the appropriate
number come to them (*RFM*, V, 14). There are many
more such examples, merely mentioned or briefly discussed, throughout Wittgenstein's *Remarks*.[4] They are all
intended to be analogous in various ways to the "possibility" that someone might go on "1004" right after "1000"
in continuing the series "+2."

When first presented with these examples it seems that
we can understand them, and that we can come to know
what such people would be like. We do not happen to do
things in these strange ways, but, it seems, we could. If
these examples represent clear alternatives, then why
doesn't it follow that our calculating, counting, measuring, and so forth, as we do is purely a matter of convention?
If this is not a matter of convention, how can these examples be perfectly intelligible to us? In suggesting answers
to these questions I will have begun to show how Wittgenstein can escape between the horns of the above
dilemma.

When we look more closely at the examples, are they
really as intelligible as they seemed at first? For instance,
consider the people who sell wood at a price proportionate
to the area covered by the pile of wood and who defend
their doing so in the way described earlier. Surely they
would have to believe that a one-by-six-inch board all of

[4] E.g., *RFM*, I, 136, 139, 152, 168; II, 76, 78, 81, 84; III,
15, 17; IV, 5; V, 6, 12, 27, 29, 36, 42, 43, 44.

a sudden increased in size or quantity when it was turned from resting on its one-inch edge to resting on its six-inch side. And what would the relation between quantity and weight possibly be for such people? A man could buy as much wood as he could possibly lift, only to find, upon dropping it, that he had just lifted more wood than he could possibly lift. Or is there more wood, but the same weight? Or perhaps these people do not understand the expressions "more" and "less" at all. They must, if they can say, "Now it's a lot of wood, and costs more." And do these people think of themselves as shrinking when they shift from standing on both feet to standing on one? Also, it would be possible for a house that is twice as large as another built on exactly the same plan to contain much less wood. How much wood is bought need have no connection with how much wood is needed for building the house. And so on. Problems involved in understanding what it would be like to sell wood in this way can be multiplied indefinitely.

If so, then so far we do not really know what it would be like for us to sell wood, and to try to justify our doing so, in the way Wittgenstein has described. And we have already noted the difficulties in trying to understand the example of continuing the series "+2." I think the initial intelligibility and strength of Wittgenstein's examples derive from their being severely isolated or restricted. We think we can understand and accept them as representing genuine alternatives only because the wider-reaching consequences of counting, calculating, and so forth, in these deviant ways are not brought out explicitly. When we try to trace out the implications of behaving like that consistently and quite generally, our understanding of the alleged possibilities diminishes. I suspect that this would happen with most, if not all, of Wittgenstein's examples, but I do not need to prove this in general, since if my interpretation is right these examples will fulfill their intended role whether or not this point holds.

The reason for this progressive decrease in intelligibility,

I think, is that the attempt to get a clearer understanding of what it would be like to be one of these people and to live in their world inevitably leads us to abandon more and more of our own familiar world and the ways of thinking about it upon which our understanding rests. The more successful we are in projecting ourselves into such a world, the less we will have left in terms of which we can find it intelligible. In trying to understand these alleged possibilities, we constantly come across more and more difficulties, more and more questions which must be answered before we can understand them. But this is not to say that we do not understand them because they are "meaningless" or "contradictory," or because what they purport to represent is "logically impossible."

Wittgenstein's examples are intended to oppose Platonism by showing that calculating, counting, inferring, and so forth, might have been done differently. But this implies no more than that the inhabitants of the earth might have engaged in those practices in accordance with rules which are different from those we actually follow. It is in that sense a contingent fact that calculating, inferring, and so forth, are carried out in the ways that they are—just as it is a contingent fact that there is such a thing as calculating or inferring at all. But we can understand and acknowledge the contingency of this fact, and hence the possibility of different ways of calculating, and so forth, without understanding what those different ways might have been. If so, then it does not follow that those rules by which calculating, and so forth, might have been carried out constitute a set of genuine alternatives open to us among which we could choose, or even among which we could have chosen. The only sense that has been given to the claim that "somebody may reply like a rational person and yet not be playing our game" is that there might have been different sorts of beings from us, that the inhabitants of the earth might have come to think and behave in ways different from their actual ones. But this does not imply that we are free to put whatever we like after "1000" when

given the instructions "Add 2," or that our deciding to put
"1002" is what makes that the correct step. Consequently,
Wittgenstein's examples do not commit him to a "radical
conventionalism" in Dummett's sense. In trying to explain
more fully why he is not committed to this I will return to
the sense in which he can be called a "conventionalist."

In several places Wittgenstein describes what he is doing
in some such way as this:

> What we are supplying are really remarks on the natu-
> ral history of man: not curiosities however, but rather
> observations on facts which no-one has doubted, and
> which have only gone unremarked because they are al-
> ways before our eyes [RFM, I, 141].

What facts does he have in mind here, and what role do
they play in his account of logical necessity? The reason
for calling them "facts of our natural history" is to emphasize both what I have called their contingency—that is,
that they might not have obtained—and the fact that they
are somehow "constitutive" of mankind—that is, that their
obtaining is what is responsible for human nature's being
what it is.

Part of human behavior consists of calculating sums,
distances, quantities, of making inferences, drawing conclusions, and so forth. It is a fact that we engage in such
practices: "mathematics is after all an anthropological
phenomenon" (RFM, V, 26). There are various facts
which make it possible for calculating to occur at all. For
example, our memories are generally good enough for us
not to take numbers twice in counting up to 12, and not
to leave any out (RFM, V, 2); in correlating two groups
of five strokes we practically always can do so without
remainder (RFM, I, 64); somebody who has learned to
calculate never goes on getting different results, in a given
multiplication, from what is in the arithmetic books
(RFM, I, 112); and so on. The inhabitants of the earth
might have lacked these and other simple abilities, and if

so there would be no such thing as calculating at all. In that way the possibility of calculating depends on such contingent facts. These are examples of what Wittgenstein calls the "physical," "psychological," and "physiological" facts which make activities such as calculating possible (*RFM*, V, 1, 15).

A contingent fact which is responsible for our calculating as we actually do is the fact that we take "1002, 1004, . . ." to be going on in the same way as putting down "996, 998, 1000, ..." It is a fact that we naturally go on in this way, but people might not have done so. Since they might naturally have followed the rule in a different way, our rules alone do not logically guarantee that they will not be taken or understood in deviant ways. A rule itself does not make "strange" ways of following it impossible, since a rule is not something which stands apart from our understanding of it, and which mysteriously contains within it all of its future applications. How we naturally understand and follow the rule determines which applications of it are correct, and the way a rule is followed will depend in part on what we take to be "going on in the same way." "The use of the word 'rule' and the use of the word 'same' are interwoven" (*PI*, 225). It is because people might not share our natural reactions, or might not be in accord with us in their "judgments of sameness" that their understanding the instructions does not rule out their taking a different step from ours at some point while still finding what they have done to be in accord with the rule. So understanding the rule in the way we do depends on such things as finding it natural to go on to "1002" right after "1000." That we take just the step we do here is a contingent fact, but it is not the result of a decision; it is not a convention to which there are alternatives among which we could choose. And that we share any such "judgments" at all (whatever they might be) is also a contingent fact, but without this agreement there would be no understanding of any rules at all.

If language is to be a means of communication there must be agreement not only in definitions but also (queer as this may sound) in judgments. This seems to abolish logic, but does not do so [*PI*, 242].

Those described as "not playing our game" are the people who are not in accord with us in the "judgments" on which the possibility of language and communication rests. Wittgenstein's examples of the possibility of people like this serve to bring out the contingency of the fact that, as things are, we are in accord in these "judgments." Anyone who did not go on as we do need not be simply continuing a different series (for example, "Add 2 up to 1000, 4 up to 2000," and so forth), and in that way be "playing a game" different from the one we happen to be playing; nor need he have misunderstood the instructions in a way that can be pointed out to him by more careful explanations. But someone like this would not be fully intelligible to us. Our relation to him would be like our relation to people who naturally reacted to the gesture of pointing by looking in the direction of the line from fingertip to wrist, or who sold wood in the way described earlier. It is not simply that they happen to have chosen to do things one way, and we happen to have chosen to do them differently, but that they would be different sorts of beings from us, beings which we could not understand and with which we could not enter into meaningful communication. They would ultimately be unfathomable to us (compare, for example, *RFM*, I, 34, 61, 66, 152). In order to have a "clear concept" of what it would be like to think and behave as they do we would have to be able to abandon many, if not all, of those "judgments" on which our being able to think or conceive of anything at all rests.

What I have been saying will explain what would otherwise be a puzzling distinction which Wittgenstein makes in a well-known passage:

I am not saying: if such-and-such facts of nature were different people would have different concepts (in the sense of a hypothesis). But: if anyone believes that certain concepts are absolutely the correct ones, and that having different ones would mean not realizing something that we realize—then let him imagine certain very general facts of nature to be different from what we are used to, and the formation of concepts different from the usual ones will become intelligible to him [*PI*, p. 230].

The point of Wittgenstein's examples of people who do not "play our game" is only to show that our having the concepts and practices we have is dependent upon certain facts which might not have obtained. They show only that "the formation of concepts different from the usual ones" is intelligible to us; but it does not follow from this that those concepts themselves are intelligible to us. And since the intelligibility of alternative concepts and practices is required by the thesis of radical conventionalism which Dummett ascribes to Wittgenstein, I think that thesis is not borne out by Wittgenstein's examples.

The "shared judgments" (for example, of sameness) upon which our being able to communicate rests, and which are responsible for our calculating, inferring, and so forth, as we do are not properly seen, then, as the results of free decisions in the manner of the logical positivists. They might have been different and, if they had been, then calculating, inferring, and so forth, would have been done differently. But this does not make them conventions in the positivists' sense. In defending the claim that we had made the correct move after "1000" in following the rule "Add 2" we could ultimately get back to something like our "shared judgment" that putting down "1002" is doing the same as we were doing earlier. There is nothing further we could appeal to. These "judgments" represent the limits of our knowledge, and thus they have a role similar to the explicit conventions of the positivists.

From what has been said so far it might still look as if our "sharing judgments" is nothing more than our all agreeing that certain propositions are true or unassailable. But

the "agreement" of which Wittgenstein speaks here is not
the unanimous acceptance of a particular truth or set of
truths.

> "So you are saying that human agreement decides
> what is true and what is false?"—It is what human be-
> ings *say* that is true and false; and they agree in the
> *language* they use. That is not agreement in opinions
> but in form of life [*PI*, 241].

This "agreement" is the universal accord of human beings
in behaving in certain ways—those "natural reactions"
which we all share, or those human practices the engaging
in which makes a creature human. Those are the "facts of
our natural history" which he is appealing to. The correctness of steps in calculating is not ultimately established on
the basis of their agreeing with or being entailed by certain
truths which we have accepted without foundation, or
which are "self-evident":

> The limits of empiricism are not assumptions un-
> guaranteed, or intuitively known to be correct: they
> are ways in which we make comparisons and in which
> we act [*RFM*, V, 18].

This distinguishes Wittgenstein both from the Platonist
and from the standard conventionalist. I shall comment
on only one other aspect of this difference.

I have said that it is a "fact of our natural history" in
Wittgenstein's sense that we agree in finding certain steps
in following a rule "doing the same." In some cases we all
naturally go on in the same way from the steps which have
already been taken. This is what makes it possible for us
to follow any rules at all.

> And does this mean e.g. that the definition of
> "same" would be this: same is what all or most hu-
> man beings with one voice take for the same?—Of
> course not.
> For of course I don't make use of the agreement of
> human beings to affirm identity. What criterion do
> you use, then? None at all [*RFM*, V, 33].

But if there is no criterion for the truth of assertions of identity, how can we know they are true? Without a proof to the contrary, might not all human beings, for all their agreement, be wrong in supposing that writing "1002" is going on in the same way as writing "1000" after "998"? Wittgenstein replies that "to use a word without a justification does not mean to use it wrongfully" (*RFM*, V, 33). And in this case, at this stage, there is no "justification" of the sort the empiricist seeks. But why not?

The correctness of particular calculations, inferences, and so forth, is decided by appeal to the rules, but can't we also ask whether those rules themselves are correct, whether our techniques of calculation, inference, and so forth, are the correct ones?

> The danger here, I believe, is one of giving a justification of our procedure when there is no such thing as a justification and we ought simply to have said: *that's how we do it* [*RFM*, II, 74].

The ultimate appeal in seeking a "foundation" for our procedures of calculating, inferring, and so forth, can only be to "ways in which we make comparisons and in which we act." That is all that an account of the "foundation" or "source" of logical necessity can achieve. This perhaps helps to explain the point of passages like this:

> What has to be accepted, the given, is—so one could say—*forms of life* [*PI*, p. 226].

Because these procedures cannot be given a "justification" it does not follow that they are shaky or unreliable, or that we are courting trouble if we decide to engage in them. We do not decide to accept or reject them at all, any more than we decide to be human beings as opposed to trees. To ask whether our human practices or forms of life themselves are "correct" or "justified" is to ask whether we are "correct" or "justified" in being the sorts of things we are.

At the end of his paper Dummett recommends inter-

posing between the Platonist and constructivist pictures
of thought and reality an intermediate picture

> of objects springing into being in response to our
> probing. We do not *make* the objects but must accept
> them as we find them (this corresponds to the proof
> imposing itself on us); but they were not already
> there for our statements to be true or false of before
> we carried out the investigations which brought them
> into being (p. 348 [p. 447 above]).

As far as I understand this, it seems to be just the picture
to be derived from Wittgenstein if my interpretation is in
general correct. Logical necessity, he says, is not like rails
that stretch to infinity and compel us always to go in one
and only one way; but neither is it the case that we are not
compelled at all. Rather, there are the rails we have already traveled, and we can extend them beyond the present point only by depending on those that already exist.
In order for the rails to be navigable they must be extended in smooth and natural ways; how they are to be
continued is to that extent determined by the route of
those rails which are already there. I have been primarily
concerned to explain the sense in which we are "responsible" for the ways in which the rails are extended, without
destroying anything that could properly be called their objectivity.

BIBLIOGRAPHY[1]

ABBREVIATIONS

A	*Analysis*
AJP	*Australasian Journal of Philosophy*
APQ	*American Philosophical Quarterly*
BJPS	*British Journal for the Philosophy of Science*
I	*Inquiry*
JP	*Journal of Philosophy*
M	*Mind*
P	*Philosophy*
PAS	*Proceedings of the Aristotelian Society*
PASS	*Proceedings of the Aristotelian Society, Supplementary volume*
PPR	*Philosophy and Phenomenological Research*
PQ	*Philosophical Quarterly*
PR	*Philosophical Review*
PS(Ire.)	*Philosophical Studies, Ireland*
RM	*Review of Metaphysics*
SJP	*Southern Journal of Philosophy*

I. CORPUS (ARRANGED BY DATE OF AUTHORSHIP)

(1913)[2] "Notes on Logic, September 1913," ed. H. T.

[1] I am indebted to Professors Rogers Albritton and K. T. Fann for most of the material contained in this bibliography. Students interested in a more nearly complete bibliography than that which follows here will find one, compiled by Professor Fann, in a forthcoming issue of the *International Philosophical Quarterly*.

[2] On the text of these notes, cf. G. E. M. Anscombe, R. Rhees, and G. H. von Wright, "Letter to the Editor," *JP*, LIV (1957), p. 484; *Notebooks, 1914–1916*, p. 93; P. W. Kurtz, "Letter to the Editor," *JP* LIX (1962), pp. 78–79.

Costello, *JP* LIV (1957), pp. 230–245; in *Notebooks*, *1914–1916*, below, pp. 93–106.

(1914) "Notes Dictated to G. E. Moore in Norway, April 1914," in *Notebooks*, *1914–1916*, below, pp. 107–118.

(1914–16) *Notebooks*, *1914–1916*, ed. G. H. von Wright and G. E. M. Anscombe, tr. G. E. M. Anscombe. Oxford: Basil Blackwell; New York, Harper & Row, 1961.

(1918) *Logisch-Philosophische Abhandlung*, in *Annalen der Naturphilosophie* (ed. M. Ostwald), XIV, Hefte 3–4 (1921), pp. 185–262; *Tractatus Logico-Philosophicus*, German-English, tr. into English by C. K. Ogden and F. P. Ramsey, intr. by B. Russell (London: Routledge & Kegan Paul, 1922, corr. reprint 1933, reprint with index by M. Black, 1955); tr. into English by D. F. Pears and B. F. McGuinness (London: Routledge & Kegan Paul; New York: Humanities Press, 1961).

(1926) *Wörterbuch für Volksschulen*. Vienna: Hölder-Pichler-Tempsky A. G., 1926.

(1929) "Some Remarks on Logical Form," *PASS*, IX (1929), pp. 162–171.

(1929 or 1930) "A Lecture on Ethics," *PR*, LXXIV (1965), pp. 3–12.

(1930) *Philosophische Bemerkungen*, ed. R. Rhees. Oxford: Basil Blackwell, 1964.

(1930–33) "Wittgenstein's Lectures in 1930–33," by G. E. Moore. *M*, LXIII (1954), pp. 1–15, 289–316, LXIV (1955), pp. 1–27; cf. "Two Corrections," *M*, LXIV (1955), p. 264. Also in G. E. Moore, *Philosophical Papers* (London: Allen & Unwin, 1959), pp. 252–324 (with "Two Corrections," p. 324).

(1933) "To the Editor of *Mind*," *M*, XLII (1933), pp. 415–416.

(1933–35) *Preliminary Studies for the 'Philosophical Investigations,' Generally Known as the Blue and Brown Books*, pref. by R. R(hees). Oxford: Basil Blackwell; New York: Harper & Row, 1958; corr. reprint Oxford: Basil Blackwell, 1960.

(1937–44) *Bemerkungen über die Grundlagen der Mathematik* (*Remarks on the Foundations of Mathematics*), ed. G. H. von Wright, R. Rhees, & G. E. M. Anscombe, tr. G. E. M. Anscombe. Oxford: Basil Blackwell; New York: Macmillan Company, 1956.

(1936[?]–45; 1947–49) *Philosophische Untersuchungen* (*Philosophical Investigations*), tr. G. E. M. Anscombe. Oxford: Basil Blackwell; New York: Macmillan Company, 1953. (Cf. G. E. M. Anscombe, "Note on the English Version of Wittgenstein's 'Philosophische Untersuchungen,'" *M*, LXII [1953], pp. 521–522.) Second edition (rev.), Oxford: Basil Blackwell, 1958.

(1938; 1942–46) *Lectures and Conversations on Aesthetics, Psychology, and Religious Belief*, ed. by C. Barrett (Compiled from notes taken by R. Rhees, Y. Smithies, and J. Taylor.), Oxford: Basil Blackwell, 1966.

(1945–48) *Zettel*, ed. G. E. M. Anscombe and G. H. von Wright, with an English translation by G. E. M. Anscombe, forthcoming from Basil Blackwell, Oxford.

II. Synoptic

Charlesworth, M. J., *Philosophy and Linguistic Analysis*. Pittsburgh: Duquesne University Press, 1959. (Cf. esp. ch. 3 pp. 75–125.)

Hartnack, J., *Wittgenstein and Modern Philosophy*, tr. M. Cranston. Garden City, New York: Anchor Books, Doubleday & Company, 1965.

Hawkins, D., *Wittgenstein and the Cult of Language*, a paper read to the Aquinas Society of London in 1956. London: Blackfriars, 1957.

Horgby, I., "The Double Awareness in Heidegger and Wittgenstein," *I*, II (1959), pp. 235–264.

Kolenda, K., "Wittgenstein's 'Weltanschauung,'" *Rice*

University Studies, L, No. 1 (Winter 1964), pp. 23–37.

Mullin, A. A., *Philosophical Comments on the Philosophies of Charles Sanders Peirce and Ludwig Wittgenstein*. Urbana: Electrical Engineering Research Laboratory, Engineering Experiment Station, U. of Illinois, 1961.

O'Brien, G. D., "The Unity of Wittgenstein's Thought," *International Philosophical Quarterly*, VI (1966).

Pears, D. F., "Wittgenstein and Austin," in B. Williams and A. Montefiore (eds.) *British Analytical Philosophy* (London: Routledge & Kegan Paul; New York: The Humanities Press, 1966), pp. 17–39.

Pitcher, G., *The Philosophy of Wittgenstein*. Englewood Cliffs, N.J.: Prentice-Hall, Inc., 1964.

Quinton, A. M., "Contemporary British Philosophy," in D. J. O'Connor (ed.) *A Critical History of Western Philosophy* (The Free Press of Glencoe; London: Collier-Macmillan Limited, 1964), pp. 530–556, esp. pp. 535–545.

Stigen, A., "Interpretations of Wittgenstein," I, V (1962), pp. 167–175. (Review of Hartnack.)

Warnock, G. J., *English Philosophy since 1900* (London: Oxford University Press, 1958), ch. 6.

Wolter, A. B., "The Unspeakable Philosophy of the Late Wittgenstein," *Proceedings of the American Catholic Philosophical Association* (1960), pp. 168–193.

III. Wittgenstein Unpublished

Ambrose, A., "Finitism in Mathematics," M, XLIV (1935), pp. 186–203, 317–340. (But cf. n.1, p. 319.)

——, "Finitism and 'The Limits of Empiricism,'" M, XLVI (1937), pp. 379–385.

——, "Wittgenstein on Some Questions in Foundations of Mathematics," JP, LII (1955), pp. 197–214.

Black, M., "Relations between Logical Positivism and the Cambridge School of Analysis," *Erkenntnis*, VIII (1939–40), pp. 24–35.

Farrell, B. A., "An Appraisal of Therapeutic Positivism," *M*, LV (1946), pp. 25–48, 133–150.

Findlay, J. N., "Some Reactions to Recent Cambridge Philosophy," *AJP*, XVIII (1940), pp. 193–211, XIX (1941), pp. 1–13. Reprinted in Findlay's *Language, Mind and Value* (London: Allen & Unwin, 1963), pp. 13–38.

———, "Wittgenstein's Philosophical Investigations," *Revue Internationale de philosophie*, VII (1953), pp. 207–216.

Moore, G. E., "Wittgenstein's Lectures in 1930–33": see entry for 1930–33 in Part I, above.

Nagel, E., "Impressions and Appraisals of Analytic Philosophy in Europe," *JP*, XXXIII (1936), pp. 5–24, 29–53 (esp. pp. 16–24).

Rhees, R., "Some Developments in Wittgenstein's View of Ethics," *PR*, LXXIV (1965), pp. 17–26.

Waismann, F., "The Relevance of Psychology to Logic," *PASS*, XVII (1938), pp. 54–68; also in H. Feigl & W. Sellars (eds.), *Readings in Philosophical Analysis* (New York: Appleton-Century-Crofts, 1949), pp. 211–221.

———, "Notes on Talks with Wittgenstein," *PR*, LXXIV (1965), pp. 12–16.

Wisdom, J., "Logical Constructions," *M*, XL (1931), pp. 188–216 (esp. pp. 201–205), 460–475; XLI (1932), pp. 441–464; XLII (1933), pp. 43–66, 186–202.

IV. The Blue and Brown Books

Bouwsma, O. K., "The Blue Book," *JP*, LVIII (1961), pp. 141–162.

Garver, N., review, *PPR*, XXI (1960–61), pp. 566–567.

Hampshire, S., "The Proper Method," review, *New Statesman*, LVI (1958), pp. 228–229.

Kreisel, G., "Wittgenstein's Theory and Practice of Philosophy," *BJPS*, XI (1960–61), pp. 238–251.

Pole, D., review, *P*, XXXIV (1959), pp. 367–368.

Strawson, P. F., review, *PQ*, X (1960), pp. 371–372.

Warnock, G. J., review, *M*, LXIX (1960), pp. 283–284.

Zuurdeeg, W. F., review, *Journal of Religion*, XL (1960), pp. 54–55.

V. The Philosophical Investigations

Ambrose, A., review, *PPR*, XV (1954–55), pp. 111–115.

Burnheim, J., review, *PS(Ire.)*, IV (1954), pp. 114–115.

Castañeda, H.-N., "Knowledge and Certainty," *RM*, XVIII (1965), pp. 508–547. (Review of N. Malcolm, *Knowledge and Certainty*. Sec. V, pp. 528–535, is a criticism of Malcolm's "Wittgenstein's *Philosophical Investigations*." Sec. VI, pp. 535–537, is a criticism of Malcolm's "Knowledge of Other Minds.")

Collins, J., review, *Thought*, XXIX (1954–55), pp. 287–292.

Davie, I., review, *Downside Review*, LXXII (1954), pp. 119–122.

Feyerabend, P., "Wittgenstein's *Philosophical Investigations*," *PR*, LXIV (1955), pp. 449–483.

Findlay, J. N., review, *P*, XXX (1955), pp. 173–179. Reprinted in Findlay's *Language, Mind and. Value* (London: Allen & Unwin, 1963), pp. 197–208.

Hamilton, R., review, *The Month*, XI (1954), pp. 116–117.

Hampshire, S., review, *Spectator* (May 22, 1953), p. 682.

Heath, P. L., "Wittgenstein Investigated," *PQ*, VI (1956), pp. 66–71.

Heinemann, F. H., review, *Hibbert Journal*, LII (1953–54), pp. 89–90.

Hutton, E. H., review, *BJPS*, IV (1953), pp. 258–260.

Lieb, I. C., "Wittgenstein's Investigations," *RM*, VIII (1954–55), pp. 125–143.

Malcolm, N., "Wittgenstein's *Philosophical Investigations*," *PR*, LXIII (1954), pp. 530–559. Reprinted in V. C. Chappell, (ed.), *The Philosophy of Mind* (Englewood Cliffs, N.J.: Prentice-Hall, Inc., 1962), pp.

74–100. Also reprinted, in slightly revised form, in Malcolm's *Knowledge and Certainty: Essays and Lectures* (Englewood Cliffs, N.J.: Prentice-Hall, Inc., 1963), pp. 96–129.

Nakhnikian, G., review, *Philosophy of Science*, XXI (1954), pp. 353–354.

Strawson, P. F., review, *M*, LXIII (1954), pp. 70–99.

Wollheim, R., review, *New Statesman and Nation*, XLVI, No. 1165 (July 4, 1953), pp. 20–21.

Workman, A. J., review, *Personalist*, XXXVI (1955), pp. 292–293.

VI. Topics in the Blue and Brown Books and Investigations

Albritton, R., "On Wittgenstein's Use of the Term 'Criterion,'" *JP*, LVI (1959), pp. 845–857.

Ammerman, R. R., "Wittgenstein's Later Methods" (abstract), *JP*, LVIII (1961), pp. 707–708.

Arbini, R., "Frederick Ferré on Colour Incompatibility," *M*, LXXII (1963), pp. 586–590. (On Ferré, 1961, below.)

Aune, B., "On the Complexity of Avowals," in M. Black (ed.), *Philosophy in America* (Ithaca, New York: Cornell University Press, 1965), pp. 35–57.

Ayer, A. J., "Can There Be a Private Language?" *PASS*, XXVIII (1954), pp. 63–76. Reprinted in Ayer's *The Concept of a Person and other Essays* (London: Macmillan Company; New York: St. Martin's Press, 1963), pp. 36–51. (Cf. Rhees, 1954, below.)

Bambrough, J. R., "Universals and Family Resemblances," *PAS*, LXI (1960–61), pp. 207–222. (Cf. Aaron, 1965, below.)

――――, "Principia Metaphysica," *P*, XXXIX (1964), pp. 97–109.

Berggren, D., "Language Games and Symbolic Forms" (abstract), *JP*, LVIII (1961), pp. 708–709.

Britton, K., "Feelings and Their Expression," *P*, XXXII (1957), pp. 97–111.

Buck, R. C., "Non-Other Minds," in R. J. Butler (ed.), *Analytical Philosophy* (Oxford: Basil Blackwell, 1962), pp. 187–210.

Campbell, K., "Family Resemblance Predicates," APQ, II (1965), pp. 238–244.

Carney, J. D., "Private Language: The Logic of Wittgenstein's Argument," M, LXIX (1960), pp. 560–565. (Reply to Wellman, 1959, below.)

———, "Is Wittgenstein Impaled on Miss Hervey's Dilemma?" P, XXXVIII (1963), pp. 167–170. (Reply to Hervey, 1961, below. Cf. reply by Hervey, 1963, below.)

Castañeda, H.-N., see entry under Rollins, C. D.

Cavell, S., "The Availability of Wittgenstein's Later Philosophy," PR, LXXI (1962), pp. 67–93. (Contains criticism of Pole, 1958, below.)

———, "Existentialism and Analytical Philosophy," *Daedalus*, XCIII (1964), pp. 946–974.

Chappell, V. C., see entry under Rollins, C. D.

———, "The Concept of Dreaming," PQ, XIII (1963), pp. 193–213.

Chihara, C. S. and J. A. Fodor, "Operationalism and Ordinary Language: A Critique of Wittgenstein," APQ, II (1965), pp. 281–295.

Cook, J. W., "Wittgenstein on Privacy," PR, LXXIV (1965), pp. 281–314.

Daly, C. B., "New Light on Wittgenstein," Part I, PS(Ire.), X (1960), pp. 5–49; Part II, *ibid.*, XI (1961–62), pp. 28–62.

Donagan, A., "Wittgenstein on Sensation," forthcoming in M.

Fairbanks, M. J., "Language-games and Sensationalism," *Modern Schoolman*, XL (1962–63), pp. 275–281.

Ferré, F., "Colour Incompatibility and Language Games," M, LXX (1961), pp. 90–94. (Cf. Swiggart, 1963, below; Arbini, 1963, above.)

Fodor, J. A., "Of Words and Uses," I, IV (1961), pp. 190–208.

———, see entry under Chihara, C. S., above.

Garver N., "Wittgenstein on Private Language," PPR, XX (1959–60), pp. 389–396.

———, see entry under Rollins, C. D.

Gasking, D., "Avowals," in R. J. Butler (ed.), *Analytical Philosophy* (Oxford: Basil Blackwell, 1962), pp. 154–169. (Cf. reply by Lean, below.)

Gert, B., "Wittgenstein and Logical Positivism," (abstract) JP, LVIII (1961), p. 707.

———, "Wittgenstein and Private Language" (abstract), JP, LXI (1964), p. 700.

Ginet, C., see entry under Rollins, C. D.

Gruender, D., "Wittgenstein on Explanation and Description," JP, LIX (1962), pp. 523–530.

Gustafson, D. F., "Privacy," SJP, III (1965), pp. 140–146. (Comments on Castañeda, entry under Rollins, C. D.)

Hallie, P. P., "Wittgenstein's Grammatical-Empirical Distinction," JP, LX (1963), pp. 565–578.

———, "Wittgenstein's Exclusion of Metaphysical Nonsense," PQ, XVI (1966), pp. 97–112.

Hardin, C. L., "Wittgenstein on Private Languages," JP, LVI (1959), pp. 517–528.

Hervey, H., "The Private Language Problem," PQ, VII (1957), pp. 63–79.

———, "The Problem of the Model Language Game in Wittgenstein's Later Philosophy," P, XXXVI (1961), pp. 333–351. (Cf. reply by Carney, 1963, above.)

———, "A Reply to Dr. Carney's Challenge," P, XXXVIII (1963), pp. 170–175.

Jarvis, J., see under Thomson, Judith Jarvis.

Kenny, A., "Aquinas and Wittgenstein," *Downside Review*, LXXVII (1959), pp. 217–235.

———, "Cartesian Privacy," in the present volume, pp. 352–370.

Kerr, F., "Language as Hermaneutic in the Later Wittgenstein," *Tijdschrift voor Filosofie*, XXVII (1965), pp. 491–520.

Khatchadourian, H., "Common Names and 'Family Resemblance,'" PPR, XVIII (1957–58), pp. 341–358.

Kretzmann, N., "Maupertuis, Wittgenstein, and the Origin of Language" (abstract), *JP*, LIV (1957), p. 776.

Lean, M. E., "Mr. Gasking on Avowals," in R. J. Butler (ed.), *Analytical Philosophy* (Oxford: Basil Blackwell, 1962), pp. 169–186. (Reply to Gasking, above.)

Levi, A. W., "Wittgenstein as Dialectitian," *JP*, LXI (1964), pp. 127–138.

Linsky, L., "Wittgenstein on Language and Some Problems of Philosophy," *JP*, LIV (1957), pp. 285–293.

Llewellyn, J. E., "On Not Speaking the Same Language," *AJP*, XL (1962), pp. 35–48, 127–145 (esp. the latter).

Long, T. A., "The Problem of Pain and Contextual Implication," *PPR*, XXVI (1965–66), pp. 106–111. (Comments on Malcolm's "Wittgenstein's *Philosophical Investigations*.")

Malcolm, N., "Knowledge of Other Minds," *JP*, LV (1958), pp. 969–978. Reprinted in V. C. Chappell, (ed.), *The Philosophy of Mind* (Englewood Cliffs, N.J.: Prentice-Hall, Inc., 1962), pp. 151–159, and in Malcolm, *Knowledge and Certainty* (Englewood Cliffs, N.J.: Prentice-Hall, Inc., 1963), pp. 130–140.

Mandelbaum, M., "Family Resemblances and Generalization Concerning the Arts," *APQ*, II (1965), pp. 219–228.

Melden, A. I., "My Kinaesthetic Sensations Advise Me . . . ," *A*, XVIII (1957–58), pp. 43–48.

Mora, J. F., "Wittgenstein: A Symbol of Troubled Times," *PPR*, XIV (1953–54), pp. 89–96.

Mundle, C. W. K., " 'Private Language' and Wittgenstein's Kind of Behaviourism," *PQ*, XVI (1966), pp. 35–46.

Munson, T. N., "Wittgenstein's Phenomenology," *PPR*, XXIII (1962–63), pp. 37–50.

Nielson, H. A., "Wittgenstein on Language," *PS(Ire.)*, VIII (1958).

Olscamp, P. J., "Wittgenstein's Refutation of Skepticism," *PPR*, XXVI (1965–66), pp. 239–247.

Passmore, J., *A Hundred Years of Philosophy* (London:

Duckworth, 1957), ch. 18: "Wittgenstein and Ordinary Language Philosophy," pp. 425–458.

Paul, G. A., "Wittgenstein," in A. J. Ayer (ed.), *The Revolution in Philosophy* (London: Macmillan & Co. Ltd.; New York: St. Martin's Press, 1956), pp. 88–96.

Paul, R., "B's Perplexity," A, XXV (1964–65), pp. 176–178.

Perkins, M., "Two Arguments against a Private Language," *JP*, LXII (1965), pp. 443–459.

Pitcher, G., "Wittgenstein, Nonsense, and Lewis Carroll," *The Massachusetts Review*, VI (1965), pp. 591–611.

Pole, D., *The Later Philosophy of Ludwig Wittgenstein.* London: University of London, The Athlone Press, 1958. (Cf. Cavell, 1962, above.)

Rankin, K. W., "Wittgenstein on Meaning, Understanding, and Intending," *APQ*, III (1966), pp. 1–13.

Rhees, R., "Can There Be a Private Language?" *PASS*, XXVIII (1954), pp. 77–94; reprinted in C. E. Caton (ed.), *Philosophy and Ordinary Language* (Urbana: University of Illinois, 1963), pp. 90–107. (Reply to Ayer, 1954, above.)

———, "Wittgenstein's Builders," *PAS*, LX (1959–60), pp. 171–186.

Richman, R. J., "'Something Common,'" *JP*, LIX (1962), pp. 821–830.

Rollins, C. D. (ed.), *Knowledge and Experience*: Proceedings of the 1962 Oberlin Colloquium in Philosophy. University of Pittsburgh Press, no date. Contains the following articles and comments:

 Garver, N., "Wittgenstein on Criteria," pp. 55–71
 Ginet, C., "Comments," pp. 72–76
 Siegler, F. A., "Comments," pp. 77–80
 Ziff, P., "Comments," pp. 81–85
 Garver, N., "Rejoinders," pp. 86–87
 Castañeda, H.-N., "The Private-Language Argument," pp. 88–105
 Chappell, V. C., "Comments," pp. 106–118
 Thomson, J. F., "Comments," pp. 118–124

Castañeda, H.-N., "Rejoinders," pp. 125–132

Rorty, R., "Pragmatism, Categories, and Language," *PR*, LXX (1961), pp. 197–223.

Siegler, F. A., see entry under Rollins, C. D.

Smart, H. R., "Language Games," *PQ*, VII (1957), pp. 224–235.

Stern, K., "Private Language and Skepticism," *JP*, LX (1963), pp. 745–759.

Stocker, M. A. G., "Memory and the Private Language Argument," *PQ*, XVI (1966), pp. 47–53.

Suter, R., "Augustine on Time with Some Criticisms from Wittgenstein," *Revue Internationale de philosophie*, XVI (1962), pp. 378–394.

Swiggart, P., "The Incompatibility of Colours," *M*, LXXII (1963), pp. 133–136. (Reply to Ferré, 1961, above.)

Tanburn, N. P., "Private Languages Again," *M*, LXXII (1963), pp. 88–102.

Thomson, J. F., see entry under Rollins, C. D.

Thomson, Judith Jarvis, "Private Languages," *APQ*, I (1964), pp. 20–31.

Todd, W., "Private Languages," *PQ*, XII (1962), pp. 206–217.

Warnock, G. J., "The Philosophy of Wittgenstein," in R. Klibansky, (ed.), *Philosophy in the Mid-Century*, Vol. II (Firenze: La nuova Italia editrice, 1958), pp. 203–207.

Wellman, C., "Wittgenstein and the Egocentric Predicament," *M*, LXVIII (1959), pp. 223–233.

———, "Our Criteria for Third-Person Psychological Sentences," *JP*, LVIII (1961), pp. 281–293.

———, "Wittgenstein's Conception of a Criterion," *PR*, LXXI (1962), pp. 433–447.

Wheatley, J., " 'Like,' " *PAS*, LXII (1961–62), pp. 99–116.

Wisdom, J., "A Feature of Wittgenstein's Technique," *PASS*, XXXV (1961), pp. 1–14.

Wolgast, E. H., "Wittgenstein and Criteria," *I*, VII (1964), pp. 348–366.

VII. Remarks on the Foundations of Mathematics

Ambrose, A., review, *PPR*, XVIII (1957–58), pp. 262–265.

Anderson, A. R., "Mathematics and the Language Game," *RM*, XI (1957–58), pp. 446–458. Reprinted in Benacerraf, P. and H. Putnam (eds.), *Philosophy of Mathematics* (Englewood Cliffs, N.J.: Prentice-Hall, Inc., 1964), pp. 481–490.

Bernays, P., "Comments on Ludwig Wittgenstein's *Remarks on the Foundations of Mathematics, Ratio*, II (1959–60), pp. 1–22. Reprinted in Benacerraf and Putnam (eds.), *Philosophy of Mathematics*, pp. 510–528.

Collins, J., review, *Modern Schoolman*, XXXV (1957–58), pp. 147–150.

Dummett, M., "Wittgenstein's Philosophy of Mathematics," *PR*, LXVIII (1959), pp. 324–348. Reprinted in Benacerraf and Putnam (eds.), *Philosophy of Mathematics*, pp. 491–509.

Duthie, G. D., review, *PQ*, VII (1957), pp. 368–373.

Goodstein, R. L., review, *M*, LXVI (1957), pp. 549–553.

Kreisel, G., review, *BJPS*, IX (1958–59), pp. 135–158. (And see entry under Kreisel in Part IV, above, pp. 251–252.)

Lewis, C. J., review, *Thought*, XXXII (1957–58), pp. 446–448.

McBrien, V. O., review, *New Scholasticism*, XXXII (1958), pp. 269–271.

VIII. Topics in the Remarks

Ambrose, A., "Proof and the Theorem Proved" (abstract), *JP*, LV (1958), pp. 901–902. (Cf. Swanson, 1959, below.)

——, "Proof and the Theorem Proved," *M*, LXVIII

(1959), pp. 435–445. (Cf. Castañeda, 1961, below.)

Bennett, J., "On Being Forced to a Conclusion," *PASS*, XXXV (1961), pp. 15–31. (Cf. Wood, 1961, below.)

Chihara, C. S., "Wittgenstein and Logical Compulsion," *A*, XXI (1960–61), pp. 136–140. (Reply to Nell, 1960–61, below.)

———, "Mathematical Discovery and Concept Formation," *PR*, LXXII (1963), pp. 17–34.

Castañeda, H.-N., "On Mathematical Proofs and Meaning," *M*, LXX (1961), pp. 385–390. (On Ambrose, 1959, above.)

Cowan, J. L., "Wittgenstein's Philosophy of Logic," *PR*, LXX (1961), pp. 362–375.

Lazerowitz, Mrs. M., see under Ambrose, A.

Levison, A. B., "Wittgenstein and Logical Laws," (abstract), *JP*, LIX (1962), pp. 677–678.

———, "Wittgenstein and Logical Laws," *PQ*, XIV (1964), pp. 345–354.

———, "Wittgenstein and Logical Necessity," *I*, VII (1964), pp. 367–373.

Nell, E. J., "The Hardness of the Logical 'Must,'" *A*, XXI (1960–61), pp. 68–72. (Cf. Chihara, 1960–61, above.)

Stroud, B., "Wittgenstein and Logical Necessity," *PR*, LXXIV (1965), pp. 504–518.

Swanson, J. W., "A Footnote to Mrs. Lazerowitz on Wittgenstein," *JP*, LVI (1959), pp. 678–679. (On Ambrose, 1958, above.)

Wisdom, J. O., "Esotericism," *P*, XXXIV (1959), pp. 338–354.

Wood, O. P., "On Being Forced to a Conclusion," *PASS*, XXXV (1961), pp. 35–44. (Reply to Bennett, 1961, above.)